INDENTURED LABOR,
CARIBBEAN SUGAR

Indentured Labor, Caribbean Sugar

CHINESE AND INDIAN MIGRANTS
TO THE BRITISH WEST INDIES,
1838–1918

Walton Look Lai

Introduction by Sidney W. Mintz

THE JOHNS HOPKINS UNIVERSITY PRESS

BALTIMORE AND LONDON

This book has been brought to publication
with the generous assistance
of the National Endowment for the Humanities.

The Johns Hopkins University Press
2715 North Charles Street
Baltimore, Maryland 21218-4319
The Johns Hopkins Press Ltd., London

Library of Congress Cataloging-in-Publication Data

Look Lai, Walton.
Indentured labor, Caribbean sugar : Chinese and Indian migrants
  to the British West Indies, 1838–1918 / Walton Look Lai.
  p.   cm. — (Johns Hopkins studies in Atlantic history and
                  culture)
Includes bibliographical references and index.
ISBN 0-8018-4465-7 (acid-free paper)
1. Sugar workers—West Indies, British—History—19th
  century. 2. Indentured servants—West Indies,
  British—History—19th century.   3. Alien labor,
  Chinese—West Indies, British—History—19th century.
  4. Alien labor, East Indian—West Indies, British—History—
  19th century.   5. West Indies, British—Emigration and
immigration—History—19th century.   I. Title.   II. Series.
            HD8039.S86W475   1993
            306.3'63—dc20   92-33812

A catalog record for this book is available from the British Library

For
my parents

Contents

Illustrations

Preface

The transition from slavery to free labor in the Americas was a general phenomenon of the nineteenth century. The motivating impulses behind the phenomenon, or the specific nature of the class and labor rearrangements after Emancipation, were, however, far from uniform. Moreover, the phenomenon of labor coercion, far from dying out, assumed new and diverse forms. One particular expression of this continuation of the forced labor tradition was the revival of the indenture system, a system of contract labor which tied the laborer to a specific employer for a fixed term of years under a contractual arrangement that often exposed the laborer to penal sanctions, including imprisonment, in the event of violation of the terms of the contract. Contract or indentured labor was not new to the Americas: indeed, it had preceded the introduction of slavery. What was new about its revival in the nineteenth century was the source of the contract labor (overwhelmingly Asian—that is, Chinese and Indian) and the more elaborate mechanisms surrounding its operation in the post-Emancipation period.

In the British West Indies, where the battle to end the system of slavery had been particularly acute, spearheaded as it had been by British metropolitan interests, the replacement of one system of labor coercion by another was attended by unique concerns and arrangements. Special regulations and safeguards surrounded the revival of this preslavery mode of labor control. The indenture system which evolved in Trinidad, British Guiana, and Jamaica in particular was markedly different in its organization and operation from its counterparts in Latin America (especially Cuba and Peru). Moreover, even within the British Caribbean itself, the extent to which it became central to the post-Emancipation production of sugar varied from territory to territory. In Trinidad and British Guiana,

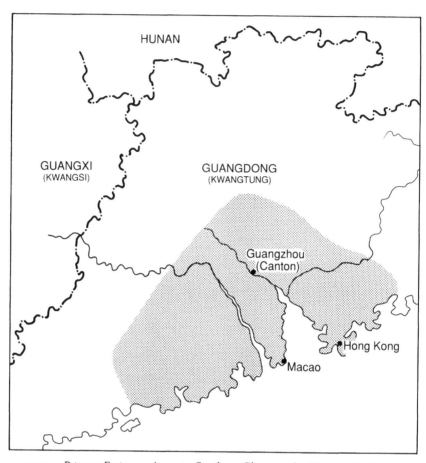

MAP I. Primary Emigrant Areas in Southern China in the Nineteenth Century

indenture was central to sugar production and the plantation economy, whereas in Jamaica and the smaller Windward Islands like Grenada, St. Lucia, and St. Vincent, it was a peripheral adjunct to a technically free labor system. (In many islands, such as Barbados and the Leewards, it was never introduced at all.)

A comparative examination of these differences within the British Caribbean system of contract or indentured labor forms one of the main focuses of this study. A second and related focus is the response of the new immigrants from Asia (Chinese and Indian) to the indenture system, and indeed to their new Caribbean (and American) social environment. The international dispersal of Asian labor was a fact of nineteenth-century life, and the Asians' arrival within the Caribbean plantation

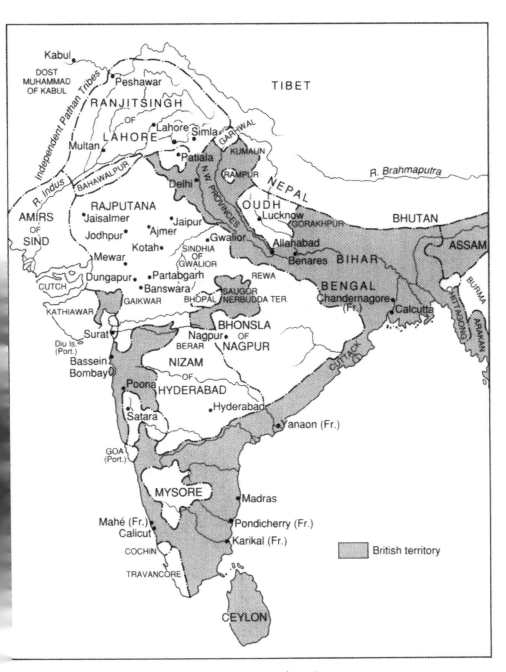

MAP 2. India in the late 1830s

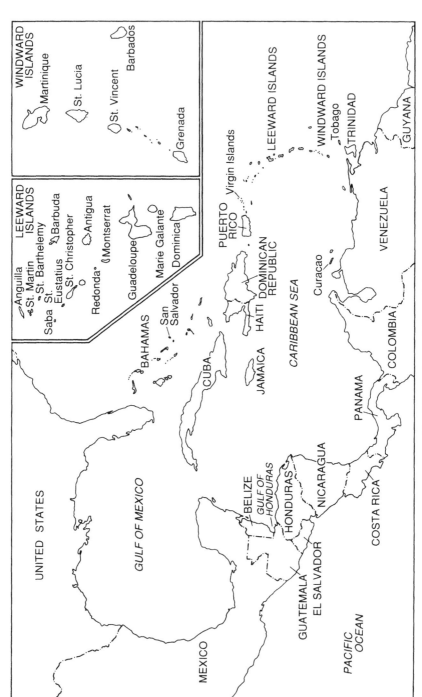

MAP 3. The West Indies and Central America

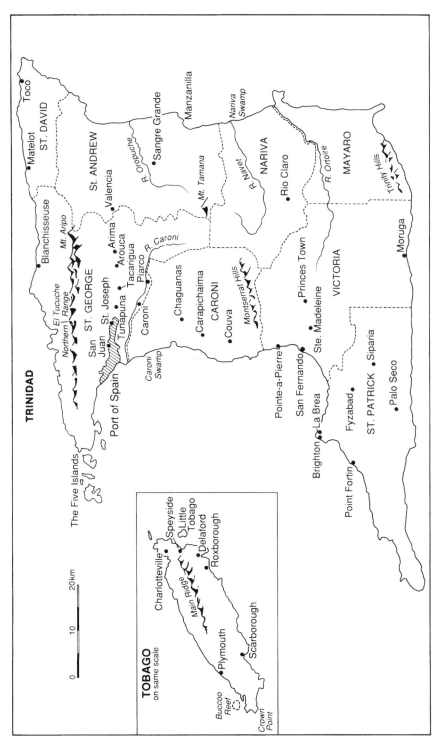

MAP 4. Trinidad and Tobago

TRINIDAD

Toco
Matelot
ST. DAVID
ST. ANDREW
Blanchisseuse
Mt. Aripo
El Tucuche
Northern Range
San Juan
ST. GEORGE
St. Joseph
Port of Spain
The Five Islands
Caroni Swamp
Tunapuna
Caroni
Tacarigua
Piarco
Arouca
Arima
Valencia
R. Oropuche
Sangre Grande
Manzanilla
Nariva Swamp
Mt. Tamana
R. Navet
NARIVA
Rio Claro
R. Ortoire
MAYARO
Trinity Hills
Moruga
Chaguanas
Carapichaima
CARONI
Couva
Montserrat Hills
R. Caroni
Princes Town
Ste. Madeleine
VICTORIA
Pointe-a-Pierre
San Fernando
La Brea
Brighton
Point Fortin
Fyzabad
ST. PATRICK
Siparia
Palo Seco

TOBAGO
on same scale

Charlotteville
Speyside
Little Tobago
Delaford
Roxborough
Main Ridge
Plymouth
Scarborough
Buccoo Reef
Crown Point

0   10   20km

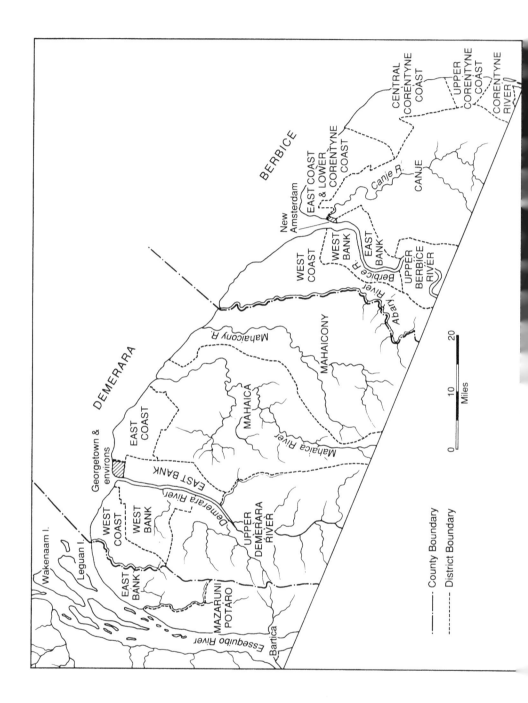

BERBICE

CENTRAL CORENTYNE COAST

UPPER CORENTYNE COAST

CORENTYNE RIVER

EAST COAST & LOWER CORENTYNE COAST

Canje R.

CANJE

New Amsterdam

WEST COAST

WEST BANK

EAST BANK

Berbice R.

UPPER BERBICE RIVER

Abary River

DEMERARA

Mahaicony R.

MAHAICONY

Mahaica River

EAST COAST

MAHAICA

Georgetown & environs

EAST BANK

Demerara River

UPPER DEMERARA RIVER

WEST COAST

WEST BANK

Leguan I.

Wakenaam I.

EAST BANK

MAZARUNI POTARO

Essequibo River

Bartica

0   10   20
Miles

——— County Boundary
- - - - District Boundary

xvi

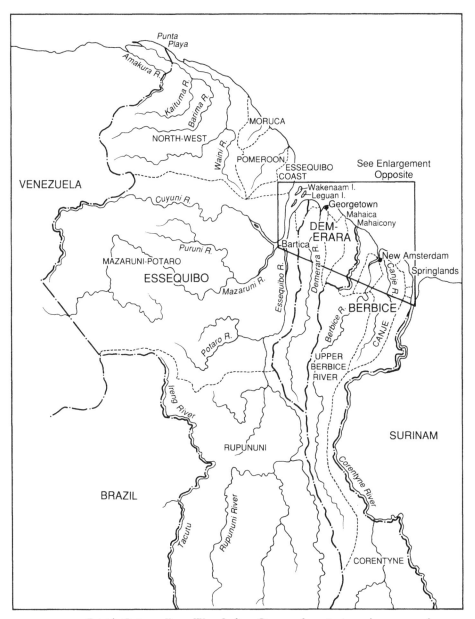

MAP 5. British Guiana. From West Indian Census of 1946. An enlargement of coastal Demarara and Berbice counties is shown on facing page.

system was part of a larger movement of peoples. But the unique nature of British Caribbean plantation society, and the dynamics of the trans-formed sugar society (i.e., sugar production minus slave labor), provided an environmental setting to an immigration and assimilation experiment which had no exact parallel elsewhere (except perhaps in Mauritius). How the immigrants coped, how they responded to West Indian planta-tion society during and after indenture, forms an important focus of this study.

There is no integrated social history to date of Asian migration to the British Caribbean region, that is, one which incorporates the experiences of both Asian groups. A number of doctoral dissertations have dealt with selected aspects of the indentured immigration. The published literature has so far been uneven, ranging from scholarly monographs like Judith Weller's *East Indian Indenture in Trinidad* to edited collections of articles of an academic and journalistic nature on the Indian experience in the Caribbean. A few well-known social histories of nineteenth-century Trin-idad and British Guiana have addressed the immigration experiment in the course of an exploration of the evolution of the larger Creole society, and there are at least two macrohistorical studies of overseas Asians in the British Empire as a whole, one on the Indians, the other on the Chinese. But an integrated and in-depth examination of Asian immigra-tion to the West Indies region, and the social evolution of both ethnic groups in this unique plantation environment, does not exist. In particu-lar, outside of Cecil Clementi's informal study *The Chinese in British Gui-ana*, published in British Guiana in 1915, the history of the tiny Chinese community in this portion of the Western Hemisphere has so far received scant attention from both Caribbeanists and Asian Americanists alike.

In this study, I address this gap in the scholarly literature and attempt to build on the published and unpublished pioneer attempts in the field, as well as to examine the official sources on both ethnic groups in a more exhaustive manner than has hitherto been attempted. I try to understand the Caribbean Asian experience as part of the social evolution of the Western Hemisphere plantation system, as well as part of the larger mi-gration movements of the period.

Chapter 1 discusses the "pull" factors at work within the post-Emancipation West Indian plantation economy leading to the multiracial immigration, and eventually Asian indenture, experiment. Chapter 2 discusses the "push" factors at work internally within Asia (China and India), and their causal interaction with growing Western imperialism in that region, leading to the emigration movements. In chapter 3 I take up the formal legal aspects of the organization of the British West Indian indenture system, identifying both regional specificity and internal differentiations within that system, ethnic as well as territorial. Chapters 4 and 5 explore the complex social experiences of both Asian groups within the New World sugar plantation system as they sought to preserve their autonomy and Subject status in the face of a large capitalistic productive system designed to denude them of these very qualities. Their successes and failures in this regard, as well as in their post-indenture efforts to preserve and enhance their social autonomy, are recorded in these chapters, as well as in chapters 7 and 8. Chapter 6 is devoted to an examination of the responses of the Creole host society (Black and White) to the issue of Asian immigration and to the indenture experiment throughout its eighty-year life span.

One hopes this study will provide new insights into a neglected theme in Latin American immigration history. It is also intended to provide comparative insights into the Asian American diasporal experience, taking place as it did in a social environment that was quite distinct: less self-consciously dynamic and expansive than its North American counterpart and constrained not only by the structural limitations of the West Indian plantation economy but also by the changed priorities of the British Empire in the new industrial age of the nineteenth century.

Acknowledgments

During the five years which it took me to research, write, and prepare this work for publication, I have been assisted by several people in small and large matters, in tangible and often intangible ways.

A grant from the New York University History Department, and a travel grant from the Rockefeller Foundation, facilitated the later stages of the preparation of this work. Professors Warren Dean and Nicholas Sanchez-Albornoz of New York University, who supervised the original manuscript in its dissertation form, made many valuable suggestions for its improvement. The editors of the Studies in Atlantic History and Culture Series at the Johns Hopkins University Press have been very encouraging in their reception of this work. I wish to thank, in particular, Professor Sidney Mintz of the Johns Hopkins University for consenting to write an introduction to the work.

I wish to thank the librarians and staff of the various libraries in New York, London, and Trinidad, where this work was researched, for their helpfulness and professionalism. These include, in particular, the personnel of the New York Public Library, the Public Record Office and British Library in London, and the National Archives and University of the West Indies Library in Trinidad. A few people assisted me in acquiring special materials at various stages in the preparation of this work. Among these I would like to mention Professor Warren Dean, Marlene Kwok Crawford, Shirley Evelyn, Brinsley Samaroo, and Maritza Hee Houng. Conversations with Marianne Ramesar often yielded useful bibliographic information and helpful insight. Kim Gransaull of the University of the West Indies library was instrumental in granting me access to the photographic collection of the West India Reference Section. Brian Chen kindly donated a valuable family photograph of his famous grandfather,

Eugene Chen. Several others, including members of my own extended family, assisted in intangible ways during the period of my research labors, and to them I am especially grateful.

Finally, I must thank Jacqueline Wehmueller and Grace Buonocore of the Johns Hopkins University Press for the professional guidance and personal interest which helped to bring this book into being.

Introduction

By Sidney W. Mintz

Walton Look Lai's book tells the story of Indian and Chinese agricultural laborers who left their ancestral homelands to cross oceans in search of economic betterment. These were primarily agricultural laborers who went off to work in distant lands. They did so in the hope of returning eventually with wealth and honor to the places of their birth, to pick up the threads of family and of village which tied them to their past lives and which their emigration had broken.

By their efforts, these Chinese and Indian workers supplied badly needed labor to the agricultural enterprises of the colonial tropical world. They came mainly from tropical and subtropical regions; they left their homes largely because they had been increasingly unable to earn their livings there. The countries to which they emigrated were dependent and colonial, countries typified by agricultural systems that had been organized and maintained on a large commercial scale by the European colonial powers, and were now—in the nineteenth century—experiencing shortages of labor.

Until nearly the middle of that century, the post-Columbian labor history of the British West Indies had been, to put it simply, slavery. It was because of the end of slavery that these migrant laborers were needed. They were brought to replace slaves, and the labor system of which they came to be a part was fashioned to fit with the slavery system that had preceded it. The migration of these people thus constituted an important chapter in the evolving saga of the world division of labor.

Look Lai shows us here how, within the global arrangements for labor supply fashioned by the imperial powers of the West, Asian workers were introduced into local West Indian economies and societies. There, many of them eventually surrendered their "sojourner" status to become citi-

zens, even as the host societies themselves were being gradually transformed from colonies into sovereign states. More thoroughly than anyone
has done before, the author enables us to see out of what milieus these
migrants had come, how their introduction into tropical plantation colonies was managed, and how they acquired in turn their own characteristic
political and social outlook in the new settings. But this movement from
the Old World to the New was in many ways only the final chapter in a
much longer story.[1]

The European agricultural entrepreneurs intent upon developing productive systems on New World lands in order to supply homeland consumers with commodities—especially certain "specialty foods" that, until
that time, had been rare and costly—must be seen in the context of
their times. It would be generally fair to say that before the sixteenth
century, the history of massed labor worldwide had been, in varying form
and degree, a history of coercion. Despite that history, when opportunities for agricultural development in the New World beckoned, beginning
as early as the sixteenth century, the rich and powerful Europeans who
were organizing new overseas enterprises were not always and everywhere
able to control the labor of the early comers. The vast lands of the New
World afforded newly arrived free laborers many opportunities to live
outside organized society—that is, outside the reach of the coercive apparatus of the state. Hence, to undertake to produce massive quantities of
salable agricultural goods for European markets in the New World tropics
would require from the first some means to control the labor force by
iron discipline. Given the relatively easy access to land for the indepen-
dent-minded individual and the relatively slow spread of police power,
free labor would never serve to man large estates. Only a system that
could effectively immobilize the laborer would work. It would take slavery, or something like it, to guarantee the discipline required.

The first enslaved Africans to reach the New World were transported
during the first decade of the sixteenth century to the earliest Spanish
colony, the island of Santo Domingo (today's Haiti and the Dominican
Republic). There, the New World's first sugar plantations were founded.
But while it was the Spaniards who thus initiated sugar production in
the Americas, they did not play a leading role in its development during
the ensuing four centuries. In the Caribbean, that leadership would soon
pass to the English and the French, with the commercial and technological initiative for such undertakings often coming from the Dutch. After
the pioneering phase initiated by Spanish colonists in the Greater Antil-

les (Santo Domingo, Cuba, Jamaica, and Puerto Rico) during the years 1510–80, Britain and France established colonies in the Lesser Antilles—Britain in Barbados, France in Martinique and Guadeloupe—where sugar production was undertaken, beginning in the 1630s. It was not until the late eighteenth century that the Hispanic Caribbean, now reduced to the islands of Cuba and Puerto Rico, would be able to reassert its primacy in regional sugar production.

Throughout the region's history, from the first plantations in Santo Domingo until the last fifteen years of the nineteenth century, the principal form of labor exaction was slavery. So intimate was the link between New World sugar plantations and slavery that these functionally unrelated institutions can be said to have become interdependent in the seventeenth century, and they remained so for more than two centuries (from about 1640 to 1880). Without slavery, there would have been some sugar, but not in the quantities, never so swiftly, and probably not at the low prices that slavery made possible. It seems quite certain that without sugar, New World slavery would have had a far shorter life and far less social importance.

These are hazardous claims, of course, both counterfactual and highly speculative. What lends them substance is the abundant evidence that slavery as a form of labor exaction was a "solution" to the lack of other forms of labor in the New World. Although it began early in New World plantation history, as Walton Look Lai explains, it was for some time only one of the means for supplying such labor, supplemented by other forms of temporary or long-term coercion. Yet a century later slavery had become virtually the only way to supply labor in the region, and it remained so for two hundred years more. Slavery, once installed, had soon proven itself successful. Once working, it acquired a systemic momentum in the hands of the planter classes and their advocates and bankers, who developed elaborate justifications for it. By its very existence it became a monstrous obstacle to any alternative labor forms. As cotton, coffee, and tobacco, among other commodities, turned out to be more or less similarly suitable to large-scale slave estate production, the system spread. But sugar was always at its base, not only in the Caribbean region but also in Brazil, the Guianas, and elsewhere.

Although there are some historically interesting exceptions, the majority of the enslaved were Africans. Their descendants, stretching over more than a dozen generations, were also slaves, born into slavery—though it was only in the U.S. South that a New World slave population may be said to have reproduced itself in growing numbers. From 1503–5, when the first African slaves are believed to have been brought to the Americas, until 1888, when the last slave was emancipated in Brazil, perhaps ten million Africans were shipped to the New World. The scale of this movement takes on great additional significance when it is framed in its time. The twentieth century has made figures of millions seem like much less to us; even the Holocaust is diminished in a world populated by billions. But when it is remembered that British Jamaica and French Saint Domingue would receive about one million enslaved Africans each, between the middle of the seventeenth century and the middle of the eighteenth,[2] then the awesome magnitude of this traffic in living human bodies at so early a period in the West's history becomes more visible.

That this activity was dedicated to the production of enormous quantities of such everyday necessities as sugar, rum, coffee, tobacco, and the like became a recognized aspect of the struggle to end the slave trade and slavery. In the awakening consciousness of the Europeans, the human cost could always be tempered by reflections on the blessed pleasures that a cup of heavily sweetened coffee, or a reassuring pipeful of tobacco, could bring. For this reason and for reason of great profit, the single greatest obstacle in the world to the progress of freedom was deliberately, even obdurately, maintained.

After the Haitian Revolution of 1791–1804, however, a growing recognition that, in the long run, slavery might be not only immoral but even politically dangerous began to seep into European consciousness. In the case of the United Kingdom, the growth of a powerful antislavery movement, the subsequent end of the slave trade, and the belief in the imminent end of slavery itself were among the background conditions that eventually made a labor importation policy nearly inevitable. From the planters' perspective, this was a rapidly approaching crisis. Events in the metropolis merely underlined the persisting need and convictions of the British West Indian planter classes. Their lives and welfare rested upon the plantation production of sugar. That production needed labor. Slave labor would soon vanish. Hence a different sort of labor would be required, and it must be labor consistent in its character with the past: if it could not be as cheap as before, then at least it would have to be more docile. If freedom for the slaves was to come, then the planters must be indemnified for the loss of their investment. And it would be up to government to figure out afterward how to supply them with labor on the same terms and at no greater cost.

It is not easy to document the persistence of deeply held convictions about the world in the face of challenges posed by a new social order.

But any observer of contemporary events in Eastern Europe, say, has ample evidence that a change in regimes need not result in any easy or compliant alteration in outlook. Nor did it in the British West Indies, as the planters were obliged to envision a world without the whip, a world in which the labor force was not manacled. Though no doubt unconscious in part, the planters' intentions to retain the peculiar privileges of the past are not difficult to understand, even if, after all, they were socially repulsive.

The "new solution" to the labor problem was the importation of impoverished laborers from agrarian societies elsewhere. India and China, among the largest, most populous, and least democratic societies known at the time, were to figure significantly in this plan. Although there is, of course, no way that they could have known it, the migrants from these societies were to be the crucial link in the continuity of planter power, for it was thanks to their brawn and suffering that the transition from enslaved to proletarian labor would be realized.

In a brief but brilliant book, the late Sir W. Arthur Lewis (1978) provides a cameo world view of migrant labor during the nineteenth century. During those one hundred years, about one hundred million persons crossed oceans seeking work. About one-half of them were Europeans, people mostly moving from a European country (e.g., Italy, Ireland) to one that had been predominantly settled by Europeans (e.g., Chile, Canada). The other half was non-European (e.g., from India or China), of whom it might be said that they left no European country and entered none.

Lewis explains elegantly why the two migrant streams flowed to different termini. In effect, he reasons, Africans and Asians were prepared to migrate to engage in wage labor at rates that could not successfully attract Europeans, who were coming from countries with relatively more efficient agriculture that yielded to its producers higher returns. But of course there was another quite efficient pruning device also at work: racism. The Chinese and Indians who ended up in British Guiana or Trinidad or Dutch Guiana or Jamaica would have been more than content to migrate to Canada or Australia or the United States, and it was not differential agricultural productivity that kept them out.

So there were two migrations, not one. While one helped to make Argentina into an ethnically heterogeneous society of a European sort, the other made Trinidad and Surinam into ethnically heterogeneous societies of a non-European sort. While one provided new human material for the educational and social systems of democratic societies such as Canada and the United States, where citizenship had a direct political meaning, the other provided the blood and muscle needed to cut and grind the sugar cane in the Guianas and West Indian islands.

Both of these migrations eventuated in second generations that included physicians, novelists, and politicians. But one did so under social and economic conditions that facilitated considerable upward mobility. The other did so under social and economic conditions that guaranteed above all the commodity harvests of sugar and coffee for the world market, and in which social and economic opportunity were severely restricted. Though less than entirely successful, the social systems of the Caribbean world were powerfully constrained to produce nothing but cane cutters, and more cane cutters, and more cane cutters.

Before the whole story of the "other fifty million" has been told, there will be need for additional careful thought and research. We are still far away from a global understanding of these events. There is little doubt, it seems to me, that the difference in our knowledge about migrations—about what happened in the West and what happened in the colonies of the West—is the result of what I would call differential political attention. Just as the Jamaican legislature had no need in the nineteenth century to answer to the Jamaican people for the immigration initiatives it sponsored with regressive taxation—by which the price of labor was driven down and the lot of the Jamaican people accordingly worsened—the metropolitan historians had no need to study the fate of millions of non-European laborers who left their countries to live out their lives in distant colonies. Now that is all changing.

Walton Look Lai's richly documented book is a building stone in the emerging saga of migrant non-European peoples in the nineteenth century. In this modern era of rapid and easy travel, it is easy to forget the awful sufferings not only of enslaved Africans in the building of today's world, but of those other millions as well who, driven by poverty or trapped by deceit, sacrificed their lives in building new worlds for their children.

INDENTURED LABOR,
CARIBBEAN SUGAR

CHAPTER I

British West Indian Society and Economy after Emancipation

The nineteenth century saw a number of dramatic developments in the world of sugar production which had a somewhat negative impact on the British West Indian sugar industry, itself largely a product of the late seventeenth and early eighteenth centuries.[1] The rapid growth of consumer demand in the metropolis, which increased with the spread of industrialization and urbanization, and the transition of sugar from a middle- and upper-class to a mass-consumption commodity inevitably led to an expansion of the regions involved with the production of this staple, even within the Caribbean region itself. New areas of sugar production in Mauritius, British East India, Cuba, Louisiana, Java, and Hawaii, among others, posed a challenge to the classic West Indian domination of this important industry, and the often superior technologies of the newcomers also exacerbated the growing problems for West Indian sugar.

As long as British West Indian sugar remained protected from competition within the British market by traditional mercantilist arrangements, and as long as the traditional command over a cheap and regular supply of African slave labor remained a reality, West Indian sugar interests could feel themselves secure against these new developments. But it was precisely these two major props of the West Indian sugar interest which fell away in the nineteenth century, opening up a whole new era in the life and development of the plantation system in these islands.

The decades after the American Revolution had seen an increasing restlessness within Britain with the traditional monopoly arrangements so dear to the West India interest. Crucial to this development was an increase in the cost of West Indian sugar, caused mainly by the increased costs of production resulting from the plantations' inability to import materials and supplies from the American market after the Revolution. Crucial, too, was the rise of abolitionist sentiment against the slave traffic and slavery itself, and the renewed efforts to terminate the institution.

An unprecedented number of works appeared in Britain between 1787 and 1807 focusing attention on the state of British West Indian society in the agitation over the slave trade. One of the best known of these works, Bryan Edwards' *History of the British West Indies,* viewing the whole debate from a pro-planter perspective, cynically suggested that the underlying cause of the abolitionist movement was dissatisfaction with the increased cost of West Indian produce resulting from restrictions on the American trade: "Discontent at the high price of sugar is called sympathy for the wretched, and the murmurs of avarice become the dictates of humanity."[2]

No small role in the abolitionist dissatisfaction with the slave trade was played by the issue of French St. Domingue in the Caribbean, which had between 1783 and 1789 leapt into the position of foremost sugar producer in the region. It supplied half of Europe with tropical produce in the last period of the century, and its exports were one-third more than those of the British West Indies combined. It became "the world's premier sugar producer, the gem of the Caribbean."[3]

A commission of enquiry into the British West Indian sugar industry in 1787 discovered that it was the British slave trade itself, via reexports of slaves from the British islands, which was helping to finance the development of Britain's rivals. Two-thirds of the annual British slave export from Africa of forty thousand slaves was heading towards non-British islands.[4] The political motives of Prime Minister Pitt for supporting the abolitionist cause were quite clear: to cut the ground from under St. Domingue and to increase sugar supplies to Britain from other new sources, such as British East India.[5]

Other vested interests within British society also found themselves unhappy with the West India monopoly, and with the philosophy of protectionism in general, as the British economy expanded quantitatively and qualitatively in the early nineteenth century. Among these were manufacturers whose raw materials were located outside the Empire, ship-owners whose vessels were restricted in the business of transporting produce from non-Empire sources (e.g., Brazilian sugar and coffee, both subject to high tariff duties unless the produce was for reexport), shipping interests which no longer revolved around the transport of slaves to American plantations, and sugar refiners who were being economically strangled by the requirement that only British West Indian sugar enjoyed preferential treatment in the home market, or who were being outpriced in the European market, with its cheaper sources of sugar.

All of these economic complaints gave extra fuel to the vigor of the humanitarian agitation over slavery, spelling doom for the cherished West Indian institution. The link between the new economic needs of nineteenth-century industrial Britain and the vibrant abolitionist movement was best summarized by Eric Williams: "When British capitalism depended on the West Indies, they ignored slavery or defended it. When British capitalism found the West Indian monopoly a nuisance, they destroyed West Indian slavery as the first step in the destruction of the West Indian monopoly."[6]

As British wealth and global needs were transformed and expanded in the early nineteenth century, as new territories were annexed into the British Empire proper, as new sources of sugar inside and outside the Empire held out new prospects for the expanding home market, the British West Indies gradually lost the pride of place they had held in eighteenth-century Britain and found themselves less able to defend the indefensible.

First came the abolition of the British slave trade in 1807, disrupting the easy and regular flow of African slave labor to the plantation system. Then, after further agitation from the abolitionist movement, came the Emancipation Act of 1833 and the formal end of British slavery on the 1st of August 1834. The political blow was softened as the West Indian slave owners were compensated to the amount of £20 million, and a formal transitional period known as apprenticeship was legally established which bound the ex-slave to the plantations for a number of years (six, later reduced to four) in order to minimize the potential disruption that might accompany a mass exodus from the plantations.

But a new era had dawned for the West Indian plantation system with the end of slavery, as the totalitarian hold over the labor force reluctantly gave way to a free labor relationship of nominal equals, and as the discipline of the whip and brute force gave way to the need for persuasion, conciliation, and bargaining characteristic of a free labor system (at least in theory). Whatever the historical motivations of the abolitionist movement (humanitarian, economic, political), it left the West Indian planter with a new and unprecedented situation and placed sugar production on a new and unaccustomed footing.

The decade after Emancipation was a period of prolonged and troubled adjustment to the new realities. Inevitably, the freed slaves took the opportunity to work out new forms of relationships with the planter class and with their new range of societal options. Inevitably, the plantation regime underwent a period of social and financial travail as the new relationships worked their way out. The situation actually varied from one island plantation system to the other, as the range of available options open to both planters and freedmen, and the manner of actually choosing between these, differed from one context to another. As visiting American journalist William Sewell put it in 1861, "Emancipation was an isolated experiment in each of the different colonies. Precedents and rules of action for one were no precedents and rules of action for another. *Here* there were obstacles to overcome and difficulties to surmount which *there* did not exist, or existed only in a mitigated form."[7]

As far as the ex-slaves were concerned, the differences lay in the extent to which they were willing to exercise their options to move away from the plantation environment—mainly to form an independent peasant sector—and the precise levels of relationship with plantation labor which they actually retained whenever they did move away. Where the availability of land was great, as in the newly acquired territories of Trinidad and British Guiana and in the old colony of Jamaica, the exodus from the plantations was great. Where land was scarce and the plantation system dominant over the island, Black labor remained largely on the estates, as in Barbados, Antigua, and St. Kitts. In most of the other smaller islands, the exodus assumed an intermediate course between the Jamaica–Trinidad–British Guiana option and the Barbados–Antigua–St. Kitts option.

There is an existing debate on the ex-slaves' motivations in moving away from the plantations: whether they sought to escape the memory of the brutality of slavery—extending on the resistance tradition, as it were—or whether they were reacting to specific unjust policies introduced by the planters after Emancipation in their attempts to keep the ex-slaves tied to the estates.[8] The debate does not make a great deal of sense in the context of the historical social and class struggle of the plantation. Both motivations were responses to the same planter class and its tactics of domination at different periods, and it is difficult (and not worthwhile) trying to distinguish between one motivation and the other, since both were clearly present, and indeed not easily separable, in the minds of the ex-slaves. The desire for autonomy and greater control over one's own destiny, and a willingness to explore all avenues in this direction, would seem to have been a sufficient motivation.

More significant is the discussion on the extent to which the ex-slaves who removed themselves from the plantation did or did not remove themselves totally from plantation labor itself in the process. Despite the lamentations of many planters, it is clear that the exodus from plantation to independent village life did not involve an absolute removal. Large numbers of freedmen continued to combine their new lives as peasant producers with wage labor on the sugar plantations, although it is clear that the new flexible relationship which they maintained with the planta-tion sector had altered the traditional absolute command over their movements to which the planters had become addicted under slavery. It was the freedman's newfound bargaining strength on the labor market, rather than his absolute disappearance from that market, which troubled the West Indian plantocracy. It was also with his often erratic (from the planters' point of view) use of that bargaining strength, giving or withdrawing his labor sometimes arbitrarily, and not always predictably, that the main problems arose.

A commission of enquiry appointed in 1842 under the chairmanship of Lord Stanley concluded, *inter alia*,

> the diminished supply of labor is caused partly by the fact that some of the former slaves have betaken themselves to other occupations more profitable than field labor; but the more general cause is that the laborers are enabled to live in comfort and to acquire wealth without, for the most part, laboring on the estates of the planters for more than three or four days in a week, and from five to seven hours in a day; so that they have no sufficient stimulus to perform an adequate amount of work. . . .
>
> . . . this state of things arises partly from the high wages which the insufficiency of the supply of labor, and their competition with each other, naturally compel the planters to pay; but it is principally to be attributed to the easy terms upon which the use of land has been obtainable by negroes. . . . Many of the former slaves have been enabled to purchase land, and the laborers generally are allowed to occupy provision grounds, subject to no rent, or to a very low one; and in these fertile countries the land they thus hold as owners or occupiers not only yields them an ample supply of food, but in many cases a considerable surplus in money, alto-gether independent of, and in addition to, the high money wages they receive.[9]

The actual ratios of Black exodus from the plantations in the early years varied from island to island, with Jamaica, Trinidad, and British Guiana experiencing the heaviest hemorrhages. In Trinidad, there were 16,000 ex-slaves (12,000 fieldworkers and 4,000 artisans) on the estates in 1838. In 1847, there were 10,000 "at the command of the estates," according to Governor Harris.[10] By 1851, only 3,116 of these laborers were allegedly at work regularly.[11] Sewell estimated in 1860 that about 4,000 of the ex-slaves had remained on the plantations, and about 7,000 had left, although during crop time about 4,000 to 5,000 of these spent some time on plantation labor.

In British Guiana, there were about 38,000 ex-slaves still on the plantations in the mid-1840s, 43 percent of the work force at Emancipation. Between 1832 and 1852, the plantation work force fell from 88 percent of the employed population to 43 percent.[12] The exodus in Jamaica was no less decisive. Sewell estimated that in 1860, 40,000, or 9 percent of the total population, worked on the Jamaican sugar estates.[13]

Descriptions of the actual impact of the labor withdrawal on the plantation system abound. In 1851, Henry Mitchell, Superintendent of Immigrants in Trinidad, reported as follows about Victoria County in South Trinidad:

> The County of Victoria, from which one half of the staple crop is shipped, is at present cultivated almost entirely by immigrant labor, either African or Coolie. . . . The former Creole population amounting to upwards of 4,000, has disappeared from the labor market. . . . During my recent inspection I found that this portion of the inhabitants had, in almost every instance, withdrawn from its former locality; not, as is sometimes asserted, because they were driven out by the competition of cheaper and imported labor, but because the former peasantry had either individually or as families, acquired sufficient means to purchase portions of those abandoned properties which the distress of former years among the proprietary body had thrown into the market at a nominal rate. On these lots of land the former peasantry now reside, and when once settled in this way no inducement will make them return to daily labor.[14]

William Burnley, the leading spokesman for the planter class in Trinidad in the 1840s, complained to the 1842 Stanley Committee about the degeneration of the work habits of many freed slaves who remained on the plantations:

> [The planter] suffers, not so much from the amount of expenses incurred by the wages, high as they are, as from the neglect and the waste, and the damage which take place upon the estate, which you cannot protect yourself against, and which you hardly dare attempt, in many instances, to find fault with. One witness before the Trinidad Committee [of 1841]

spoke to the great additional expense in the loss of laboring cattle, the oxen, from the bad treatment that they now receive, not being properly fed and attended to, and being beaten and knocked about cruelly. . . . The greatest loss arises from the deterioration in the quality of the sugar. A man is placed to skim a copper, and to attend to the work; he does not attend to the work, and you cannot compel him. And the same witness stated that the loss in this particular alone amounted to £4 a hogshead, which was 1,200 pounds sterling in the annual crop, simply from the deterioration in the quality of the sugar; and in every other department, losses arise continually from the negligence of the laborers. . . . It arises directly from the want of labor, which enables the laborer to do as he pleases, and you cannot find fault with him, because if you do he leaves your service, and you would rather have him to do his work badly than not have him at all.[15]

Such large-scale withdrawal and declining work standards were repeated in the other territories, with varying degrees of intensity, even allowing for much planter exaggeration.

One labor innovation introduced by the ex-slaves in some territories was the practice of organizing themselves into mobile task-gangs, collectively negotiating with individual estates to perform specified tasks at mutually agreed-on wages. These task-gangs roamed the countryside and brought the collective principle to bear on the new relationship in the plantation work environment.

Actual wage levels for collective or individual field labor varied widely from island to island, with wages tending to be highest where it was scarce and most needed, namely, in the new territories of Trinidad and British Guiana. The following is a list of minimum and maximum daily wage levels for field labor in the 1840s:[16]

Trinidad	40–50 cents (1s.8d.–2s.1d.)
British Guiana	33–48 cents (1s.4½d.–2s.)
Jamaica	18–42 cents (9d.–1s.9d.)
Barbados	14–30 cents (7d.–1s.3d.)
Antigua	12–50 cents (6d.–2s.1d.)
St. Kitts	12–32 cents (6d.–1s.4d.)
Nevis	10–24 cents (5d.–1s.)
Montserrat	4½–12 cents (2¼d.–6d.)
St. Lucia	20–44 cents (10d.–1s.10d.)
St. Vincent	16–48 cents (8d.–2s.)
Dominica	9–20 cents (4½d.–10d.)

| Grenada | 15–28 cents (7½d.–1s.2d.) |
| Tobago | 14–32 cents (7d.–1s.4d.) |

The processes by which large numbers of freed Blacks acquired lands beyond the sugar plantation regimen were not at all uniform, particularly if the phenomenon is viewed regionally. Land hunger was sometimes actually satisfied in collaboration with the authorities (planters and colonial governors), as a means of keeping the laborers allied to estate work. This happened in the Leeward Islands, to keep workers from migrating to the expanding territories like Trinidad and British Guiana. But individual planters in these two territories also engaged in the practice, to keep their labor force tied to their own estates. More often, land hunger was satisfied against the broad consensus of planter opinion, but with the collusion of desperate individual planters anxious to divest themselves of estates undergoing financial stress and facing impending ruin. Even more drastically, it was often acquired illegally, through the widespread practice of squatting on abandoned estates, on the unoccupied fringes of plantations, or on Crown lands. More rarely, it was acquired through purchase of Crown lands, but the existence of stringent regulations and expensive formalities introduced after apprenticeship, mainly with a view to discouraging such sales, often acted as a brake on widespread sales of public lands to all but a handful until late into the century. Up to 1868 in Trinidad, 320 acres was the minimum purchase allowed on Crown lands; in British Guiana, it was 100 acres until as late as 1898.

The new peasantry generally remained close to the plantations themselves, in a proliferation of new villages, to retain the option of working on the estates whenever they wished. Sometimes the villages sprang up haphazardly and spontaneously, as in Trinidad. Sometimes, as in Jamaica, they were established with help from sympathetic missionary elements. Sometimes, as in British Guiana, they were the product of totally independent Black coooperative initiatives, that is, group purchases of declining plantations (mainly cotton and coffee, but also sugar). Many of the new villages in British Guiana in the 1840s and 1850s were also the result of individual or group purchases of the front portions of existing plantations, acquired from their owners as primarily residential lands.

Most of the lands purchased in Trinidad and British Guiana, though acquired often at bargain prices, were much more expensive than lands farther into the interior, beyond the reach of the plantations or towns. William Burnley told the Stanley Committee in 1842 that in Trinidad some of the ex-slaves "paid very high prices indeed . . . but it is not for the purpose of cultivating them, but as a residence in the vicinity of the towns. To avoid such a trifling distance as four or five miles, they have preferred giving forty, fifty or even one hundred dollars for an allotment, which they might have bought one of the same size in the interior for, for four or five dollars."[17]

The Governor of British Guiana also reported in mid-1843 that up to then not more than two sales of Crown lands had been made to the freed laboring population. They preferred, he said, to purchase for high prices land situated in the vicinity of estates, schools, and churches, rather than buy unappropriated lands of the Crown, "which would separate them from civilization."[18] By 1848 only 1,387 acres of Crown land had been purchased by ex-slaves. The difficult and restrictive regulations surrounding the purchase of Crown lands were not the only reason for this. Ex-slaves bought private lands on the coastal areas at £50 an acre, usually collectively, with money saved from high wages earned during apprenticeship.

Sugar production fell drastically between 1839 and 1846 in some territories (for example, Jamaica and British Guiana), fell slightly in others (Barbados), remained reasonably stable in some (Trinidad), and even improved in a few (Antigua and St. Kitts).[19] The labor exodus was felt most severely where the regularity of plantation labor from the new peasantry was less predictable or where early immigrant replacements in the first years did not suffice to stabilize the work situation. William Burnley told the 1842 Committee that despite the problems the Trinidad planters faced, production in that island had been kept stable with the aid of African and other West Indian immigrant labor.

High prices for West Indian sugar on the protected British market after Emancipation also helped to cushion the plantations somewhat. Sugar sold for less than £30 a ton in the last years of slavery but fetched over £30 a ton between 1834 and 1846, with the price even passing the £39 mark in some years (£40 16s. in 1836, £39 3s. in 1839, £49 2s. in 1840, £39 13s. in 1841). This factor was directly responsible for an artificial escalation of wage levels beyond the dictates of prudent management on many individual plantations in Trinidad and British Guiana, as planters struggled to attract and keep Black labor on the estates, often in competition with one another.[20]

Despite this, many individual plantations fell by the wayside, some sold off for much less than the market value to new owners, some taken over by creditors, many parceled out and sold to the ex-slaves in small allotments (in British Guiana, whole estates to Black collective purchasers), and many simply abandoned and left idle, to be occupied by squatter elements or left to waste away as tragic symbols of failure.

It was the decision by the British Parliament to pass the Sugar Duties Act in 1846 which effectively ended the old order for the West Indian sugar industry, putting the final seal on a process that had begun with the act abolishing the slave trade in 1807 and the Emancipation Act in 1833. The 1846 Act brought an end to protection for West Indian sugar by admitting all sugar from Empire and non-Empire sources (even slave labor societies like Cuba and Brazil) on an equal basis into the British market, without preference. Prices for sugar automatically dropped in the ensuing years, even though the Act became fully effective only in 1854. The British consumers got their cheap sugar, but the West Indian planters had to struggle with the consequences of free trade. Sugar prices returned to the £20 range, where they remained effectively until the crisis of 1884, when prices sank still further, into the £10 range, due to competition from subsidized beet sugar from Europe.

The years 1847–48 were also years of a financial collapse in Britain, and the crisis of the ailing sugar industry doubly heightened, as credit sources in the metropolis dried up temporarily, with the collapse of many merchant houses engaged in West Indian trade and finance, including their branches in the West Indies. Wages dropped dramatically in Trinidad and British Guiana. In the latter colony, a racially bitter resistance waged by Black workers in a strike lasting three months (January to March 1848) failed to arrest the downward trend in wages.

Plantation failures multiplied, as did sales of viable properties far below their market value. Trinidad, which had had only about 13 of 206 estates abandoned up to 1847, saw the total multiply to forty by 1850. The Attorney General of Trinidad reported, concerning the period between 1846 and 1848: "nearly all the English and Scotch houses connected with this colony have been struck down. . . . 64 petitions of insolvency have been filed; estate after estate thrown upon the market, and no purchaser found. Even where there has been no insolvency, many estates have been abandoned from the inability to raise money on the faith of the coming crop."[21]

One writer pointed out in 1866 that all the sugar estates of at least seven districts in Trinidad, which had together produced 8 percent of the 1836 sugar crop, had since been abandoned, sold off cheaply, or taken over by the Crown and that no sugar at all was being produced in these districts by the 1860s (Mayaro, Guapo, La Brea, Irois, Erin, all in the south, plus Toco and Carenage in the north).[22]

In British Guiana, 72 sugar estates had been totally abandoned by 1850. The number of all estates (sugar and nonsugar) had been reduced from 308 in 1838 to 196 by 1849.[23] An American official resident in the colony described the crisis years after Emancipation as witnessing "the downfall of the old proprietary body" and the emergence of a plantation system where many estates were held by English creditors hoping for better times, and many others by "industrious coloured men" buying them and dividing them up among themselves.[24]

Indeed, changing ownership patterns dominated the industry in the latter half of the century. In both territories, the traditional family-owned plantation (resident or absentee) gradually gave way to metropolitan-based corporate entities with greater commercial expertise, credit access, and technological dynamism. These developments eventually ensured the relative modernization and ultimate survival of the West Indian sugar industry and brought it partially into line with modern world developments. The old plantocracy did not disappear, but their ranks were depleted and their socioeconomic functions quite altered as the century progressed. Many went out of sugar altogether, some transferring to new plantation products (such as cocoa in Trinidad) or into mercantile activity, some leaving for other pastures within the West Indies or elsewhere.

Apart from Jamaica, which was a special case, the sugar industry did not remain sick for very long, despite the large number of estate failures in the 1840s. Writing in the 1860s, William Sewell was able to point out that all the sugar societies had in fact increased their output by that decade, with the sole exception of Jamaica, whose industry, he maintained, had been ailing before the end of slavery. British Guiana in particular managed to overcome its severe crisis to become by the late 1850s the premier sugar-producing country in the British West Indies, second in the region only to Cuba. In the early 1850s, it was already producing one-quarter of British West Indian sugar; by the late 1880s, two-fifths. As the century progressed, the British West Indian share of total world production of sugar progressively declined, but its output kept rising.[25] By 1859–60, that share was 15 percent (198,600 tons) of the world total, and by 1894–95, it was 7 percent (260,211 tons). However, with Cuba included, the Caribbean region still produced 51 percent of the world's sugar in 1859–60 and 41 percent in 1894–95.[26]

Central to the recovery of British Guiana, and to the steady upward expansion of Trinidad from mid-century onwards, was the issue of immigration.[27] Barbados and the Leewards, with sufficient command over their own labor force, did not have to resort to this policy option in order to increase their output. New ownership patterns, technological innovation, and easier access to metropolitan capital and credit had enhanced the competitive standing of the West Indian industry in an age of lower sugar prices, but it was the labor question that was paramount and, in the final analysis, decisive.

Sewell, an American, was a pro-abolitionist and pro–free labor advocate, and when he wrote, he did so with half an eye on the unfolding debate over slavery in his own country. His was an undifferentiated praise for the "success" of freedom over slavery in the West Indies in stimulating increased production. The superiority of the free labor experiment was demonstrated by the statistics on production. However, he conveniently underplayed the fact that in Trinidad and British Guiana (if not the others) it was not free labor, but an alternative form of unfree labor—contract or indentured labor—which came to the rescue of the sugar industry in these two plantation systems.

Jamaica (as indeed some of the small Windward islands) experimented too with both free and unfree labor migration in an attempt to keep its sugar industry afloat, but its commitment to a uniform immigration policy was not firm, and the plantation system there evolved away from the classic sugar-dominated model of the eighteenth century. By the 1890s, it had the most diversified nonsugar base of all the West Indian islands, not to mention the most vigorous and successful of the post-Emancipation Black peasantries.[28]

The issue of immigration had been raised by the planters just after slavery and remained a persistent policy imperative for the embattled ex-master class. Immigration was seen not only as a way of expanding a sparse population in an underdeveloped frontier environment (which Trinidad and British Guiana essentially were in relation to the older sugar islands), but also as a weapon in the class struggle against the newly freed Blacks. It was the ultimate way that they could be disciplined and controlled to suit the needs of the plantation system.

Even the 1842 Stanley Committee in its recommendations had made the objectives of immigration policy quite explicit: to introduce a fresh laboring population whose purpose would be to act as a competitive element against the Black labor force and thereby to depress wages to what the plantocracy would consider manageable and reasonable levels. Thus the main recommendations were not for a new pioneer farmer class, but a new estate labor force, and as the policy debates evolved, not even a free labor force, but one that was tied to the estates by legal and contractual mechanisms that severely constricted its nominal freedoms.

Another commission of enquiry, chaired by Lord Bentinck, which had been appointed in 1848 to investigate the effects of the Sugar Duties Act of 1846 on the region, reiterated the point and called for financial assistance to help the planters with the immigration project.[29]

Immigration after Emancipation

In the years immediately after Emancipation, quite a significant flow of spontaneous voluntary immigration into Trinidad and British Guiana emanated from the smaller West Indian islands to the north. The mobility that freedom brought led many small-island Blacks to opt for migration to other islands rather than to inland settlements. The densely populated islands like Barbados and the Leewards contributed heavily to these movements, but the outflow was not confined to them. The higher wage levels of the two new sugar territories were a natural magnet, and many came without direct or indirect encouragement from the local plantocracy there.

Gradually the planters began to intervene more directly into the process, and they did so in a number of different ways: paying the passages of the immigrants, sending their own private vessels up the islands to ferry them down to the two territories, paying captains of independent vessels a bounty (from $5 to $15) on each laborer introduced, making contracts in the islands with the immigrants for specific terms of service.

The semiorganized influx encountered several problems. The small-island governments took objection to the activities of the recruiting agents, enticing their laborers away as they were, and a few enacted legislation to curb their enthusiasm (St. Kitts, Tobago, Grenada, St. Lucia, St. Vincent in 1838). This did not have any significant impact, however, as the Colonial Office disallowed legislation intended to curb the freed Blacks' freedom of movement. The outflows continued, both organized and unorganized, throughout the century. The practice of giving bounties to vessel captains was discontinued in Trinidad when it was discovered that they were in the habit of reintroducing many of the same people year after year and collecting a bounty each time they were brought back to the island.

Between 1839 and 1849 alone, 10,278 islanders were estimated to have migrated to Trinidad, 7,582 to British Guiana, and 790 to Jamaica.[30] It is difficult to quantify this migration (which never really terminated), but it is accurate to say that those who stayed did not become a permanent part of the plantation work force, being in the habit of opting for alternative nonplantation occupations much like their fellow Black laborers in Trinidad and British Guiana. In 1847 about 3,000 of them were said to be working full-time on the sugar plantations of Trinidad. Barbados alone is estimated to have contributed about 40,650 immigrants to British Guiana between 1835 and 1893, and the Trinidad census of 1891 recorded 13,890 Barbadians out of 30,689 West Indian immigrants. White Creole historian Louis De Verteuil stated that most of the interisland private vessels brought back laborers from Grenada, St. Kitts, Nevis, and Montserrat to Trinidad.[31]

However, the total immigrant group came from everywhere, virtually. A look at the annual reports of the Superintendent of Prisons in Trinidad in the 1850s reveals that, of those who fell afoul of the law at some point in this period, there were people from as far afield as Bermuda, the Bahamas, Anguilla, St. Thomas, St. Croix, Tortola, St. Barts, St. Martin, and Martinique.[32] In British Guiana, there were as early as 1839–40 about a hundred Dutch ex-slaves from Saba, St.Eustatius, and Curaçao, whose freedom had been bought by their Guianese planter-employers.

The 1851 census of Trinidad recorded 10,800 British West Indian immigrants, 15.5 percent of the island's population of 69,609, and the largest single immigrant group in that year. The British Guiana census of the same year recorded 9,278 West Indians (4,925 from Barbados alone); they were 7 percent in a population of 135,994, and the second largest group of immigrants next to the Africans (divided into 7,083 "old Africans," and 7,168 new immigrants).[33]

After 1851, West Indian island immigration became largely spontaneous and voluntary (the planters having turned to India for regular labor), and more to Trinidad than British Guiana. Most never went to the plantations, and squatting on Crown lands in Trinidad was a major "pull" factor in the pre-1870 years. By the end of the nineteenth century, West Indian immigrants were arriving in Trinidad at the rate of 5,000 to 9,000 a year.[34] In 1911, there were 47,802 British West Indians in Trinidad and 12,268 in British Guiana.

Other sources of Black immigrant labor were the United States and West Africa (Sierra Leone and Liberia). From the former source came a very minor stream that did not develop into anything significant. The immigrant population from the latter was made up of a tiny stratum of free voluntary migrants, plus a large number of Africans liberated from slave captors on their way to the New World and relocated to Sierra Leone or the island of St. Helena, where they were housed under the supervision of an international body prior to embarking for various destinations in Africa or elsewhere. Liberated Africans were also housed at centers in the New World, Rio de Janeiro and Havana in particular.

The following figures are given by Roberts and Byrne on the arrival of these immigrants into the West Indies during the period of early immigration experimentation:[35]

United States	1,333 to Trinidad (all arriving before 1848)
	73 to British Guiana (in 1840)
	258 to Jamaica (before 1845)
	178 to British Honduras (in 1867)
Africa	39,332 in all arriving between 1834 and 1867:
	8,854 to Trinidad
	14,060 to British Guiana
	11,391 to Jamaica
	5,027 to Grenada, St. Vincent, St. Lucia, St. Kitts–Nevis, Dominica

The Americans were free Blacks living mainly in the mid-Atlantic states of Maryland, Delaware, Pennsylvania, New Jersey, and New York. Harassed by the racism that stifled free Blacks in the cities of the antebellum North, a minority had advocated (and a few practiced) migration to Black nations outside the United States. Some had gone to Liberia since its founding in 1819, a few to liberated Haiti, and the debates about the merits of overseas migration were always a vibrant part of free Black discourse on Black options in the antebellum North.

The Trinidad planters, led by the New York–born William Burnley, tried to tap into this tradition, visiting the mid-Atlantic states in 1839. Edward Carberry of British Guiana did the same in the same year. The African-Americans themselves even sent a two-man delegation of their own in 1840, Nathaniel Peck and Thomas Price, to survey the prospects and the terrain of the two colonies.[36] They both seemed to prefer British Guiana, but as it turned out, most actually went to Trinidad (and these mainly in the years preceding their own delegation).

The migrations were not popular with the African Americans, however. Most of them were artisans and quasi-urban elements. Agricultural labor in a tropical Caribbean environment was not an experience the majority of them relished, and most soon returned to the United States. In 1848 there were 148 of them still on the estates of Trinidad.[37] In 1851 Trinidad passed an ordinance (No. 8 of 1851) designed to encourage free Blacks and colored immigrants from the United States and British North

America into the colony, but there is no evidence that much resulted from this legislation. The records indicate that only about five men arrived with their families.[38]

The Africans (so-called "liberated") were the products of the British campaign to enforce the ban on the slave trade, in a period when key slave states such as Cuba, Brazil, and the U.S. South continued to exist, and by their mere existence to encourage the continuation of the trade, clandestine and open. Africans liberated from captured slave ships were rehabilitated in Sierra Leone and on the Atlantic island of St. Helena, and marginally at Rio and Havana in the Western Hemisphere. Those who came to the West Indies in the 1840s and 1850s often had little real choice, given the pressures to which they were subject in Sierra Leone and elsewhere, but to indenture themselves for a period of years to the West Indian plantations.

In Trinidad they were utilized by both sugar and cocoa planters. The first year, 1833–34, saw applications for more Africans than were available, from as many as 184 planters. These included 53 cocoa planters, 12 sugar planters, 1 cotton and rice cultivator, 13 employers engaged in artisan activities, 76 householders wanting domestics, and 29 unspecified. The total number of Africans applied for by these 184 owners was 1,051.[39]

By the time of the 1851 census, Trinidad had 8,097 Africans in a population of 69,609, 11.6 percent and the second largest immigrant group after the West Indian small islanders. British Guiana recorded 14,251 in a total population of 135,994, 10.5 percent and the largest immigrant group in the colony in that year.

For a time, the Africans, who were a diverse lot, did assist the plantation system to survive and grapple successfully with the labor shortage dilemma, but many tended to duplicate the attitudes of the ex-slaves and escape into the interior of the colonies, often to regroup by themselves or with fellow Africans into villages with distinct identities, less Creole than the normal village communities. A sizeable portion of Trinidad's squatter communities in the 1860s consisted of African immigrants. As late as 1870 there was a squatter settlement in South Naparima known as Krooman Village, with surviving members of the Kroo tribe from Liberia and their families still living in community.[40] As time went by, however, most of them intermarried with the Creole Black population and merged into the general Black community.

Next to Black labor, the 1840s and 1850s experimented with various kinds of White immigrant labor. They included immigrants from Britain (including Ireland), France, Germany, Malta, and Portuguese Madeira. Outside of the Portuguese, all were very minor and insubstantial, barely making an impact on the life of post-Emancipation society in the West Indies. Most went to Jamaica (4,087 out of 4,582); British Guiana received 381; and a mere handful went to Trinidad.[41] Portuguese immigrants from Madeira, Cape Verde, and the Azores were more significant and mainly destined for British Guiana, which received the lion's share of this ethnic influx (32,216 out of 40,971), which actually lasted from 1835 to 1881. Most arrived, however, in the 1840s and 1850s, the decades of multiethnic experimentation. Trinidad received a mere 1,298 of this group, less than islands such as Antigua, St. Kitts, and St. Vincent.[42] After 1858, the Madeiran immigration to British Guiana was free and voluntary and not encumbered by any system of indenture.

The European immigrants who did not make their way into the small managerial or overseer class and who were utilized as field laborers did not remain there for very long. Heavy mortality and unwillingness to work in that capacity in a tropical milieu led to early abandonment of plantation life. Some became urban déclassé elements, like some of the French in Trinidad and the Maltese and Irish in British Guiana. Some became small businesspeople. Many migrated to the United States after a short spell in the tropics.

The Portuguese-speakers from Madeira, Cape Verde, and the Azores (actually, the Cape Verdians were Black, not White) remained on the estates for slightly longer, on various terms of indenture (five-, three-, two-year contracts) and later on even as free laborers, but they gravitated out of estate agriculture into the petty trades and small farming very rapidly. Their color, and the desire of the colonial society to encourage the formation of some kind of stable buffer class between the ruling Whites and the mass of Blacks, assisted in their rapid rise as a colonial small-trading middle class, not without some hostility from the larger Black society. There were major anti-Portuguese riots in British Guiana in 1856 and 1889, during periods of severe economic hardship and social stress.[43] The Trinidad Portuguese, 537 of whom were actually Protestant refugees from Catholic Madeira, met with less societal hostility or attention when they did move upwards into the small trades.[44] Many relocated to Brazil and to the United States. Many also moved to British Guiana, where they could find greater ethnic and cultural companionship with their compatriots, who lived in large close-knit communities in that colony.[45]

The 1840s to 1860s were the main period of multiethnic immigration experimentation. These years also saw the beginnings of experimentation with Asian immigrant labor. Chinese immigration commenced in 1853, lapsed, and revived again in 1859. Here, too, like the other migrant flows described above, the experiment was short-lived and not successful as a substitute for the regular Black work force that the planters craved. The migration effectively terminated in 1866, with sporadic arrivals afterwards. During this period a total of 17,904 Chinese laborers entered West Indian society, 13,533 to British Guiana, 2,645 to Trinidad, 1,152 to Jamaica, and 474 to British Honduras in Central America.

It was not until the decision to regularize the importation of contract laborers from British India, after initial experiments in 1838 in British Guiana, and 1845–48 in British Guiana, Trinidad, and Jamaica, that a solid replacement for the Black ex-slave work force was finally found by the West Indian plantocracy. The following chapters are devoted to an examination of the arrival and social adjustment of both kinds of Asian labor, the small and marginal Chinese group and the more than 400,000 Indians who eventually came to the British West Indies every year from 1851 to 1917.

CHAPTER 2

Push Factors and Migration Trends in India and China

A total of just over half a million (536,310) immigrants made their entry into the British West Indian plantation system between 1834 and 1918. (This figure does not include the interisland movements of the West Indian Blacks themselves.) Of these immigrants, 83.5 percent came from Asia alone, 80 percent (429,623) from India and 3.5 percent (17,904) from China. British Guiana alone absorbed 56 percent (300,967) of the total migration, 55.6 percent (238,909) of the Indians, and 76 percent (13,533) of the Chinese. Trinidad absorbed 29.4 percent (157,668) of the total migration, 33.5 percent (143,939) of the Indians, and 15 percent (2,645) of the Chinese. Jamaica received 10 percent (53,940) of the total migration, 8.5 percent (36,412) of the Indians, and 6.4 percent (1,152) of the Chinese total.[1]

The Asian migrations to the Caribbean region were but a small fraction of a much larger global dispersal of Asian labor from India and China in the nineteenth century. Indian immigrants went in large numbers to Ceylon, Burma, and Malaya in South and Southeast Asia; to Mauritius, Reunion, and Madagascar in the Indian Ocean; to Fiji in the Pacific; to Natal in South Africa, as well as East Africa. Within the Americas, they went not only to the British Caribbean, but also in reasonably significant numbers to Dutch Guiana (Surinam), and to the French West Indian territories of Martinique, Guadeloupe, and Cayenne.

The Chinese continued their steady stream of migration to the countries of Southeast Asia, traditionally the major destinations. But in the nineteenth century they flocked in large numbers to new destinations: to Australia, New Zealand, and the Pacific islands (Hawaii, Tahiti, Western

Samoa), to Mauritius in the Indian Ocean, and to the Americas. Unlike those of the Indians, their movements into the Americas were totally dispersed, covering North America (the United States and Canada), Spanish America (mainly Cuba and Peru, and, later in the century, Mexico), and Portuguese Brazil in addition to the French, Dutch, and British Caribbean plantation societies.

The migrations to the British Caribbean must therefore be seen in both specific and global comparative terms, particularly in any discussion of the "push" factors which propelled the migrants out of their original societies and into the expanding world economic system of the nineteenth century. Like their European counterparts of the period, the immigrants were both victims and products of new global social forces and realignments taking decisive shape after the end of the eighteenth century, propelled by the modernization momentum of northwestern Europe and the aggressive expansionism that accompanied this dynamism.

British Colonialism and Indian Emigration

India was the first major non-Western civilization to feel the impact of the imperatives created by the British Industrial Revolution. During the seventeenth and eighteenth centuries, up to 1757–63—the years of the establishment of a decisive political presence in India—the British East India Company had been largely confined to the trading enclaves of Fort William (Calcutta), Madras, and Bombay. From this base the profitable trade with the East was carried on, with the British economy importing much more from India than it was exporting to it, right up to the end of the eighteenth century.[2]

The Industrial Revolution transformed Britain from a net importer into an aggressive exporter of manufactured goods. It also expanded its raw material imports (foodstuffs and industrial raw materials) not only from India but from an ever-widening global environment. The internal disintegration of the Mogul Empire, which had been taking place during the eighteenth century, enhanced the prospects for political-territorial expansion by the British East India Company, and relations between the two countries underwent a decisive turn after the capture of Bengal in 1757 and the defeat of the French claim to a share of India in the Seven Years' War ending in 1763.

From this expanded and expanding political base, British imperialism proceeded to create the administrative and military framework required to meet the needs of the new industrial metropolis. One of the lasting consequences of the changes thus introduced in the nineteenth century was the erosion of the traditional Indian village community, with its high degree of self-sufficiency and its delicate balance of agriculture and handicraft industry which had served it well for centuries, and especially in the early period of its relationship with the Western traders.

British imperialism's reorganization of the traditional Indian village economy and society, beginning with the so-called Permanent Settlement of Bengal in 1793, involved three major elements: (1) the establishment of a land revenue and taxation system that imposed greater hardships on the village community than those to which it had been accustomed under the Mogul Empire or before; (2) the introduction of the notion of private property in land, paving the way for the expansion of a vast intermediary landlord class, who increased the burden of economic and social exploitation of the peasantry; (3) the imposition of trade and tariff policies that guaranteed free entry of British products into India but levied prohibitive duties on Indian products entering Britain, resulting in the severe disruption of traditional Indian handicraft manufactures and an unprecedented displacement of millions of producers in the countryside.

Taxation introduced by the British was of two kinds, one indirect and one direct: the *zamindari* system introduced in Bengal in 1793, and the *ryotwari* system introduced in South India in 1812 and later extended to the northwest and northeast. The zamindar in traditional Mogul India was a local chieftain or elite figure whose claims to exercise personal revenue collection rights over a specific territory were left untouched by the Mogul bureaucracy, so long as he surrendered a fixed portion of those revenues to the central authorities. The British arrangement went a step further: it not only endorsed his authority as an intermediary and revenue collector, but also extended it by granting him Western-style private property rights in the lands under his control, thereby transforming him into a landlord.

Thus under the British system, the peasantry found itself at a dual disadvantage. Not only was the collection system made more "efficient" and more brutally extractive than the lax Mogul system,[3] but the zamindar-landlord was now free to subject the new tenants to all manner of rental payments. These often escalated to unbearable levels, driving many of the peasants to local moneylenders, who themselves extracted their own pound of flesh from the helpless villagers. The moneylender in the Indian village system predated the British, but his power over the debtor was always circumscribed by village tradition and customary law: he could not seize the debtor's land, or transfer it to outsiders, nor could

Chinese immigrant and wife, 1890s.
From Henry Kirke, *Twenty-five Years in British Guiana, 1872–1897* (London, 1898).

he deny the tenant's traditional rights over the land.[4] These circumscribed collection rights were vastly extended with the British recognition
of private property rights in land and their readiness to protect these
rights, and enforce debts and mortgages, in the new colonial court system. Village debtors were often at the mercy of their creditors. The result
was frequently bankruptcy and eviction, in a process that constantly
multiplied the numbers of landless laborers living on the edge of starvation in a generally depressed and nonvibrant agricultural milieu.

Often, there were further layers between the zamindar-landlord and
the tenant-cultivator, as tenants themselves subdivided and rented out
portions of their lands to other tenants. This produced a complicated

pyramid of landlordism throughout the countryside (the process is called subinfeudation), not to mention an intense fragmentation of the land.

Under the *ryotwari* system, the government collected the taxes directly from the tenant-cultivator, or ryot, and not through a *zamindari* class. This direct relationship did not relieve the tenants of the crushing burdens of payment imposed by the government, and the levels of displacement caused by the moneylenders and the landlords (in this case subsidiary peasant proprietors) were no less acute.

Together, both systems succeeded in bringing to an end the underlying communalism that lay at the heart of traditional village life, despite its internal occupational and caste stratifications. In its place was erected a system which was a mix of feudal landlord-tenant relations and an uneven system of commercial agriculture, growing crops for the market beyond the horizons of the village structure, and indeed for the British metropolis.

In addition to the tax collection system and land tenure laws, the British imposed a trade tariff policy which was pro–free trade as far as British products entering India were concerned, but protectionist in relation to Indian products entering Britain. By this means, the substantial cottage-type industrial production of India, producing the finest silks, cottons, and muslins, which Britain had imported in great quantity before the Industrial Revolution, was gradually stifled, while British-made cotton textiles flooded the colonial market. This specialized home manufacturing sector of traditional India, which had supplied both domestic and export markets and provided employment for millions of artisans in towns and villages, gradually crumbled against the onslaught of British trade policies.

With the introduction of the railway after 1853, cheap British machine-made products penetrated the remotest villages of India, permanently altering the domestic market and handicraft industry production patterns and throwing millions of people back into agriculture at the very moment that this sector was itself undergoing its own traumatic transitions under the new colonial empire. Lord William Bentinck, Governor-General of India, commenting in 1834 on the dilemma of the Indian cotton weavers, pronounced his famous (and now classic) condemnation:

> the misery hardly finds a parallel in the history of commerce. The bones of the cotton weavers are bleaching the plains of India.[5]

A local newspaper, the *Bengal Hurkaru,* recorded the following comment in 1835:

> The calamity was not felt by the weavers only, but it continued to be felt by all sections of people. Because, it is well known that cloth would formerly be manufactured not only for home consumption but also for exports, from thread spun by native women of every class. From Brahman to the Hary—from the wealthy zamindar and merchant's wife to the wife of the poorest ryot, every woman had a charka for herself and every female in the family. Return of profit to each woman was more than sufficient for her subsistence, and thus one half of the population used to live by spinning. Since the introduction of European thread so superior in quality and cheap in price, scarcely a charka is to be seen in the country. Not only that the return of this rude spinning machine is not now enough to maintain the spinner, but it cannot cover even the cost of cotton. Under these circumstances, it is no wonder that a poor family that used to command the industry of four hands, having two rendered altogether unproductive, must suffer penury. Hence the increase of poverty among the ryots and other poorer classes.[6]

India thus became the first classic colony of the Industrial Revolution: deindustrialized consumer of imported British products, and vital supplier of primary products required by the industrial metropolis.[7]

The social displacement and consequent population pressure on the land were felt more acutely in some areas of India than in others. The North Western Provinces and Oudh in the Indo-Gangetic Plain (combined in 1877, known after 1902 as the United Provinces of Agra and Oudh, and still later as Uttar Pradesh), Bihar within the westernmost end of the Bengal Presidency (today a separate province), and the Madras Presidency in South India were the areas most affected by the disruption of traditional economic life. The phenomenon of the landless laborer or the socially oppressed peasant was no invention of British colonialism, but British policies certainly intensified the phenomenon—in some areas to unprecedented levels—and upset the delicate hierarchies of traditional village India in a way that the Mogul rulers themselves had never succeeded in doing.

One example of an oppressive social tradition which predated the British arrival was a form of praedial servitude existing in various parts of northern India which bound peasants to their landlords through unpaid debts. In Bihar this debt bondage system was known as *kamiuti* and the debtors or bond slaves as *kamias*. In exchange for a loan from the landlord-moneylender, the *kamia* executed a bond pledging his services for a specified period. There were three types of servitude arrangements. The most severe involved binding himself and his descendants in perpetuity to the creditor; the children were born slaves of the estates and were disposed of at the proprietor's will. The second arrangement involved slavery for life for the *kamia*, but his children were not slaves. The third arrangement involved being bound to the landlord-creditor until the repayment of the debt. This was very often longer than anticipated, considering the accumulation of interest payments, low wages, and other devices (including further loans) which the landlord would conjure up in order to enslave the debtor as long as he could. Often the only alternative for the debt slave was to flee to another district or province, or even overseas, to escape the clutches of his master.[8]

In South India, moreover, slavery proper was widespread in the early nineteenth century. The pariahs, or "untouchables," were said to number about one-fifth of the population of the vast Madras Presidency, and their conditions were declared by European residents to be worse than those of slaves elsewhere. An active slave trade from South India to overseas destinations such as Malaya, as well as Mauritius and Reunion in the Indian Ocean, existed in the eighteenth century. In 1800 there were as many as six thousand slaves on the estates of Mauritius and a sizeable number on the island of Reunion.[9]

The central dilemmas facing large sections of the Indian peasantry in the disruptive years of the early nineteenth century, therefore, were partly traditional, partly British-inspired: oppressive social relations in the countryside, ranging from traditional slavery in all its forms to feudal exploitation by landlords and moneylenders; and displacement of millions of artisans who were thrown back into agriculture, swelling the ranks of the landless from about 1815 onwards. The result was intense population congestion and strain on available land resources. This was exacerbated by low productivity, itself the result of natural infertility in some areas, as well as agricultural nonexpansion and conservative utilization stemming from feudal relations, and continual fragmentation of landholding units (subinfeudation) mentioned above.[10]

Added to these factors were the periods of intense famine caused by crop failures or the ravages of nature (drought or floods) which occurred with great regularity, striking some areas more often than others during the century. Major famines occurred in the North Western Provinces in

1860–62; in the United Provinces (North West Provinces and Oudh) in 1877–78; in Bengal, Bihar, and Orissa in 1865–67; in Bengal and Bihar in 1872–75 and 1884–85; and in the Madras Presidency in 1876–79.

A few things must be emphasized in relation to these general "push" factors. In the first place, the mobility of labor which they occasioned in the nineteenth century flowed more towards destinations within India itself than towards overseas destinations. The main areas of migrant labor absorption (much of it seasonal) were the provinces of Bengal and Assam, the former with its jute mills, coal mines, and other industries, the latter with its tea plantations. Labor also migrated to the textile mills of Bombay and to coffee, tea, and cotton plantations in the south and west. In addition, government public works and railway construction employed thousands of laborers from several provinces.

Second, the people who were caught up in the inland migration process were from the same areas as those involved in the overseas migrations. Provinces such as the United Provinces (North West Provinces and Oudh), Bihar, and Bengal in the north and Madras in the south generally provided the most mobile labor force internally as well as externally. The overseas migrations are to be seen as an extension and overflow of an internal labor fluidity within the colonial Indian economy itself, as it adjusted to the British imperial impact, and not as a separate phenomenon. Indian migration was more the product of "push" factors than "pull" factors, important though some of these latter may have been, especially in the later years.

Third, the overall mobility of labor, both inland and overseas, was very small in comparison with the total population, even within the provinces where labor was most mobile. The Indian peasantry was traditionally, and continued to be throughout the nineteenth century, an extremely inward-looking and immobile social class. The 1891 census of India revealed that 89 percent of the people were still residing in the districts in which they were born, and as many as 98 percent were still resident in the provinces of their birth.

A variety of social inhibitions operated to keep Indian peasants rooted to their environment, despite often overwhelming hardship. Among these were fear of caste defilement, religious conversion, loss of tradition; ignorance and apprehension of life beyond the support systems of family, caste, and village; fear of the unknown beyond the *kala pani*, or dark waters; and last but not least, a strong suspicion of the overseas recruiters and their motivations.

There were some notable exceptions to the rule. In some districts, emigration overseas was not feared but was actually popular. Shahabad and Patna in Bihar had such a reputation.[11] So, too, did Chota Nagpur, the home of the non-Hindu tribal people in South Bihar and West Bengal who emigrated en masse to the tea plantations of Assam, the indigo factories of Bihar, and the overseas sugar colonies in the 1840s and 1850s. South Indians were also less generally inhibited about overseas migration than North Indians, and indeed, next-door Ceylon was to the South Indian what inland Assam or Bengal was to the North: a major destination for seasonal migrant workers.

Fourth, there were often "push" factors at work which were more than simply socioeconomic. Some were political, others were compounded by personal motivations of a complex and varied nature, and still others involved a measure of trickery and fraudulence practiced by recruiters on the gullible. The most important political "push" factor in the migration years was the Indian Mutiny of 1857–58, a widespread insurrection against the British which erupted, exactly one hundred years after the conquest of Bengal, in neighboring North West Provinces, Oudh, and Bihar. This was the most important, and was to be the last, organized native rebellion against British imperialism in nineteenth-century India.[12] A Hindu and Muslim alliance of dispossessed sectors of the traditional elite, landlord-zamindars, the peasantry, and the Indian soldiery within the British Army engulfed the north from Delhi to Patna in a sixteen- to eighteen-month conflict, which was put down finally with great loss of life and great social dislocation in the areas directly affected by the confrontation.

Emigration to the colonies from Calcutta shot up by more than three times in the years 1858–59. Most of the emigrants went voluntarily to the emigration depots, and most were from the districts most affected by the disturbances (e.g., Shahabad, Patna, Gaya in Bihar, Ghazipur in Oudh). Many were high-caste ex-soldiers from the disbanded native army denied jobs in the British Indian Army; many were mutineers fleeing from the prospect of arrest and deportation to Port Blair, the convict settlement in the Andaman islands. Mauritius was the main destination of the increased tide, but Demerara (British Guiana) also experienced a significant jump in immigration. Trinidad was less affected, but by no means totally immune from this politically inspired surge in emigration from Calcutta.[13]

Personal and domestic motivations for migrating overseas ranged from the typical to the unusual to the highly eccentric. Typical examples were individuals who felt personally oppressed or stifled by the joint family or

village community life. This would include those who had lost caste for
one reason or another, those who had quarreled with relatives, those
with a sense of adventure, and widows who felt tyrannized by the expectations and demands of the traditional household. Some individuals might
be avoiding the long arm of the law or the stranglehold of a creditor.
Many may have migrated to urban Bengal in search of employment there
but were frustrated in their efforts. British official G. A. Grierson, in his
report on emigration from Bengal submitted in 1883, said as much: "I
believe that the bulk of the people registered there [the 24 Parganas
district in Calcutta] are up-country men, who have come down to Calcutta to look for work, and have failed to find it."[14]

There were the unusual migrants, like the batch of dancing girls and
their male attendants who found their way to Surinam in the 1870s, or
the odd schoolmaster who had fallen on hard times.[15] There was the
poignant, like the case of the migrant arriving in Trinidad in 1899 looking for a rich brother already settled in the island, and whose indenture
was immediately commuted by that brother upon being found.[16] Then
again, there was the downright idiosyncratic, like the young woman who
arrived in Jamaica in 1891 on board the *Erne*, claiming to be a princess,
the daughter of the Maharaja of Nepal, who had escaped overseas with
a palace servant only to satisfy her curiosity about the new country.[17]

Dr. D. W. D. Comins, an Indian government official who visited the
Caribbean region in 1891 and wrote a series of reports on the social
conditions of the Indians in the various territories, told the story of the
adventurous Luchmon, who migrated, deserted, and remigrated to British
Guiana no less than three times between 1879 and 1888, constantly
eluding his planter-employers and the authorities, before disappearing
from the colony for good after his third return and desertion.[18]

Not all the migrants left for overseas destinations on their own volition. Cases of illegal detention or kidnapping or other coercion were
frequent enough to warrant the attention of the authorities in India,
even as late as the 1870s.[19] More often, the seductive promises of the
native recruiting agents enticed their more gullible brethren into accepting contracts of indenture which many regretted after arrival in the
new societies. Intending migrants were often misled on the issue of wages
or conditions of work, especially in the early years. As late as 1909,
one witness before the Sanderson Commission of Enquiry into Indian
Emigration, held in London, himself a manager of a British Guiana
estate, had this to say about the recruiters of his day:

I do not believe the present recruiters in India care twopence whether the men are good men for agriculture or not, so long as they get their commission. . . . I do not mean the magistrates and the white men, I mean the men who go about recruiting. They tell the coolies lots of nonsense I am quite sure, because a coolie has often told me he was told so and so, and in fact he thought all he had to do was to lie on his back and the cocoanuts would drop into his mouth, and the gold, and everything else.[20]

As late as 1905, four Brahmins who arrived in Trinidad refused to work and demanded to be returned to India, claiming that they had been deceived by their recruiters about what to expect in their new home.[21]

In most districts, many of the villagers were so suspicious of the recruiters that they were often bullied by the local district policemen as they went about their recruiting operations.[22] Even the local district magistrates, whose duty it was to formally register the recruits after establishing their willingness to emigrate, often did their best to dissuade the villagers from their decisions, with insinuations about the dangers of kala pani crossings or life in the sugar colonies.[23] Trinidad's Protector of Immigrants, William Coombs, told the Sanderson Commission hearings that sometimes as many as 5 or 6 percent of the migrants were people who refused to work after arrival, claiming some deception or misrepresentation in the recruitment process.

We get high-caste Brahmins, we get priests and Sadoos, and all sorts of people who are really no use at all. These men go on the estate, and directly they get there they say "No, I did not come here to work; I was told I would get a place as a clerk", or something. Then we have occasionally people who are educated men who come over, certainly we cannot find out why, but very often being under a cloud in India, and they refuse to work also.[24]

Where, then, did most of the migrants actually come from, where did they go, and in what numbers? Was there any correlation between province or district of origin and overseas destination? Were there preferences and priorities among the various destinations, or was migration a haphazard affair? What percentage of the overall total went to the British Caribbean plantations?

The broadest distinctions are between those who left via the North Indian port of Calcutta in Bengal and those who did so via the various South Indian ports of the Madras Presidency (mainly Madras proper, but

Newly arrived immigrants, 1890s.
Courtesy University of the West Indies (Trinidad) Library.

also from Pondichery and Karikal for the French colonies). Up until
1865, an attempt was made to make Bombay on the west coast an emigration port, but only about 31,761 made their way to Mauritius via this
route. Local "pull" factors, such as the rise of industry in Bombay, absorbed much of the floating labor around this port. The objections of the
government of Bombay to emigration also played a part: its claim was that
there was no significant population pressure in the Bombay Presidency to
justify colonial emigration schemes.[25]

The initial years of the overseas migration (1830s to mid-1850s) relied
mainly on recruitment from among the non-Hindu aboriginal tribes living
in the hilly Chota Nagpur district in southern Bihar (known collectively
as *Dhangars* or *Kols* or "Hill Coolies"); from floating déclassé elements in
the cities of Calcutta or Madras; and from the pariah, or "untouchable,"
elements of the districts surrounding Madras, many of whom were in a
position of slavery or semislavery. A significant number were also from
the northwestern regions, driven to the cities by famine in the early
1840s in Upper India.

Between 1834 and 1841, Mauritius absorbed 15,753 migrants from
Calcutta, 9,955 from Madras, and 272 from Bombay. Alone of the British

Caribbean territories, British Guiana received 396 in 1838 (the year apprenticeship ended) in two ships, the *Whitby* and the *Hesperus*, brought over by private enterprise and distributed over six estates (the numbers actually embarked from Calcutta were 414).[26]

It is difficult to estimate the exact ratio of tribals to Hindu elements in these early shipments. A recent study suggests that in the 1840s and 1850s, about two-fifths to one-half of the overseas migrants were *Dhangars* from Chota Nagpur and neighboring districts.[27] The British Guiana contingent of 1838 consisted of 150 tribals from Chota Nagpur. Of the Burdwan and Bankurah districts near Calcutta, it is not clear how many were tribals. The 1843–45 shipments of 32,000 from Calcutta to Mauritius comprised about 53 percent Hindus and 47 percent tribals. It has been pointed out by one writer, though, that in the early official lists of the overseas migration, many people described as *Dhangars* or "Hill Coolies" were often low-caste Hindus, identifiable as such by their names.[28]

During the first years of the Caribbean migrations (barring the 1838 arrivals), a total of 22,202 left Calcutta and Madras between 1845 and 1848 for British Guiana, Trinidad, and Jamaica (11,071 from Calcutta and 11,131 from Madras). The percentage of tribals among the North Indians must have been about 50 percent. From the early 1850s onwards, the emphasis of the recruiting operations shifted farther westwards as the *Dhangar* component began to decline, partly because of the heavy mortality they experienced at sea and on the overseas plantations, but mainly because the expanding tea plantations of Assam proved to be a more attractive option for Chota Nagpur laborers.[29] During the season of 1853–54, of 14,368 who embarked from Calcutta, only 2,234, or 15.5 percent, were from Chota Nagpur. One official estimate made in the early 1870s put the total number of "aboriginals" migrating overseas between 1842 and 1870 at 17 percent of the total North Indian contingent (54,956).[30] Declining by the 1860s to virtually zero, the tribal element would resurface in the final two decades of the migration (1900–1917), but only as a tiny, unquantifiable segment of the whole. In Trinidad they were known as "janglis."

Throughout the nineteenth century and beyond, there were a number of specific districts within the major provinces of recruitment which tended to produce more recruits than others. The main districts in the United Provinces tended to be the easternmost ones, many within Oudh: Ballia, Ghazipur, Azamghar, Fyzabad, Basti, Gonda, Gorakhpur, Benares, Mirzapur, Jaunpur, Lucknow, Cawnpore (Kanpur), Allahabad, and Agra. The main districts of Bihar were Shahabad, Patna, Gaya, Saran, Muzaffarpur, and Champaran. Each of these districts had between one and two million inhabitants in the 1870s and 1880s, and the population density ranged from 217 per square mile in Mirzapur to 870 in Saran.

A minority of recruits came from other North Indian provinces: Central India, the Punjab, Rajputana, and Orissa.[31] The main districts in Central India were Bilaspur, Jubbalpore, and Raipur; in the Punjab, eastern districts such as Delhi, Ambala, and Rohtak.

From South India, the sprawling Madras Presidency provided the bulk of the southern migrants, from both the Tamil-speaking districts and the Telugu-speaking districts to the north of Madras city. Among the former, Tanjore, Trichinipoly, South Arcot, Chingleput, and Madras city stood out among the early contributors to the migrant flow; among the latter, Vizagapatam, Ganjam, Rajahmundy, and Godavari.

By far the greater number of the mobile labor force of the North Indian provinces found themselves gravitating towards more industrialized Bengal. In 1881, out of a total population of 69 million, Bengal recorded 593,292 immigrants, 352,693 of whom were from the North West Provinces and Oudh. In 1891, there were 200,000 migrant laborers in Bengal from the Bihar district of Gaya alone. Many of those recruited in Calcutta proper for overseas colonies were actually from outside Bengal. In 1880–82, out of 4,736 recruited in the 24 Parganas district of metropolitan Calcutta, only 74 were local men.[32]

The dominant province in the overseas migration before the 1870s tended to be Bengal (including Bihar). After that period the United Provinces (North West Provinces and Oudh) became the major recruiting ground. John Geoghegan, Under-Secretary of the Agriculture, Revenue, and Commerce Department in the government of India (which handled the emigration portfolio), wrote a comprehensive report on emigration from India which was published in 1873–74. In it, he reported that between 1842 and 1871, the United Provinces contributed 29.3 percent (100,433) of the Calcutta emigration. Bihar alone contributed 45.2 percent (155,399). The other areas specified in the report were western Bengal, 18 percent (62,113); central Bengal, 3.8 percent (13,224); Orissa, 1.3 percent (4,409); eastern Bengal, 0.5 percent (1,713); and "elsewhere," 1.9 percent (6,391).[33] Emigration from the Bengal Presidency as a whole (including Bihar) thus constituted 68.8 percent.

Total emigration from Madras and the French ports of Pondichery and Karikal between 1842 and 1870 amounted to 159,259 (29.8 percent), and from Bombay 31,761 (6 percent). Hugh Tinker has pointed out that these Madras figures did not include the vast spontaneous and unregulated migration from South India to next-door Ceylon and to Malaya and Burma, which was impossible to quantify and involved about half a million or more (many returning to India).[34]

Of these total figures, the breakdown for the Caribbean alone suggests that the United Provinces (including a small number from Central India) contributed a slightly higher percentage than the overall percentage figure of 29.3 mentioned above (which would of course have included the Mauritius contingent). Calcutta departures for Trinidad up to 1871 included 41.7 percent from the United Provinces and 29.3 percent from Bihar, with the overall total from the Bengal Presidency (including Bihar) being 56 percent. British Guiana had 37.3 percent from the United Provinces, 36 percent from Bihar, and 61 percent from the Bengal Presidency (including Bihar). The Jamaican contingent included 35 percent from the United Provinces, 33.7 percent from Bihar, and 62.2 percent from the Bengal Presidency (including Bihar). Geoghegan stated that up to 1870 the main districts of recruitment were Arrah (Shahabad), Gaya, Patna, Allahabad, Ghazipur, and Oudh.[35]

Soon after 1870 the dominance of the United Provinces as the main provider of overseas migrants to the sugar colonies was established. In the 1872–73 season, it contributed more than three times the number of emigrants as the whole of the Bengal Presidency: 12,263 as opposed to 4,327 (of whom 3,360 were from Bihar). In 1878–79 it contributed 12,869 as opposed to 2,727 from the Bengal Presidency. In the 1881–82 season, out of a total of 11,000, only 1,800 were registered in the Bengal Presidency. This pattern continued throughout the rest of the century, with the United Provinces providing 63.7 percent of the emigrants for 1888, 65.1 percent of those for 1889, 83.1 percent for 1890, and 81 percent for 1896.[36]

There were individual seasons when the normal percentage patterns were reversed, because of special developments. Thus, in the 1883–84 season, due to the semifamine in Bengal and Bihar, the recruitment figures from these areas were higher than usual, with 6,795 as compared with 8,599 from the United Provinces. In the 1884–85 season, this figure escalated to 12,775, more than the 8,461 from the United Provinces. This pattern continued throughout the last nine months of 1885.

During the 1890s, moreover, there was a steep increase in the number of migrants from the Punjab, most of whom were going to Fiji. The census report of India tells us that between 1891 and 1901, Punjabis were actually the second largest group of emigrants after those from the United Provinces, with Madrasis third and those from the Bengal Presidency fourth. Again, the annual report of the Calcutta Protector stated that in 1904, while 62 percent of the migrants were from the United Provinces, 17 percent were from the Central Provinces (an area not normally associated with large-scale recruiting, although many were going to Assam in the 1900s), 8 percent were from the Punjab, and 6 percent from Bihar.

Special occurrences could also occasion dramatic increases in the annual departure figures. The most dramatic was the period immediately after the Indian Mutiny, when 27,779 left Calcutta in the 1858 season, and 25,337 in the 1859 season. These were the only two years when the annual departure figures from Calcutta rose above the 25,000 level.[37] The main districts affected by the social disruptions—Shahabad, Ghazipur, Gaya, Patna—provided more than 50 percent of this sudden increased outflow. Mauritius received the lion's share of this dramatic exodus, but British Guiana figures also leapt from a 2,000 annual average to over 4,000 in the years between 1859 and 1861, and even Trinidad crossed the annual 1,500 average to an over-2,000 figure between 1858 and 1861.

Years of famine could also cause the emigration rate to rise above the normal. In 1860 and 1861, when famine prevailed in the North West Provinces, the number of departures from Calcutta was 17,899 and 22,600, respectively. In 1865–66, the year of the famine in Orissa and Bihar, the departure total was 19,963. In 1873–74 and 1874–75, famine in Bihar and severe scarcity in Oudh and the eastern districts of the North West Provinces caused the totals to rise to 24,571 and 20,109. The same occurred in 1877–78, when famine in the eastern United Provinces lifted the numbers departing to 13,342 from 6,620 in the previous season.

By 1910 the Sanderson Commission of Enquiry into Indian Emigration was stating that most of the overseas-bound Indians were recruited in three districts in the eastern United Provinces—Fyzabad, Basti, and Gonda—and that 80 percent were born in twenty-one districts of Bengal and the United Provinces, with a combined total area of 55,000 square miles and a population of thirty-four million: north and south Bihar, the Benares, Gorakhpur, and Fyzabad divisions.[38]

The general trends described above for the post-1870 period were also true for Trinidad and British Guiana individually. A recent study on Trinidad concluded that between 1875 and 1917, of 92,243 migrants, 75 percent came from the United Provinces (23 percent from Oudh alone), 13 percent from Bihar, 4 percent from Central India, 3 percent from Nepal and the native states, 2 percent from the Punjab, 1 percent from

Bengal, and another 1 percent from places like Orissa, Ajmere, and Bombay.[39] A full 91 percent of the 1908 season (2,231) were from the United Provinces, with 5 percent (121) from Bihar and Bengal and 4 percent (95) from the smaller provinces.[40] Another study concluded that between 1865 and 1917, the migrants to British Guiana were 70.3 percent from the United Provinces and 15.3 percent from Bihar.[41] In 1898, a full 83 percent of the 3,450 destined for British Guiana from Calcutta came from the United Provinces, with only 7.8 percent from Bihar and 7.2 percent from Bengal proper, and the remaining 2 percent from elsewhere.

Outside of the North Indian provinces, the main contributor to the migration outflow was the Madras Presidency in the south. Most of the South Indian exodus, however, was not to the sugar colonies, but to the tea, coffee, and rubber plantations of Ceylon and Malaya and the rice fields and rice mills of Burma. Only a mere 8 percent of the vast Madras emigration was directed towards Mauritius, the Caribbean, Natal, and Fiji.[42] When Geoghegan wrote his report on Indian emigration in 1873–74, his estimate of the Madras outflow to the sugar colonies was 29.8 percent (159,259) of the whole for the years 1842 to 1870. Of these, 110,825 had left for Mauritius, 11,459 for British Guiana, 4,992 for Trinidad, 2,792 for Jamaica, and 5,437 for Natal. A full 16,341 had gone to the French West Indian colonies of Guadeloupe, Martinique, and French Guiana, departing from Madras proper as well as the neighbor ports of Pondichery and Karikal.[43]

The Madras contribution to Indian labor in the Caribbean was fitful and sporadic, with most of it confined to the pre-1863 period. Apart from difficulties on the recruiting end, the Madras emigration was never very popular with the Caribbean planters, all of whom preferred the North Indians as laborers. The Immigration Agent-General for British Guiana, Robert Duff, who told the Sanderson Commission in 1909 that he liked the Madrasis as laborers, some of the men from Ganjam district being "magnificent men," was definitely going against the prevailing view of the South Indians held in the West Indies (if not necessarily elsewhere).[44]

Trinidad received no Madrasis in the nineteenth century after 1871 (a single shipment of 322 arrivals after the last one in 1860).[45] But in the twentieth century there was a brief revival, and quite a sizeable number came to the island in the years 1906, 1910, 1911, 1912, and 1916, the last years of the traffic. Eight vessels, most of them calling at both Calcutta and Madras, brought 3,375 Madrasis alive to Trinidad in these closing years.[46] There is also some indication that a trickle may have arrived in the intervening years as part of the Calcutta contingent. Though it was never large in dimension, it was not that unusual for a few Madrasis to emigrate via Calcutta to the colonies. During the 1877–78 season, for example, when there was a famine in the south, about 1,594 of these casual emigrants from the Madras Presidency left via Calcutta for various destinations.[47] A few even found their way to Trinidad in that year.[48] The reports on emigration from the port of Calcutta for 1905–8 also show that 9 Madrasis (6 men, 3 women) left for Trinidad via Calcutta in 1905, 6 (5 men, 1 woman) in 1907, and 1 woman in 1908.

After the last arrivals in 1862, British Guiana received a few shipments of Madrasis between 1884 and 1886, then no more until the traffic was again reopened in 1912. Dr. Comins estimated in his 1893 report to the government of India that up to 1890, British Guiana had received 14,026 Madrasis as against 156,995 "Calcuttans," or 8.93 to every 100. He estimated the Madras population in 1890 to be about 6 percent of the immigrants.[49] In 1905, there was actually one lone Madrasi laborer still indentured to Non Pareil estate in East Coast Demerara.[50] About thirty-one estates had small contingents of ex-indentured Madrasis still resident in that year. Then, in 1913, 46 Tamils and Telugus were brought in on the *Indus*, and in 1914–15, 314 more Madrasis arrived in British Guiana. Jamaica, in the meantime, had received ten shiploads of Madrasis up to 1863, then none until the very last vessel in 1916, the *Dewa*, which called at both Calcutta and Madras and brought 258 Madrasis alive out of 617 to the island in June.

The minor provinces fluctuated in their contributions to the migrant outflow over time, as we have seen. The *Alnwick Castle* during the 1861–63 seasons to Trinidad had included people from Baluchistan, West Punjab, Bhopal in Central India, Kashmir, and even Kabul in Afghanistan. On board the *Cochin* to Trinidad in 1869–70, the passengers included a minority from the Punjab, Rajasthan, Central India, Bombay, Vindhya Pradesh, and Nepal. Several Nepalis traveled to Trinidad in the 1870s and 1880s.[51] The annual immigration reports from Trinidad in the closing two decades of the migration were full of references to newcomers: Sikhs and others from the Punjab, Pathans (Afghans), Rajputs from Ajmere, recruits from the native states of Gwalior and Jaipur, as well as Bhopal in Central India.

There were also hordes of second-time indentured immigrants ("return" migrants, they were called) hailing from the other colonies: British

TABLE 2.1

	1882	1907	Increase
Mauritius	248,000	264,000	16,000
British Guiana	88,000	127,000	39,000
Trinidad	51,000	103,000	52,000
Natal	25,000	115,000	90,000
Jamaica	11,000	13,000	2,000
Fiji	1,400	31,000	29,600

Guiana and Surinam in the Caribbean, as well as Mauritius, Natal, Fiji, the Straits Settlements or Malaya, even two from New Caledonia in the Pacific in 1910–11. Trinidad in the early twentieth century had become one of the favorite destinations of the Indian emigrants. Colonel Duncan Pitcher, in his testimony before the Sanderson Commission, placed Fiji, British Guiana, and Trinidad equally as tops on his personal list of favored destinations for the Indian emigrants.[52] Dr. Comins, in his 1893 reports, had closed his Trinidad report with the following pronouncement: "If I were a Cooly, I should like to spend my indentured service in British Guiana, and then settle down in the hills of Trinidad."[53]

A look at the size of the Indian populations in the major British sugar colonies in the 1880s, and again about twenty-five years afterwards (see Table 2.1), should give us some idea of their relative growth during the height of emigration.[54]

Of the 238,909 Indians who landed alive in British Guiana between 1838 and 1917, 31.62 percent (75,547) eventually returned to India, taking advantage of the repatriation option in their contracts. Of the 143,939 who landed in Trinidad in the same period, 23.13 percent (33,294) returned to India. The Jamaican repatriates were 32.63 percent (11,880) out of a total of 36,412. Thus 71 percent of the Indian immigrants made the Caribbean their permanent homes or final resting places.[55]

Nature and Causes of Chinese Emigration

The expansion of Chinese overseas migration in the nineteenth century, mainly from southern China, differed from contemporary Indian migration in a number of significant ways. There was the obviously wider dispersal of destinations discussed earlier, with the Chinese venturing out of the traditional Southeast Asian orbit in the late 1840s and towards expanding areas of the Western world, while Indian migrations remained confined to the Afro-Asian world, including the semi-Western plantation economies of the Caribbean region.[56]

In addition, it is not wholly inaccurate to say that the Chinese migration movements were just as influenced by "pull" factors as by "push" factors. The majority of those who emigrated were free voluntary migrants, with the contract or indentured labor element constituting no more than about 11 or 12 percent. While there was undoubtedly a significant element who had been driven to such personal desperation by conditions in China that where they went was of lesser importance than the fact that they could escape at all,[57] the total migration movement was arguably characterized by a much greater self-awareness and discrimination between destinations than was the case with the Indian indentured laborers leaving Calcutta or Madras. The destinations of many of the Indian recruits in the early years were often arbitrarily altered at the last moment by the recruiting officers at the registration (recruitment) points, simply on the basis of the relative lengths of the emigration lists before them. The gold mines of California or Australia, by contrast, were their own magnets, drawing working people from many societies and ethnic groups, including the Chinese.

Because most Chinese migration was free, moreover, the extent to which Western middlemen (state or private) were involved was much less than with the contract labor migrations. Most Chinese overseas migration movements were controlled by Chinese business intermediaries, for better or worse, acting as free agents rather than as agents of a larger state apparatus, Chinese or other.

A look at the domestic "push" factors also reveals that Chinese "push" factors tended in the main to be largely internally self-generated, and not as totally the result of Western imperialist disruptions of traditional society as they clearly were in India. The Western intervention exacerbated, but did not cause, the exodus. Chinese migrations to Southeast Asia dated from the fifteenth century and even before. Before the Anglo-Chinese War of 1839–42 (the First Opium War), which opened up China decisively to the West, Chinese imperial society had been undergoing its own internal crises, especially after the death of the Emperor Chien Lung in 1795.

The Ch'ing dynasty in the early nineteenth century became prey to widespread social illnesses: weak leadership, corrupt bureaucracy, regional fragmentation tendencies, in addition to problems of overpopulation and recurring productivity crises in many regions (many stemming from basic irrigation and public works maintenance problems caused by misuse and mismanagement of public funds at the local levels). Attempts by the imperial authorities to resolve their growing fiscal problems by increased taxation and levies on an already oppressed peasantry led to an anti-imperial peasant hostility and unrest that was widespread in the nineteenth century.

Both the fiscal and political crises of the old regime were exacerbated by the Chinese military defeats in the two so-called Opium Wars of 1839–42 and 1856–60. The Western powers, led by Britain, were interested in deepening the trade between an aloof and largely self-sufficient China and the West. Outright colonial conquest along the lines already adopted in India after 1763 was not militarily and politically feasible, but the indispensability of Chinese products and the prospects of a vast market for British goods led the British to persevere in the attempt to break down Chinese imperial closed-door policies, best characterized by the famous statement of Emperor Chien Lung to King George III in 1793:

> Our Celestial Empire possesses all things in abundance and lacks no products within its borders. There is therefore no need to import the manufactures of outside barbarians in exchange for our own produce. But as the tea, silk and porcelain which the Celestial Empire produces are absolute necessities to European nations and to yourselves, we have permitted, as a signal mark of favour, foreign *hongs* (business establishments) to be established at Canton.[58]

The overwhelming trade superiority of the Chinese was, ironically, first undermined in the eighteenth century by the illegal export of opium into China, a drug to which large sections of Chinese society had become addicted and which the imperial authorities could not stamp out. By the nineteenth century opium, grown largely in British India, was being used to pay for indispensable Chinese imports and indeed to reverse the trade balance in favor of the British. The two trade wars waged to open up China to "legitimate" free trade were also meant to further this illegal trade, out of which immense profits were made at the same time that it was succeeding in debilitating large sections of Chinese society.

As a result of the Treaty of Nanking (1842) and the Treaties of Tientsin and Peking (1860), the process of converting China into a helpless semicolony of a combined West (including the United States) and of opening up the Chinese domestic market for Western industrial products was formally completed. China's revenue imbalances became chronic, and the massive indemnity (about twenty-one million pounds) which had to be paid as a result of losing the wars made the crisis even worse.

Peasant unrest in the face of economic hardships and imperial oppression became the norm in nineteenth-century China. Hardly a year passed in the 1840s without a local uprising of some sort. The worst of these social upheavals was the fourteen-year Taiping Rebellion (1851–64), which began in Southern China, engulfed fourteen provinces, destroyed about six hundred cities, and took about twenty-five million lives before it was finally crushed with the aid of the Western powers.

In addition to this enormous rebellion, there were equally devastating interethnic conflicts in the province of Kwangtung between the native Cantonese (or Punti) and the Hakka peoples. A migratory minority ethnic and language group originally from north central China, the Hakka peoples had recently been forced to migrate farther into Kwangtung from their homes in the northeastern parts of the same province because of economic pressures. These tribal conflicts lasted from about 1854 to 1868. Whole villages were razed, and thousands of villagers were uprooted in this civil strife, particularly in the areas immediately to the west of Macao (the Sze Yup, or Four Districts, area), from which most of the migrants came.

The period of the 1850s and 1860s was therefore a period of immense internal turmoil in China, as the decaying imperial authorities found themselves caught between the growing power of Western imperialism on the one hand and widespread social unrest from below on the other— unrest that was both horizontal (interethnic) and vertical, localized in impact as well as national in scope.

About seven and a half million Chinese peasants, working people, and urban déclassé elements left China for overseas destinations in the nineteenth century in the face of these internal social conditions. The vast majority remained within the traditional Southeast Asian orbit, with a movement of about 95,000 towards Australia and about 600,000 towards the Americas. Of the American migrations, about 45 percent went to Latin America and the Caribbean, mainly as contract or indentured laborers.[59] The main destinations were Cuba (142,000, or 51 percent), Peru (100,000, or 36 percent), and the British West Indies (19,000, or 7 percent), with the remaining 6 percent siphoned off in smaller streams to Central America (Panama and Costa Rica), the Dutch and French West Indies, Brazil, and even Chile. In the last quarter of the century, after the close of the indenture period, and during the regime of Porfirio Díaz in Mexico (1876–1911), a significant movement of free Chinese immigration took place to that society, a fraction of it from California, the main destination of the North America–bound migrants.[60]

Traditionally, Chinese migrants tended to come from just two of China's provinces, Fukien (Fujian) and Kwangtung (Guangdong), both in the southeast. A British official in China writing in 1852 stated:

> it is these two provinces alone that have sent forth the myriads which have reclaimed the islands of Formosa and Hainan; introduced industry and various of the most useful arts into the countries of Cochin China, Camboja and Siam; settled many of the islands of the Indian Archipelago; and contributed more than any other race to the rise and prosperity of the European settlements in Java, the Philippines, and the Malayan Peninsula.[61]

The official identified four districts in particular as major contributors to the traditional migration: Changchow and Tseuenchow in southern Fukien, and Chaouchow and Keaying in northeast Kwangtung. They emigrated out of Amoy (Xiamen) and Swatow (Shantou), respectively.

Up until 1842, the majority of Chinese migrants were Fukienese, although traditional migrant communities in Southeast Asia tended to come from five dialect groups: Hokkien (from Amoy in Fukien), Teochiu (from Swatow in northeast Kwangtung), Cantonese (from the areas surrounding Canton in southeast Kwangtung), Hakka (the Hakkas lived in all three areas but had a subcultural life of their own), and Hainanese (from the southern island of Hainan). Prior to 1842 the Cantonese element was a subsidiary element of the migrant stream, and indeed, as late as 1852, when the British official quoted above wrote his brief report on Chinese emigration, he stated:

> Emigration from Canton, both in junks and foreign vessels, to the countries and settlements above named (not including California) has continued to increase during the late years, although the average number of emigrants—3,000 to 4,000 annually—is much below that of the other departments.

The exodus of the mid- to late nineteenth century brought the Cantonese segment (including Hakkas) into a more prominent position vis-à-vis the formation of overseas Chinese communities. This was especially the case with the migrations to the Americas, where the traditional ratios were directly reversed. In fact, about 96 percent of the migrants to the Americas came from the province of Kwangtung, especially the areas surrounding Canton, Macao, and Hong Kong in the southeast, with only about 4 percent coming from the traditional sending port of Amoy. In North America, the Cantonese percentage may have been as high as 99 percent.[62]

Even more astonishing, the main districts from which the Cantonese communities themselves came were hardly more than a dozen in all, constituting no more than 7,000 square miles. These districts can be classified under the following headings: (1) the Sze Yup (Four Districts) area to the west of Macao, made up of the districts of Toishan (Hsinning before 1914), Hsinhui (Sun Wui), Kai Ping, and Enping; (2) the Sam Yup (Three Districts) area just south of Canton, made up of Nanhai (Nam Hoy), Pan Yu, and Hsun-tak (Shunde); and (3) other districts scattered around the Cantonese Pearl River delta, but dominated by Chungshan, just to the north of Macao.

In some destinations some districts tended to dominate over others, but everywhere there was a mixture of migrants from all of these various districts. In the United States, some 60 percent of the Chinese came from the Toishan district, about 1,235 square miles in size and with a population of roughly 680,000 in 1853. In Latin America and the Caribbean, Toishan and Chungshan were two major districts, although (as elsewhere) there was a fair number from other areas of the Pearl River delta among them. The Hakka component, moreover, was always a significant but unquantifiable element within the whole.

Roughly 700 vessels made the journey from southern China to Latin America and the Caribbean between 1847 and 1884. Of these, 345 went to Cuba, 276 to Peru, and 50 to the British West Indies. Most of the migrants to the British West Indies (just under 80 percent, or 14,120) arrived during a concentrated eight-year period, between 1859 and 1866. Of the 50 vessels, 39 went to British Guiana, 8 to Trinidad, 2 to Jamaica, and 1 to British Honduras. Twenty sailed out of Hong Kong, 20 out of Canton, 2 out of Swatow in northeast Kwangtung, and 8 out of Amoy in Fukien Province.

Jamaica also received two ships from Panama with 205 Chinese in 1854. These men had gone earlier in the year from Swatow on two vessels, American and Spanish, to work on the Panama railway project, but the excessive mortality (about 50 percent) had aborted that experiment, and the rest made their way partly to the United States, mainly to Jamaica.[63]

Earlier in the century, moreover, there had been an unusual and solitary experiment in 1806. One vessel, the *Fortitude*, belonging to the British East India Company, had transported two hundred Chinese—

recruited in Macao, Penang (Prince of Wales island) in Malaya, and Calcutta in India—to Trinidad in an early attempt to found a colony of Chinese settlers on that island *before* the end of slavery. On the 12th of October, 192 arrived alive in what must surely have been the first organized Chinese settlement in the Western Hemisphere in the nineteenth century.[64] The experiment was not a success, and after a few years most of them returned to China or Bengal. There were about twenty or thirty of them on the island in the 1820s, and a mere two or three by the time slavery ended.[65]

The inclusion of this solitary pioneer vessel would bring the total number of vessels sailing directly from the East to the British West Indies to fifty-one, and the total number to Trinidad to nine. There were abortive attempts by the British to restart the migration in 1843, but the real movement did not begin again until 1853 (1847 for Cuba, 1849 for Peru). From that year there was a regular annual flow of vessels to the Caribbean region (mainly to Cuba) until 1874, the year the Latin American "coolie trade" ended, after which there were just a few sporadic arrivals in the British West Indies (1879, 1884).[66]

In contrast with the British West Indian migrations, about 75 percent of the Cuban/Peruvian migrations sailed out of Portuguese Macao. In the early years, Cuban recruiting vessels left from Amoy and from Namoa island off Swatow. In 1856–58 a few even left from British Hong Kong. Peruvian recruiting ships also left from Cumsingmoon, a small island off Canton. But local objections to recruiting irregularities and violence against recruiters led to a gradual shift of operations to Macao by the 1860s. The free migration to California and Australia, meanwhile, left mainly from Hong Kong and Canton, while the traditional diversity of origin of the Southeast Asian migrants continued throughout the nineteenth century, with an enlarged Cantonese component.

The percentage of Fukienese migrants among those who went to Latin America and the Caribbean seems to have been somewhat larger for the British Caribbean than for the region as a whole. The first three vessels which opened the traffic to British Guiana were from Amoy. In the concentrated eight-year period from 1859 to 1866, five ships out of the total of forty sailed from Amoy: two to British Guiana (the *Lady Elma Bruce* in 1862, arriving with 384 passengers from both Amoy and Swatow, and the *Light Brigade* in 1866, with 487 from Amoy) and two to Trinidad (the *Dudbrook* with 272 and the *Red Riding Hood* with 325, both in 1866). The solitary vessel to British Honduras in 1865, the *Light of the Age*, also sailed out of Amoy.[67] One other vessel, the *Jeddo*, also left Amoy in 1866 for British Guiana but never made it. A mutiny on board led to the ship catching fire and 161 of the 480 Chinese, plus 3 of the crew, losing their lives. The rest landed at Batavia.

The approximate numbers of Fukienese arriving alive in the British Caribbean from these ships were therefore something like 2,500, or 14 percent. The actual numbers were certainly larger, though probably not significantly so, since many vessels sailing out of Hong Kong and Canton contained within them sprinklings of migrants from Amoy as well as Swatow, particularly after the regular contract migrations from these ports officially ceased in the 1850s. Provincial factional fighting among the passengers was often reported on board, and on at least three vessels in 1862, the *Maggie Miller/Wanata* to Trinidad and the *Persia* and *Genghis Khan* to British Guiana, this kind of fighting created considerable disruption on the journey to the Caribbean.[68] As early as 1854 an official dispatch had warned against mixing the Fukienese and Cantonese migrants on the same vessels. "Hong Kong," it advised,

> is at too great a distance to be suitable as a depot for emigration from Fukien; and if it were not so, it would not be desirable to use it as such. The disputes and dissensions between the people of the two provinces, consequent upon the general dislike entertained by all other Chinese to the Cantonese; their clan feuds; the great difference of dialect—would render it highly dangerous to embark them together in the same vessel.[69]

The two vessels which left from Swatow in 1853 for Trinidad (*Australia* and *Lady Flora Hastings*) also carried a small number of emigrants from Amoy among them, about 143 in all.[70]

For Latin America and the Caribbean as a whole, one recent estimate of the Fukienese contingent stands at 11,402, or 4 percent of a rough total of 275,511. According to this estimate, the breakdown of departures for the whole region from different Chinese ports between 1847 and 1874 was as follows:[71] Macao, 205,626; Swatow, 24,953; Canton, 13,262; Amoy, 11,402; Hong Kong, 10,934; Cumsingmoon island (off Canton), 5,137; Shanghai, 485; Ningpo, 47; Singapore, 615; and Unknown, 3,050.

The minuscule Shanghai contingent may have been larger than this estimate. In 1857, 331 out of 355 landed in Martinique in the French West Indies. The rest, probably another 700 to 800, went to Cuba and Peru.[72]

One major difference between the systems of immigration from China and British India lay in the relative complexity of the former. There were basically three ways one could emigrate from China. One could pay one's own way. One could have the passage money advanced on loan by a sponsor and gradually repay that loan with interest after arrival. The sponsor could be a family member, a local Chinese broker, or a veteran Chinese immigrant based in the new country. This system of emigration was known as the credit-ticket system and was the primary method utilized by Chinese migrants to the United States, as well as Canada, Australia, and Southeast Asia.

The third arrangement, that of contract or indentured immigration, was a minority phenomenon in the history of Chinese immigration but was the primary method utilized by those who went to Latin America and the Caribbean. Contract migration to Australia, the United States, and the Pacific was not uncommon, but it was not the main trend in these destinations. Among the contract migrants, moreover, there were fundamental differences between the private enterprise–operated schemes to Cuba and Peru, for example, and the state-sponsored, state-regulated, and state-supervised system of indentured immigration which was typical of the British system.

In this respect, there was a similarity between the Chinese and Indian migrations to the British Caribbean plantations, which made them both quite distinct from the more traditional indenture experiments of the nineteenth century, particularly the infamous Latin American "coolie trade" in Chinese labor. Apart from having to obtain a license to import laborers from the China coast, the Latin American importers (whether shipping firms operating the traffic as a speculative profiteering venture, or specific planter-employers chartering vessels to bring back specified amounts of laborers) were only minimally affected by the state and its agencies in their operations. In fact, many of the shipping firms involved in the China coolie traffic were veterans of the African slave trade, shifting their attention to the China coast in the mid-nineteenth century.

By contrast, apart from a few early attempts to allow private enterprise to participate in the traffic to British Guiana, the entire British operation was state-sponsored and state-controlled, just like the more large-scale operation in India. The British government established its own recruiting agencies in Hong Kong, Canton, or smaller temporary locations in Amoy and Swatow and had a paid government official in charge of the entire operation in China, acting in consultation with the Chinese authorities at Canton (the official Chinese ban on emigration from China, on the books from time immemorial and honored more in the breach than in the observance, was altered by the 1860 treaties).

The British also preferred to utilize the services of voluntary friendly recruiting elements like China-based British and European missionaries. Strict (although not always successful) attempts were made to avoid the method of recruiting potential migrants through the activities of paid professional recruiters (or crimps, as they were called), who were the main contacts relied upon by the private speculators. The activities and methods of the professional recruiters, more often than not, involved all manner of fraud, trickery, and intimidation of the kind associated with the earliest indentured migrations from seventeenth-century Europe, and indeed African slavery itself. Interestingly, even the state-supervised recruiting system employed in India was not widely utilized in China. Here the British preferred a system of voluntary individual recruitment, assisted by missionary elements and sympathetic local Chinese officials rather than by an army of local intermediaries, whether responsible to the state or not.

One interesting difference between the Chinese and Indian migrations was the ratio of females among the migrants. Some analysts have made much of the difficulties faced by the British in getting a satisfactory proportion of women to migrate from India to the sugar colonies. The overall percentages (authorized and actual) would seem to have been somewhere between 30 and 40 percent. The Geoghegan Report revealed that up to 1870, about 21 percent of the British West Indies–bound migrants, and 19 percent of the total migration to the sugar colonies, were women (not including female children).

Reasons advanced for the recruiting difficulties centered around the traditionally conservative family role of the Indian peasant female, in a population notorious for its immobility, even within the borders of India itself. Yet in comparison with the Chinese migrations, even to Southeast Asia, these percentages seem quite large. Chinese emigration was always technically illegal before 1860, and for the Chinese female, throughout the nineteenth century, emigration continued to be so rare as to be noticeable when it did occur at all. Part of the reason stemmed from the traditionalism of Asian male/female roles, but part of the explanation must also stem from the nature of the Chinese emigration process itself.

Most Chinese who left for Southeast Asian and American destinations did not leave with the intention of settling permanently in their new societies. Indeed, there was throughout a large-scale movement back and forth to China, controlled by native Chinese middlemen, which institutionalized the temporary attitude to the migration process. This applied just as much to Malaya as it did to California, and the "sojourner" attitude prevailed for a long time, regardless of the actual realities of many immigrants' situations in the new societies.

The British Consul at Canton wrote, somewhat exaggeratedly, in 1852:

> Chinese women never emigrate. There is not a China woman in the Straits Settlements, nor an honest one in Hong Kong.[73]

Another official wrote in 1851:

> Extensive emigration has been going on for many years to almost every island in the Indian Archipelago, to Manila, to Borneo, to Java, where there are several hundred thousand; to Singapore, Malacca, and other places, but in every case the emigration has been of men alone, and there is hardly one solitary instance of the emigration of women or families. In all these cases the Chinese have formed connexions and intermarried with the Malay or other women of the country where they have settled, and the want of female emigration has consequently not been felt.

> The men appear to me to be domestic and fond of their families and children, and yet, while they emigrate by the thousands, there is hardly an instance of any woman having left the country. Many of the Chinese settled in Singapore, Java and elsewhere are comparatively wealthy; but instead of sending for their families they prefer making remittances to them, and the connexion is kept up by occasional visits to their native land.[74]

With the Western-controlled contract or indentured migration schemes to far-off Latin America, the incentives for female emigration were even less. Not only was the prospect of a return to China not as clear-cut as it was in the free migration process, but in addition the uncertainties (and downright illegalities) surrounding much of the "coolie trade" to Latin America did not act in favor of encouraging women to emigrate in large numbers. Only in the British system (and to some extent in Dutch Surinam) do we find a comparatively larger number of Chinese females among the migrants.

This was the result of deliberate British efforts to encourage family emigration, assisted by missionary elements helping the relocation efforts of villages destroyed in the ethnic feuds of southern Kwangtung in the nineteenth century. It was also the result of the decision to conform to the Chinese custom of wife purchase by granting prospective migrants a $20 gratuity for wives brought to the West Indies. This policy seems to have worked better in Canton than in Amoy, and here again a large number of the women were widows whose husbands had perished in the social disturbances of the period.

Even here, however, high as the percentages might have been in relation to the rest of Chinese migration, they were nowhere near what was actually achieved in the Indian indentured migrations (unsatisfactory as these latter may have seemed to contemporary and later observers). A mere total of 3,121 Chinese women accompanied the slightly over a quarter of a million migrants who departed for Latin America and the Caribbean. Of these, a full 3,053 were destined for the British, Dutch, and French Caribbean (2,669 for the British), a mere 62 to Cuba, and 6 to Peru during the whole period of the indenture experiment (i.e., up to 1874 for Spanish America, and 1884 for the British Caribbean).[75] The percentage for the non-Latin Caribbean was roughly 14.7 percent, whereas for the whole of Latin America and the Caribbean it was a mere 1 percent.

Chinese contract migrations to the British West Indies were virtually over by 1866. This was the year that the Anglo-French-Chinese Convention to regulate the engagement of Chinese emigrants by British and French subjects (the Kung Convention) was signed in Peking. Articles VIII and IX of the treaty granted to every emigrant the right to a return passage home for himself and his family at the end of his term of indenture, or a cash grant in lieu of passage. Article IX further specified that in the event that the migrant reengaged himself for a second five-year term, he should receive a bounty equivalent to half the amount of his return passage, while still retaining his right to a free passage at the end of the second term.

Complaints were raised by the West Indian planters, and also by the Colonial Office (which apparently had not been consulted beforehand on these provisions by the British Foreign Minister who negotiated the treaty, Sir Rutherford Alcock), to the effect that this would make Chinese contract emigration too expensive, at twice the cost of the Indian indenture scheme.[76] Further negotiations dragged on over the years, until finally the Chinese government accepted a modified convention in 1872, guaranteeing migrants a cash grant of $50 in lieu of return passage after five years.

But by that time, most of the initial impetus had gone out of the Chinese indenture experiment. The Trinidad planters in particular had been extremely disappointed with the immigrants who came in the 1860s and preferred to stay with Indian indentured labor.[77] The British Guianese planters were ambivalent about Chinese usefulness as laborers (some were for, others against), but in the final analysis it was the relatively prohibitive cost of the Chinese scheme, not to mention the stability of the arrangement with another British colony (British India), which led to its discontinuance.

Only two ships sailed to British Guiana after 1866, one in 1874 from Canton, the *Corona*, with 388 passengers, and one experiment in free migration from Hong Kong in 1879, the *Dartmouth*, with 515 passengers. Single individual migrations continued throughout the century to both colonies, but organized group migrations ended with the *Dartmouth* in 1879. Jamaica, however, which had remained relatively untouched by the Chinese indenture experiment since 1854, received the last formal group of indentureds from Hong Kong in 1884, 680 on the *Diamond/ Prince Alexander*. Interestingly, these migrants were from a totally different district nexus, east of Canton and also just north of Hong Kong (Tung-Kuan, Pao-An, and Hui-Yang), and a large number of them were of Hakka origins.

Meanwhile, the discontinuance of migration to the British West Indies after 1866 scarcely had an impact upon the Cuban/Peruvian operations out of Macao. Up to 1874, when the "coolie trade" was finally banned in Macao after intense pressure from China, the Western countries, and finally from the inhabitants of Macao itself, the traffic flowed unabated: 116 ships to Cuba and 110 to Peru, with about 93,150 passengers, roughly half each. Chinese (and Cantonese) migrations to and within Latin America did not end in 1874, however, as we have mentioned earlier, but the indenture experiment had come to an end.

CHAPTER 3

The Formal Organization of the British West Indian Indenture System

The plantation labor regime which emerged in Trinidad and British Guiana after Emancipation, and which survived until the end of the First World War (1838–1920), was dualistic and hybrid in nature, combining elements of both semifree and free labor, imported foreign indentured labor and Black Creole free labor. The sugar plantation itself came to rely almost exclusively on indentured immigrant labor for its survival and continued vitality throughout the century. Indeed, the institution indenture in the West Indies as a whole came to be identified overwhelmingly with the fortunes of the sugar industry, even though a minority of importers came from the nonsugar sectors, mainly cocoa planters in Trinidad and Grenada and banana planters in Jamaica. The immigration ordinances passed in 1891 in British Guiana, and 1899 in Trinidad, gave the government departments of both colonies the right to import laborers on their own account, but there is no indication that they did so in any significant number.[1] A handful of private individuals also applied for, and engaged, indentured immigrants in domestic-type duties, but these were always a minority.

In Trinidad, especially after the 1880s, the expansion of cocoa production came to provide a healthy counterpoint and alternative to the dominance of the sugar industry, and in British Guiana gold mining emerged as an industry of some significance by the 1890s.[2] Neither of these sectors, however, ever depended on bound immigrant labor to the extent that sugar did, although cocoa expansion in Trinidad relied heavily on the labor of the ex-indentured or freed Indian immigrant. Gold mining in British Guiana remained throughout a Black Creole enclave, with no major intrusions from the immigrant labor force, indentured or freed. In Jamaica, which saw a steady decline in the importance and output of the sugar plantations after Emancipation and the emergence of not only a significant small farmer and peasant class but also a vibrant banana industry by the 1880s, indentured labor from India came to form an important, though not exclusive, part of both the sugar and banana sectors.

Eric Williams has described the indenture system as the nineteenth-century West Indian plantation counterpart of the encomienda. This is only symbolically accurate as a description of the nineteenth-century labor regime. In fact, the British West Indian indenture experiment embodied many unique features that distinguished it, not only from earlier forms of unfree labor in the region, but even from many other indentured labor experiments taking place simultaneously during the period in other parts of the world, and even in the Americas.

The crucial factor here was the central role played by the state and its agencies in regulating and supervising the entire system. From recruitment of laborers in the East, to transportation of immigrants to their destinations, to allocation of laborers to specific plantations, to ensuring that plantation management, labor utilization, and labor relations remained faithful to the requirements laid down by the law—the entire system was regulated by a three-way collaboration and interaction between the British Colonial Office (and its agencies, such as the Colonial Land and Emigration Commission before 1876), the government of India, and the individual colonial governments. (The Chinese arrangement contained modifications which are discussed below.)

The elaborate immigration laws passed, the number of state agencies involved, and the careful keeping of records on the progress of the immigrant population on (and often off) the plantations all created an institutional network and procedure that—if not perfect by any means in practice, as we shall see—were at least distinct in demonstrating the complexity of state regulation and supervision accorded to one indenture experiment in an age when various other kinds of indenture arrangements under purely private auspices were more normal.

In this chapter we examine the evolution of the formal framework—institutional and legal—which governed the British West Indian indenture experiment. In chapters 4 and 5, we shall see how this formal framework often operated in actuality—the tension and discrepancy between theory and practice. We shall also look at the Asian immigrants themselves: their arrival and adjustment to the rhythm of the plantation regime and their attempts to preserve and maintain their humanity and autonomy within a system that was designed—especially in the early stages, before 1870—to reduce them to mere objects, abstract units of production, rather than to groom them for citizenship and assimilation into a new society.

The main characteristics of the British West Indian indenture system can be summarized as follows: (1) the five-year contract of indenture, binding the laborer to a specific plantation for a specified time period at a fixed rate of wages, with severely limited rights of physical mobility outside the workplace environment; (2) the elaborate regulations contained in the various colonial immigration ordinances, governing the reciprocal rights and obligations of planters and laborers, all backed by criminal sanctions (fines and imprisonment); (3) active state involvement at the points of recruitment and transportation in the East, as well as at the points of arrival and distribution in the Caribbean, and the total exclusion of all privately sponsored immigration schemes; and (4) state subsidization of the financial expenses involved in operating the indenture scheme (paid public immigration, rather than free voluntary immigration).

Indenture Contracts

The final introduction of the five-year contract of indenture, binding the migrant laborer to a specific plantation for the full term of five years at an official rate of daily wages (generally 24 cents or 1 shilling in British Guiana, 25 cents or 1 shilling half pence in Trinidad), did not take place until 1862, a full twenty-four years after the first Asian laborers made their appearance on the Demerara plantations (the 396 "Gladstone Coolies" of 1838). Prior to that date, the contractual arrangements under which immigrants of all races arrived in the West Indies varied widely with the policy fluctuations to which the whole experiment in free labor remained subject in the early years.

The story of these early years was essentially one of gradual shifts over time in the colonial labor policies of the British government, a shift from an extreme liberal commitment to the humanitarian protectionism of the abolitionist lobbies and to the ideal of free labor, to a gradual recognition of the necessity for some form of paternalistic control over the labor force, as a concession to economic pragmatism and to the pressure-group demands of the West Indian plantocracy.[3] The indentured immigrant labor force, half free and half tied, became the backbone of the revival of the sugar industry in Trinidad and British Guiana and remained a marginal but important part of the labor force of the other territories to which these immigrants migrated.

The cornerstone of the early post-Emancipation labor policy of the Colonial Office was two Orders-in-Council passed in July and September 1838. They were known as the Stephen Code regulating the rights and duties of Masters and Servants (after Sir James Stephen, Parliamentary Under-Secretary of State for the Colonies). They prohibited the making of labor contracts outside the colonies where such labor was to be utilized and effectively limited the duration of such contracts, when made before a local magistrate, to one year. Immigrants not working under contract were not bound to work for more than one month.

This policy was primarily designed to ensure against the possible revival of "a disguised form of slavery" through the practice of private traders or speculators coercing or seducing overseas laborers (in the West Indian islands, Africa, or elsewhere) into signing contracts that would then be sold to planters in Trinidad or British Guiana for a profit. Under the 1838 Code, a local magistrate would be required to supervise and endorse the making of local contracts for immigrants after their arrival, to ensure their voluntary and noncoercive character.

The prohibition on overseas contracts severely hampered the efforts of planters attempting to resolve their labor problems with the ex-slaves through the recruitment of contract labor particularly from the smaller West Indian islands. Free and spontaneous immigration to Trinidad and British Guiana, in their view, was not sufficiently reliable as a mechanism for ensuring the regularity and cheapness of much-needed labor. Colonial Office fears of a new form of slavery, they insisted, were exaggerated, and the new policies in fact constituted an interference with the overseas laborers' own movement and freedom of choice. It was this clash of viewpoints which constituted the heart of the early dilemma over immigrant labor, with the Colonial Office being particularly solicitous over the issue of Black immigrant labor. Even when the use of public funds or bounties was authorized in 1839 to help stimulate free immigration from nearby destinations, the ban on overseas and long contracts continued.

To be sure, there were officially endorsed exceptions to these stringent regulations, and these tended to increase over the years, until new policies came into focus in the 1850s, beginning with the period of the passing of the Sugar Duties Act in 1846. The earliest exception was in 1838 itself, when a special Order-in-Council had to be passed to enable the Guianese planter John Gladstone to arrange for the first importations

Oyster vendor in nineteenth-century Trinidad.
Courtesy University of the West Indies (Trinidad) Library.

of labor from India. The "Gladstone Coolies," distributed over six estates, arrived on specially endorsed five-year contracts of indenture, with a free return passage guaranteed at the end of that period. This arrangement was similar to the practice then in operation in Mauritius, where Indians had been imported on five-year contracts since 1834. The practice was terminated in 1839 after official investigations, made after protests from the Anti-Slavery Society revealed significant abuses against the laborers in both Mauritius and British Guiana.

Between 1841 and 1844, further modifications were allowed, mainly on the ground that the prospective immigrants concerned were competent to make contracts overseas on their own account, and also that many of them would not emigrate without such contracts. Thus in 1841

Europeans, in 1843 North American Blacks, and in 1843–44 the Chinese were permitted to enter into valid overseas contracts. The Chinese option in fact did not materialize, for continued lack of public funds and the reluctance of private interests to undertake the financial risks themselves. There is some indication also that not enough numbers of Chinese were available for the projected venture. But the other immigrants did enter the West Indies, under contracts concluded overseas. Further special exceptions were allowed for the importation in 1842, on public funds, of liberated Africans on one-year contracts, and for the private importation of Madeirans in 1844 on two-year contracts to Trinidad.

The shipment of Indians between 1845 and 1848 to Trinidad, British Guiana, and Jamaica entered the West Indies under the strict labor regulations of 1838. Promised a free return passage after five years in the region, they were not permitted to make other than verbal one-month contracts or written one-year contracts after arrival. No regulations existed for the control of their physical movements after this period, and as a result, desertion and widespread vagrancy became common among these immigrants, unaccustomed as most of them were to regular agricultural labor of the kind being offered to them, and more often than not being the victims of various kinds of abuse and ill-treatment on the plantations to which they had been assigned.

The planters, supported by the local governors, agitated for some kind of long-term indentures for the Indian immigrants and for some kind of regulations which would help them to control their propensity to wandering and abandonment of the plantations. Their efforts came up against a reluctant but increasingly sympathetic Colonial Office. The years between 1846 and 1854 were taken up by the frictions and disagreements between the colonies and the Home Government over the issue, marked by the passage of many local regulations and laws which were disallowed by the Colonial Office but marked also by a gradual shift of sentiment and concrete policy at the center on the desirability and duration of overseas compulsory terms of indenture for immigrants imported on public funds.

Three-year overseas contracts for all immigrants (including West Indian Creoles) were actually authorized in 1846, but the controversy over their applicability to the two specific groups of Africans and Indians extended somewhat longer. Verbal contract arrangements with all immigrants without exception were also extended from one to six months. The Colonial Office proposed in 1846 that Indian immigrants be retained on voluntary one-year contracts but that they be charged a monthly tax (on pain of imprisonment for nonpayment) for any period during their five-year term of residence when they were not actually at work on the plantations. Trinidad passed an ordinance in 1847 based on these recommendations, with a monthly tax of 5 shillings and a 2-pence-a-day penalty for absence from work without authorization. This, however, proved unworkable in practice, as the taxes and penalties proved uncollectible and the offenders difficult to physically apprehend.

This failure increased the call for compulsory three-year contracts. British Guiana actually tried to legalize three-year contracts in 1848, and Trinidad five-year contracts in 1849, but this legislation was disallowed by the Home Government. By 1848, however, the Colonial Office was prepared to concede on the desirability of three-year written contracts for the Indians, provided they were voluntary (i.e., could be voluntarily terminated by the laborer), but again it exempted the Africans from this concession. The metropolitan economic crisis which took place in that year, however, and the financial difficulties surrounding the Indian immigration caused a temporary suspension of the flow from India.

When the immigration was resumed in 1850, the planters in British Guiana agitated for a further extension of the Indian contracts from three to five years, or failing that, for a part payment of the return passage costs by the immigrants. The Home Government resisted the idea of the extension but consented to an exaction of monthly sums from those immigrants who would not consent, after their first three years, to enter into further work agreements during their two-year additional period. This again proved to be a failure, as it had in Trinidad.

A new stage in the agitation came about after the visit in 1852 to British Guiana and Trinidad of the emigration agent at Calcutta for both territories (also Mauritius), Thomas Caird. As a result of his favorable portrait of the immigration and the condition of the Indian population on the plantations, the Indian government consented to extend the official term of industrial residence from five to ten years—that is, the free return passage could be claimed only after ten years instead of five. An attempt by the Guianese legislature in 1853 to extend the indenture term to five years was met with a compromise arrangement, with the Colonial Office prepared to allow a three-year contract, followed by a further two years of one-year indentures with employers of the laborers' own choosing, or a commutation payment by the immigrants who preferred other arrangements of $12 per annum. The return passage was to be available after ten years under the new arrangement. This new proposal for a de facto five-year indenture period became official in 1854.

An early attempt to include a $35 contribution by the Indian to his return passage after ten years was abandoned in 1856 after early evidence of reluctance to emigrate under these conditions. During the second five-year period, the immigrant could voluntarily choose to enter into further one-year contracts with employers of his own choosing or pay a $12 fee for any year in which he remained free from such contractual obligations. (This fee was also later abandoned.)

The 1854 laws on Indian indenture marked a decisive shift away from the policy imperatives of the early years, when the protection of the laborers from possible abuse by the planters and neo-slavery was a matter of paramount concern to the Colonial Office, influenced by the liberal humanitarianism of the antislavery agitation. By the early 1850s, and indeed after the passage of the Sugar Duties Act in 1846, the recognition of the need for immigration, and for some form of control over the immigrant labor force, as an indispensable condition for the healthy recovery of the West Indian sugar industry had become integral to official reasoning. Only the precise forms of the new relationship remained to be agreed upon. Even the prohibition on overseas contracts for Africans was lifted. Two-year contracts were allowed in 1850, and three-year contracts in 1853. The years after 1854 were years of stability in the supply and regulation of the mainly Indian immigrant labor force, and years of stability for the sugar industry. When the final legal alteration was made in 1862, and the five-year term of service to the single employer made absolute, the line of official thinking on the immigration question had already moved a long way from the anxious protectionism of the early 1840s.

The formal contract of indenture, technically a civil contract between equal parties—the emigration agent at Calcutta or Madras and the prospective emigrant—assumed a standard format.[4] Its provisions dealt with the basic conditions of the engagement: free passage to the West Indies; the five-year term to be devoted to agricultural labor; the authority of the Colonial Governor and the Immigration Agent-General to assign the laborer on arrival to a specific plantation; the six-day workweek; the length of the working day (in Trinidad nine, in British Guiana seven hours for field laborers, and ten hours in both for work in the factory buildings); the amount of daily wages (25 cents in Trinidad, 24 cents in British Guiana for timework, and more but not less for taskwork, that is, work by specific assignments); method of payment, generally weekly; a supply of rations for the first three months in British Guiana, twelve months in Trinidad, the cost of which was to be deducted from wages;

free housing and medical attendance; and finally, a guarantee of a free return passage to India after a continuous residence of ten years in the colony.

A special word has to be said about the Chinese contracts of indenture, which had not only a different format, but also a more fluctuating history. While evolving against the background of the larger policy concerns discussed above, their specifics tended to be subject to many fluctuations. The principle of overseas five-year contracts for Chinese had been accepted as early as 1843, but the different recruitment exercises initiated over the years—in 1853, then in 1859–66, and then finally in the 1870s after the modifications imposed by the Kung Convention proposals—saw many different variations on the actual contracts offered to prospective emigrants, quite unlike the relatively standardized version offered to the Indians after 1854, and certainly after 1862.

Although at least two contract versions came to dominate the migration in the 1860s, this writer has been able to identify no less than ten different versions used with the Chinese during the relatively brief period of their migration to the British West Indies. In addition to this, Ordinance No. 4 of 1864 in British Guiana, the main immigration law in force until its replacement in 1873, actually authorized the Immigration Agent-General to make local alterations of contracts concluded in China as he saw fit, without necessarily getting the formal approval of the parties involved. Section 46 stated:

> Every indenture made in China shall, on the arrival in this colony of any Chinese immigrant, be submitted to the Immigration Agent-General, who shall, if necessary, make such alterations therein for the benefit of the immigrant as he shall judge requisite to render the same conformable to the provisions of this Ordinance; and the employer to whom the immigrant may be allotted shall sign such indenture as so altered, and the same, being signed also by the Immigration Agent-General, shall be binding on the said employer and immigrant, and valid, in the same manner as if made originally in China.

The very existence of this provision in relation to the China-concluded contracts testified to the somewhat unsettled environment in which the migrations were taking place. A report of an official investigation commission into immigration conducted in British Guiana in 1870–71 accused the colonial legislature of "bad faith" towards the Chinese and of interfering with some contracts "in the most extraordinary manner."[5]

The main distinctions between the various contracts were between those which gave the immigrant the option to cancel or redeem his obligation after a year (or more), provided he repaid a proportionate part of his passage moneys from China to the West Indies (one-fifth of $75 for any single year commuted), and those which made the five-year term of service absolute and unredeemable. The initial 1853 contracts to both British Guiana and Trinidad belonged to the latter category, at a time when the Colonial Office was just conceding five-year contracts, redeemable in three years, for the Indians.

When the Chinese immigration was resumed in 1859, the contracts actually made in China were canceled after arrival in British Guiana, and new ones substituted, on the ground that their terms did not conform to the specifications laid down by Ordinance No. 17 of 1858, reopening the migration. The China contracts were for five-year terms of service, redeemable after a year on repayment of the appropriate part of the passage money spent on the immigrant. The substituted contracts made the indenture redeemable only after three years and made the repayment sums quite specific: $50 for two years, $25 for any single year. The rate of wages promised in the contracts, moreover, which was $4 a month plus free rations (or $6 a month without rations), was also changed to "the same rate of wages as is paid to the laborers not under contract or indenture, working on the same plantation," to be paid weekly.[6] There seemed to have been no resistance on the part of the Chinese to these changes.

Between 1860 and 1862, when J. Gardiner Austin was the emigration agent in China, the contracts were all for five-year terms of service, redeemable after a year (or later), similar to the disallowed provisions of the 1859 contracts, although the format was more elaborate. A local law in 1860 had facilitated this change. This was again replaced in 1862, when the absolute five-year contracts came into force generally; some 1862, and all 1863, contracts were rephrased accordingly. Ordinance No. 4 of 1864 endorsed these contracts but allowed contracts made in China in the previous form (permitting commutation after one year) to remain legitimate. Thus after 1862 there were two versions actually in force, and even after 1864 this duality continued. Even the Trinidad migrations, which were not directly affected by the Guianese legislative mood swings, reflected the same duality at the level of the kinds of formal contracts which were being signed by the prospective emigrants in China. The 1862 *Maggie Miller/Wanata* contracts allowed the redemption-after-one-year option, as did the 1865 *Montrose* and *Paria* contracts, but not so the 1866 *Dudbrook* and *Red Riding Hood* contracts, which made the five-year term of service absolute.[7]

There were other important variations on the Chinese contracts. There were those that specified the amount of wages to be earned monthly, those that left the amount unspecified, to correspond with wages of free laborers, and those that gave the migrants the option of choosing between timework at specified wages and taskwork at unspecified wages, again corresponding with those of free laborers. All three versions were utilized in the 1860s. Whenever wages were specified, they were generally $4 a month plus free rations (or $6 without). However, the 1853 contracts, made under private auspices and before the state supervision system had been regularized, were more inconsistent. One, the *Clarendon* to Trinidad from Canton, offered $5 plus rations ($7 without rations). Another, the *Glentanner* to British Guiana from Amoy, seems to have offered $2 plus rations ($4 without).[8] In addition, most of the post-1860 contracts to British Guiana, where the issue seems to have been a contentious one, omitted references to free rations and made mention only of unspecified wages, to correspond with those of free laborers. Even the 1860 contracts appeared to have been changed after arrival in British Guiana, to delete the promises of free rations promised to the Chinese, on the ground that this arrangement, different from the arrangement with the Indians, would prove unworkable.[9]

These inconsistencies in the actual contract terms, combined with the general power of the Immigration Agent-General in British Guiana allowed by the 1864 law to effect changes in the China-concluded terms as he saw fit, led the 1870–71 Commission to comment that the contracts made in China seemed to be regarded in the colony as "necessary evils, to be got rid of somehow or other."[10]

Compared with the standard Indian contracts, the Chinese contracts (all versions up to 1866) differed in the following respects:

1. There was no provision for a return passage to China at the end of the five-year term.

2. The five-year contracts were in force since 1853 for both, but the commutation or redemption provisions were not the same: the Indian contracts were generally redeemable before 1862 in three years, from 1862 not at all (though this was not observed strictly in practice); the Chinese contracts were at first nonredeemable (1853), then redeemable after three years (substituted 1859 Guiana contract), then redeemable after one year or more (after 1860), then nonredeemable once more after 1862 (with both forms being allowed after 1864 in British Guiana and always in Trinidad).

3. The wage clauses were generally less precise or standardized in the Chinese contracts.

4. The workday was generally seven and a half hours in the Chinese contracts, but nine hours in the Indian contracts for Trinidad, and seven in those for British Guiana.

5. Advance allowances ranging from $10 to $20, repayable in monthly wage deductions of $1, were allowed to the Chinese emigrants, though not to the Indians.

6. $20 bounty payments for accompanying wives were authorized in the later Chinese contracts, with no similar concessions to the Indians.

7. Rations provided after arrival, whenever the Chinese contracts did mention them at all, were meant to apply to the full period of indenture, whereas the Indian rations, which were always mentioned in the contracts, applied for a limited initial period (three months in British Guiana, twelve months in Trinidad), and these had to be paid for in the case of the Indians.

8. Many of the Chinese contracts also mentioned free garden grounds, in addition to the normal benefits such as free housing and medical attention, but it is not clear how many of the migrants actually benefited from these provisions.

9. Most important, Chinese women were not allowed to enter into contracts of indenture, but instead into what were called contracts of residence, which bound them to their designated plantations for the full term but did not oblige them to do any work whatever. Failure to remain on the plantations, however, technically left them open to being charged (and possibly imprisoned) for the offense of desertion.

Finally, there were the post-1866 contracts, formulated after the negotiations on the 1866 Kung Convention treaty. These were probably utilized only with the *Corona* to British Guiana in 1874 and the *Diamond/ Prince Alexander* to Jamaica in 1884. Under these contractual terms, a return passage payment of $50 was guaranteed to the emigrants at the end of their five-year terms. If they decided not to return, the cash was to be given to them. If they decided to reindenture for a second five-year term, they were to receive a $25 bounty, while still retaining their right to the $50 return passage contribution.

Immigration Ordinances

The indenture contract was technically a civil contract between equal parties. Never mentioned in the document itself, but central to the whole system of indenture as it evolved in the British West Indies, were the elaborate local immigration ordinances, which outlined in much more rigorous detail the nature of the duties and obligations of both employee and employer and which governed their relations throughout the indenture period. The most important feature of these laws as they affected the immigrant was the fact that criminal penalties (fines and imprisonment) were automatically applicable for various breaches of work discipline and other violations and, most important, that the immigrant was required by law to be physically bound to his plantation milieu during the whole term of his indenture, not allowed to move freely beyond a 2-mile radius without a specific written permit from his employer.

This stringent pass-law system made the laborer a de facto prisoner of his specific plantation and was the major distinguishing mark of difference between an immigrant contract laborer and a free laborer. Regardless of how the pass-law system operated in practice—and there were wide de facto variations from period to period, from plantation to plantation— the fact was that the laws gave the planter-employer a formal power over the immigrant laborer and his physical movements which clearly violated his abstract status as a free agent, and which could be utilized either for the paternalistic protection of the immigrant in a new and strange environment or for the abuse of his labor power by unscrupulous plantation officials.

The fact was that the system of indenture which emerged was a curious legal anomaly—a civil contract enforceable mainly with criminal sanctions, historically a hybrid creature of the nineteenth-century plantation need to replace free Black labor with some alternative form of bound labor, not as extreme as chattel slavery, but certainly not free in the increasingly accepted metropolitan liberal sense of the term.

The first pass-law regulations were originally introduced in Trinidad in 1846 by the Governor, Lord Harris, and Major Fagan, an official appointed to protect the interests of the early Indian immigrants.[11] They were introduced in an attempt to curb the widespread vagrancy and desertion of the first Indian arrivals to the island. These regulations, which were disallowed by the Colonial Office on a technicality, after loud protestations from the Anti-Slavery lobby, stated that laborers could not temporarily leave their allotted plantations without a ticket of leave and required that those who had terminated their term of service carry with them an official certificate of discharge from their ex-employers. Given the climate of opinion in the metropolis and in the Colonial Office at that time, such attempts to tie immigrants to their place of work, and to regiment the new labor force, could not succeed. The Harris-Fagan regulations, and subsequent efforts to achieve the same result with the imposition of a monthly tax on idlers or unemployed immigrants (discussed earlier), never got off the ground. Yet in the final analysis it was this very feature that became the cornerstone of the whole system, and the indispensable corollary to the five-year contract.

The 1899 Trinidad Immigration Ordinance, formulated during the high point of the indenture experiment, phrased the prohibition as follows:

Immigrants unlawfully at large [Section 136]

Where any immigrant is found on a public highway, or on any land, or in any house, not being the land or house of his employer, or in any ship, vessel or boat within the waters of the island, any of the following persons, that is to say:

(1) The Protector, or any person authorised in writing by him;

(2) Any estate constable attached to the plantation to which the immigrant is under indenture; and

(3) The employer of the immigrant or his manager or overseer,

may without warrant stop such immigrant, and in case he fails to produce a certificate of industrial residence or of exemption from labor or a ticket of leave may, if there be reasonable cause to suspect the immigrant is under indenture, arrest him and take him to the nearest police station, there to be detained until he can be taken before a Stipendiary Justice of the Peace.

If upon such immigrant being brought before a Stipendiary Justice of the Peace it appears in respect of which plantation his services are due, and he fails to prove that at the time of his being arrested he was absent from such plantation by virtue of a ticket of leave, the Stipendiary Justice, if he sees fit, may order such immigrant to be returned to the estate to which he is indentured, or to be imprisoned with or without hard labor for any term not exceeding seven days; but if it does not appear in respect of what plantation the services of such immigrant are due, and such immigrant does not prove to the satisfaction of the Stipendiary Justice that he is not an immigrant within the meaning of this Ordinance, or that he has completed his term of industrial residence, the Stipendiary Justice may if he sees fit make an order for the imprisonment of such immigrant with or without hard labor for any term not exceeding three months.

The parallel 1891 Immigration Ordinance in British Guiana covered the same offense in Section 127, but the penalties in British Guiana were not separate from the penalties connected with the charges of unlawful absence or desertion, described below. Trinidad's Section 136 seemed to have imposed a distinct set of penalties in addition to the others. In case of immigrant noncooperation after apprehension, in both colonies, a penalty not exceeding £1 in Trinidad ($5 in British Guiana), or imprisonment with or without hard labor, for any term not exceeding fourteen days, was imposed.

Penalties for unlawful absence or desertion were as follows:

—Unlawful absence from plantation: fine up to £2 in Trinidad, $10 in British Guiana; if female, £1 in Trinidad, $5 in British Guiana.
—Desertion (unauthorized absence for three days or more in Trinidad, seven days or more in British Guiana): fine up to £5 in Trinidad, $24 in British Guiana, or imprisonment up to two months, or both penalty and imprisonment.

Immigrants were, however, entitled by law to a free pass of one day and one night for every fortnight of unbroken labor, twenty-six such passes being the maximum to which they were entitled in any one year. Moreover, arrest for unreasonable cause, if proven, could result in a compensatory award to the immigrant of up to £20. The immigrant was also entitled to absent himself, with or without a pass, if his intention was to go to the immigration authorities with a reasonable complaint, but complaints deemed frivolous, or going off to do so with five or more immigrants, could still leave him open to prosecution.[12]

The vagrancy and desertion laws described above were the indispensable accompaniment to the labor laws proper, governing work discipline, and during the mature phase of the indenture experiment after the mid-1850s constituted the legal basis of the overall social regimentation imposed on the movements of the contract laborer. Laborers were to be bound physically to their plantations, and laws of a criminal nature had to be formulated to reinforce the purely formal civil contractual agreements contained in the formal contract of indenture made in Asia. In this way, the notion of freedom of contract was given a unique twist, all in the service of an economic imperative deemed to be appropriate to a colonial plantation environment.

The labor laws themselves imposed a distinct set of criminal penalties affecting work performance: a worker not performing his job properly was not subject to possible loss of job or income and job benefits (housing, medicine), but to fines and imprisonment of a penal nature. Thus the following penalties were standard by the 1890s:[13]

—Absence from work without lawful excuse, or refusal/neglect to begin or finish an authorized work assignment: up to £2 in Trinidad, $10 in British Guiana, or imprisonment for any term up to one month.

—Refusal to amend work rejected for improper performance: up to £1 in Trinidad, $5 in British Guiana, or imprisonment up to fourteen days for a first offense, and for a second or subsequent conviction on the same offense, up to £2 in Trinidad, $10 in British Guiana, or imprisonment up to one month, plus forfeiture of portion of wages due to such work assignment as the magistrate may see fit.

The offense of habitual idling, defined as unauthorized absence from work for twelve days in any one month or any two consecutive months, was punishable by a prison term of up to three months.

There were also penalties attached to other minor on-the-job offenses, such as drunkenness at work, fraud or wilful deception in the performance of work, abusive or insulting language or behavior to superiors, and wilful disobedience to lawful and reasonable orders. For all of the above, a fine of up to £1 in Trinidad, $5 in British Guiana, or a prison term of up to fourteen days, was imposed.

For more serious offenses, such as threatening language or behavior to superiors, damage to plantation property through negligence or improper conduct, unlawfully selling off plantation property, hindering or molesting any other immigrant in his work performance, and persuading (or attempting to persuade) any other immigrant to absent himself from work or refuse work, there were higher penalties: fines up to £5 in Trinidad, $24 in British Guiana, or a prison term up to two months.

These were some of the major penalties affecting the immigrant laborer under indenture. They tended to change over time. For example, the regulations in British Guiana before 1873, under Ordinance No. 4 of 1864, were often far more stringent.[14] There was one offense frequently resorted to by the Guianese planters, that of insufficient work, that is, not completing a stipulated quantity of work within a week (five tasks or five days' labor), for which the penalty was anything up to $24 (equivalent to five months' wages) or one month's imprisonment with hard labor. This offense was over and above the other offenses for refusal to work, neglect of work, unauthorized absence from work, or refusal to finish assigned work, and it kept the specter of punishment perpetually above the heads of the immigrants, since the stipulated number of five tasks per week was seldom completed weekly by many immigrants. In fact, the 1870–71 Commission of Enquiry revealed that only about 44 percent ever did so regularly.

Under the 1864 law, moreover, all of the above offenses carried with them the additional penalty of forfeiture of wages of up to one week, at the discretion of the magistrate. Every one carried the same penalty as well: up to $24 or one month in prison with hard labor. Desertion also carried the same penalty for first offenders, and up to $48 or two months for subsequent offenders, with a possibility that both fine and prison term could be imposed together in all cases. An amending law in 1868 made the penalties for all these offenses even harsher, extending the incarceration period from one to two months and even removing the magistrate's discretion to forfeit wages, making such a penalty automatic in the case of unfinished work. The 1870–71 Commission was critical of the severity of these laws, and substantial revisions were made in 1873, following on its recommendations.

Regardless of the content of the regulations, however, or the quantum of the penalties imposed for various offenses, the philosophical basis of all the immigration ordinances was the same: indenture imposed civil obligations with criminal sanctions on contract violators or unsatisfactory workers; plantation discipline and regimentation were enforceable, like criminal actions, in courts of law. To be sure, the employers themselves had obligations and duties under the law towards their laborers, also punishable in similar fashion, but there was a noticeable difference in the scale of penalties involved which only served to prove the point: only in one single offense (discussed below) did the threat of imprisonment exist on the books for an offending plantation official; the rest were all punishable by fines.

The major obligations of the employer towards his indentured workers under the 1891 British Guiana and 1899 Trinidad Immigration Ordinances were (1) to provide suitable dwelling free of charge for all immigrants under contract, set to detailed specifications; default led to penalties ranging from fines of up to £5 in Trinidad, $24 in British Guiana, all the way to removal of immigrants from the offending plantation; (2) to provide regular rations for the first twelve months in Trinidad, and the first three months in British Guiana, according to the specified schedules laid down in the regulations, deducting 6 cents in Trinidad, 8 cents in British Guiana, a day from the immigrant's weekly or fortnightly wages, in payment; (3) to provide suitable hospital accommodation on the plantation at the rate of roughly 10 percent of beds for the number of immigrants on the plantation, with separate accommodation for male and female patients. Default in the proper maintenance of these hospitals led to fines of up to £10 in Trinidad, $48 in British Guiana. Employers who neglected to send their sick workers for medical treatment or needed hospitalization were also subject to fines of up to £5 in Trinidad, $24 in British Guiana.

Other employer obligations included payment of appropriate wages for full day's labor either by the task or by the day, weekly, or fortnightly, according to fixed procedures (taskwork was roughly equivalent to a seven-hour day's work). Disputes over amount of wages due or over employer withholding of wages were settled in court. (Before 1873 in British Guiana, the immigrant had virtually no remedy in this matter.)[15] Employers or plantation officials found guilty of unauthorized withholding of wages were liable to fines of up to £10 in Trinidad, $48 in British Guiana. In addition, on any plantation in Trinidad where average daily earnings for a year fell below 12 cents for more than 30 percent of the male adults, the Protector of Immigrants had the option to refuse further allocations of immigrants to that plantation for the following year, unless the Governor was satisfied that the deficient earnings could be justifiably explained. Plantation officials were also forbidden to keep any shop on or within 5 miles beyond the plantation; violation of this prohibition made offenders liable to fines of up to £10 in Trinidad, $48 in British Guiana, in the case of overseers, drivers, and other minor officials, and up to £20 in Trinidad, $100 in British Guiana, in the case of planters and managers.

Employers were also forbidden to oblige any immigrant to work for more than six hours extra time in any one day, although extra-time work was allowed by agreement. Failure to comply could lead to fines of up to £2 in Trinidad. Also forbidden was the employment of immigrants indentured to another planter. This offense led to fines as high as £50 in Trinidad and a maximum of $48 in British Guiana. Damages to the planter deprived of the immigrant's labor also involved an additional 4 shillings ($1 in British Guiana) a day for the number of days missed by the absentee worker. Related to this offense was the prohibition on employing any free immigrant without asking him to produce his certificate of exemption from labor before hiring, in order to verify his legal status. Violation of this provision led to a fine of up to £5 in Trinidad and $24 in British Guiana.

Reindentures of time-expired immigrants after five years' service were permitted, however. The planter, whether the same or a new one, was obligated to pay the immigrant a bounty or premium of mutually agreed value—usually $10–$11—in exchange for a new contract of indenture to last not more than one year. In British Guiana before 1873, five-year reindentures were legal and quite common. They were officially disallowed in 1873 after charges of abuse and exploitation during the 1870–71 investigations, and one-year reindentures became normal soon after that. However, reindenture as a mode of employment died a natural death in British Guiana around 1875, when the reindenture fee to be paid by the planter was raised by the legislature to prohibitive levels.

In one case only was the employer made vulnerable to a potential prison term in addition to a simple money penalty. This was where plantation officials were found guilty of physically assaulting or ill-using an immigrant. The offender could be fined up to £10 in Trinidad, $48 in British Guiana, or imprisoned, with or without hard labor, for up to two months. He could also be fined and imprisoned.

This situation contrasted with that of the immigrant laborer, who was vulnerable to a whole range of potential prison terms for a variety of large and small offenses, in addition to the money penalties imposed. In this sense, the imbalance integral to the immigration laws was obvious, despite the technically impartial regulations outlining the rights and duties of both parties to the indenture contract.

The regulations outlined above are quoted from the Immigration Ordinances of 1891 (British Guiana) and 1899 (Trinidad). These were the main consolidating laws passed during the mature phase of the indenture experiment. They introduced hardly any important new provisions themselves: most of the regulations contained within them had been in force for at least twenty years or more in both colonies. The main rules had been formulated before the 1870s, but trial and error, plus criticisms of British Guiana's Ordinance No. 4 of 1864 (as well as the actual harsh enforcement practices of the Guianese planters), compelled a certain amount of streamlining which took place in the 1870s.

British Guiana passed Ordinance No. 7 of 1873 following on the exhaustive investigation and critique of the 1870–71 Commission. Trinidad passed a consolidating ordinance, No. 13 of 1870, after many years of piecemeal legislation on various aspects of the immigration process. Jamaican regulations, discussed below, were largely embodied in Ordinance No. 23 of 1879. A broad grasp of the evolution of the immigration regulations over time can be gained by mentioning some of the more notable changes in the law between the 1870s and the mid-1890s.[16] They included:

—the cessation of five-year reindentures in British Guiana;

—the phasing out of the "insufficient work" offense unique to the 1864 law in British Guiana;

—the introduction of procedures for the recovery of wages unjustly withheld by employers in British Guiana, almost impossible before 1870;

—the abolition of the "livret," a detailed daily work routine record first introduced in 1873 in British Guiana but found difficult to operate in practice;

—the reduction of the term of indenture for female immigrants from five to three years;

—the exemption of females from punishment as habitual idlers;

—the extension of the immigrant's term of service to include all days lost through absence, desertion, or imprisonment (not strictly observed);

—banning the practice of enlisting indentureds and their descendants, especially in Trinidad, for work in nearby foreign countries (e.g., Venezuela);

—introduction of a Government Medical Service, partly in order to free medical officers from dependency on the planters, among other reasons;

—making provision for newly arrived immigrants to be allotted to domestic, rather than agricultural, work, if the Immigration Agent-General thought them physically incapable of the latter;

—introduction of measures designed to protect wives from physical violence committed by jealous immigrant husbands, as well as for the punishment of seducers of immigrants' wives;

—laws for the administration of intestate estates of indentured and unindentured immigrants; legalization and regularization of marriages and divorces among the immigrants performed according to their own religious laws;

—the regularization of Indian festivals conducted publicly.

After the 1890s legislation, the main change in the immigration regulations concerned the question of the free return passage to India. These changes were the result of local planter agitation and the pressures of the depression years for sugar (mid-1880s to 1890s), but they were endorsed by Dr. D. W. D. Comins, who had visited the West Indies on behalf of the Indian government in 1891 to observe the conditions of life for Indians in these territories. After 1895–96, new immigrants were expected to pay a portion of the return passage: for those arriving between 1895 and 1898, a quarter (one-sixth for females); for those arriving after 1898–99, a half (one-third for females). Wives and children of returning immigrants, however, retained free passage rights.

In the closing years, following on the recommendations of another Indian government delegation which visited the West Indies in 1913 (Messrs. James McNeill and Chimmam Lal), and in the context of growing criticisms of the whole indenture system of immigration in those years, there were late modifications. Fines for absence from, or refusal to, work were reduced to 10 shillings, payable by installments of up to one-third of weekly wages, and imprisonment for breaches of the labor laws was even abolished in 1916. However, these were all introduced when the indenture system was already on its last legs.

State Regulation and Supervision

A central feature of British West Indian indenture was its state-regulated and state-supervised nature. By the time Asian immigration was systematized, the experimental mixture of private and public involvement in recruitment and distribution which had characterized the early immigration movements of the other ethnic groups had given way to a unique state-controlled immigration scheme, to remain this way until the termination of the whole venture in 1920.

Even the Asian groups, however, had had earlier bouts with privately sponsored immigration. The "Gladstone Coolie" experiment to British Guiana in 1838, and the first year of Chinese immigration to both colonies (1853), had been conducted with minimal state involvement. The mature immigration program involved state recruitment agencies in the East as well as state allocation and distribution agencies in the colonies themselves. The Indian operations were similar to simultaneous immigration schemes directed to the sugar colonies in the Old World. The Chinese immigration was quite exceptional and confined to British Empire destinations (mainly the West Indies), contrasting sharply with the free voluntary movements to North America, Southeast Asia, and Australia on the one hand, and the privately sponsored indentured immigration schemes, mainly to Latin America, on the other.

RECRUITMENT IN CHINA

The Chinese emigration depots in the East grew in an atmosphere different from the ones in India, China being a sovereign country and not a colony, and the emigration movements being more multifaceted and open to interference by many nationalities. The British attempt to establish a viable state-controlled contract immigration flow from China, while mildly successful within its short life span, never really got off the ground properly and floundered constantly on numerous obstacles. Chief among these was the lack of stability of its personnel in the East. Between 1853 and 1866, the post of emigration agent was held by three different persons.

The first was James White, originally the British Guiana emigration agent based in Calcutta, who was connected with the 1853–54 efforts. He succeeded in formally dispatching only one vessel, the *Epsom* to Jamaica in 1854, the six others (three each to both colonies) actually being handled by private elements—Messrs. Booker in British Guiana, Messrs. Hyde, Hodge and Company in China—with Mr. White marginally involved in a few of these departures. The 1859 resumption was actually handled privately by Thomas Gerard, the West India Committee agent sent to the East that year. (He also made the immigrants out to have been recruited in Hong Kong, when they had been actually recruited from the infamous Macao barracoons, center of the Latin American "coolie trade" recruitment efforts. He was recalled after this discovery.)

Stability and state control only began with the 1859 appointment of J. Gardiner Austin, former Immigration Agent-General of British Guiana, who kept his main agency at Hong Kong, with a subimmigration agency based at Canton under his deputy, Theophilus Sampson. Austin himself held this post for only three seasons, until 1862, when he became Lieutenant Governor of British Honduras. The post then fell to Sampson, who shifted the main headquarters to his own base of operations at Canton. During the 1861–62 season, Austin had established smaller subagencies at Hang-Tsai, 50 miles from Hong Kong; O-Tau, near Swatow; Tat-Hao-Pu, situated near Chao-Yang, a district town in the Chao-Chou Prefecture, near Swatow; as well as in Amoy in next-door Fukien Province. Hang-Tsai depot was run by W. Maxwell; Tat-Hao-Pu by James Jones, a missionary; Amoy by M. Fitzgibbon, a person with missionary connections. After Austin's departure, all recruiting by Sampson was confined to Canton (ships often left from Whampoa downstream), with a few ships sailing from Amoy in 1866, two to Trinidad and one to British Guiana. No ships left Hong Kong after Austin's departure, at least not until the departures in 1879 and 1884.

In 1866 came the Anglo-French-Chinese Emigration Convention (the Kung Convention) with its disputed proviso about free return passages for the immigrants at the end of their indenture term. During the seven years or so while diplomatic wrangling went on over the retention of this clause, the agency was maintained in China at considerable expense (£1,600 a year), without recruiting a single emigrant for the British West Indies. The 1870–71 Commission of Enquiry into the condition of the immigrants in British Guiana was still lamenting in that year over the situation:

> the emigration establishment is still kept up in China, at considerable expense to this colony, with little prospect of the emigration of a fair class of agricultural laborers from thence being renewed, as long as California and other parts of the United States hold out to the Chinese who are willing to emigrate the inducements they at present have to offer, in the shape of high wages and great facilities of returning to and communicating with their native country, by means of the large steamers now plying monthly between San Francisco and Hong Kong.[17]

The agency was finally closed down in 1873–74.

Competition from free migration ventures handled mainly by Chinese business intermediaries and the bad reputation surrounding foreign-controlled contract emigration efforts (derived from the Macao-based Latin American recruiters) were the main factors hindering and inhibiting the British recruitment efforts in Hong Kong and Canton. The ambivalent Chinese attitude towards foreigners, and particularly the British in the wake of the two so-called Opium Wars (Kwangtung Province, and Canton in particular, was occupied by Anglo-French forces during 1858–61), did not improve matters either. The Chinese agents in Hong Kong handling the California and Australia routes did not take too kindly to the British efforts to encourage voluntary contract migration to dubious destinations like the West Indies, and the migrants themselves were highly influenced by the direct and effective information they were receiving about the possibilities in the two gold-mining destinations.

The statistics for departures from Hong Kong between 1854 and 1880 compiled by one recent study bear out the point.[18] Of 543,097 who left via Hong Kong in this period, approximately 186,109 went to various Southeast Asian destinations, 177,415 to the United States, 93,709 to

Australia, 5,191 to New Zealand, and 2,394 to Canada. British Guiana received around 6,808, Cuba 4,991, Surinam 1,869, and Peru 763. Other destinations included Hawaii (3,120), Tahiti (1,035), and India (2,385).

The British agency tried to avoid the practice of recruiting via Chinese recruiters (crimps) working for a fee on each emigrant brought in. Much effort and expenditure went into the business of advertising and publicizing British destinations and terms of service in the surrounding districts, in the effort to encourage potential migrants to come voluntarily to the agency offices. Austin talked about having "depots in every direction," and "Europeans communicating directly with the people in their villages."[19] He also estimated the whole operation—salary accounts, depot accounts, ration accounts, and general expense charges—to come to about $57.22 per head (an underestimate, as it turned out). He compared this method favorably with the Latin American practice of maintaining one depot and a small European staff at Macao and paying out sums of money to Chinese recruiters to go out and do the recruiting in the Chinese countryside for them, indirectly financing the infamous recruitment tactics employed by the Chinese crimps.

Some of the British information, ironically, was not immune from the same kind of misrepresentation which they claimed to be trying to avoid. The picture of average daily wages for free laborers held out in the public notices in China and in some of the British Guiana contracts—2 to 4 shillings for men, and 1 to 2 shillings for women—constituted nothing more than an officially endorsed misrepresentation of the true state of earnings for field laborers in the West Indies at the time. Many of the Chinese did in fact complain after arrival that they had been deceived about the true level of wages they could earn in the new environment.[20]

The British agency did succeed, however, in enlisting the cooperation of local Chinese officials in the effort to legitimize the recruiting effort, and the voluntary appearances of potential emigrants were jointly supervised by British and Chinese authority figures. The Governor of Kwangtung Province, Po Kwei, under the promptings of the Allied Commanders in charge of Canton, had declared voluntary emigration officially lawful, going against centuries-old Chinese attitudes towards emigration. The provincial authorities then proceeded to collaborate with the Western powers in attempting to stamp out crimping and kidnapping (unsuccessfully, as it turned out) and to regularize proper emigration procedures. This included assisting the British with their efforts to encourage a voluntary recruitment for their contract emigration program in Canton. The official proclamation of Governor Po Kwei, dated 9 April 1859, had read as follows:

> Wherever in the province of Kwangtung, mercantile classes are found mingled with the people, a densely crowded population is the result. Among them may be found those who are compelled by want to search for a living wherever they can obtain it; while others, in order to drive a trade, quit for a time their homes and cross the seas; or, accepting the employment offered by foreigners, obtain by going abroad a profitable remuneration for labor. Permission for their doing so should not, it is clear, be withheld in any of these cases, provided the parties themselves really consent to the arrangements.

The proclamation also denounced the "pig trade"—kidnapping—and warned the crimps of the penalties to which they exposed themselves. A further proclamation in October 1859 by the Acting Governor-General of Kwangtung and Kwangsi declared:

> It has been formally intimated to me by the Allied Commissioners that the British Government has sent an authorised agent to these provinces to establish an emigration house for the reception of emigrants for the British West Indies. To this end it is proposed that those Chinese who wish to obtain employment in the said colonies should go to the Emigration House and there negotiate for themselves all the conditions of service as well as their exact destination, and that these conditions, when accepted by both parties, should be recorded in a formal contract, and joint inquiry be held by the foreign agent and a Chinese officer specially deputed for the purpose, in order that the circumstances of each case may be clearly ascertained, and thus all the abuses attendant on kidnapping may be eradicated.[21]

The work of European missionaries, such as the Reverend William Lobscheid, who took a direct personal interest in the West Indian emigration effort, even traveling to British Guiana and Trinidad in 1861–62, was also very influential in recruiting families, and sometimes whole villages uprooted by local strife or famine, for the British agency. Reverend Lobscheid recommended a number of policy approaches for the British recruiters and carriers in a letter to Austin in February 1859:[22] to prepare and circulate a paper outlining the details of the engagement, to hire one or two men at $10 a month to circulate these in the surrounding districts, and to ask them to keep in touch with him; to employ a Chinese preacher on each ship at a monthly salary of $10–$12; to pay attention to the power of Christianity as a bond attaching the laborer to the plantation milieu; to educate the children after arrival in the colony, as some would return to China to educate their peers in turn; to keep the various clans separate (the Punti and the Hakka, for example) to prevent quarrels on the ship; to refrain from "touching females in a joking manner," because the Chinese were not accustomed to such things and would consider it a gross insult. Reverend James Jones, a missionary in the Swatow region, was another minor recruiter for the British effort. He acted as subagent for the Tat-Hao-Pu agency and recruited migrants in the Swatow region between 1862 and 1863.

Despite the cooperation of the Cantonese authorities, the recruiting efforts were often attended by severe personal dangers, given the social atmosphere prevailing in southern China, and Austin had the following comments to make on this:

> Even in Hong Kong . . . money had to be brought into the office under the charge of a sepoy with a loaded musket, and I have often sat with a loaded revolver at my side to guard the dollars, which were being paid out. I never crossed to Hang-Tsai but with the greatest caution, concealing my movements as much as possible, and never parting from my revolver by day or night, holding it repeatedly in my hand during the whole of the latter. On one occasion two piratical junks were placed to intercept me. On another Mr Maxwell was beaten and robbed of everything he possessed, and then a price was set upon the head of every foreigner. Was it to be wondered at that the insurance offices would charge myself and the other agents more than the ordinary China risk?[23]

Not all the British recruiting efforts were free from the questionable methods they ostensibly tried to avoid. Gerard's efforts in 1859 have already been mentioned. Sampson's 1866 shipments from Amoy were also reportedly done via a mercantile firm utilizing questionable procedures at Amoy, while Sampson himself remained based at Canton. The matter was cause for some official correspondence, and the complaints of the planters about the 1866 arrivals seemed to confirm the criticisms leveled at Sampson's carelessness.[24]

RECRUITMENT IN INDIA

The system of recruitment of laborers in India combined the overarching state supervision principle with a system of direct recruiting by paid recruiters responsible to a number of regional subagents based in different areas of the North Indian countryside and the Madras Presidency in the south. Unlike the local recruitment in the Chinese experiment, the role of the local recruiting agency was not simply to wait for voluntary emigrants to turn up at the office for further information, but to actively seek out potential migrants through a network of paid local recruiters roaming the Indian countryside. To prevent them from degenerating into the kind of people who created multiple headaches for the South China authorities (kidnappers and crimps), a system of local district supervision and licensing of recruiters was developed, involving the local district magistrate and the local emigration subagent. India being a British colony, networking of provincial and central state agencies and officials was easier than in nominally sovereign China.

A comprehensive consolidation act was passed by the government of India (No. 13 of 1864), which streamlined the various regulations in force for about twenty years, scattered among about nineteen different acts. Its purpose was mainly consolidatory, although a few important new procedures were introduced. The regulations it contained remained the basic law governing the recruitment of emigrants in India for the British sugar colonies up to the end of indenture.[25]

The hierarchy of emigration officials involved the Calcutta- and Madras-based Protectors of Emigrants (responsible to the government of India), the emigration agents for each of the different colonies (paid by the respective colonial governments), and the medical officers on the ground and on the transporting vessels, in addition to the provincial or district-based emigration subagents, with their cadre of licensed recruiting officers, and the local district magistrates whose job was to supervise recruiting in the course of their normal judicial activities. Meanwhile, at the receiving end, in charge of the allocation and distribution of the immigrants after arrival, there was the government immigration department, headed by a chief immigration officer who went by various names over time (Protector of Immigrants, Agent-General of Immigrants, Immigration Agent-General), assisted by a Sub-Protector (or Senior Immigration Agent), a number of immigration inspectors (or immigration agents)—three in Trinidad, four in British Guiana—plus clerical officers and interpreters. The activities of the colony-based immigration officials were regulated by the relevant local immigration ordinances.

Indian Act No. 13 of 1864 specified how recruitment in India was to be conducted. All recruiters were to be licensed, and no recruiting by unauthorized persons was to be permitted, on pain of fine or imprisonment. Sections 24 to 29 empowered the Protector, on the application of an emigration agent, to license as many persons as he might deem necessary for the purpose. Each license was valid for one year, on payment of a fee of ten rupees, and had to specify the colony for which the recruiter proposed to act. The license had to be countersigned by the magistrate of the district or Presidency town where the recruiter proposed to operate. Licenses could be withdrawn for misconduct, and recruiters had to wear badges identifying themselves as such.

Under Sections 30 to 35, all potential migrants had to be brought by the recruiter before the district magistrate (or the Protector, if recruited in a Presidency town) for registration. The magistrate (or the Protector) was required to examine each intending emigrant as to his comprehension of the proposed engagement and willingness to fulfill it. The entry on the register, a copy of which was to be furnished to each emigrant, had to specify his name, his father's name, his age, his village, the depot for which he was bound, and the "rate of wages and period of service . . . agreed upon between the emigrant and the recruiter." The magistrate (or the Protector) would refuse to register the proposed emigrant if he felt that he did not understand the nature of the engagement or had been induced by fraud or misrepresentation to enter into it. Upon registration, a fee of one rupee was payable, and a copy of each registration was to be forwarded by the district magistrate to the Protector and the emigration agent concerned (if by the Protector, then to the agent).

The intending emigrants were to be transported soon after registration to the relevant emigration depot in Calcutta or Madras, accompanied either by the recruiter or some other approved person, and provided with food and lodging during the journey. The emigration agent and the Protector were to be notified immediately on arrival, and medical examinations of each emigrant were to be made. (Sections 36–40.)

Within two days of arrival, the Agent and the Protector had to examine each emigrant, and upon being satisfied of their fitness, both were required to countersign the register and deliver to each emigrant a pass signed by both officials, with his name, age, and father's name, certifying that he was in a fit state of health to emigrate. If the Agent should reject a particular emigrant without the consent of the Protector, he was responsible for the expense of returning him back to the original district where he was registered. (Sections 41–43.)

The provision for separate depots for each colony, and for the licensing of each depot by the Protector, was an innovation. This had become necessary because, prior to this separation, the practice of recruiters luring away emigrants enlisted for other colonies was quite common and was a cause of grievance for recruiters and emigrants alike. The Act of 1864 also defined the duties of the Protector more precisely and forbade him from combining his post with other occupations, as had been the case prior to 1864. Before then, the Protector used to be also the master attendant (port controller) at Calcutta and consequently devoted his energies to diverse functions, to the detriment of proper supervision over the emigration process.

Intending emigrants were generally examined in groups, rather than individually, which led to all kinds of abuse. The Protector's defined duties included a visit, with the medical inspector, to each depot at least once a week, to examine the state of the depot and the manner in which emigrants were "lodged, fed, clothed and otherwise provided for and attended to." It also included the inspection of outgoing vessels as well as vessels returning with immigrant laborers from the colonies. In the case of the latter, he was to enquire into their treatment both in the colonies and on the voyage back.

With this procedural and institutional streamlining, the recruitment process largely remedied the main abuses which had attended the experiment before the 1860s: deception, intimidation, or kidnapping of illiterate villagers by unscrupulous recruiters; direct transportation to Calcutta or Madras without local supervision, often also illegally housing them in private residences in Calcutta or Madras without properly informing them of their destinations until very late; and careless and perfunctory group examinations by a busy Protector with ill-defined responsibilities. Some abuses were not very easy to eradicate, and these continued, though on a diminishing scale, throughout the indenture period. They involved mainly recruiting people with highly colored informal accounts of prospects for self-enrichment in the colonies, sometimes even deceiving some about the level of hard work actually required on a sugar plantation in the West Indies.

As late as 1898, twenty-seven recruiters had their licenses revoked for a variety of offenses and irregularities. One was involved in a case of rape and murder. One was deemed to have detained two persons against their will who did not want to emigrate. Two had attempted to recruit Nepalese contrary to orders. Two tried to defraud the railway company by sending prospective emigrants to the central depot without buying rail tickets for them. One tried to deceive the registering officer or magistrate. Two had disposed of some immigrants without following the legal procedures. One brought a false charge. One induced a woman to emigrate under false promises. One released a woman who had been duly registered and then readmitted her and sent her off to Calcutta without the knowledge of the emigration agent. One was implicated in a case of rape and wrongful confinement. One kept a mistress in his depot. One was reported by the emigration agent as being frequently guilty of misconduct. The rest had their licenses revoked because subsequent to their grants the holders were found to bear bad or indifferent characters.[26]

A further point to be made about the recruiters themselves was that the practice of utilizing unlicensed recruiters (including women) did not die out, despite being technically illegal. But they were responsible to the licensed recruiters, who paid them a portion of their own fees and on whose head would fall the wrath of the law in the case of gross irregularities. Recruiters generally received about 2 and 4 rupees for a man and a woman, respectively, in the 1850s, and 10 and 14 rupees in the 1880s. Emigration subagents based in the local districts, whose activities were not covered by the 1864 Act but whose services were invaluable to the main emigration agents based in the big cities, coordinated the transportation of emigrants to the main depots with the recruiters and were legally entitled to a regular salary, although the Grierson Report stated that they were usually paid according to the number of emigrants recruited (18 and 26 rupees for men and women in 1883). Often, they were not full-time agents, and combined recruiting portfolios for several colonies.

There was also a systematic institutional deception entrenched in the whole system, in that no one ever informed the intending emigrants (or was ever required to by law) about the harsh disciplinary laws imposed unilaterally by the planter-controlled colonial legislatures contained in the immigration ordinances, the whole apparatus of criminal penalties attached to small and large infractions of the contract or of basic work discipline. This omission remained basic to the entire immigration experiment and thereby defined the indenture system as a quasi-servile labor system, despite its other legal safeguards and the paternalistic policy pronouncements of the policy makers in the Colonial Office and the colonies. It would be well to note also that the official attitude of the Indian government itself towards emigration throughout the whole experiment was one of "benevolent neutrality," that is, facilitating and supervising the process, but in no way actively encouraging it or proselytizing to migrants in its favor. An attempt by Lord Salisbury, Secretary of State for India, to get the Indian government in March 1875 to adopt a more activist emigration policy was flatly rejected. The official reply said in 1877: "After a careful consideration of the past history of Indian emigration and of the probable effect on the native mind of a direct intervention on the part of Government to encourage its subjects to emigrate, we are clearly of opinion that any material departure from the permissive attitude which has hitherto been observed would be extremely impolitic."[27]

Complementing the activities of the China- and India-based emigration officials were the officials of the Immigration Department in the West Indies. The Protector of Immigrants (Immigration Agent-General) was charged with all matters connected with the indentured immigrants, from their arrival to their allocation and distribution to the individual plantations, and supervision over their progress and functioning during their five terms of indenture. The main functions associated with these powers were described in an official report to the Sanderson Commission in 1909:

> The Protector may at any time visit estates, inspect condition and treatment of immigrants and their dwellings and hospital accommodation, enquire into complaints of all kinds, lay information against employers or any other persons, and at all hearings before the magistrate act on behalf of the immigrant as if he were the principal in the matter, and report to the Governor. The Protector is responsible for the proper carrying out of the provisions of all immigration laws, and may deal with employers generally in respect of any breaches of the provisions of the ordinances then in force. He is assisted by a Sub-Protector and such other Inspectors as the Governor may appoint, of whom there are now three in various parts of the island, to each of whom is given power to visit every plantation on which indentured labor is employed, and to enquire into all complaints of or against immigrants, to give advice, conduct investigations, institute prosecutions, and assist the magistrate, if required, in the estimation of wages.
>
> The Protector or any Inspector may grant warrants for the arrest of any person who upon investigation may appear to him to have been guilty of any offence under the immigration laws, may summon witnesses and take evidence of any enquiry instituted by him, and may order the production of the employer's books of account showing the wages paid to indentured immigrants.[28]

The execution of the major functions of the Immigration Department was often influenced by the personality of the particular Protector or Agent-General. Certainly the confidence reposed in the Department by the Asian immigrants depended often on this factor, and in the history of the indenture experiment, certain officials stood out more than others in terms of the image they projected as humane and impartial administrators. Such, for example, were people like British Guiana's James Crosby, who held this post for most of the crucial years of the indenture system, 1858 to 1880. So revered was he by the Indian community that the office of Agent-General was popularly known as "Crosby" long after his departure and death.[29] Less personally lionized but equally well known was Trinidad's early Agent-General, Dr. Henry Mitchell, who held office from 1850 to 1883 and of whom Arthur Gordon (later Lord Stanmore), who governed Trinidad between 1866 and 1870, said: "He never lost an opportunity . . . of turning the scale in favor of the immigrant."[30]

More colorful and controversial was Major James Fagan, a retired army officer from India who was appointed Trinidad's "Coolie Magistrate" in 1845–48, a post which was a precursor to the Protector or Agent-General office. His denunciations of official and planter neglect of the Indians arriving in this formative period earned him many friends and enemies, until his post was abruptly terminated in 1848 by the Governor, Lord Harris.[31] Other influential figures who held this position in the later period included Robert Duff of British Guiana (1905–12), and the more ambivalent Commander William Coombs of Trinidad (1896–1914). Robert Duff has been described by a modern Guyanese scholar: "Mr Duff had a high conception of Indians and drew attention on several occasions to the part played by them in developing the agricultural resources of the colony. He was instrumental in causing a reduction of the high percentage of prosecutions for labor offences, and did a great deal in other respects for their benefit."[32]

Commander Coombs was involved in a celebrated case in Trinidad in 1897, soon after his arrival, against an influential manager, Peter Abel, who was charged by Coombs for physical maltreatment of six Indian laborers (tying them together with rope as a disciplinary measure). Abel was found guilty and fined a grand total of £60, £10 for each victim of abuse.[33] Later in his administration, Coombs developed into a conservative disciplinarian towards the immigrant community, less sympathetic or liberal than the other figures mentioned above.[34]

There was one other important administrative agency involved in the immigration experiment in the early years: the London-based Colonial Land and Emigration Commission, an agency of the Colonial Office which functioned from 1840 to 1878. Its specific portfolio was the overall supervision of the emigration movements involving Britain and the British Empire and the formulation of recommendations concerning these processes to the Colonial Office. Asian indentured immigration was just a part—although an important part—of its administrative preoccupations, the migrations to North America and to the white Dominions being of greater import during the high point of its influence.

Created in 1840, it functioned with a staff of thirty officers in 1849. The Commission advised the British government on all aspects of immigration, drew up regulations, critiqued and reviewed all colonial legislation touching on immigration matters, and prepared an annual report on emigration which was printed as a parliamentary paper. In those emigration movements where the transportation took place in state-supervised vessels, it was responsible for appointing medical officers and providing supplies, making sure that the provisions of the Imperial Passengers Act were observed and even chartering some of the vessels required. After the Australian and North American migrations began to wind down, its own activities were downscaled in the 1860s. But the Asian migration movements within the Empire formed a crucial part of its preoccupations right up to 1876, when the Indian immigration portfolio was transferred to another agency within the Colonial Office. The Commission itself was formally dissolved in 1878.[35]

IMMIGRATION REGULATIONS IN JAMAICA

Thus far the discussion on the formal organization of the British West Indian indenture system has centered on the apparatus and laws of Trinidad and British Guiana. Jamaica, with its somewhat more marginal and erratic experience of Asian immigration, developed a number of unique rules which distinguished it from the others, even though the overall framework remained similar.

The main element of uniqueness centered on the powers of the Protector of Immigrants. Unlike in the other two territories, the Protector retained a judicial function in addition to all his other welfare and administrative responsibilities. Up until 1899, he and his inspectors had the sole authority to adjudicate on all offenses against the immigration laws. After Law 4 of 1899, district magistrates were given concurrent jurisdiction to try cases affecting immigrants. In this sense, the Protector in Jamaica was similar to the "Coolie Magistrate" in Trinidad in 1845–48, a post which Major James Fagan held before the formal post of Protector was created in 1850.

Another distinctive feature was the absence of a requirement for planters employing indentured laborers to construct and maintain their own estate hospitals to look after sick immigrants. Because of the smaller numbers, it made sense to require the immigrants to be treated at public hospitals rather than estate hospitals, with the planters having to meet the expenses thereby incurred. Estate hospitals were in existence until 1879, when they were abolished.

The method of sourcing funds for the Immigration Fund also evolved distinct traits after 1891. Until then, the general pattern of doing so via a combination of indenture fees paid by the planters plus export duties on produce (mainly sugar and its by-products) remained true for Jamaica as well. After Laws 14 and 20 of 1891, export duties were abolished, and indenture fees raised to £15 per immigrant (or £17 10s. over five years), contrasting with the £5 fee payable in the other territories. From 1891, employers of free immigrants who had completed their indentures but not their ten-year residence were also required to contribute to the Fund: 1 shilling per week for each week their services were engaged. (After 1905 the free immigrants themselves had to report their places of residence on a quarterly basis to the police or the Protector.)

These requirements were unique to Jamaica and were criticized by some external observers, such as Dr. Comins. But they remained in force to the end, on the ground that the Jamaican situation did not permit the same kinds of financial levies allowed by the other colonies.

The equally distinct method of apportioning the total immigration expenses between the planter-funded Immigration Fund and the general revenues is discussed below. In Jamaica the contribution from the general revenues was much less than that payable in the other two territories.

The main laws affecting Jamaican indenture over time were No. 34 of 1869, No. 23 of 1879, and later Nos. 14 and 20 of 1891. The 1879 law (the Immigration Protection and Regulation Law) was the main consolidatory law, whose provisions remained in force up to the end of indenture (this did not include financing immigration expenses). There was a provision introduced in 1891 for special one-year indenture contracts to be extended to natives of Jamaica, that is, Black Creoles. However, this never worked, as no one attempted to take advantage of the provision.[36]

State-Funded Immigration

The last feature of the indenture system to be examined is its method of financing. In the earliest years, private importers of immigrants were expected to assume on their own the entire burden of the expenses incurred. In 1839, public bounties were introduced, subject to the restrictions on contracts discussed earlier. When the immigration began in earnest in the mid-1840s, a loan from the British government helped to tide over the initial difficulties. By the 1850s, the expenses of immigration were divided between the planters and the general revenue. Up until 1860, however, the exact proportions for which each sector was responsible remained unsettled, with the planters generally being expected to pay roughly one-third of the total expenses incurred in importing labor to the colonies, about $50 in indenture fees per immigrant ($80 for a Chinese immigrant).

Under the system introduced with the creation of an Immigration Fund in 1862, the planters' contribution was raised to two-thirds of the total expenditure, with the remaining one-third payable by the general revenue. This arrangement, with minor substantive changes and modifications from time to time on the concrete sources of the financial contribution, remained the basic division of financial responsibility between the planters and the colony in general, up to the end of the system in 1920. It was criticized constantly from many quarters inside the colonies themselves, by those who for various reasons felt that immigration designed to benefit the sugar interests should not be subsidized by other producing sectors or by the general taxpayers. However, the arrangement remained intact up to the end.

When the Sanderson Committee reported in 1910, the Trinidad Immigration Fund consisted of (a) indenture fees, (b) immigration tax, and (c) vote by the Legislative Council in aid of immigration.

A special memorandum prepared for the Committee in 1909 stated:

(1) Every employer pays £5 as indenture fees for each immigrant not a minor, and £2 10s. for each minor, payable by five equal annual payments, and such payments shall be made although the immigrant shall have died, become incapable, or have deserted, unless the indenture shall have been cancelled by the Governor. All indenture fees become a first charge on the plantation to which the immigrant is indentured.

(2) Immigration tax is regulated each year by Ordinance, and varies according to the amount required. For the current year it is as follows:

Upon Sugar	3s. 6d. per	1,000 lbs
" Molasses	3s. 1d. "	100 gallons
" Rum and Bitters	9s. 4d. "	100 gallons
" Cocoa and Coffee	8d. "	100 lbs
" Cocoanuts	8d. "	1,000 nuts
" Copra	2s. 7d. "	1,000 lbs

(3) The vote in aid of immigration consists of a charge of one-third of the total annual cost of immigration against general revenue, but this year the

amount actually paid from general revenue will not greatly exceed one-fourth of the total cost by reason of the casual receipts.

(4) Casual receipts consist of advances, arrears, redemption, added percentages on default, passages of immigrants paid by themselves, and miscellaneous.

The receipts under the above heads are estimated for the current year as follows:

Indenture Fees	£10,000,	paid by planters
Immigration Tax	£32,496,	paid by planters
Vote in Aid	£16,458	
Casual Receipts	£3,102	

The planters will therefore contribute £42,496, against the total expenditure of £62,056, for the current year, and general revenue £16,458.[37]

In British Guiana, in place of the export tax on produce, there was an acreage tax on sugar lands introduced in 1903: $1.50 per acre if under cane cultivation, 2 cents per acre if empoldered but not under cane cultivation. This was applied to lands held by the planters, and not to those held by small farmers with small leases. Also reintroduced in that year was an earlier method (1873–78) of passing the one-third annual immigration expenses on to the general revenue. The salaries and office expenses of the Immigration Department, including the salary of the emigration agent based in India—amounting to about £6,800 a year—were paid from the general revenue. So too were the expenses of the Government Medical Department connected with indentured immigrants. (Estates usually had their own hospitals, however, and immigrants treated in public hospitals were paid for by the planters.) The other expenses connected with immigration (recruitment, introduction, and repatriation) were paid for from the Immigration Fund, funded by indenture fees and acreage taxes on sugar estates after 1903.

In 1907–8 the Guianese immigration expenditures connected with recruitment, introduction, and repatriation looked as follows: the expense of introducing 1,766 statute adults was $138,243, and of back passages $65,843, making a total charge on the Immigration Fund of $204,086. To meet this expenditure the receipts were as follows: indenture fees $99,360; acreage tax $113,186; miscellaneous sources, $922; a total of $213,468. The Fund therefore had a surplus that year of $9,382.[38]

In Jamaica, where the sugar interest was not dominant in the late nineteenth century, and where the planters consequently had less influence on the colonial legislature, the sugar planters were compelled to pay more than the usual two-thirds for their labor imports after 1879. The public pressure to remove the public subsidy, and to impose the entire burden of immigration on the sugar interest, was more successful in Jamaica than elsewhere. The Immigration Finance Law (No. 18 of 1879) divided the overall expenses connected with immigration as follows: (a) medical expenses spent on maintaining and caring for immigrants in public hospitals to be borne by the general revenue; (b) salaries and expenses of the Immigration Department on the island and elsewhere, including repatriation costs for immigrants indentured before the 1st of January 1878, to be borne by the Immigration Fund (export duties on sugar and by-products); and (c) all recruitment (minus salaries of the emigration agent in India), introduction, and post-1878 repatriation expenses to be borne by the planters themselves.

This arrangement remained in force until Laws 14 and 20 of 1891 made further readjustments. Under these laws, the general revenue became responsible for the salary and office expenses of the Immigration Department on the island and elsewhere, in addition to the existing financial responsibilities on medical expenses. Recruitment, introduction, and repatriation expenses were chargeable to the Immigration Fund. Export duties on sugar and rum were also abolished and replaced by an escalated indenture fee of £15 (or £17 10s. in five years) payable by the planters for each immigrant indentured, plus the 1 shilling weekly fee for the employment of individual free immigrants mentioned above.[39] This would have had the effect of shifting a good share of the financial expenses on to the banana planters, who were major importers of immigrant labor after 1890.

While a small amount of public protest at the continuation of the subsidy continued to the end of indentureship, the Jamaican method of financing the later stages of its small indentured immigration experiment was clearly quite distinct from that of the other two main colonies.

CHAPTER 4

Life and Labor on the Plantations:
The Chinese

Drawn from diverse nationality sources, the immigrant labor force became overwhelmingly Indian only by the 1870s. When the Commission of Enquiry into conditions on the British Guiana plantations met in 1870–71, the plantation work force there was still quite multiracial, although most of the Portuguese had already left for other pastures. Trinidad's immigrant work force was also losing its polyglot character by 1870, lesser numbers of Portuguese having emigrated to that island, and most Chinese having already left plantation life by that year—many indeed having absconded from their duties, but many also having commuted their indentures before the full term had expired.

In this chapter and the next, we examine the arrival and adjustment processes of both groups of Asian immigrants to Caribbean plantation life, and their experiences of what one recent writer critical of the indenture system called the gap between "the facade of governmental regulation and the reality of plantation neglect."[1] The Chinese are discussed first, even though the first contingent of Indian arrivals had preceded their arrival in 1853.

When the Cantonese region began to show increased emigration activity in the years following the first so-called Opium War (1839–42), Western importers began to pay active attention to the prospect of recruiting cheap labor from this source. A British parliamentary committee had tried to revive the issue of Chinese immigration to the West Indies as early as 1811, but there was no follow-up. In 1843, licenses for the importation of 2,850 Chinese were actually granted (six for British Guiana for 2,150 immigrants, one for Trinidad for 300, and one for Jamaica for 400). But the projects were never undertaken because at this point the importers were expected to bear the financial risks themselves, and their agents in the East could not get many Chinese to migrate to the West Indies voluntarily.

The idea remained dormant until 1850–51, when the local legislatures of both British Guiana and Trinidad passed legislation authorizing the revival of the Chinese labor importation efforts, and the British Guiana emigration agent in India, James White, was dispatched to China to survey the prospects. His reports were favorable. On the 19th of July 1851, he wrote from Hong Kong:

> I have no reason to alter the opinion formerly expressed that the Chinese are admirably adapted as laborers for the West Indies; they are strong, active and intelligent, disposed to work and to make money. The climate here, at least at this season of the year, is very similar to that of the West Indies, and I think they would enjoy health and strength in their new location. The extensive cultivation of rice and sugar in the lowlands of the two provinces of Canton and Fukien would seem to qualify them for a residence in Trinidad and Demerara, and I believe they will be found hardy and industrious.[2]

The organized migration of laborers from China which commenced in 1853 was plagued throughout, as we have seen, by difficulties. Many of these difficulties stemmed not only from problems at the recruiting end, but also from problems at the receiving end. Compared with the migrations to Cuba, which, after a fitful start in 1847, resumed in 1853 and saw vessels leaving the China ports for Havana every single year until 1874, the demand for Chinese laborers in the West Indies was not as constant. This was partly due to the supply instability at the China end, but also partly due to the varied reactions of the planters to the Chinese actually sent.

Most important, it was caused by the factor of competition from India, whose supplies were more regular, better organized at source, and less expensive. The requirements imposed in 1866 by the Kung Convention regulations virtually priced Chinese labor out of the West Indian market (about £35–£37 per immigrant), even though the Cuban planters continued to import Chinese on eight-year contracts at almost double that figure up to 1874.[3]

The immigration, as we have seen, was eventually broken into three periods: the 1853–54 seasons, the 1859–66 period, and the last sporadic shipments of 1874, 1879, and 1884. Of the seven vessels that sailed to the British West Indies in the first two seasons of 1853 and 1854, six were organized under private auspices under the umbrella of a government bounty ($100 a head), and only one was dispatched by White.

The *Glentanner*, the *Lord Elgin*, and the *Samuel Boddington* arrived in British Guiana with 647 Chinese from Amoy in Fukien Province between January and March 1853, all on five-year contracts. In the same year, the *Australia*, the *Clarendon*, and the *Lady Flora Hastings* brought 988 Chinese to Trinidad, between March and June. The *Clarendon* was dispatched from Canton (downstream Whampoa),[4] and the two other vessels from Swatow (Namoa island) in northeast Kwangtung, close to Amoy and the Fukienese border.

White's first vessel, the only one for which he was fully responsible, the *Epsom*, left Hong Kong for Jamaica in April 1854 with 310 passengers, 267 of whom survived the voyage. This was the first attempt to encourage a direct voluntary engagement of contract emigrants by the British, the others having gotten their recruits via the questionable indirect methods then in vogue with all private importers, that is, through paid Chinese freelance recruiters on the ground.

White, in his report on the departure of the *Epsom*, recounted some of the difficulties he encountered in his first efforts, with aspiring native recruiters attempting to frighten off the Chinese with tales of evil British intentions to enslave them if they went on board voluntarily and individually. It took several days before fears and suspicions were allayed and emigrants began to come forward on their own. White was able to report: "The greater number of the emigrants on board the *Epsom* may be considered as voluntary emigrants; and this is the only instance in which the advances paid have been received by the emigrants themselves, and expended as they thought proper. Hitherto the crimps have always managed, by fair means or foul, to appropriate the largest portion of the advance." As testimony to the general community goodwill surrounding the *Epsom* voyage, he reported that the vessel sailed out of Hong Kong "amid the firing of crackers and the uproar of gongs and drums" from shore.[5]

The entire British Guiana contingent was recruited at Amoy, where up to 1852 most of the early private importers for Latin America were conducting their recruiting operations. In November 1852 there was an ugly riot of Amoy Chinese against the British firms conducting recruiting operations for Cuba and elsewhere, over the unscrupulous activities of the crimps in their employ. British troops got involved, and several lives were lost in the confrontations which ensued.[6] Some of the private mercantile firms then shifted their activities to next-door Namoa island off Swatow, and it is there that two of the Trinidad-bound ships received their own contingent of emigrants.

The passengers were a motley lot, most of them between the ages of twenty and thirty-five. Many had been agricultural laborers before, but many were déclassé elements, with somewhat unreliable potential as sugar cultivators. The surgeon on the *Samuel Boddington* to Demerara did not attempt to conceal his prejudices against the Chinese aboard his vessel. He wrote in his journal: "The greater part we have on board are quite savage, many of them never having seen a European before coming to Amoy to go away, and having as little idea of right and wrong as the wandering savages of the wildernesses of America. They are fierce, cunning, ill-natured, revengeful and hypocritical; and we have far more to do to keep anything like order among them than if they were so many monkeys."[7]

He also wrote of ominous signs of mutiny being planned by the Chinese during the voyage, and he seemed somewhat fearful himself. However, an official letter of the Colonial Land and Emigration Commission Office, written a few months after the vessel had docked at Georgetown, seemed to cast doubt on the surgeon's fears, suggesting that they might have been imagined.[8]

The judgments of the West Indian planters were far more favorable towards the newcomers. The Guianese contingent was distributed over ten estates, in detachments of sixty to one hundred, and the Trinidad contingent over forty-six estates, in smaller detachments, varying from sixteen to thirty-three. Reports submitted on their performance in the early months described some of them as turbulent, others as cheerful and docile. One planter enthused: "I have very little hesitation in predicting that in a short time they will be the most efficient laborers we have. They appear to have the strength to do all kinds of work required of them, and at present they exhibit a ready will to try anything they are told to do. They jump at the first call, and the merry, noisy way in which they tumble out to their work reminds me of the 'scaling' of a school."[9]

These sentiments were echoed by Guianese and Trinidadian planters alike.[10] Governor Barkly of British Guiana reported one instance where about forty of the Chinese laborers turned out to work on a Sunday morning on one estate, insisting on being given the opportunity to earn seven days' wages a week if they wanted. Their enthusiasm had to be restrained.[11]

The *Australia* contingent to Trinidad (or part of it) received praise as being "the best immigrants hitherto imported." These Chinese from the region surrounding Swatow, all previously employed in cane cultivation, were described as good-natured though stubborn, "their muscular development more pronounced than that of any set of immigrants . . . yet seen, whether European or Asiatic."[12]

The Cantonese who came with the *Clarendon* to Trinidad—the only recruits from the Canton region in these two years, apart from those who went to Jamaica on the *Epsom*—were described as "smarter and more civilised," though "much more difficult to control."[13]

The adjustment to the plantations was not without its frictions and discordances. Not all the newcomers responded favorably to their new social environment and conditions of work. On some estates, the laborers refused to work the required number of hours per day, while insisting on full rations and wages. Often, many would feign illness, some going so far as staying in bed for the entire fourteen days allowed for illness, then turning out to work for the fifteenth day, and returning to bed for the rest of the month, all the while insisting on a full month's wages despite the formal nonperformance.

There were disagreements in Trinidad over repayment of the advances made in China, some believing (or claiming to believe) that these were not repayable from wages, but were given as bounties. Attempts to deduct these sums from wages caused such "endless strife and vagrancy" that many planters paid the sums themselves, and in many cases it was never recovered.

Moreover, the contingent of Chinese from the Swatow region which arrived in Trinidad on the *Lady Flora Hastings* was of a different and more unstable social element than those on the other two vessels. Many of them were also chronic opium smokers. They were deemed by many of the planters as "utterly worthless," giving proper satisfaction on only one of the seventeen plantations to which they had been assigned. According to one annual immigration report, they proved a source of continual annoyance to the estates that received them, and before six months had passed, they suffered so severely from dysentery and sores that the local government had to make the matter a subject of special enquiry.[14]

In addition to this, they often fought among themselves, since it would appear that a number of Fukienese were among them. (About 107 had come on the *Australia,* and about 36 on the *Lady Flora Hastings.*) Two people were killed in this kind of factional fighting. Later reports recorded that while the transition to plantation work discipline was impossible with many, a few from this third group of Trinidad immigrants did nevertheless make the transition eventually.

One major factor complicating (and in some cases probably causing) the overall adjustment frictions was the language factor, the inability to communicate between laborers and managers, and the small number of those who could act as interpreters. The migrants to British Guiana had among them only two people—a man and a boy—with a limited knowledge of English, and one other who had picked up a few words of French in Mauritius. The surgeon on the *Lord Elgin,* Dr. Shier, could understand Chinese when spoken but could not converse in the language himself. Those who came to Trinidad were no better off, although a later report stated that a few of them became towards the end of their indenture residence fairly fluent in both French and English, the popular languages of the island in the nineteenth century.[15] The Jamaica-bound Chinese were only slightly better off, with about four to six of them possessing some knowledge of English. One of them could even speak Bengali, having lived for some time in India.[16]

British Guiana and Trinidad employed one official Chinese interpreter each for their immigration departments: one Ho-a-Sing for the former, and Ong Soong Seng, a Chinese native of Penang, for the latter. They were both fluent in English, but the former could only speak the Cantonese dialect, and the latter the Fukienese (Hokkien). This did not eliminate the communication problem with the immigrants, since the Guianese group were all Fukienese. Ho-a-Sing, however, could write the Chinese language, which was standard throughout China, despite the differences in the spoken dialects. This alleviated matters for those few who could read, probably not very many. Ong Soong Seng could not write Chinese but could converse with the Swatow contingent, since their spoken dialect, Teochiu, resembled that of the Fukien province. Difficulties persisted, however, with the Cantonese group from the *Clarendon.*[17]

There were other problems of adjustment for a minority of the immigrants. The habit of opium smoking, widespread in China at the time, debilitated and often killed those prone to taking too much of the drug. A few of them reportedly even picked up the vice of excessive rum drinking. The Immigration Agent-General in Trinidad commented that a few from the *Australia* contingent, who had been allocated to Jordan Hill estate, had shown a stronger predilection for rum drinking "than might have been predicted from tea drinkers."[18]

There was also the climate, the rainy season during the last six months of the year often playing havoc with the health of some of them. Managerial cruelty, a problem that surfaced regularly with the migrants who came in the 1859–66 period, especially in British Guiana, seems not to have played a great role in the problems of the 1853 groups, although there were many reports of managerial frustration at the turbulent behavior of some of them in the first few months after arrival. On at least ten plantations in Trinidad, a number of the Chinese had to be relocated to other plantations.[19]

Relations with the Black Creoles also caused some early minor friction. In British Guiana some of the Chinese on Plantation Blankenburg in West Coast Demerara were involved in a huge fight with some of the free Blacks from the neighboring village of Den Amstel. Six Chinese were jailed by the authorities as a result of this confrontation.[20] In Trinidad a few of the *Australia* group allocated to the Friendship estate in Naparima got into a scuffle with their fellow Black laborers, and two Chinese and one Black ended up with head wounds from stick blows. After a magistrate's hearing, the Chinese were removed to nearby Williamsville estate.[21] Generally, however, race relations seemed to have been free of friction, especially in Trinidad, and the official reports, at least, carried few accounts of further interracial incidents.

The Chinese who arrived in Jamaica on the *Epsom* in 1854 were allocated to estates in Clarendon and to the Caymanas estates near Kingston. Not long afterwards, they were joined by a fresh contingent of 205 by way of Panama, all from the Swatow and Amoy regions. Earlier in the year, about 1,040 of them had left Swatow to go to Panama to work on the Panama railway project. Climate, deadly fevers, and gross managerial cruelties (some of these at the hands of Chinese headmen) caused the mortality rate to rise to a horrendous 50 percent.

According to the account of Wang-Te-Chang, one of the Chinese interpreters from the *Epsom* who was taken on a Jamaican mission to Panama to speak to them, some of the Chinese thought that they were originally bound for California, not Panama.[22] After their tribulations in Panama, a small number—just over thirty—did manage to leave for California, but half of them died within a few months after arrival in Panama, about thirty or forty of them from suicide. About two hundred were in the hospital at the time of the Jamaican mission. The survivors were only too anxious to leave Panama and relocate to Jamaica as agricultural laborers. In November, they arrived on the island on two vessels, the *Vampire* and the *Theresa Jane*.

The fortunes of these early Chinese in Jamaica were quite mixed, the Panama lot faring much worse than the *Epsom* lot. Many disputes over conditions of work took place between the planters and the new laborers, and there was a very high desertion rate. Many congregated in Kingston and Spanish Town, some drifting into vagrancy and having to be housed in the hospitals or almshouses of the urban centers. Some were relocated on government initiative on a small land settlement scheme, where they were encouraged to grow sweet potatoes. The experiment collapsed, however, and the government stopped subsidizing the settlement. Many remained on the estates, some long after the formal indenture term was over. As late as 1866 there were twenty Chinese laborers on an estate in St. Thomas-in-the-Vale. A small number gravitated towards small-scale trade in Kingston.[23]

The overall total of 2,107 migrants to the three Caribbean sugar colonies proved to be the only shipments the British could manage in the initial phase. The attempt to establish an agency in Hong Kong did not come to fruition, partly because of the expense involved and the competition from other nationalities now participating in the China traffic, partly because of problems with the proposed agent, James White, who was recalled in 1854 after attempting to recruit migrants at Namoa (off Swatow) in violation of the treaties with China. The project was left in abeyance, and not until five years later was the China effort resumed.

This second phase proved to be the most productive, lasting eight years, after which there was another abrupt termination, and, as it turned out, a more or less decisive one. During this period thirty-four vessels sailed to British Guiana, and five to Trinidad, bringing about 80 percent of the Chinese who migrated to the British West Indies in the nineteenth century. The year 1859 saw 699 migrants arriving on the *Royal George* and the *General Wyndham* in British Guiana, officially from Hong Kong, but actually recruited via Macao (discussed in chapter 3). Between 1860 and 1866, thirty-two vessels brought 11,290 Chinese to British Guiana, sixteen of them from Canton, fourteen from Hong Kong, and two vessels registered as sailing from Amoy. The Trinidad-bound vessels, five in all with 1,657 passengers, arrived in 1862, 1865, and 1866, one from Hong Kong, two from Canton, and two from Amoy.[24]

Just under 2,000 females came to British Guiana in the eight-year period from 1859 to 1866, 17 percent of the whole, with the first group arriving on March 11, 1860, aboard the *Whirlwind* from Hong Kong (56 women and 4 girls). About 309 females landed in Trinidad in the five ships, 18 percent of the passengers, with the first group of 125 (124 women and 1 girl) arriving from Hong Kong on the *Wanata* on July 3, 1862. The mortality rate aboard the *Maggie Miller/Wanata* had been very high, and the 125 females who made it safely to Trinidad were survivors of an original contingent of 174 females who had embarked at Hong Kong on February 12.[25]

Most of the sugar plantations in British Guiana received an allotment of Chinese (116 out of 153 plantations in the 1860s). Demerara received about 64 percent, Essequibo about 21 percent, and Berbice about 15 percent. The Trinidad Chinese were allotted to a total of 70 to 76 plantations, between 1853 and 1866.[26]

The experience of these immigrants was very much an enlarged version of the 1853 experience, but with significantly new developments, not necessarily favorable. The flood of Indian immigrants to both colonies was now an established fact, and so was the stabilization of sugar production. The intense supervision of the Anti-Slavery Society and its friends had long subsided, as the normality of indenture came to be accepted by the Colonial Office in the 1850s. In this context, the gaps between the formal regulations of the immigration laws and the actual management practices of the planters and their agents were often quite wide. It took a series of scandals and a formal Commission of Enquiry in 1870–71 to clear up some of these discordances in British Guiana.

The Chinese arrivals were not immune from these larger influences alive in the plantation system. Of course, there were many reports of favorable treatment and favorable work performance, as before. The shipment from Swatow and Amoy which arrived on the *Elma Bruce* in 1862 was described by the Guianese planters as "without exception the finest body ever introduced into the colony." A number of them—about ten— were also Christian converts, and they proselytized among their brethren on the voyage and on the estates.[27]

Some accounts adjudged the Chinese to be the best plantation workers in the colony for "expertness and really natty work." The British Guiana Commission Report of 1871 had this to say about the Chinese as laborers:

> The Chinese laborer possesses greater intelligence than either the Indian or the Negro, and is much quicker at learning to manage machinery than either of them. He is also very careful and neat in his work in the field or buildings; is much more independent than the Coolie, and not so easily led away by discontented persons; rarely making a frivolous complaint. . . . Possessing a keen sense of justice where his own rights are concerned,

he is very capable of strong resentment at anything that appears to him unjust.[28]

Again, in another section:

> The Chinese have proved, in the hands of those employers who took pains to study their temperament, valuable as field laborers, and unmatched as artisans; and the success with which the finer processes of sugar-making by the vacuum pan method have been conducted in Guiana, is in some measure attributable to their neat-handed industry.[29]

By the same token, the 1871 report acknowledged that general planter reactions to the Chinese were quite mixed, "some regarding them as splendid labourers and good fellows, while some can make nothing of them, and would gladly be rid of the whole lot."[30]

In Trinidad, the Cantonese who arrived in 1865 on the Montrose and Paria came in for singular praise from the planters to whom they had been assigned. When the Agent-General of Immigrants wrote his annual report a year later, he recorded that not a single person from this contingent of 380 men and 205 women had been reported as missing from their allotted estates. One planter, to whose estates a large portion of the Paria arrivals had been allotted, recounted in a newspaper article the immigrants' eagerness to get to work immediately on arrival on the estate:

> the first thing they did when they reached the estate was to wash themselves, then wash their clothes, and afterwards to thoroughly scour and cleanse the rooms they were to occupy. The men presently asked for their hoes, and expressed a wish to go to work at once. When Saturday night came around, and the women saw their husbands receiving payment of the wages they had earned, they too expressed a wish to be sent into the field, which was of course readily complied with.[31]

The newspaper, Port-of-Spain Gazette, commented:

> This is the only instance, we believe, of Chinese female immigrants here voluntarily offering themselves for field work. In Demerara the Chinese women cannot be induced to perform any labor at all in the field.[32]

Despite these generally upbeat reports, the discordances were also clearly there. In Trinidad, the balance sheet in the final analysis did not appear favorable to the planters, since three out of the five shipments which arrived in these years turned out to be a disappointment for immigrants and planters alike. The Wanata, which was the only vessel to get to Trinidad in 1862—in contrast with the seven vessels that made it to British Guiana in the same year—arrived with a mixed group of 467 passengers from the Cantonese Delta area, the Swatow region, and Amoy.[33] They had also been fighting among themselves on the voyage over.

When they got to Trinidad, the healthy survivors were distributed over twenty-three to twenty-four estates. They included among them the first Chinese women to arrive in Trinidad, 124 adults and 1 girl, 115 of whom were formally allotted to the estates.[34] Within a year and a half after arrival, about 200 had deserted the estates, including about 104 of the females, who had not been indentured in the first place, but had arrived officially as companions or "wives" of the males on board.

About these women, the Annual Immigration Report for 1862 (submitted in 1863) had this to say:

> incapacitated . . . from earning by agricultural toil a sufficiency for self-support, [the men] have, for the most part, repudiated the wives whom they picked up at Hong Kong, more with a view of sharing in or appropriating their advance money, than with any intention of permanent connection. These unfortunate females, bound by no indenture, have been thus thrown for support on most precarious resources. They do not, as a rule, appear willing to work, although many are physically able. Some have found employment among their previously settled countrymen, others have found a temporary asylum in the public hospitals, while the balance remain on the estates whither they were originally sent, working little and eking out a bare existence in doubtful ways.

A year later, the Agent-General of Immigrants lamented that the women, having been imported at enormous expense, had turned out "worse than useless." He advised in the future that only bona fide wives "able and willing to help the husband" be imported, since the men could not do much more than support themselves, especially in their first year of residence.[35]

The adjustment problems of the men varied with their district origins. Those from the Swatow and Amoy regions were peasants, whereas the Cantonese were mainly urban artisan and déclassé elements. The severe pressures of plantation labor after arrival, earnings below the immigrants' expectations, and the onus of the debt of $10 advanced in China led to widespread desertion, and in at least four cases, to suicide. The Immigration Report for 1863 recorded that out of 326 who owed an aggregate of £900, only two had repaid £10 each, and they were household servants.

On some estates the average daily wage was as low as 6 cents, on others about 20 cents. At the end of 1864, prior to the arrival of the *Montrose,* there were only 179 Chinese officially indentured to the estates in Trinidad and 3 nonindentured residents, presumably female.[36]

The 1866 arrivals from Amoy on the *Dudbrook* and the *Red Riding Hood* were considered nothing short of a disaster, and the experience sealed the attitudes of the Trinidad planters towards the Chinese indenture experiment, despite the favorable performances of the previous year's arrivals. Recruited by Sampson via the services of private mercantile firms, the 1866 migrants were almost all urban and highly rebellious by nature. Unaccustomed to agricultural labor, they had been enticed into migrating by a bounty of $20. Of 597 who arrived alive, only 7 were women (including 1 girl), in stark contrast with the year before. Six came on the *Red Riding Hood,* and 1 woman achieved the extraordinary feat of traveling from Amoy to Trinidad on the *Dudbrook* alone with 271 men.[37]

The desertion rate soon after arrival was a startling 40 percent, and none of the thirty-four estates involved had much to praise in the performance of these immigrants. The Immigration Report for 1866 had this to say:

> [The employers] have in several instances prayed to be relieved from them even while continuing to pay the indenture fees. This is not to be wondered at, as between vagabondage and theft they have stocked the public gaols, and as a necessary consequence, the hospitals, the return from the former, and the abode in the latter, being alike sources of expense to employers. Scenes of violence with occasional murder of their own countrymen or of others have occurred, while their constant depredating at night in the provision grounds, and misconduct by day, have tended greatly to demoralise their otherwise well-disposed fellow laborers.
>
> One estate is actually paying at the rate of £800 per annum for public hospital accommodation on vagrants who have never been, and never will be, remunerative in their turn—for men, in fact, who when discharged from hospital as cured, prefer being committed to gaol as vagrants and fed at the public expense to making the slightest exertion to earn their living.[38]

The owner of Perseverance estate in Couva, who had received allotments from both the 1865 and 1866 shipments, differentiated them by saying that the former had the appearance of agricultural peasants, the latter that of "skulkers about towns." He complained bitterly about the money wasted on the latter.[39] Another planter lamented:

These Chinese are quite averse to steady labor, many strong and able men will not work and perform the task of weeding that frail coolie women go through by one or two o'clock in the afternoon. Early in the morning they will secrete themselves in the canefields, or in the neighborhood, to return in the night to rob the industrious laborer of his poultry and provisions, or to entice away a few of their friends to disappear altogether.

Kindness or legal proceedings have been quite a failure; the leniency shown by His Excellency on a recent occasion has rendered them more uncontrollable—more have run away. They are not only refractory but violent sometimes. Within one month I have been obliged to send before the magistrate two cases of assault upon a sub-manager, one case upon an overseer, without the least provocation on the part of either the overseer or the sub-manager.[40]

These reports highlighted a factor that seemed to loom fairly prominently among the 1859–66 Chinese migrants to both colonies: the tendency of a significant minority to engage in praedial larceny, often alone, but more frequently in organized armed gangs, as a means of sustaining themselves outside the wage labor system, and perhaps as a form of rebellion against it. These elements were considered a perpetual nuisance and menace by the planters, but even more so by the plantation laborers themselves, both Chinese and non-Chinese, who were often the victims of this kind of predatory activity. Official reports stated that ordinary laborers, whose carefully cultivated gardens were despoiled by these nocturnal raiders, would often become demoralized in their attempts to supplement their wages with small-scale farming.

The 1866 arrivals to Trinidad had a large number of such elements among them,[41] and so did many of the British Guiana Chinese, despite their overall good work performance rating among the planters there. Lives of villagers and watchmen were often lost in the clashes between the Guianese and these roving Chinese gangs of twenty to fifty, armed with knives attached to long sticks. Henry Kirke, a magistrate in British Guiana for twenty-five years, later described some of them in his memoirs as "powerful ruffians [who] always carried a large, sharp, two-edged knife, which they never scrupled to use to avoid capture" and called them "a terror to all law-abiding citizens."[42]

Flogging ordinances had to be passed in 1862 and 1865 in British Guiana to curb the stealing of plantains and other produce.[43] The guilty parties might receive as many as thirty-nine lashes, but apprehending them when they moved in such large numbers would often be a problem.

Still others would desert and support themselves in various dubious ways: rum smuggling, illicit rum distillation, keeping gambling houses and brothels. Many deserters would seek asylum among their compatriots in a settlement of free Chinese up the Demerara River. Kirke stated that "it would be a bold policeman who would attempt to execute a warrant in their midst."[44]

After the 1870s, however, these praedial larcenies and other illicit activities tended to subside, as the rebellious elements became acclimatized to the new society, and individuals found other forms of remunerative and orthodox economic activity.

Another prevalent social weakness, and more widespread among the community of laborers, was the habit of chronic opium smoking. The 1870–71 British Guiana Commission Report stated: "Opium smoking is carried on by some to great excess, and it is not uncommon to see many of them quite emaciated, and almost unfit for work, from excessive use of this drug. . . . The wretched appearance of some of the votaries of this habit has more than once misled strangers into conclusions unfair to the planters and the immigration system."[45]

The report went on to say that even a few Indians had picked up this habit from the Chinese. Fatal drug overdose was a frequent cause of death among the Chinese. Between 1865 and 1879 it seems that at least twenty-nine suicides among them were attributable to opium overdose.[46] Even in Trinidad it was felt that the deaths of most of the Chinese up to 1864 were "indirectly attributable to the dysenteric affections which generally attend the abuse of opium."[47]

Suicide, drug addiction, refusal to work, desertion, and vagrancy, plus the occasional strike and act of violence against management personnel or property—all of these were symptoms of a deeper adjustment problem with plantation life which existed among a significant minority of the Chinese population. British Guiana experienced these symptoms on a larger scale, simply because the Chinese immigrants there were larger in number, but the evidence suggests that managerial cruelties and insensitivity were higher in that colony than in Trinidad, particularly before the 1870–71 investigations.

Ex-magistrate William Des Voeux, whose letter to the Colonial Office in 1870 was the spark that led to the official Commission of Enquiry initiated later that year, stated in that letter that the Chinese were even more discontented than the Indians with the peculiar defects of the Guianese plantation system. The report itself described the Chinese laborer as "silent, observant and capricious, ready to hang himself or desert at a moment's notice, for reasons inappreciable to a European."[48]

Disputes over wages and work loads were frequent. So was physical abuse of the laborers by the plantation staff. In 1860 a Chinese laborer was forcibly bound and his "pigtail" cut off on the orders of the manager, as a means of intimidating his fellow workers.[49] The 1871 report re-counted the case of the murder in May 1868 of Low-a-Si, a Chinese "boxman" (a person wheeling away trucks containing megass in the build-ings), by a head overseer and a driver at Plantation Annandale, the latter of whom was later tried for manslaughter and acquitted.[50] It also recalled the physical assault of another laborer, Wong-Ting-Fat, by a manager.[51] Des Voeux's letter recounted the case of a Chinese worker who was severely beaten by an Indian watchman when caught stealing, and who subsequently died from his wounds because he was turned out of the estate hospital prematurely.[52]

Such cases of physical brutality were far more frequent than the au-thorities acknowledged, and not all of them ever reached their attention. In Trinidad, on Lochmaben estate in Cedros in 1865, the manager, Mr. Johnston, was arrested and charged with a brutal assault with a hunting whip on a Chinese worker who had been demanding payment of several weeks' wages in arrears. The Port-of-Spain Gazette reported: "The man fell insensible; and while on the ground several more blows were given. . . . The blow completely smashed in the bridge of the man's nose, inflicting a wound that endangered life."[53]

Legal action, followed by incarceration, for the slightest violation of the immigration laws was also a common tactic of imposing discipline on recalcitrant workers of both Chinese and Indian groups. In 1866, a local Guianese newspaper observed that the number of Chinese incarcer-ated in the Georgetown jail was out of proportion to their numbers in the colony.[54] Quite a few of the Chinese, we have seen, often preferred to endure the trials of imprisonment rather than the trials of plantation life, this in itself being a commentary on the rigors of plantation work discipline, as well as on the persistent rebelliousness of some of the Chinese.

Occasionally, their discontent with life on the estates would trigger fears of a possible rebellion or uprising, and alarm and unease among the local elite. Such an occurrence took place in Trinidad in March and April 1866 in the Couva area, following a number of disturbances there, and particularly one on Perseverance estate which resulted in the dispatch

of armed police detachments and the arrest of thirty-nine Chinese workers. Six of the ringleaders were eventually jailed, and the rest were sent
back to the estate.[55]

Henry Kirke recalled many personal anecdotes of some of the rebellious elements he encountered in British Guiana. One character who had
been condemned to death in Essequibo went to the scaffold cursing and
railing in Chinese against the authorities right up to the very last moment, even after the mask was put over his face and the rope around his
neck.[56]

Despite the undoubtedly large number of discordances at work in the
relationship between the Chinese immigrants and the plantation system,
a surprisingly fair number of them did tolerably well within its confines
and limitations, and a small handful even managed to do very well. In
British Guiana, where the controversial practice of second-term five-year
reindentures was legally allowed after 1856, many Chinese remained on
the plantations after their initial terms of service, lured by the $50 bounty
offered for reindenture, as well as by the knowledge that mobility avenues
outside the plantation were quite rare.

In British Guiana, unlike Trinidad, rural small trader activities were
monopolized by the Portuguese until the late 1870s (the 1871 report
stated it to be as much as nine-tenths), and independent small farmer
production was severely constrained both by the nature of the coastal
terrain, with its expensive drainage and irrigation requirements, and by
government policies on Crown land acquisition in the interior (no less
than 100 acres).

Between 1865 and 1870, 6,359 Chinese reindentured officially. When
the 1870–71 investigations were held, there were still 5,210 contract
laborers, as well as 1,159 free laborers, among the Chinese on 101 estates.
Six of the 101 estates had only free Chinese. Of the 5,210 still on
indenture, 1,383 were on their first five-year term, 3,254 on their second,
489 on their third, and 84 on their fourth or later terms of service.[57]

Many absconded after receiving the $50 bounty, a practice which was
supposedly common among the Chinese. The 1871 report claimed that
the Chinese would often take bounty in the day, lose the entire sum in
gambling during the same night, and desert the next morning in disgust.[58]

A small number managed to save enough to buy off the remaining last
years of their indenture, although paradoxically some of them did so in
order to claim the $50 bounty for a second reindenture term. Those who
managed to acquire a certain level of savings in both colonies did so from
wages on extra work or on sale of farm produce grown on small plots of

planter-donated land, from illegal bribes taken from fellow workers in the case of Chinese headmen or drivers, and occasionally from gambling, a major pastime among the Chinese which was responsible for many small fortunes being made or lost.

Opportunities for post-plantation mobility were more favorable in Trinidad than British Guiana as early as the 1850s and 1860s, and many Chinese there chose to leave the plantations early in order to avail themselves of these options (discussed in chapter 7). About 230 of the 1853 migrants managed to buy off the last two years of their indenture in this fashion, striking out on their own and establishing themselves in the society well before the arrival of the second batch of immigrants in 1862. The practice of reindenture, common in British Guiana, was less popular as an option in Trinidad, and only a small number availed themselves of it. In any case, the contractual term was confined to one year at a time, which made it less oppressive. By the 1870s, whether through commutation, completion of service, or desertion, most of the Chinese in Trinidad were off the plantations, unlike their Guianese counterparts. Of the 1,190 arriving in 1865 and 1866, no more than 476 were still officially on the estates in 1870, and by the next year the Agent-General of Immigrants was complaining that only 303 were on the estates' books, and 175 of these were runaways.[59] The Immigration Report contained no references to death rates among the Chinese of this group. By 1875 the Chinese had left plantation life completely.

The planters in both colonies made halfhearted and unfruitful efforts to recruit more Chinese indentured laborers in 1871–72, 1872–73, and again in 1883. The British Guiana planters applied for 1,225 in 1871–72, and 3,000 in 1872–73; the Trinidad planters applied for 400 in 1872–73.[60] Tentative requests to allow a China-based businessman named Tong-King-Sing, of the China Merchants' Steam Navigation Company, to encourage a migration of free settlers to Trinidad in 1883–84 fell through. Mr. Tong had been engaged in negotiations with the Brazilian government and Brazilian coffee planters for a similar migration of free Chinese workers to Brazil, and the Trinidad planters wanted to be included in the proposed project. The whole proposal proved abortive, however.[61]

Emigration agent Sampson had tried unsuccessfully in 1866 to relocate 2,500 Hakkas from Toishan district to   British Guiana. Around 1870 there had also been some official correspondence conducted by the Colonial Office about the possibility of initiating a migration of Chinese from the northern regions of China, some of whom were then migrating to

Manchuria. This never materialized, and in any case the British Guiana Commission of 1870–71 warned against encouraging it for reasons of possible acclimatization problems for the northern Chinese, who were accustomed to a more temperate climate. One attempt to explore the possibility of recruiting laborers from San Francisco for British Guiana in 1877 also remained stillborn.[62]

British Guiana did receive two more shipments of Chinese laborers after 1866: the *Corona* in 1874 from Canton, and the solitary contingent of free migrants from Hong Kong on the *Dartmouth* in 1879. After this, Chinese immigration to the two colonies was confined to small individual voluntary movements, unconnected with plantation labor. However, as late as 1896, the West India Royal Commission of that year recorded that 109 Chinese (76 men and 33 women) were still employed on seven plantations in British Guiana, all belonging to the Colonial Company.[63] Curiously, the Trinidad census of 1891 also recorded that there were 7 Chinese, out of a China-born community of 1,006, still resident on the sugar estates in that year: 3 agricultural laborers, 2 overlookers, a shopkeeper, and a market gardener.[64]

Actually, the last ship to reach the British West Indies from China with indentured laborers did not go to Trinidad or British Guiana, but to Jamaica in 1884. This colony had not imported any Chinese laborers since the semi-disastrous experiments of 1854. A few ex-indentureds had been recruited from the other two colonies in the 1860s to work on the banana, sugar, and coconut estates of a few American companies, but they did not amount to more than 200. On July 12, 1884, thirty years after the original shipment, the *Prince Alexander* arrived in Jamaica with 680 passengers (including 122 females and 3 infants), a transfer ship from the *Diamond* which left from Hong Kong in May. Only about 20 of these migrants seemed to have come from the Sze Yup (Four Districts) region.[65] Most were from Tung-Kuan, Pao-An, and Hui-Yang to the east of Canton, and north of Hong Kong—districts that had not sent any migrants to the West Indies before. Most were also of Hakka origins.

They were allotted to sugar estates, and the same diversity of response to work conditions which had characterized their counterparts' behavior in the other sugar colonies repeated itself here. After two years, about 179 of them were deserters. One of them, Wen Choy Pai, a boy of nine in 1884 and still alive in Jamaica in the 1950s, recounted later how about 100 of them were allotted to Tuck and Field sugar factory in St. Thomas in 1885. He recalled that they were required to work from 6 A.M. to

6 P.M. and that the Chinese staged a sit-down strike to protest these hours. The planters gathered about 60 Blacks and 100 East Indians to force the Chinese to work, and in the ensuing scuffle, 1 Black ended up dead, and several people, including 7 Chinese, were injured. After negotiations, the hours were reduced, from 7 A.M. to 4 P.M.[66]

Absenteeism, however, seemed to be the norm. In January 1889, of 647 officially still attached to the estates, 287 had deserted, while another 129 had apparently been "relieved and commuted."[67] It is clear that soon afterwards the Chinese left plantation life altogether and took up their traditional occupational preferences as small shopkeepers and peasant farmers. Sixty-one percent of the Chinese population of Jamaica were residing in the urban centers of Kingston and Port Royal by 1891. Only 8 percent were still in St. Thomas and St. Mary, where the 1884 migrants had been distributed after arrival.[68] According to a recent chronicler of the Chinese progress in Jamaica, Lee Tom Yin, there were 2 survivors of that 1884 voyage still alive in Jamaica in the 1950s: Wen-Choy-Pai, mentioned above, and the widow of one Hu-Lai, who was herself only nineteen years old when she landed in Kingston.

We may close this chapter with a brief account of the fate of the solitary shipment of Chinese from Amoy to the Central American colony of British Honduras in 1865. The experiment had been the result of a request for laborers sent by the Lieutenant Governor, J. Gardiner Austin, formerly emigration agent in China in 1860–62. The *Light of the Age* arrived in that colony on June 12 with 474 immigrants (including 14 adult women and 2 girls), and all were allotted to the estates of the British Honduras Company. A year after arrival, official reports recorded that 100 had absconded, seeking refuge among the Santa Cruz Indians in the interior. Soon after that, another 55 joined them. The reasons for their discontent centered on the nature of the work they were expected to perform (tree felling), as well as on the bad treatment they encountered from estate personnel: "cruel neglect," questionable wage deductions and stoppages for advances reportedly made in China, unsatisfactory food. The Chinese were ordered removed from the estates of the British Honduras Company and were transferred to other employers.[69]

By late 1868 there were still 193 of them on five estates in the colony, reportedly working well and in good health and spirits; 108 had died (most within a year after arrival), 17 had commuted their indentures, and 1 was in the lunatic asylum.[70] The next year some of them were reported to be earning more than Black laborers, and on only one estate was their appearance described as unsatisfactory. This was attributed to their "gambling propensities, to gratify which they sell their clothes and rations in the neighbouring Indian villages."

While recording this solitary shipment of Chinese laborers as a mild success, the official reports doubted that it would be renewed by the British government, or by the colonists of this small Central American British colony.[71]

CHAPTER 5

Life and Labor on the Plantations: The Indians

The East Indian influx into the British West Indies took place in three phases: the initial experimental period, which began fitfully in 1838 in British Guiana and then resumed briefly between 1845 and 1848 in all three sugar colonies; the period of multiracial immigration (1851–70), when Indians were the major but not the exclusive source of overseas labor; and the final developed phase after 1870, when they were the exclusive element in the indentured immigration, arriving when most of the early rough edges of the system had been ironed out. Moreover, in this last period, Indians were being seen—first in Trinidad, later in British Guiana—not only as abstract units of temporary plantation labor, but also as potential settlers and citizens of the new societies into which they were being imported.

The total number of Indians arriving in the first period was 22,889; in the second, 116,141; and the third, 290,593. Thus most of the Indians (67.6 percent) came to the British Caribbean in the third period, when the indenture system had been more or less stabilized. Of the individual territories, the breakdown was as given in Table 5.1. A small number also went to the islands of St. Lucia, Grenada, St. Vincent, and marginally to St. Kitts.[1]

In Trinidad, a minority of these migrants found their way to the cocoa estates, especially in the third period, when cocoa exports began to take off.[2] However, the numbers were always small, even during the period of the industry's highest development. As early as 1863, there had been a few assigned to two estates in Arima (Mount Pleasant and Verdant

TABLE 5.1

	First Period (1838–48)	Second Period (1851–70)	Third Period (1871–1917)
British Guiana	12,770	64,277	161,862
Trinidad	5,568	35,572	102,799
Jamaica	4,551	9,924	21,937

Vale),[3] and in 1876, three cocoa estates, also in the northern county of St. George, had a total of forty-five indentured Indians (including eleven women) among their workers (Maracas Bay, Mon Desir, San Antonio).[4] By 1890, there were fifteen cocoa estates and two coconut estates, as compared with seventy-eight sugar plantations, employing Indian indentured labor. According to the Comins Report of 1893, out of ten thousand indentured laborers in 1891, there were about six hundred functioning on cocoa and coconut estates.[5]

This number escalated at the turn of the century, the period of the cocoa boom in Trinidad. By 1904, there were 1,269 indentured and 565 unindentured Indians on roughly forty-eight cocoa estates, while roughly thirty-five sugar estates employed 8,250 indentureds and 7,533 unindentureds.[6] By 1910, six years later, there were eighty cocoa estates, thirty sugar estates, and three coconut estates employing a total of 11,551 indentureds and 13,516 unindentureds. Of these, 2,757 indentureds and 851 unindentureds were on the cocoa estates, and 137 indentureds and 150 unindentureds on the coconut estates.[7]

Significant as was the increase in the number of cocoa estates employing indentured labor, and the number of indentured workers on these estates, the vast majority of cocoa estates on the island continued not to employ any indentured laborers at all. They relied instead upon free labor of various nationalities, principally Venezuelan mestizo immigrants, but including the Indians. In 1910 there were more than seven hundred cocoa estates—large, medium, and small—in Trinidad, a number of which were even owned and worked by Indian peasant proprietors on their own initiative.

All the sugar plantations, by contrast, in Trinidad as well as British Guiana, depended on indentured labor, and it was around the fortunes and vicissitudes of sugar that the fate of the Indian migrants revolved. In this sense the evolution of the sugar plantation in these two territories assumed not only a sociolegal, but also an ethnic coloration absent in most of the rest of the Caribbean region (except Dutch Surinam, where similar processes were at work). The Jamaican sugar plantation remained

overwhelmingly Black Creole, though with an added new ethnic dimension; but the Black sugar worker was not displaced or replaced in the
same manner.

The first imports of immigrants from India preceded the Chinese arrivals discussed in chapter 4, with the solitary shipments to British Guiana
in 1838 on the *Whitby* and the *Hesperus* preceding the 1845–48 shipments
to the three colonies. The 1838 arrivals were generally known as the
"Gladstone Coolies," having been imported on the initiative of the
planter John Gladstone, father of William Gladstone,[8] and owner of two
plantations in Demerara, Vreed-en-hoop and Vreedestein. Both vessels
arrived from Calcutta on May 5, with 396 passengers (including 14
women and 18 children), and they were distributed on six plantations,
Gladstone's own taking 101 of them.

The experience of these first Indians was quite mixed. There was
evidence of severe brutality against them, in the tradition of slavery, on
two of the estates. A commission of enquiry appointed to look into the
allegations of abuse confirmed this, and its report resulted in the dismissal
and imprisonment of one overseer and the fining of three others. There
was also evidence of a severe mortality rate among them, almost 25
percent. Guyanese scholar Dwarka Nath, however, provided information
on the other laborers and concluded that many of them actually prospered
during their five years in British Guiana. Of the 396, 236 returned to
India in 1843, at the end of their term of service, carrying with them
£5,296 8s. 6d. It seems that those on Plantations Anna Regina and
Waterloo did very well, taking home an average of £37 and £33 per head,
respectively. Roughly 100 died in the five-year period, and 60 decided to
remain in the colony.[9]

The 1845–48 arrivals were a mixture of North Indians, mainly from
Bengal, and Madrasis from the South, roughly fifty-fifty. Their fortunes
were just as contradictory, and for many of them, somewhat more calami-
tous. The new regulations from the Colonial Office had forbidden the
making of contracts outside the colony and had limited verbal agreements
to four weeks' validity. Most of the migrants had refused to enter into
written agreements (valid for one year) after arrival, so that after one
month the planters had virtually no control over the new labor force.

The Indians' own responses to Caribbean plantation life were not
uniform, but the absence of formal controls, combined with the widely
divergent social backgrounds of the immigrants (most of the Madrasis
had been urban vagrant elements, the social refuse of the city's population), led to widespread desertion and wandering. This tendency was less

marked among the Calcutta recruits. In all three colonies, the situation was the same.

A report prepared in January 1848 by Dr. G. Bunyun of the British Guiana Medical Service stated that, of 3,985 Madrasis imported since 1845, 1,249, or 33.5 percent, had either died or deserted the estates; of 3,668 Calcutta coolies, only 265, or 7.2 percent, had thus disappeared.[10] Many deserters flocked to Georgetown and New Amsterdam, hiring themselves out as grass cutters, domestics, cow keepers, even fishermen. Many became beggars, no doubt following the same activities that they had followed in Madras prior to embarkation. The 1851 census estimated that Georgetown had 210 Calcutta coolies and 661 Madrasis, and New Amsterdam 33 Calcuttans and 120 Madrasis.[11]

The eating habits of some of the more destitute Madrasis in British Guiana were described by Dr. Bunyun as follows: "[The Madrasis] are very much given to vagabondage, and are extremely filthy in their persons and habits, eating every species of garbage, even to the extent of picking up the putrid bodies of animals from the nearest trenches, cooking them and eating them mixed with curry." Dr. Bunyun maintained that the general appearance of the Madrasis was very inferior to that of the Calcutta Indians but suggested that there were two distinct social elements among the Madrasis: "I am not aware whether these people are vagabonds and beggars in their own country or not, but I am induced to think that two distinct classes of them have been brought here: for those on Plantation Albion in Berbice, and Plantations Paradise and Enmore, appear to me to be a superior class, irrespective of the state of health they were in." He was of the opinion that the inferior caste was not worth the trouble and expense of acclimatizing. The laborers from Calcutta, on the other hand, appeared to be generally of a higher caste of Indians, "more cleanly in their persons, stricter in their religious observances with regard to food, fonder of dress and more industrious than the Madras laborers." Seen in separate bodies, he continued, the Madrasis had "a dirty, lurid, ragged appearance," contrasting sharply with the "bright, clean and gay aspect" of the North Indians.

In Trinidad, the desertion, vagrancy, and widespread mortality of the 1845–48 arrivals seemed to have reached alarming levels. Governor Lord Harris lamented that skeletons of wandering Indians were being found every week in the woods and the cane fields.[12] From the large numbers being found destitute, sick, and starving on the roadsides, he had had to establish two special hospitals for their reception. Between June 1847 and February 1848, some 250 had died in the public hospital. "In no

Usine St. Madeleine Sugar Factory, Trinidad.
Courtesy University of the West Indies (Trinidad) Library.

country," he declared, "has greater suffering been undergone than by these poor, unfortunate people, in the shape of disease, starvation and ultimate death."

Many of the deserters had no doubt strayed off the plantations on their own volition, reacting negatively to the unaccustomed rigors of agricultural labor. Many, however, were callously ejected from them by the planters themselves, dissatisfied for one reason or another with their labor, some of them being stricken with sickness and disease and consequently considered a burdensome expense to their employers. This was often done to the womenfolk as well. A few instances of startling brutality were exposed in Trinidad. Governor Harris reported in 1848 that thirty to forty Indians from one estate in a distant part of the island had all died after being ordered to the hospital in Port-of-Spain, having received neither wages, clothing, nor medical aid, nor "the smallest modicum of food." He commented that this was the worst instance to have come to his knowledge: "It would appear so palpably the interest of the planters looking at the matter even in the lowest point of view viz. as to pecuniary return, to take a proper care of the immigrants, that a stranger to the facts will hardly credit the negligence which has been manifest in this respect."[13]

In 1847, instances of cruelty on the Clydesdale Cottage estate in the Naparimas and on the Carolina estate also came to light.[14]

While Major Fagan, the "Coolie Magistrate" specially appointed to look after the welfare of the Indians, made a great noise over the inhumane treatment he felt was being meted out to the new immigrants,

Governor Harris himself tried to be more euphemistic about the general situation. He considered such cases of deliberate maltreatment exceptional, although he was willing to concede that "neglect of proper managerial duties," due to "ignorance," was quite widespread.[15]

Not all the desertion from the plantations was spontaneous or unsystematic. Some of it, done individually or in groups, was more related to a search for better work and wage conditions by the immigrants rather than a desperate or malicious escape from the plantation as such. A report from Dr. Henry Mitchell, the newly appointed Superintendent of Immigrants in 1851 (the name was changed in 1854 to Agent-General, still later to Protector), had this to say about some of the Indian immigrants in Trinidad:

> The Asiatic, unless controlled, invariably leaves the estate upon which he has been located by Government, and seeks another domicile of his own choosing. His selection does not appear to be guided by any fixed principle, for he quits the second estate as speedily as the first. The Coolies, taken generally, have wandered in search of labor over every estate in the island. To this rule there have been very few exceptions.
>
> It does not appear . . . that their wandering habits could be traced to any ill-treatment received on the estates they left; on the contrary, some of these properties, on which only forty or fifty had been located by Government, after the entire departure of the original number, have in some instances found themselves replaced by accessions of seventy and even ninety. This erratic tendency of the coolie laborer has been frequently a source of serious annoyance and loss to the planter. Generally speaking, however, when a gang of coolies leaves an estate on a Saturday evening, they are replaced on the subsequent Monday by another gang of nearly equal numbers from some distant quarter. There appears to exist among them some kind of association by means of which the news of one district is immediately communicated to all the others.[16]

The migrants clearly made a difference to the plantation economy, since their presence helped to push production levels up in both Trinidad and British Guiana, despite the overall atmosphere of crisis which overshadowed the industry in these years due to falling prices, loss of metropolitan credit, and loss of preferential status in the British market after 1846. The average annual production between 1845 and 1852 is given in Table 5.2.[17]

In British Guiana, a general strike of Black workers in 1848 was actually defeated, and production maintained, because of the refusal of the

TABLE 5.2

	Trinidad	British Guiana (in tons)
1844	13,729	34,125
1845	18,207	34,681
1846	17,664	22,935
1847	19,676	41,307
1848	19,583	46,784
1849	21,220	29,672
1850	18,311	32,692
1851	22,088	37,655
1852	24,192	48,737

Indian and Portuguese immigrants to desert the plantations in support of the strike—an incident that did not endear the new immigration to the Afro-Guianese any more than it already had.[18]

Lord Harris of Trinidad, originally lukewarm to the idea of Indian immigration, admitted that the exports from Trinidad for the five years ending in 1851 were greater than in any previous five-year period, and that the crop of 1852 was the largest ever shipped, while cost of production had diminished by at least one-third. Similar progress was also recorded in British Guiana, where the immigrants formed a quarter of the rural population and did about a third of the plantation work in these years.[19]

There were many mistakes in this initial experiment from India, however, as Lord Harris himself had pointed out earlier, in 1848. These included the too hasty adoption and execution of the scheme; the recruitment of too many who were unfit for such a migration; and the fact that proper officers were not sent at the same time, and there was not enough government supervision before or after. Planter ignorance of the mores and language of the immigrants also undermined the experiment, as did the fact that immigrants were unable to voice their complaints adequately and were easily seduced from the plantations by some of their compatriots. Finally, lack of regular inspection of plantation conditions made government improvement initiatives difficult. Many of the immigrants in search of work were often left to collapse and die unattended to, unless discovered by the police.[20]

The Indian immigrants themselves were equally ambivalent when questioned about their early experiences in the West Indies. A group of Madrasis returning to South India in 1851 on the Zenobia spoke well of their treatment on the Guiana estates, which they said was humane and fair. Their main complaints were not about people, but about the climate and environment of British Guiana, and especially about the species of worm known as the "jiggah," which penetrated the skin and, if not tended early, could require amputation of limbs. They themselves would not want to return to the colony and would not recommend the place to their compatriots. They reported that a number of the others, however, particularly those who had saved no money, had accepted the $50 bounty offered for reindenture and stayed on for a second five-year term.

The returnees reported that they themselves had been regularly paid, some by the week, others by the month. On their first arrival, laborers had been much in demand, and they themselves had received as much as $1.00 (4s. 2d.) a day, but as many estates were then abandoned and sugar prices went down, 32 cents (1s. 4d.) a day was more normal. Until then, a hard worker could save as much as $5–$7 a month and live well on $7 a month. A small minority were employed on coffee plantations, and some were allowed to cultivate small plots of land adjoining their abode, where they grew local items such as plantains and cassava, as well as pumpkins, onions, and garlic. Some Bengali immigrants, they reported, had even made a tentative start with rice cultivation. They were not allowed to cremate their dead, but they themselves had had no objection to burial in the Western style, as the planters had provided the coffins necessary. They were not allowed to celebrate festivals, but they tried to observe their other religious customs and ceremonies as usual. They themselves were not at a loss to communicate, as they had had a good interpreter.

On their relations with the Blacks of Demerara, they "spoke of them with the greatest disgust, saying that they are a coarse woolly-headed race, more like monkeys than human beings, and that they never associated with them in any way." They acknowledged, however, that the contempt was mutual, but since they were generally kept apart, they were never "ill-used or beaten" by the Blacks.[21]

Those who returned to Calcutta from Trinidad in the same year on the *Eliza Stewart* had favorable comments on the island and their experiences of the authorities there. They went so far as to say that they had never heard of any instances of cruel treatment of coolies by employers while they were there. Some of them intended to return to establish themselves as traders; some wanted to consult with their families in India before deciding whether they would return with them to the colony. They did not express the aversion to returning which the Madrasis on the *Zenobia* had.

Their main complaints were about some of their own, two interpreters who they claimed exploited the Indians and distorted their statements to the authorities unless they were bribed beforehand. One of them, it seems, had wound up in jail.

Asked about the vagrancy problem, they declared that only about four or five of the Bengalis to their knowledge had become deserters or beggars, most Bengalis being hard workers, whereas almost half of the Madrasis were beggars. There was plenty of work for them, and at the same rate of pay as the Bengalis, but the Madrasis did not work because they were "bad men."[22] This basic division between North and South Indian, discussed later in this chapter, was never completely overcome and remained a constant throughout the indenture period and after.

Meanwhile, the Jamaican contingent had not fared any better or worse than its counterparts in the two other colonies. Many had become deserters and been reduced to a state of abject mendicancy in the towns of Kingston and Spanish Town. John Bigelow's *Jamaica in 1850* provided one of the earliest nonofficial descriptions of their condition in these years:

Those that I saw were wandering about the streets, dressed rather tastefully, but always meanly, and usually carrying over their shoulder a sort of *chiffonier's* sack, in which they threw whatever refuse stuff they found in the streets, or received as charity. Their figures are generally superb, and their eastern costume, to which they adhere as far as their poverty will permit of any clothing, sets off their lithe and graceful forms to great advantage. Their faces are almost uniformly of the finest classic mould, and illuminated by pairs of those dark swimming and propitiatory eyes, which exhaust the language of tenderness and passion at a glance.

But they are the most inveterate mendicants on the island. It is said that those brought over from the interior of India are faithful and efficient workmen, while those from Calcutta [sic] and its vicinity are good for nothing. Those that were prowling about the streets of Spanish Town and Kingston, I presume, were of the latter class, for there is not a planter [sic] on the island, it is said, from whom it would be more difficult to get any work than from one of these. They subsist by begging altogether, they are not vicious, nor intemperate, nor troublesome particularly, except as beggars. In that calling they have a pertinacity before which a Northern mendicant would grow pale. They will not be denied. They will stand perfectly still and look through a window from the street for a quarter of an hour if not driven away, with their imploring eyes fixed upon you, like a stricken deer, without saying a word, or moving a muscle. They act as if it were no disgrace for them to beg, as if the least indemnification which they are entitled to expect, for the outrage perpetrated upon them in bringing them from their distant homes to this strange island, is a daily supply of their few and cheap necessities, as they call for them.

I confess that their begging did not leave upon my mind the impression produced by ordinary mendicancy. They do not look as if they ought to work. I never saw one smile, and though they showed no positive suffering, I never saw one look happy. Each face seemed to be constantly telling the unhappy story of their woes, and like fragments of a broken mirror, each reflecting in all its hateful proportions the national outrage of which they are the victims.[23]

Judging from the two main indicators of the immigrants' progress in the colonies—the amount of money which they took back to India with them, and the number who voluntarily chose to remain in the Caribbean for a second term—the conclusion has to be drawn that, despite the unquestioned weaknesses and abuses involved in the initial experimentation, many of the Indians themselves had progressed individually, however limited the total picture might have appeared. In fact, a foreshadowing of all the contradictory benefits and horrors of the indenture system can be seen in this first period: much of what came after 1851 was a development on the same themes struck here, themes that would extend all the way through to the demise of the system in 1920.

The 300 who returned to India on the *Zenobia* supposedly returned with about $30,000 (about £20 apiece). One man who landed at Madras was reported to have returned with about 1,000 Spanish dollars and 30 rupees.[24] Those who returned on the *Eliza Stewart* (354 of them, including 49 women and 34 boys and girls) carried back £3,532, about £10 a head on the total number. Twenty sirdars (foremen) who went back on the *Eliza* in the same year from Trinidad returned with £1,074, more than £50 a head.[25] (The maximum expected earnings of an indentured immigrant during the five-years period was $350, or just under £73, during the high period of the system.)

Of the approximately 22,000 Indians who were introduced into the Caribbean in the 1845–48 period, the numbers sent back (including children born in the colonies) were just over 5,000 by early 1856.[26] This suggests a high level of reindenture and postponement of return passages, despite the heavy mortality. Of the 4,551 introduced into Jamaica, about 1,597 (35 percent) had died or disappeared by the mid-1850s. Several hundred were also said to have migrated to Central America, following the trail of Black Jamaicans, to work on the Panama railroad.[27]

In Trinidad, too, Indian immigrants had gone over to next-door Venezuela in such numbers that the official reports were unable to estimate the exact mortality among the Indians in Trinidad up to 1855.[28] A report dated December 31, 1855, estimated that there were still 1,190 of the 1845–48 contingent still on the estates (681 on five-year reindentures, and 509 on one-year contracts), plus about 2,000 in the towns and villages of Trinidad living independently of the plantations, by and large.[29] The British Guiana census of 1851 recorded 7,682 Indians still in the colony (4,017 North Indians, 3,665 Madrasis). With about 1,170 repatriated between 1850 and 1851, this left approximately 3,000 unaccounted for. The statistics were notoriously unreliable, so this need not indicate more than a very rough picture of the true mortality figures.

Immigration after 1851

With the resumption of Indian immigration after 1851, there was a regular annual influx to Trinidad and British Guiana right up to 1917. Jamaica experienced the renewed immigration in fits and bursts, resuming not in the 1850s but in 1860–63, then 1867–85, 1891–95, 1899–1900, and finally in 1903–1916. It was during the 1850s and 1860s that the Indian character of the sugar plantation became more and more pronounced, until by the mid-1870s the terms "sugar worker" and "Indian worker" became virtually synonymous in Trinidad and British Guiana. And yet the Black Creole workers were never totally displaced from the industry; indeed, they continued to perform vital roles within it throughout, despite the dramatic shift in racial percentages by the mid-1870s. The skilled factory positions, and many field operations, still depended on them as before. Some percentages will be of help here.

In 1858, after eight years of renewed immigration, Indians were 34.6 percent of the estate-resident work force on 140 sugar estates in Trinidad; the overall Black percentage was 63.1 percent (Afro-Trinidad, West Indian and African immigrants), with the local percentage being probably no more than 25 percent. In some areas, such as Couva in Central Trinidad, the Indians would seem to have been already numerically preponderant on many estates. In the main sugar-producing county of Victoria, the Superintendent of Immigrants, Dr. Mitchell, had noted that the Black Creole work force of the island had almost completely withdrawn as early as 1851, with the estates being manned sometimes by African immigrants, sometimes by Asiatics, often a mixture of both.[30] By 1872 Indians were about 75.3 percent of the total plantation adult work force, resident and nonresident (24,598). By 1889 the percentage was about 81 (of 27,599), and by 1895 about 87 (of 26,958).[31]

The same "creeping majority" syndrome was at work on the Guiana plantations. In 1851 the Indians represented roughly 16 percent of the estate labor force. Twenty years later, the percentage of Asians was some-where between 57 and 60 percent, and by 1891 the Indians alone consti-tuted 80.4 percent of the 90,000 or so full-time workers on the planta-tions.[32]

It must be noted that, despite these percentages, as many as 17,808 Black Creole workers were still residing on the estates in 1871. The numbers remained roughly the same in 1891. In Trinidad, the numbers of Black estate residents (as opposed to Black sugar workers, resident and nonresident) were 3,308 in 1876, 2,462 in 1889, and 1,682 by 1917.

The division of labor between Blacks and Indians on the sugar estates of Trinidad was described by the Protector of Immigrants in 1891:

> During the first years of immigration, immigrants were principally em-ployed with the hoe in weeding and other field work, also in the mill-gang work, which requires considerable powers of endurance, while cutlass or axe work, with draining, were chiefly performed by the Creole laborer. The work of carting canes, and the handling of mules or horses was monop-olised by the latter class of laborers. But, as time went on, the Indians and their descendants gradually acquired the use of cutlass, spade or axe, and on sugar plantations and cocoa estates may now be seen using these implements side by side with Creole laborers. The use of the axe was perhaps more slowly acquired by them than that of any other implement; but it is now commonly used by them in cutting wood for the manufacture of charcoal, and, in some cases, for clearing forest land for their own plantations. The stock-keepers on sugar estates are now, in most instances, coolies, and they may often be seen driving cane carts or their own donkey carts, on the estates and public roads of the colony. The use of the fork, which was at first confined entirely to Creole laborers on sugar estates, is now common to the Indian laborer also.
>
> It may, I think, be assumed that the reason why the Indian immigrant did not more speedily acquire the use of implements, other than the hoe, was that they were generally required to perform the work which the Creole male laborer did not care to do. At the present time, when, on some large plantations, trucks and locomotives have to a great extent

taken the place of cane carts, the loading of these trucks (where they are weighed as they pass into the mill yard, and the laborers paid so much a ton) is perhaps the most severe kind of work to be found on sugar estates, and one which taxes considerably the powers of endurance of the laborer; this kind of truck-loading is confined almost entirely to male indentured Indian immigrants, as Creoles and Indian immigrants not under indenture can seldom be found to do it.[33]

Sir Neville Lubbock, Chairman of the West India Committee, testifying before the Sanderson Commission on Indian Emigration in 1909, had this observation to make on racial attitudes towards labor:

> I think it is a remarkable instance of the vanity of the Negro . . . that there are certain classes of work in Trinidad that the Negro will not look at . . . it is quite "infra dig" for a Negro to throw canes on to a cane carrier . . . [carrying] the canes up to the mill mouth . . . that is coolie work . . . not negro work. . . . Nothing will induce a Negro to weed a field. He will not mind digging drains . . . but weeding is quite beneath the dignity of a Negro . . . putting manure on the fields (though that is women's work) . . . a negro would not look at. . . . They have a great choice of work in Trinidad . . . and they select just what pays best.[34]

The specific roles of the Black Guianese sugar workers by the last quarter of the century were not much different. They remained sparsely represented in the lowest-echelon field work (weeding, manuring, forking, banking, cleaning trenches) and intermingled with the immigrants in the upper-echelon field work (cane cutting, punt loading, trench digging, and other jobs requiring the use of the shovel). They also dominated the skilled jobs in the factory. In Jamaica, as has been intimated before, the sugar industry—crisis ridden and well past its high point achieved in the eighteenth century—utilized immigrant labor to a far less degree. The Black Jamaican sugar worker continued to be the major figure, but there was hardly any major sugar estate where Indians were not also to be found. Even so, in the parish of Trelawny, the smaller sugar estates were all totally reliant on Black labor.[35]

Thanks to steady Indian immigration and a favorable international market, sugar production in the two main colonies stabilized in the 1850s, and production and earnings began a steady upward trend not disturbed until the depressions of 1884–85 and 1894–97. In Trinidad, where the value of sugar exports had dropped from £409,416 in 1841 to £294,248 in 1851, that value rose to £938,000 in 1871, £668,153 in 1881, and

£662,789 in 1891. In British Guiana, from a similar drop in earnings—
£953,113 in 1841 to £643,134 in 1851—it was £2,190,510 in 1871,
£2,019,257 in 1881, and £1,662,741 in 1891.[36]

There was a corresponding expansion in sugar cultivation: in Trinidad,
from 28,507 acres in 1845 to 47,319 acres by 1871 and 58,500 acres by
1891; in British Guiana, from 24,850 acres in 1841 to 75,944 acres by
1871, and 78,307 acres by 1891.[37] In Trinidad, there was a simultaneous
rapid rise in the acreage under cocoa cultivation, in which, as we have
said, a sizeable number of ex-indentured Indians, and also increasingly
indentured Indians, played a contributory role: from 18,935 acres in 1871
to 94,500 acres in 1891, reaching a peak with 290,200 acres in 1911.
Despite the rise in cocoa production after 1880, however, it was not until
the turn of the century that sugar took second place in Trinidad as an
export earner. In 1897, when the Royal Commission investigating the
state of the West Indian sugar industry (Norman Commission) met, the
contribution of cocoa and sugar sectors was still about 40–60.[38]

The size of the Indian labor force increased correspondingly, with the
post-1870 influx responsible for about 67.6 percent of the total Indian
immigration. As the years progressed, however, and larger and larger
numbers of immigrants tended to remain in the West Indies after their
total ten-year period of industrial residence was up, the ratio of indentureds in relation to ex-indentureds or unindentureds tended to decrease,
despite the continuous inflow of new arrivals. In Trinidad, where indentured workers were 74 percent of a total Indian community of 13,488 in
1861, they were only 38.7 percent of a total of 27,425 by 1871, and 15.3
percent of a total of 70,242 by 1891.[39] In British Guiana, where the
practice of a second five-year reindenture was legal (and popular with
many immigrants) until it fell into disuse in the mid-1870s, the ratio of
indentureds to ex-indentureds tended to remain higher for a longer period. Thus, indentureds constituted about 72 percent of the Indian population of 48,363 in 1871, falling by 1881 to 26 percent of 87,988, and
by 1891 to 15 percent of 108,484.[40] Indentureds were, of course, always
a slightly higher percentage of the formal estate dwellers, since a high
percentage of the free immigrants lived off the plantations and in the
neighboring villages, even when they continued to work for the sugar
plantations.[41]

After the dramatic drop in the market price of sugar in 1884–85,
declining still further in 1894–97,[42] there were severe pressures on the
sugar industry, and these affected wage levels of both indentured and
free laborers, regardless of the statutory wage minimum. Despite these

pressures, the planters continued to import large numbers of Indians into the society, as a means of further depressing wage levels in the industry generally. Their rationale was that there was a labor shortage, with not enough free Indians being available to the sugar work force, even though there was clearly a surplus.

Controversy over their abuse of the immigration system, and calls for a reduction in the number of imports, resounded through both societies with increasing vigor in the last decade and a half of the nineteenth century.[43] The indentured immigration continued, however, and the Indian communities continued to expand in numbers. By 1911, there were 110,120 Indians in Trinidad (50,585 India born, 59,535 Trinidad born) in a total population of 333,552; and 126,517 in British Guiana (59,849 India born, 66,668 Guiana born), in a population of 296,041.[44]

Social Conditions on the Plantations

What was the quality of life like for the indentured worker on the sugar plantations? What was the relationship between the formal laws and the way in which the institution of indenture actually operated on the ground? Was the indentured immigrant, in the final analysis, a beneficiary or a casualty of this unique system of forced labor operated by British colonialism and the West Indian plantocracy? To what extent was he Subject, to what extent Object, within this particular mode of production?

Edward Jenkins, a British writer, wrote in 1871:

Take a large factory in Manchester, or Birmingham, or Belfast, build a wall around it, shut in its work people from all intercourse save at rare intervals with the outside world, keep them in absolute heathen ignorance, and get all the work you can out of them, treat them not unkindly, leave their social habits and relationships to themselves as matters not concerning you who make money from their labor, and you would have constituted a little community resembling in no small degree a sugar estate village in British Guiana.[45]

Within the confines of this self-enclosed world, apart from the difficulties involved in getting accustomed to the indenture system—its rules, its work rhythms, its hierarchies, its contradictions—the Indian immigrants had first to get acclimatized to their own fellow immigrants in the work force. They were not a homogeneous group, and there were many differences of background and custom among them. A major difference lay between the North and South Indians, who did not speak the same languages or dialects.

A British missionary, the Reverend W. H. Gamble, had this to say in 1866:

> The Bengalis speak Hindustani and Bengali, while the inhabitants of the Madras Presidency speak Tamil, a totally different language. When these people meet in Trinidad, it strikes me as somewhat strange that they have to point to water and rice, and ask each other what they call it in their language. So totally different are the languages, the Hindustani and the Tamil, that English has to become the medium of communication.[46]

The encounters between the two groups were not always that innocent or cordial. Indeed, there were many instances of friction and animosity between them, in the midst of their mutual problems with the plantation hierarchy and plantation life generally. The Annual Immigration Report for 1912–13 in Trinidad observed, in relation to the last contingent of Madrasis arriving between 1906 and 1916, "Most of the disturbances that do occur on the estates are between the people themselves. The Calcutta and Madras people do not seem to agree, and outbreaks between them sometimes take place." The next year's report suggested that these frictions had abated somewhat, "due in great measure to the tact displayed by the estate's authorities and the inspectors."

Similar frictions were recorded in British Guiana, with a riotous clash between the two groups on Non Pareil estate in 1889. Several instances were also recorded of one group refusing to support strike action or work stoppage undertaken by the other—for example, at Diamond estate in 1917, when Calcuttans refused to support striking Madrasis, and at La Bonne Intention estate in 1919, when it was the turn of the Madrasi laborers to refuse to support strike action by their Calcutta fellow workers.[47] One group of newly arrived Madrasis went on strike on Non Pareil estate in Trinidad in 1916 because no one understood their language and they did not like being surrounded by Calcutta people. They were transferred to another estate.[48]

On occasion, these regional-cultural frictions would erupt into major group clashes. The mixed group who landed in Jamaica on the last ship, the *Dewa*, in 1916, broke out into uncontrollable fighting right at the receiving station in Port Royal. Seventeen immigrants were seriously wounded in the fracas, and damage was done both to the building and to hospital equipment.[49]

More usually, however, these group frictions would tend to be sub-
merged within the daily routine of plantation life, affecting simple social
relations and choice of social companions rather than infecting group
activity in relation to the plantation hierarchy. The rough and dark-
skinned Madrasis often tended to be at the receiving end of North Indian
caste disdain. The differences in their original social backgrounds in India
also exacerbated the problems caused by regional attitudes. This was
often remarked upon by colonial officials and metropolitan social commentators. The Reverend Gamble commented as follows about the early
mixed arrivals of the 1850s and 1860s:

> The difference in the people is almost as great as the difference in the
> languages; the coolies from Calcutta proving valuable, steady laborers,
> while those from Madras are for the most part useless. This is accounted
> for by the fact that those who embark from Calcutta have come from the
> interior, and have been used to the cultivation of rice or indigo all their
> lives. No better laborers than these prove, can be desired. The Madras
> coolies appear to be, with few exceptions, the scum and refuse of the city
> of Madras—stray waifs who have sunk very low in their lives before they
> find their way into the hands of a shipping agent. Some of these, however,
> make very good house servants, as butlers and cooks, and some of them
> turn out good grooms.[50]

The Agent-General of Immigrants expressed his own opinions in his
1859 annual report:

> It would seem that the [Madrasis], however healthy during the passage,
> and apparently superior to the Bengalis in muscular development, are,
> unless carefully selected from the agricultural ranks, little adapted to the
> exigencies of our sugar districts. No doubt seven months almost continuous
> rain was somewhat trying to the constitution of people newly arrived, but
> the climatic influences were, in the case of the Madrasi, seriously aggra-
> vated by their own intemperance, idleness and despondency.
>   They are greatly deficient in the docility of the Bengali; and although
> members of ablebodied men, particularly since Mr Warner's agency at
> Madras commenced, have been thence introduced into Trinidad, they are
> as a rule turbulent, and so difficult to manage, that of the few employers
> who have been exceptionally successful in ruling them, not one would
> receive a Madras coolie into his employment if he could engage a Bengali.
> As domestics they might probably give satisfaction, but they are undesir-

able as workers in the field, and are quite cunning enough to know that there exists no species of legal coercion capable of ensuring their efficiency.[51]

As early as 1848, Dr. Bunyun of British Guiana had made similar observations about the social character of the Madrasis arriving in the West Indies,[52] and these stereotypes would persist throughout the entire immigration, a mix of planter prejudice, North Indian regional and caste disdain, and actual fact, deriving from the nature of those migrants actually arriving. It must be mentioned that the West Indian attitudes stood in marked contrast with the attitudes of planters in other sugar colonies, such as Mauritius and Fiji, where the Tamil laborers were often prized for their sturdy, reliable qualities as laborers.

Plantation officials, of course, were not above exploiting these regional-cultural frictions among the Indians to their own advantage. Most of the sirdars (headmen, drivers, foremen) in pre-1870 British Guiana were Madrasis (a large number were also Black Creoles). The British Guiana Immigration Commission of 1870–71 described them as "generally men of strong character and thriving circumstances, separated in interest from the great mass of Calcutta coolies, and much trusted by managers." But it also characterized the Negro driver as "apt to be violent and brutal," and the Indian one as often "corrupt."[53]

Similar regional and religious differences existed among the North Indians themselves, but these never seemed to have had an impact on plantation life in any significant way. An example is the Muslim-Hindu difference: the Geoghegan Report had calculated that up to 1870, at least 49,860, or 15.4 percent, out of the 323,877 migrants embarking from Calcutta for the sugar colonies in general had been Muslims.[54] During the later stages of the migration, immigration regulations were routinely translated into Hindi and Urdu for the benefit of those incoming migrants who could read (less than 6 percent) and distributed in pamphlet form. There is no indication from the official records that the general rapprochement between these two groups which existed in North India in the nineteenth century did not also transfer itself to the West Indian plantations.

Occasionally there were stereotypical references to certain regional types. Pathans, for example, were considered dangerous in British Guiana if allotted in too great numbers to any single estate.[55] The Trinidad authorities did not want too many Punjabis and Sikhs in the 1900s, since they tended to be somewhat troublesome. Nepalese and "Calcuttans" clashed on Plantation Non Pareil in British Guiana in 1888.[56] Often, too, frictions existed between India-born and Caribbean-born Indians, or between long-standing immigrants and newcomers, but these were not chronic or deep-rooted.[57] In the last decades of the migration, the authorities had many problems with return migrants (those who had been indentured before, either in the West Indies or elsewhere). The Immigration Department often felt them to be too assertive and a bad influence on the other workers, and some of these tensions must have rubbed off on intragroup relations, positively or negatively.

The most important social division among the migrants, and one that was decisively remolded under the conditions of plantation life, was that of caste. Delicate and complex, rooted in the occupational and color stratifications of village India, and filled with infinite intricacies of inter-pretation and application, the caste system of social differentiation could not survive the rough equalizing discipline of the modern plantation system. (Indeed, the experience of semimodernization embodied by the Caribbean plantation was only a foreshadow of other complex moderniza-tion processes at work within India itself, and these too have had a similar disruptive impact, albeit more slowly, on traditional stratification norms.) Dr. Comins wrote in 1893 that caste was "not a subject which troubles coolies long after their landing, and in most cases many of the prejudices disappear or become much modified."[58] The Protector of Immigrants also stated, "Its rules are not much observed by the children of immigrants born here. . . . If immigration from India were to cease now, caste as known in India would in fifty or sixty years be a thing of the past, except perhaps among a few 'Brahmins' or 'Chuttrees.'"

Be that as it may, there were numerous examples in the records of high-caste Indians, especially Brahmins, utilizing their status to exploit their fellow Indians in the new environment for monetary gain. One official testifying before the Sanderson Commission stated in 1909: "A Maharaja is a Brahmin priest. We do not like them to come amongst the coolies at all. They rather rob them, and they do a little harm now and again, especially in taking money from them that they should not take."[59]

A common confidence trick practiced on gullible newcomers who were dissatisfied with the new society was to extract money from them and take them into the bush, purporting to find an overland route back to India for them. There they would be abandoned and left to starve. An-other witness complained of priests and headmen: "[They were] making slaves of the ordinary coolie. I heard of one case of a man on one of our estates who had been working for fifteen years for one of these Indian Babus, and merely getting his keep, and could not get free of him."[60]

Occasionally, the rough social equalization of the New World would lead to dilemmas for those returning to the Old. One man was reported to have married a woman of higher caste in the West Indies, living with her happily on the plantation for ten years before they both returned to India. On their return, the wife turned him adrift, with the words, "You low caste man, I will have nothing more to do with you." She took his money and abandoned him, whereupon he returned to the estate in the West Indies, vowing that he would never marry a high-caste woman again.[61] Dr. Comins also recounted the case of a high-caste man abandoning his low-caste wife and child at the Howrah railway station in Calcutta soon after their return to India.[62]

Authority positions in the plantation hierarchy, however, paid almost no attention to caste as time went by. In 1883, the sirdars in British Guiana were about equally divided: 120 high-caste Brahmins, 110 middling castes, 118 low castes, and about 95 Muslims.[63] There were indeed many incidents of individual immigrants objecting to working under a lower-caste sirdar, particularly if they could not get along otherwise, but the selection of supervisory personnel continued to be influenced by other criteria.

There does seem, however, to have been a comparative advantage shared by the higher-caste Indians with respect to the postplantation mobility process. A report entitled "Wealthy Coolies" in the *Trinidad Chronicle* in January 1877 stated:

> We understand the majority, the bulk we may say, of the natives of India who acquire wealth in the colony, carry the stamp of superior caste in bearing, manners, honourable dealing, and generally too in build. No doubt men of the higher castes, being honoured and trusted by the lower caste coolies, have superior opportunities of making money among them. The poorer caste men appear generally to settle down as cultivators, laborers, cowherds, grass sellers, porters, etc.[64]

Far more crucial than the contradictions and conflicts among the immigrants themselves were the repressive laws and social practices which kept the indentured workers under a rigid system of semiservitude for at least five years. Several levels of hardship were involved: those formally sanctioned by the law (the immigration ordinances and their various amendments over time, plus the obligations of the contract); those arising in the course of day-to-day plantation life, many involving actual breaches, abuses, or circumventions of the formal laws; and finally, many infractions not covered by the law at all, and widely practiced, even though clearly repressive.

The most important of the formal laws were those that provided a variety of criminal penalties for violations by workers of their obligations, and those that sought to confine them to the environment of the plantation under a rigid pass-law system of regulations. One writer described the laborer's basic condition under these laws as one of insulation and immobility.[65] The oft-quoted remark by the planters of pre-1870 British Guiana was that the place of the indentured laborer was to be either "at work, in hospital, or in gaol."

It must be said that the notion of imposing penal sanctions for breach of a civil contract was not unique to the West Indian indenture system and indeed existed in various milder versions in nineteenth-century Britain itself.[66] However, its social function in the Caribbean context was clearly to find a sociolegal mechanism for regulating and controlling the supply of labor for sugar production in an environment where an untrammeled free labor system would have wreaked havoc on the viability of a plantation economy accustomed to slavery. A quotation from British Colonial Secretary Herman Merivale cited in Karl Marx's *Capital* helps to make the point: "In civilised countries (i.e. Europe) the laborer, though free, is by a law of nature dependent on capitalists; in colonies this dependence must be created by artificial means."[67]

The main objections, moreover, were to the frequency of these punishments in routine plantation discipline. George William Des Voeux, the official whose letter to the Colonial Office led to the 1870–71 enquiry in British Guiana, contended that the immigrants were governed "not by kindness and good treatment, but through fear of the severity of the law."[68] Between 1865 and 1870, in nine out of twelve districts in British Guiana, 32,876 cases were heard—all but a handful against indentured workers—with 49.3 percent (16,222) of them resulting in convictions. The yearly average was between 6,000 and 7,000 cases.[69] The main infractions were neglect or refusal to work, absenteeism, desertion, vagrancy, and insufficient or incomplete work. Convictions for failure to perform the required five tasks per week—an offense that was seldom prosecuted in Trinidad—amounted alone to 23.7 percent of the total convictions.

While it is true that the viciousness of planter-laborer relations was particularly acute in pre-1870 British Guiana, this tendency to resort to legal action and penal sanctions for often minor infractions continued right down to the demise of the system. As late as 1909, the Sanderson Commission felt compelled to comment on the practice and to enquire into its causes. In 1907–8, with an indentured population of 9,784 in British Guiana, there were no less than 3,835 complaints by employers against immigrants, 2,019 of which ended in convictions. The percentage of complaints against the indentured population was 39.2 percent, and of convictions 20.6 percent. A similar picture obtained in Trinidad, where the number of convictions in 1901 was 1,010 out of a total indentured population of 7,359 (about 14 percent); in 1902–3, 1,730 out of an indentured population of 8,800 (about 20 percent); and in 1907–8, 1,869 out of an indentured population of 11,506 (about 16.5 percent).[70] Between 1898 and 1905 the total number of prosecutions amounted to something like 11,149.

The Commission Report observed as follows:

> It seems clear that on the best managed estates prosecutions are rarely resorted to, and as the general tenor of the evidence is to show that the mass of the immigrants is contented and easy to manage, we cannot resist the conclusion that many trivial cases must be brought before the courts, and that many of the estate managers must be too ready to adopt this means of enforcing their strict legal claims against the immigrants, and not sufficiently patient in attempting to attain their object by milder and more humane methods.[71]

The McNeill-Lal delegation in 1913 was advised by local Indian spokesmen that managers should try to exercise more control over the arbitrary actions of overseers and headmen, who had direct control over the laborers.

It is just possible that the managerial motivation for enforcing such heavy legal discipline on the laborers was not the same in the early and later stages of the indenture system. The general cruelties of pre-1870 British Guiana—not duplicated in Trinidad during the same period—stemmed from the difficulties of the Guianese planters in making the transition from a tradition of slavery to a new labor relationship. It stemmed also from the general political atmosphere in post-Emancipation British Guiana, one in which the antagonisms between Black labor and White capital were much more acute than in the other territories.[72] Some of the hardened planter attitudes towards Blacks were transferred to the new immigrants, but there was a general atmosphere of planter intransigence which was quite specific to that colony. The imperatives of the economic revival obviously also played a role in the harshness of the discipline imposed.

During the post-1870 period, and especially after the mid-1880s' economic depression which affected the sugar industry, it is arguable that the laborers themselves began to exercise a greater degree of independence in relation to their commitment to plantation duties and that this independence often presented management with a problem. Many new options outside the plantation were being explored, and a vigorous small peasantry was on the move. In British Guiana this development came a bit later than in Trinidad, but the growth of rice farming after the turn of the century was sufficiently important to create the same dual loyalties among the indentured laborers as had already been the case in Trinidad for some time.[73] Indentureds were constantly being encouraged by their compatriots in the nonsugar sectors either to abscond or to surreptitiously divide their time between their duties to the sugar estates and other profitable openings elsewhere.

It is possible that the rigorous enforcement of the penal sanctions of the labor laws in these last decades of the system was an attempt by the planters to control the vigorous independence of their laborers, rather than simply a continuation of a philosophy of forced labor derived from earlier times. The laborers here, in other words, may have been not simply passive victims of an unjust system, but rather active conscious subjects of their own progress, engaged in a continual battle of wits with their employers over the creative utilization of their labor.

In Jamaica, by contrast, where alternative labor was always available for those estates that did utilize immigrant labor, it is noticeable that this method of disciplining the Indian indentureds hardly existed at the time of the Sanderson Commission. The report stated that two Indian deserters were apprehended in 1908, six in 1909. In March 1909, there was just one immigrant undergoing imprisonment for desertion; the year before that, there was none. However, total complaints against immigrants violating the labor laws in 1907–8 numbered 239 (11 percent), of which all but two ended in convictions, most of them punishable only with a fine. During this period about 7,500 of the Indians—just over half the total on the island—lived or were employed on the estates; of these, only 2,200 were under indenture, the remaining 5,300 being free laborers.[74]

Closely allied to the laws regulating the work performance of the laborers were the provisions seeking to keep them tied to the estate, relatively shut off from the rest of the society, during the period of indenture. The "pass-law" system authorized officials—public and plantation related—to intercept immigrants off the plantation and turn them over to a court or police station if found to be without authorization to be where they were. This system acted as a complement to the other rules described above.

Quite apart from the merits or demerits of this law, or even from the fact that it was supposedly never enforced as rigorously as it was formulated, the reality was that it often exposed the immigrants to a number of abuses which were not contemplated by the formal legislation but which took place frequently nevertheless. One of these was the immigrants' exposure to intimidation and threats of arrest from officials, such as policemen, if found without a pass, unless they paid the officials a bribe.[75] Immigrants leaving their estates, even under the greatest emergency, and even though they may have completed their day's work, were liable to be arrested and imprisoned if they did not have an official pass on their persons. A related irregularity was the frequent need to bribe a plantation official (usually a sirdar) in order to acquire a pass to leave the estate at all. The granting of passes was often made arbitrarily and thus treated not as a right, but as a privilege that could be withheld at will or granted on "good behavior," subjectively defined. Although this practice may not have been the norm and may have been more intense in some periods than in others, nevertheless the legal loopholes were there to be abused, and they often were.

The withholding of a pass could also be used to prevent workers from finding out the wage levels of other estates, in cases where there were uneven payment of wages and infringements of the legal minimum wage requirements. More insidiously, it could be used to prevent workers from having access to the Immigration Department in order to make legitimate complaints against individual planters and their management. Even though they were formally allowed to do so by the law, instances abounded of immigrants being arrested for vagrancy and for nonpossession of passes when they were actually on their way to the Immigration Department to lodge formal complaints on one issue or another. In one case, an immigrant was arrested and imprisoned after having been to court to answer a subpoena.[76] As late as 1897, the West India Royal Commission into the state of the regional sugar industry actually heard of one case in Trinidad where a laborer named Gangadeen, indentured to Williamsville estate in Victoria County, was arrested for vagrancy while on his way to the nearest police station to obtain permission to play a drum at his own wedding banquet, due to take place later the same day![77]

Another example of the way in which the practices of the planters tended to violate the spirit of the law can be found in the pre-1870 British Guiana attitude towards reindenture. Under the law, reindentures for a second five-year term were permissible on payment to the immigrant of a cash bounty of $50, equivalent to just under a full year's wages. Despite the harsh conditions of life on the West Indian plantations, many immigrants felt sufficiently attracted by the offer to remain on the plantations for a second term, and a significant minority reindentured more than once, some as many as three, four, or more times. In 1870, out of 40,227 under indenture, almost 18,000 were persons who had reindentured, some for an incredible fifth and sixth time. Between 1871 and 1875, when the practice was discontinued after it became too expensive (the reindenture fee was raised to $200 in 1875), a further 10,957 immigrants reindentured. Yet the 1870–71 enquiry accused the planters of British Guiana of coercing a large number of the immigrants into reindenture through excessive recourse to the labor laws on absenteeism, refusal to work, and insufficient work. A large number of the complaints filed against the immigrants—almost 50 percent—were never actually heard in court. It seems that they were filed more often as an act of intimidation, and also as a way of piling up a long list of offenses against indentured immigrants, who could then be pressured into reindenturing in exchange for a withdrawal of the charges. In 1870 alone, about 57 percent of the charges were withdrawn.

As with reindenture, so with other matters. The most notorious violations took place on the issue of wages and wage payments. Real wage levels were almost never what the contracts or the ordinances stipulated that they should be, and in some periods, such as the depression years of the mid-1880s through the 1890s, they often reached scandalous levels. The legal minimum wage rate for male indentureds was 25 cents a day after the mid-1870s, but the depression a decade later created great discordances in earnings, as planters sought to reduce wages either by lengthening the size of the daily task or by cutting down on the number of tasks a single laborer could perform in a day, or—more effectively—by insisting on a continued importation of labor despite the depression, with a view to creating an artificial surplus on the estates and thereby depressing wages through severe competition.

There were always conflicting estimates on the actual earnings of the immigrants. The Sanderson Commission heard in 1909 different estimates from the Trinidad Protector of Immigrants and anti-immigration lobbyists like the representative of the Trinidad Workingmen's Association (T. W. A.) and Black legislators. The T. W. A. representative claimed that Indians did not earn the stipulated $1.25 a week, but more like 72 cents. The Commission accepted the view that wages had fallen from a high of 30 to 40 cents a day during the early 1850s, to a low of about 20 cents a day during the depressed 1880s, but that they had stabilized around the stipulated 25 cents.

Evidence indicated, however, that there were uneven wage fluctuations among the individual estates, and that a wage of lower than 20 cents a day was not unusual on many estates for certain workers. The Comins Report itself had uncovered some wages that had dwindled to miserable levels in 1891. A significant number of workers were clearly earning less than 12 cents a day in 1895–96. The Protector of Immigrants reported in 1895 that half of the sugar estates were paying 34 to 59 percent of their workers less than 6 pence (12 cents) a day.[78] The McNeill-Lal delegation reported that Trinidad wages were between 90 cents to $1.20 a week in 1913, and that on at least three estates visited, more than 30 percent of the male adults earned less than 12 cents daily.

Despite these appalling violations of the minimum wage stipulation, planters often tended to excuse their actions by reminding critics that in India the daily wage rate was hardly more than 4 cents.[79]

In British Guiana the picture was not much different. The 1871 report had estimated that about 40 percent of the male indentureds did not earn as much as 5 shillings ($1.20) a week, though the average daily wage tended towards 28 cents. The trend in wage rates continued downwards, and during the depression years some startling low levels were recorded: on Plantation Turkeyen in 1885, as low as 4 to 8 cents a day, despite the official minimum wage rate of 24 cents. Messrs. McNeill and Lal estimated the average weekly earnings per worker between 1908 and 1912 as follows: Berbice County, $1.13 to $1.23; Demerara County, $1.17 to $1.23; Essequibo County, $1.09 to $1.14.[80] Thus by the early twentieth century the Guianese rates were slightly higher than those in Trinidad. However, the variations between individual estates were just as prevalent, as the county comparisons demonstrate.

And there were always startling reminders of horrible individual cases of exploitation, such as that of the immigrant Govinder from Plantation Johanna Cecilia, who died in 1889 after having apparently lived for a considerable period on a wage of 8 cents a day. The Immigration Department had refused to act on his complaints on the ground that his earnings were not much lower than those of other immigrants on the plantation. There was also the testimony before the West India Royal Commission in 1897 of the immigrant Bechu, who gave direct confirmation of the inability of workers to earn the minimum daily wage, even after a day's work of nine or ten hours.[81]

Closely allied to the dilemma of fluctuating wage levels was the practice of wage payment delays and arbitrary deductions as fines for alleged infractions; neither was officially sanctioned by the law, but both were widely resorted to in day-to-day plantation life. Wages were often arbitrarily delayed or partially withheld for any of a number of reasons: absenteeism without authorization, damage to plantation property, minor disciplinary violations, debt on rations. Dr. Comins recorded in 1891 that on many estates it was common practice to withhold one week's wages from laborers as a guarantee for good behavior and regular work, even though this practice was not sanctioned by the law.

In the early years of the indenture system, there were frequent examples of vindictive refusal to pay the workers their wages, often for months, in both colonies. Compounding the problem was the inadequacy of the law itself on the issue of worker action for the recovery of wages. In British Guiana the law of 1864 regulating the immigration and indenture system made no mention of the subject, though earlier legislation had provided for an appeal to the Protector of Immigrants or a civil action under the Petty Debt Ordinance of 1858 (which itself was severely circumscribed and inapplicable where the dispute concerned the wage rate). In Trinidad, however, there was provision for wage recovery in a summary manner before any magistrate.

The entire apparatus of the courts, however, was organized on this and all other matters in a manner that militated against the interests of the indentured laborer. While more blatant in British Guiana before 1870, the situation remained basically the same throughout the indenture period. Magistrates were generally biased in favor of the plantocracy, linked as they often were by race, class, social intercourse, and cultural-ideological prejudices against the alien Asiatics in their midst. In pre-1870 British Guiana, the often vindictive solidarity of the planter class, and its influence on the political directorate of the colony—more cohesive than in culturally divided Crown Colony Trinidad—made the pressures from the top just that much more solid.

Immigrants were disadvantaged by legal procedures, quite apart from the subjective biases of many magistrates. Lack of acquaintance with the law and its procedures, inability to communicate effectively to an often impatient magistrate, exploitation by interpreters of their own race who often solicited bribes in order to be effective and truthful translators, difficulty in getting fellow laborers to testify against employers for fear of future victimization and loss of earnings, inability to pay for adequate legal representation due to poverty—all of these contributed to the atmosphere of intimidation and mystification which was the immigrants' experience of the law in action. The court, in the final analysis, functioned more often as an extension of the instruments of labor discipline than as an impartial arbiter of industrial disputes between equal parties, or a mechanism of grievance redress on the laborer's behalf, although officially it was designed to function as an embodiment of all three objectives under the immigration ordinances.

Many exceptions to this generalization about the judiciary stood out in the history of the indenture experiment. Outstanding among these were the two who were at the center of the British Guiana scandals which led up to the 1870–71 investigations, William Des Voeux and Chief Justice Joseph Beaumont, but there were others, many unnamed. Des Voeux, in his memoirs written many years later, recalled a letter he received during the 1870 scandals informing him that many magistrates were silently happy about the revelations he had made about injustices in that colony, but they were unable to be as visible or vocal as he had decided to be.[82] Chief Justice Beaumont's own dismissal and untimely departure from the colony in 1868 was somewhat reminiscent of the earlier fate of Major Fagan in Trinidad. His frequent overruling of harsh magistrates' decisions, his open criticisms of the shameful discrimination against and exploitation of the Asian immigrants, and his defiant attitude towards Governor Hincks as well as the general body of planters had culminated in the inevitable demotion and dismissal. Moreover, the scandal surrounding his own departure from the colony had also led to a few resignations among his colleagues on the Bench.[83] In the 1880s, Magistrate Hastings Huggins was often accused by Guianese planters of leniency and favoritism towards the laborers.[84]

In Trinidad, too, which was never as scandal ridden as its sister colony, a few names stood out. There was of course Major Fagan, the first "Coolie Magistrate," whose energetic and impassioned outbursts on behalf of the Indian newcomers in the 1840s eventually led him to be dismissed from his post prematurely. There was also Magistrate Thomas Shirley Warner, who developed a reputation in the 1860s as someone whose decisions always tended to "favour the working classes." A letter writer to the *San Fernando Gazette* complained, "No matter what amount of evidence is brought to bear on a case, he invariably finds a hitch, and in nine cases out of ten the culprit is allowed to go scotfree."[85] There was also Chief

Justice John Gorrie, whose rebellious social activism earned him an enduring image as a working-class champion in the late nineteenth century.[86]

In the final analysis, however, the judgment about the courts acting more against than for the interests of the indentured laborers was not an exaggeration. As late as 1913, Messrs. McNeill and Lal were confronted in both colonies with virtually the same list of objections to court "impartiality" as those described above, more than forty years after the extreme scandals of 1870. The delegation did not accept these criticisms, and clearly 1913 was not 1870 on the issue of blatant planter intransigence and exploitation, but the fact that the inbuilt structural and existential dilemmas were still being experienced, though admittedly on a more low-keyed level, was a testimony to the imbalances inherent in the indenture experiment. And it must not be forgotten that it was the raising of some of these very issues by anti-immigrationists within India itself that led to the sudden termination of the system, just four years after the McNeill-Lal visit.

Finally, there was always the question of physical violence against the laborers, more intense in some periods than others, and on some plantations than others, but always an ever-present underlying reality in the social relations of plantation life. Drivers were often in charge of voluntary henchmen who would be ready, in extreme situations, to inflict beatings on "difficult" laborers in order to bring them into line. Managers and overseers were often guilty of personally beating individual laborers. Sometimes offenders would be brought before the law for these violations, but often the matter would not be reported, and it became an incident "all in the day's work." The 1845–48 period in both colonies, and pre-1870 Guiana generally, recorded the worst episodes of this kind of cruelty, but it was always an element in everyday plantation life which never quite died, regardless of how well employer-employee relations were functioning in any given period.

As late as 1897 in Trinidad, there was a celebrated case in which a manager of the large Usine Ste. Madeleine estate, Peter Abel, was brought to trial by the Protector of Immigrants, William Coombs, for tying up an indentured worker named Sitaram and five of his co-workers with pieces of rope and leaving them to stand in the sun, allegedly for neglecting their work duties. The case occasioned a great deal of public attention and comment. He was found guilty and fined a total of sixty pounds, ten for each laborer.[87]

With all the operating defects of the indenture system catalogued

East Indian market, British Guiana.
From *Handbook of British Guiana, 1922.*

above, it becomes valid to ask the question, were the indentured laborers wholly victims within this system, as some writers and critics of the system have sought to portray them? Or were they, like most workers entrapped within an unfree labor system, part casualties and part beneficiaries, simultaneously Object and Subject in a labor regime that was preoccupied only with maximum production output and maximum control over labor at minimum overall cost? In what ways, and to what extent, were they able to manifest and exercise some degree of creative autonomy within the totality of the constraints surrounding them?

One fact that stands out in the midst of all the harshness of indenture and plantation life was that the vast majority of the immigrants who came to the West Indies—71 percent—elected to make these colonies their permanent home. Much of the reason for this was the hope they held out to most immigrants of some kind of viable post-indenture economic and social mobility, especially in the post-1870 period, when the trend towards permanent settlement became quite marked.

The Indian community spokesman from Trinidad at the Sanderson Commission hearings in London in 1909, George Fitzpatrick, indicated

that Indians had been willing to bear the intolerable hardships and frequent injustices of indenture because they saw it as a prelude to a better
life in the society later on. He also recorded that the Indians in Trinidad
were generally in favor of a continuation of indentured immigration,
though they were also for a correction of the many abuses still rampant
within the system (this in 1909, when anti-indenture lobbyists in India
itself were agitating to bring the system to an end).

Writers and commentators of British and Euro-Caribbean origins during the nineteenth century mainly tended to stress the brighter side of
the picture, emphasizing the contentment of the immigrant communities
rather than revealing the festering sores described above. There were
some notable exceptions, but by and large, the picture painted of the
Indian community's responses to conditions in the West Indian colonies
presented a favorable image, which ironically may have been just as
accurate and truthful as the darker side of the immigration.

Early comments came in the 1860s from two missionaries, the Reverend E. B. Underhill and the Reverend W. H. Gamble. The former visited
Trinidad in 1859 and recorded as follows:

> There may be cases of oppression, but I did not hear of them; and I am
> sure that some of the parties with whom I had intercourse would have told
> me had they known of their existence. My own observation, on such
> estates as I visited, or passed through, quite corroborates the testimony of
> parties in the island. The huts of the coolies, to say the least, are better
> than the cabins they usually inhabit in India. The people look well fed,
> happy and contented. I spoke with men from many parts of India, from
> East Bengal, Bihar, the North West Provinces, and from Oudh, and that
> away from the estates, on the roadside; everyone expressed himself as
> pleased with his lot. "This good country," was a frequent reply to the
> question put.[88]

He went on to quote from the Annual Immigration Report for 1859:

> Not only have many immigrants, who availed themselves of free passages
> back to Calcutta from the West Indies, returned hither, with full knowl-
> edge that their renewed contract was for a residence of ten instead of four
> years, as in the first instance; but others have paid their own passage fares,
> and that of their wives, from India, to enable them to return to the West
> Indies, free from contract towards either the colony or the employer.[89]

The Reverend Gamble lived in Trinidad for nine years, and his judg-

ment was that "a fairer system for the laborer could not well be devised."
Of the Indians he commented,

> As a rule, they are well conditioned, happy and cheerful, having their
> own rooms, living comfortably with their wives and children. They are,
> moreover, allowed to cultivate a patch of ground, or (which they much
> prefer) to keep a cow or a pig. Of cows the coolies are very fond, and
> certainly they know how to take care of them. It is true, that sometimes
> an irate overseer or driver may strike a coolie, and so may any angry man
> strike another in any country, and irrespective of their relative positions;
> but there is as much redress for the coolie as any one else. . . . In leaving
> their country, the coolies have most certainly bettered their condition;
> and what is of higher importance, they have been delivered, to a great
> extent, from the intolerable yoke and curse of caste, and, as a conse-
> quence, the coolies in Trinidad are in a much better position to receive
> the Gospel . . . than they are in their own country.[90]

Conditions in pre-1870 British Guiana were not quite as rosy as the
pictures painted here, as the main works to come out of this period clearly
indicated. These included two books published in London in 1871, Edward Jenkins' *The Coolie: His Rights and Wrongs* and ex–Chief Justice
Beaumont's *The New Slavery: An Account of the Indian and Chinese Immigrants in British Guiana;* and George William Des Voeux's two books of
memoirs, published much later, *Experiences of a Demerara Magistrate,
1863–1869,* and *My Colonial Service in British Guiana, St. Lucia, Trinidad,
etc.* Beaumont's own stinging condemnation reverberated through the
century and was often quoted by critics of the indenture system:

> This is not a question of more or less, of this or that safeguard, of an
> occasional defect here, or excess there. But it is that of a monstrous, rotten
> system, rooted upon slavery, grown in its stale soil, emulating its worst
> abuses, and only the more dangerous because it presents itself under false
> colours, whereas slavery bore the brand of infamy upon its forehead.[91]

The 1871 report, though not accepting all of Des Voeux's harsh accu-
sations against the indenture system in British Guiana, was nevertheless
muted in its endorsement of the system. On the Indians it suggested,
somewhat ambiguously,

> their love of saving and desire to return to their own country, rather than
> wish to make themselves comfortable during their temporary absence from
> the land of their birth, induces them to work.[92]

It suggested also that the experience in the new environment was liberating for the traditionally servile Indian peasant:

> the coolie, after he has been here for some time, gives up to a great extent the habit of saluting his superiors that he had on arrival, and becomes much more independent in his bearing. The difference of bearing between immigrants about to return to India and those who have arrived in this colony, is very marked in this respect.

Underlying all its criticisms of the operating defects of the system was a reminder:

> whatever may be the hardships of a coolie in Guiana, it must not be lost sight of that thousands of them have been here from fifteen to twenty years, and have had many opportunities, had they wished, of returning to India. Not having taken advantage of the free passage to India to which they are entitled, and which is open to them almost every year, we may safely infer that they consider their position here at least equal to what it was in India.[93]

Commenting on the somewhat strained relationship between the Indians and the Blacks, the report noted,

> there will never be much danger of seditious disturbances among East Indian immigrants on estates as long as large numbers of Negroes continue to be employed with them.[94]

Des Voeux himself remained convinced in his later years that his intervention had done some good, even though he admitted that his own performance before the commission of enquiry had been lackluster and shoddy, leading the commissioners to be critical of his initial outbursts against the system. He recalled that during the hearings, a few friends and sympathizers came to him in secrecy and under cover of night, but that with the exception of the Immigration Agent-General Mr. Crosby and a merchant named Perot, "not a single white person, and very few others except coolies, dared to visit me in the daytime."[95]

He recorded also that during the several months that had elapsed after the announcement of the Commission, the planters had made great exertions and had expended large sums (estimated at hundreds of thousands of pounds) with a view to improving the condition of the estates before the arrival of the commissioners.

> Hospitals were enlarged and improved, water tanks erected, coolie barracks built or improved, and yards cleansed, so that, as Mr Crosby and others

informed me, some of the inferior estates had had their aspect entirely altered.

In the final analysis, the legislative improvements introduced subsequently, and the increased executive vigilance not only in British Guiana but also in Mauritius and other colonies after 1871, "must have added at least something to the comfort and happiness of several hundreds of thousands of indentured immigrants."

The later period of immigration saw some generally favorable comments coming out of both colonies. A British schoolmaster resident in Trinidad, J. H. Collens, remarked on the large sums being taken back to India from Trinidad in the 1880s and compared the Indians favorably with the downtrodden English peasant.

> In 1887 upwards of 678 returned to India, taking with them the sum of £12,065 in bills and specie, besides gold and silver ornaments which they were wearing to the value of another £1,000, and £200 in gold which they had entrusted to the Surgeon Superintendent for safe keeping. Fancy the wife of an English peasant having a dozen silver bangles, or a beautiful and valuable necklace of gold coins! The thing is incongruous, and as difficult to imagine as it is unlikely, and yet it is a common occurrence with these people.[96]

Marveling at their frugal and thrifty nature, which enabled them to save huge sums while "living on the plainest and coarsest of diet," he recalled the case of one Moolchan, who was originally indentured on Ste. Madeleine estate in 1853 and died in 1878 a respectable Port-of-Spain merchant, with total assets valued at $60,000 (£12,500). He suggested that this was no exceptional case either.

The sentiment that indentured immigration had been a good experience for the Indians was expressed by the Protector of Immigrants in Trinidad in the early 1870s:

> If the prosperity of the planter has been increased, the laborer on whose exertions so much depends has reaped corresponding advantages, as shewn by the increased rate of wages, and I think may be recognised in the more independent self-reliant attitude of the people who now begin to feel themselves a power; their increased self-respect is even more perceptible in their gait and dress. The number of strong, hearty men who would inevitably have perished from famine in their own country, the number of women who have been rescued from a life of degradation worse than death, and turned into industrious wives and mothers of children, the troops of

healthy and intelligent children springing up to furnish a valuable addition to the labor supply of the next generation, are living instances of the beneficial results of our system of immigration.[97]

Dr. Comins, visiting from India, compared the relative merits of the two main sugar colonies in 1891:

> Of all the colonies of the West Indies, Trinidad is the favored home of the coolie settler, where he can easily and rapidly attain comfortable independence, and even considerable wealth with corresponding social position. British Guiana, in consequence of the long continued efforts of successive generations of legislators and planters, has brought its system for the beneficial control of indentured labor to a higher pitch of perfection than any other colony, but it has no such solid advantages to offer the settler as Trinidad.[98]

Reverend John Morton, founder of the Canadian Presbyterian Mission in Trinidad in 1868 and resident in the island into the 1910s, insisted to the Sanderson Commission that the indenture system was beneficial, rather than harmful, to the Indian immigrants.[99] A well-known writer on labor systems in tropical colonies in the nineteenth century, W. Alleyne Ireland, who lived in British Guiana for a while and worked there in 1895 as an overseer, also insisted, "Of all the men I have ever met in the world, no man is so highly protected in all the relations of life as the East Indian immigrant in Demerara."[100]

It is clear from an examination of the opinions of contemporary writers on the indenture system that there was a tendency to take positions according to one's social and political beliefs. The distance between an Alleyne Ireland and a Joseph Beaumont was absolute. Part of the explanation lay in the time period that formed the framework of each writer's observations, and the extent of the social injustice which may have been present during the period commented on. But the ideological presuppositions of the writers were by no means a negligible issue. Their largely metropolitan and often planter-related backgrounds did predispose them to gloss over the deep irregularities of plantation life and to stress its fairer sides. (It was not until much later that the grandchildren and great grandchildren of these very immigrants would emerge to tell a slightly different tale and to try to express a somewhat less apologetic perspective on the whole system.)[101]

The immigrants themselves demonstrated a resilience and creativity— but also a defeatism—which sometimes transcended, sometimes reinforced, the heavy impositions of plantation life. Simultaneously Object and Subject, they responded to their social circumstances in a variety of often contradictory ways, ranging from passive resignation, to self-destructive in-group attitudes, to sporadic rebellion (small and large scale), to diverse efforts to carve out spheres of autonomy for themselves in the midst of all the constricting limitations of the system.

Acts of creative resistance can be divided into on-the-job responses of an individual or collective nature, and the more frequent attempts to effect some measure of escape from the plantation regime itself. The most typical of the former involved conscious individual acts of violation against the requirements of work stipulated by the management and protected by the law. The statistics on the many violations of the labor laws which were brought before the courts might have told the tale not only of harsh management, but also of the depth of the class struggle on the plantations.

More overt and identifiable would be the various acts of physical rebellion, either against an authority figure on the estate, against plantation property (e.g., acts of incendiarism), or by way of collective action such as a strike. Overseers and drivers were often the targets of outbursts of physical violence, and the motivations for these outbursts could range from retaliation for various acts of petty tyranny against the laborers to disputes over women.

This latter problem was by no means a minor one. Management exploitation of Indian women was described by an immigration report in British Guiana in 1897–98 as "the secret source of dissatisfaction and disturbances." The immigrant Bechu who testified before the West India Royal Commission of 1897 specifically spoke about the sexual immorality that was an integral part of the plantation environment, and of the difficulties some laborers faced in finding suitable and reliable wives, when women were being "kept" with such frequency by authority figures on the estates. Eight out of ten of the overseers tended to be white, so when these disputes involved overseers, the racial resentment would clearly be an exacerbating factor.

So serious did this problem seem to be that as late as 1916, a formal petition was presented to the authorities in Trinidad by a group of indentured laborers on the dilemma of "Christian males" keeping Hindu and Muslim females as paramours and concubines. It described the practice as a "burning shame, and a grave cancer of a disgraceful and scandalous nature."[102] (Strangely, the McNeill-Lal delegation from India reported in 1914 that the problem—in Trinidad, at any rate—was not one on which there was much concrete information or evidence.)

Even the 1869 disturbances in British Guiana on Plantation Leonora which triggered Des Voeux's letter to the Colonial Office and led to the 1870–71 enquiry, rooted though they obviously were in the injustices rampant in that period, were not completely immune from the poisonous influences of sexual exploitation as one source of worker grievance. The 1871 report hinted ominously, in paragraph 309: "It is our belief, founded on good authority, as well as on incidents which have come to our knowledge, that the recent disturbances have been originally due, in a far greater degree than is supposed, to some interference with women on the estate."

Official regulations banning such liaisons were clearly ignored in real life, and despite the resentment which the practice generated among many Indian males, it is obvious that many managerial elements were not inclined to take these objections seriously. Indeed, some may even have been amused by the whole thing, as the following remark by William Campbell, Chairman of the West India Committee, to the Sanderson Commission demonstrated:

> We have had some . . . trouble with some of the overseers living with coolie women . . . that is now very much less than it used to be. . . . Speaking to our headman about the overseers . . . he said it was all very well to blame the men; they are after all human, and you do not know how oftentimes some of these coolie women take a fancy to an overseer, and simply pester his life out. Actual cases of it have been given to me by senior men who are men now well on in years and of position in the colony. They have told me how they have been persecuted when they were young men. Therefore it is very difficult for me to believe that the coolie women as a class are all so very high-minded. As a whole I do not think we have much trouble with them. . . .
>
> It would be a very great thing if we could have in more women, but that has always been a very difficult subject with the Indian government, and I think they are right too, because they have to take care that women are not imported from India into the colonies simply for immoral purposes. [103]

One of the most scandalous examples of exploitation was related by a medical doctor who wrote an account of his experiences in the 1845–48 period. He related that the Governor of Trinidad, Lord Harris, once told him of an estate manager who had had seven Indian women simultaneously with child, all by him![104]

One offshoot of the sexual immorality and instability which surrounded plantation life—by no means confined to the racial exploitation described above, although that was clearly a major fact of life—was the very high number of crimes of passion committed by jealous immigrant husbands against their wives. The internalization of this violence within the family was a form of social response by the Indian immigrants which became almost a stereotype of Indian male behavior towards their women. The phenomenon of "wife murders" among the Indians was so widespread that the immigration ordinances had to legislate for the physical protection of women from spouse violence, as well as against the practice of seduction of immigrants' wives. It provoked much comment from high officials in the society, some theorizing that it was the low ratio of women to men which encouraged this practice of "wife murder" and jealousy among the men, others pointing out that the practice was also widespread among the peasantry in India itself and was connected to traditional attitudes towards women as well.[105]

Some indication of the level of the problem can be gleaned from the following statistics: between 1872 and 1898, out of 109 murders committed by Indians in Trinidad, 63 were murders of wives by jealous husbands;[106] in British Guiana, between 1886 and 1890 alone, there were 31 murders of women, of which 25 were murders of wives by their spouses.[107]

Another regular feature of plantation life was strike activity, although it was not legal. Its extent is difficult to measure from the official records, even the annual immigration reports, since the local officials tended to gloss over the difficulties involved, in the attempt to appear to scrutinizing Indian and British government officials to be running a reasonably normal ship of state. However, many acts of collective discontent did reach the official tallies, some more serious than others. Most of them were confined to individual estates rather than involving several estates at the same time, although there were some occasions, as in 1869, when the disturbances transcended individual estate grievances and spilled over into a larger collective expression of discontent.

The 1869 disturbances in British Guiana which eventually led to the enquiry may have been the most widespread, embracing the largest number of estates in a short span of time. Triggered on each estate by different immediate grievances, they were clearly manifestations of a deeper social grievance held by the indentured laborers during that period. Thus from late July to December, riots and acts of physical violence occurred on

Plantations La Jalousie, Leonora, Malgre Tout, Mahaicony, and Enterprise. Armed police and military detachments had to be dispatched to quell the Leonora riots.

The use of armed force to quell worker discontent occurred on several occasions in British Guiana, the most well known incidents being at Devonshire Castle in 1872, Non Pareil in 1896, Friends in 1903, Lusignan in 1912, and Rose Hall in 1913.[108] All of them resulted in loss of life among the Indians, the Rose Hall clashes ending with fifteen dead. The strike at Friends arose directly out of grievances over the sexual exploitation of Indian women by the managers and overseers.[109]

Minor work stoppages, often accompanied by assaults on plantation officials, as well as acts of incendiarism on cane fields and plantation property, occurred regularly, with some periods being more intense than others. In July–August 1873, there were fourteen strikes; between 1886 and 1889, as many as one hundred such stoppages were officially recorded. In 1888 alone, there were nine incidents of riot and assault of plantation personnel heard in the courts.[110] In 1903 there were eleven, including the most serious one at Friends estate. A witness before the Sanderson Commission claimed that there were "only six strikes" in British Guiana in 1908.[111]

Strike activity in Trinidad was just as much a normal part of plantation life as anywhere else, though it was largely confined to the second category of disturbance (localized and not involving armed clashes with the police). Indeed, the most famous incident of an armed clash between the police and the Indian immigrants in Trinidad did not arise out of a strike, but out of a public religious procession held annually by the immigrants, known as Muhurrum or Hosein. This Shiite Muslim festival, transferred by the North Indian Muslims to almost all their overseas destinations, had become syncretized into a multireligious, and even multiracial, occasion. It provided an outlet not only for legitimate expression of religious fervor but also often for the release of much pent-up frustration among the celebrants, usually against one another.

During the so-called Hosein riots of 1884, when religious celebrants chose to defy an official proclamation placing restrictions on public procession and celebration that year, the clash which ensued between the celebrants and the police resulted in twenty-two dead and hundreds seriously injured. A commission of enquiry had to be launched to investigate this disturbance, the only one of its kind in the history of indenture in Trinidad.[112]

During the depression years of the 1880s, there seems to have been a marked increase in collective work stoppages. One writer calculated that between 1870 and 1901 there were at least fifty-two strikes, with seven occurring in 1882, six in 1883, twelve in 1884, four in 1891, and four in 1895. The major grievances revolved around reduced wages, forced labor on Sundays, and excessive tasks.[113] Even the Hosein riots, while they had not taken place on the plantation as such, clearly arose out of the background of the sudden recession and its social effects upon the community of plantation laborers.

However, not all the disturbances emanated from purely economic factors. In 1891 an overseer, Hilton Christian, the son of the proprietor of Caparo estate, had been beaten by workers, who claimed during the subsequent trial that he had, in addition to being a hard taskmaster, dishonored Indian women by taking one of the estate women as his mistress.[114]

During the final years of indenture, at the turn of the century, there seems to have been an increase in the militancy of the indentured laborers in both colonies, many of whom were return migrants (i.e., second indentures) from other sugar colonies, including Natal, Fiji, and Mauritius. The annual immigration reports often complained about these return migrants, deeming them too "knowledgeable" about the general indenture system and too rebellious, a bad influence on the more innocent and malleable first-timers. Protector of Immigrants William Coombs told the Sanderson Commission that all the serious troubles in Trinidad in the previous ten years could be traced to the "pernicious influence" of returned immigrants.[115] He complained in his annual report for 1900 of the influence of a return immigrant from Demerara as being responsible for the Harmony Hall estate strike of that year. The reports often complained too about specific groups, such as Pathans, Punjabis, and Sikhs, as well as about the influence of high-caste elements. The McNeill-Lal Report specifically stated that some of the newly arrived "dislike the indentured system, purvey journalistic and other literature of an unsettling kind, and conduct an agitation both on and off the estates."[116]

In Trinidad there were several minor strikes, at Harmony Hall in 1900, Orange Grove in 1901 and 1906, and eight strikes in 1916 alone (three at Orange Grove, two at Non Pareil, and one each at Waterloo, Camden, and Caroni). The three at Orange Grove and one at Non Pareil involved newly arrived Madrasis, and they were all minor.[117] There was also a major strike at Harmony Hall in 1903, described by the Protector of Immigrants as "the longest and best engineered strike in this colony" (though curiously, it was not officially recorded or discussed in the formal annual reports). It seems to have originated as a protest against an attempted reduction of wages and soon embroiled the whole estate when a delegation to the Immigration Department was arrested and imprisoned. When it was over, many indentured laborers were transferred to other estates, many of their terms of indenture terminated, and the leader of the strikers, a Chattri by the name of Daulat Singh, was sent back to India. Blaming return migrants for the incident, the Protector of Immigrants also suggested that there was "an unscrupulous Black lawyer" behind the disturbances, without elaborating.[118]

Additional incidents during these years involved the beating to death of two overseers on Waterloo and Perseverance estates in 1907—the latter by a mixed group of newly arrived Punjabis and Madrasis—the killing of an Indian driver on Ste. Marie cocoa estate in 1910, and the wounding of another overseer on La Compensación cocoa estate in 1912, the ringleader of the eleven attackers in this last incident being a return migrant from Natal.[119]

Even in Jamaica, where the immigrants because of their small numbers were always in a generally more vulnerable and uninfluential position, there was evidence of some strike activity and restlessness in the last years—for example, on Moreland estate in 1908 and Worthy Park estate in St. Catherine in 1914. One study asserts that after 1900 there were reports of at least one strike per year.[120]

Far less dramatic, but in the final analysis much more significant as a response to the indenture system, was the attempt by the immigrants to carve out some measure of independence for themselves either within the plantation itself or outside it altogether. Under the former option, it was a question of acquiring with or without the cooperation of the plantation management an added source of income to supplement their meager wages from sugar. Quite frequently, during the term of indenture, a planter might allow individual migrants to cultivate small plots of land on the estate on their own behalf. There they could grow root crops, vegetables, and rice for their family's subsistence and for the small domestic market beyond the plantation. In British Guiana, with its spacious plantation acreages, this practice was more widespread than in Trinidad, but it was common to both. The immigrants who chose to reindenture for another term could also use the cash bounty to buy a cow, which brought in added income through milk sales to the plantation or the village markets. The grants of land from the planters were often, in such cases, for cattle grazing as well as food production. Here again, British Guiana's practice in this respect was well in advance of its sister colony.

Quite often, even from the early years, but especially after the 1880s, indentured immigrants would acquire some interest in land cultivation off the estate—individually or in collaboration with others—and would steal away for several days from their plantation duties to work these lands before returning home. The statistics on desertion and absence without leave give us an indicator of how frequent this practice became after profitable alternatives such as cocoa in Trinidad and rice in British Guiana began to produce split loyalties within the indentured laborers' perceptions and work habits.

It was also not uncommon for laborers to actually work for wages on the estate of a second landowner during such illegal and unauthorized periods of absence. Many of these secondary landowners might be Indians themselves, ex-indentured folk with small (and sometimes large) estates of their own, engaged mainly in nonsugar activities. (Many in Trinidad were small sugar cane farmers in need of hired hands.) False "free certificates"—belonging to dead or third parties—would often be provided to the absconding immigrants, to enable them to "steal time off" and move from one estate to the other without detection for long periods of time.[121] Some of the landowners utilizing the labor of deserters might themselves be indentured immigrants still tied to their own estates![122]

The practice was not without its hazards. British Guiana's Agent-General of Immigrants, Robert Duff, told the Sanderson Commission that some cunning rice farmers often refused to pay the deserters after their work was complete, thereby leaving their compatriots in the lurch after exploiting their illegally acquired labor.[123]

A great deal of desertion involved actually breaking the five-year indenture term and striking out on an independent path in an illegally acquired freedom. In Trinidad, the options facilitating this kind of premature termination of the five-year obligation were always greater than in British Guiana, because of the nature of the terrain and the easy access to off-estate properties. Thus it is difficult to estimate what percentage of the overall desertion patterns in Trinidad belonged to the first category (temporary desertions) and what to the second category (attempted permanent desertions). It is possible to say, however, that the first category was widespread during the depression years of the mid-1880s and beyond and provides a clue to the extremely high rate of prosecutions against indentureds which puzzled the Sanderson Commission investigators.

Within the second category Trinidad experienced a relatively high exodus even before the 1870s. One major source of attraction enticing the indentured immigrants away from the plantations, and which was a constant and insoluble headache for the Trinidad authorities, was the option of spiriting away to neighboring Venezuela. From as early as the 1850s, all the way through to the end of indenture sixty-odd years later, the annual immigration reports kept up a constant lament about the large numbers of Indians who were being encouraged by their free compatriots to abort their indentures and find their way to the Spanish Main, to settle there or, more often, to work at much higher wages there for a number of years before returning to Trinidad, or possibly to India.

It is curious how little mentioned is this secondary migration by the Indians to Venezuela in the existing literature on indenture in Trinidad, for the evidence indicates that it was quite a substantial, though unquantifiable, hemorrhage on the labor supply over the years. As early as 1855, an official report from the Immigration Department was declaring that it was impossible to give a true estimate of the size of the Indian community still alive in the colony because of the large numbers who had deserted and gone over to Venezuela up to then and who could not, therefore, be accounted for. An 1857 report by Charles Warner, Chairman of the Legislative Council Chamber, called attention to the phenomenon and suggested that high wages paid by Venezuelan planters were responsible.

Throughout the 1860s, the annual immigration reports kept referring to the exodus, often with considerable cynicism.

Many of [the absentees] still abscond to the Spanish Main, although the wretched condition of such as have lately returned should deter others from the same course.[124]

[There is an] increased demand for field hands on the neighboring shores of the Spanish Main, where the natives have deserted the cocoa estates and other usual culture, to escape service in the miserable struggles that desolate Venezuela. This causes a heavy drain on both contract and free labor, which must continue in the absence of any extradition treaty with that Province, to enable the planters of this colony to trace and bring back their fugitives.[125]

Agents . . . from the Spanish Main offer fabulous wages to such as will engage in their cocoa cultivation, and although those who return thence have generally done so in great misery and destitution, numbers still flock to the same fate, decoyed by the free coolies who are always well paid and fed by their employers.[126]

The 1865 Immigration Report described the migration as "the one great source of vagabondage over which neither the employer nor the government possesses any control"; it declared further, "The exodus is on the increase, and must continue while the high price of cocoa induces the Venezuelans to pick and care their produce at our expense." The fare to Venezuela was $2 in 1876, and the distance a mere 25 miles from Port-of-Spain and 8 miles from the extreme western end of the island.

The attractions outweighed whatever hazards were involved, and there were definitely many of these. Immigrants were often robbed of their possessions by those who transported them out of the island and back. In 1893, Dr. Comins, referring to the phenomenon, mentioned that Indians returning to Trinidad with gold would often be at a risk of being robbed by the Venezuelans themselves. Nevertheless, they continued to go, and in large numbers. A special ordinance (No. 21 of 1878) was passed to try to "prevent fraudulent enlistment of immigrant laborers to foreign parts." But the illegal exodus continued unchecked.

The 1889 Immigration Report had an interesting account of some of the migrants living in Venezuela.

> During last year several immigrants returned from the Spanish Main, some of whom have taken contracts on cocoa estates and are doing remarkably well. One of these men, the father of a family of five or six grownup children, all of whom returned with him, informed me that there were at Guiria, where he resided, about one hundred coolies from Trinidad who nearly all had small patches of cocoa on contract. He himself had a contract of nearly 3,000 trees about four years old, which, with several other small plantations, were entirely destroyed by locusts. This, he says, caused him to return here. This man has since returned to the Main and brought back with him a pony and other property, showing thereby that he must have been well-to-do.

In 1897 there was the case of four Indians, all still under indenture, actually being caught by immigration officials on the Cocorite wharf with "all their worldly possessions" while waiting for transport to the mainland. They were prosecuted, punished, and afterwards returned to their estates.[127] Occasionally a boatman would be apprehended for taking or attempting to take immigrants over.[128] In 1902 someone was actually caught and convicted and fined £10 for trying to entice four indentureds over to the mainland, an offense for which it was normally very difficult to arrest anyone, despite its widespread practice, usually by mainland Indians receiving a bounty in Venezuela for each immigrant actually recruited.[129]

The 1904–5 Immigration Report confessed to impotence on the matter: "There is no means of preventing this, a man has only to go across in a boat on a dark night, and on landing he is free." In the final analysis, it is impossible to quantify this sixty-odd-year clandestine migration (which of course supplemented the legal movements of free Indians). It is even more difficult to quantify the numbers (legal and illegal) who may have actually made the Venezuelan mainland their permanent home.

The largest number of absentees and deserters remained in the colonies, however. Those who attempted to abandon their original estates permanently relied upon the multiple options available elsewhere in the system, always more numerous in Trinidad. There were lands to be acquired, legally or illegally, in the public or private domain. There were others who were willing to employ them, even though it was technically illegal for them to do so. Every prospective employer, estate owner or otherwise, was supposed to request the immigrant to produce a certificate of exemption from labor, or "free certificate," to make sure he or she was not a deserter. But the employment of deserters continued and was often not rigorously followed up even by the original owners.

In both colonies, many planters often found the process of legal recovery of the immigrant so cumbersome, time-consuming, and expensive that they did not pursue the matter through to its legal conclusion, particularly when the plantations involved were very distant from each other. Besides, it often seemed a waste of time to be tracking down unwilling immigrants, since their future productivity was not assured. So widespread was this practice of employing deserters, knowingly or unknowingly, that even a former Chief Justice in Trinidad was convicted in the 1900s for the offense.[130]

An analysis of the background of the deserters done in the 1860s suggested that they tended to be either newcomers seduced away by older hands, or old immigrants who had served out their indenture and reindentured for another term, taking a bounty with them in the process without any intention of fulfilling their second agreements. It pointed out, however, that the problem tended to be more acute on some estates than others, thereby pointing the finger of culpability also at the estate management. In 1864, for example, 55 out of 150 estates had no absentees at all. Deserters or absentees tended also to come from those with nonagricultural social backgrounds, whether beggars and urban déclassé elements or those accustomed to lighter occupations in India. This apparently even included, in the early 1860s, "retired Mohammedan soldiers or Sepoys . . . inferior in domestic and social relations to every grade of Hindoo and utterly unfitted for agricultural pursuits, whose reticent venom towards a Christian master is something altogether inconceivable to the European mind."[131]

Not all absentees or deserters acted for purely economic reasons. This was very obvious with the pre-1850 arrivals, but the phenomenon continued throughout the indenture period, although with diminishing frequency. First-year arrivals were particularly prone to this kind of desertion, particularly if they had been misled in India about the exact nature of the labor that was required of them, or if maltreatment of one kind or another (including acute lack of sanitary conditions) existed on the plantations to which they had been allotted. The 1864 Immigration Report for Trinidad talked about "much annoyance from the attacks of insects." The caste of the laborer could often influence his level of impatience or dissatisfaction with the rigors of plantation life.

Many of the ignorant or innocent were duped by their fellowmen into trying to find an overland route to India, to escape their tribulations on the plantation. As late as the 1880s such cases were still frequent in British Guiana, as the Comins Report revealed. Many would wind up in a state of semiservitude to their own landowning compatriots, bound by debt or other obligations for indefinite periods of time.

Others simply sought to express their personal sense of freedom by the act of abandoning plantation life. As early as 1851, there was one report of an Indian youth found far in the Guianese interior, 200 miles up the Berbice River, living and working with the local Amerindian community.[132] Dr. Comins recounted the unusual story of one Indian by the name of Luchmon who seems to have been a compulsive deserter, and a somewhat romantic and adventurous figure. He arrived in British Guiana on the ship *Silhet* in 1879 as a return migrant of Jamaica and was allotted to Plantation Goedverwagting. He deserted in December 1880 and was apprehended two years later, in September 1882. He was charged and convicted the following year with attempting to leave the colony without a passport. Nevertheless, he managed to obtain one in 1884, and, his employer not objecting, he left for India on the *Ganges*. The next year he was back on the *Allanshaw* and was allotted to Plantation Greenfield. After one year, he again deserted, in April 1886, and a few months later his employer heard from him by letter. The letter came from England, where he had gone by ship from Demerara as a lascar. He told his employer he was on his way back to India. In 1887 he was back a third time on the *Rhine*, but under an assumed name and posing as a return migrant from Natal. Allotted to Plantation Albion, he was soon recognized by an immigration official and reported. He escaped from Albion but was soon arrested trying to cross over to Surinam. He was reallotted to Green-field but deserted again in mid-1888. After that, he was never appre-hended or heard from again.[133]

From the official statistics, which were not always consistent, it would seem that the average annual desertion rate from the 1880s to the last years was somewhere around 500 to 550 in British Guiana and 400-plus in Trinidad. In the latter colony, it was generally between 200 to 300 between 1870 and 1880 and around 400 in the decade before that. The desertion rate in the pre-1870 period in British Guiana was high. Between 1865 and 1869 alone, the Commission Report of 1871 stated that 4,258 desertions had taken place, ranging from more than 1,000 a year in 1865–66 to between 600 and 700 in 1868–69.[134]

Looked at as a whole, the historical evidence clearly indicates that the Indian immigrants' responses to the indenture system were complex and multifaceted, providing a picture of themselves as simultaneously Object and Subject, simultaneously cooperative and rebellious, defeatist and resigned or fiercely independent and self-motivated. Never totally Objects, they constantly struggled to make their humanity manifest in a milieu that was not designed with their own best interests in mind. In the final analysis, their many successes and failures in the face of large odds presented a picture of the immigrant experience which was perhaps not untypical of the larger immigrant experience in nineteenth-century America, even though they functioned in a much less self-consciously dynamic and expansive sociocultural milieu.

CHAPTER 6

Critics of Indenture: Alternative Voices in Creole Society

The establishment and consolidation of the state-aided indenture system after Emancipation was primarily a planter and Colonial Office joint initiative. Marked by many changes of detail and policy shifts over time, this dualistic labor regime—combining bound contract immigrant labor on the one hand with a nominally free labor system of Black labor and ex-indentured immigrants on the other—constituted the primary mode of labor organization in the larger territories up to the end of the First World War, when a full free-market labor system was finally introduced.

At no time during its seventy-year existence, however, was its legitimacy as a mode of labor organization accepted by the broader plantation society. Throughout the entire period, there were persistent criticisms and attacks coming from a variety of social elements, more intense in some periods than in others, but always an ever-present fact of life in these plantation societies. Some criticisms were leveled at the very basis of the indenture system; some were concerned with the abuses, flagrant and minor, which accompanied the operation of the system; still others were leveled at the character of the immigrants themselves, questioning their worth as plantation laborers and as potential settlers in the host societies.

Given the political influence and power of the plantocracy, these attacks never succeeded in shaking the system, especially since the success of the experiment seemed to be demonstrated concretely by sugar production figures for the second half of the century. These figures appeared to speak for themselves, when viewed against the immense crisis which had afflicted the sugar industry in the decade just after Emancipation.

British Guiana, which produced 47,983 tons of sugar in 1838 and 22,935 tons in 1846, was producing 80,132 tons in 1866, 104,667 tons in 1876, and 107,073 tons in 1896. Trinidad, with a production of 14,312 tons in 1838 and 17,664 tons in 1846, was producing 40,666 tons in 1866, 42,600 tons in 1876, and 54,800 tons in 1896. Only in Jamaica was there a continued steady decline in sugar production after Emancipation, due to the progressive diversification of the production system on that island in the nineteenth century: from 52,659 tons in 1838, to 28,641 tons in 1846, to 23,260 tons in 1876, to 22,995 tons in 1896.[1]

From time to time, the concerns of the government of India and of the Colonial Office were sufficiently activated—whether by criticisms coming from the colonies themselves or by policy initiatives emanating from their own centers of decision making—to appoint investigative enquiries into the conditions of the immigrant laborers in the West Indies and elsewhere. Some of them were colony specific, coming on the heels of some scandalous series of revelations within the territory concerned, like the Commission of Enquiry into the Treatment of Immigrants in British Guiana in 1870–71. Most were broad investigations into the social conditions of indenture in several territories, like the Geoghegan Report in 1873 on Emigration from India; the several reports by Dr. Comins in 1893 on Emigration from India to Trinidad, British Guiana, Jamaica, St. Lucia, Surinam, and the French West Indies; the wide-ranging London-based Sanderson Commission hearings on Emigration from India to the Crown Colonies and Protectorates, whose report was issued in 1910; and the McNeill-Lal Report to the Government of India on the Conditions of Indian immigrants in the Four British Colonies (Trinidad, British Guiana, Jamaica, and Fiji) and Surinam, issued in 1914–15.

All of these investigative exercises, however, tended to give the overall indenture experiment a relatively clean bill of health, after critiquing various abuses and malpractices in its day-to-day operations in specific territories. Some were harsher than others, such as the 1870–71 British Guiana enquiry. But the irony was that, right up to the end of the indenture experiment in 1920, the official investigations were themselves recommending its continuation and generally dismissive of the variety of harsh criticisms coming from within the colonies themselves, certainly the West Indian colonies. Even more ironically, the end of indenture came as a result of Indian-inspired nationalist agitation within India itself, highlighted by abuses in places like Natal and Fiji, but driven largely by the moral humanitarian arguments of the new Indian nationalist leaders Mohandas Gandhi and Gopal Krishna Gokhale and of India-based missionaries like the Reverend Charles F. Andrews, and finally by a sympathetic Indian colonial government, then headed by Viceroy Lord Hardinge.

It did not come from the initiatives of London officialdom or London-based social activist organizations (like the earlier abolitionist movement), nor did it even come from the initiatives of Indian community spokesmen in the West Indian territories, some of whom testified before the Sanderson Commission in London and spoke with Messrs. McNeill and Lal during their visit in 1913. These spokesmen generally tended to favor continued immigration, but they argued for the elimination of certain abuses, as well as for more formal communal representation in the colony's official bodies.

It is true, as we have mentioned in chapter 5, that many of the incoming immigrants in the last years of the system, no doubt fired by the agitation which had been going on within India itself, betrayed a restlessness and rebelliousness which extended to their activities on the plantations (McNeill and Lal talked about some of them peddling subversive literature). But the mass of the Indian community in the West Indies did not appear to diverge in opinion from its formal spokesmen on the question of support for continued indentured immigration.

Whatever opposition there was, in the mid- to late nineteenth century, to the indenture system came from a variety of diverse elements, mainly within the colonies themselves. As we shall see, they were not always motivated by the same social impulses, and often not even by the same arguments. Together, however, they formed a strand of public opinion inside the various colonies which demonstrated that, despite their ultimate political weakness in the overall scheme of things, there were always many people who disagreed with the planter–Colonial Office alliance on the direction that the plantation society was taking, and on the desirability of the dualistic labor regime that had been introduced to effect the transition from slave to free labor.

The earliest attacks upon the indenture system began with the first arrivals in 1838 in British Guiana, the "Gladstone Coolies." The official organ of the Anti-Slavery Society of Great Britain, the British Emancipator, carried a report in its issue of January 9, 1839, of severe maltreatment on two of the six plantations to which the first batch of 396 had been allotted, including one of the plantations of John Gladstone. The charge was shortly afterwards taken up with the Governor of the colony by three members of the Anti-Slavery Society, including the Secretary, John Scoble, and a commission of enquiry was appointed to investigate the charges.

Witnesses confirmed the practice of severe flogging and physical brutality meted out against the laborers by their Anglo-Indian superintendents (overseers) on Plantations Vreed-en-hoop (belonging to Mr. Gladstone) and Belle Vue (belonging to Andrew Colville). One of them, Charles Jacob, was accused of flogging laborers and rubbing salt into their wounds, as well as extorting money payments from laborers for not administering corporal punishment on them. Jacob was fined and imprisoned, and three others were fined with suspended sentences.[2]

The second batch of laborers from India between 1845 and 1848 stirred up the first organized opposition to the new immigration from within the territories. In Trinidad, that opposition came from colored middle-class elements, backed by limited public support. It came also from colonial officials themselves in the form of severe criticisms of abuses perpetrated by planters. In British Guiana, it came from an alliance of progressive British missionary elements and a militant ex-slave mass movement, in a social atmosphere of class tension and hostility which was specific to that colony. In Jamaica, there was no organized opposition to the new immigration in the 1845–48 period.

About two months after the first Indians arrived in Trinidad, a petition protesting the new immigration policy was presented to Governor McLeod, signed by Thomas Hinde and 140 other signatories. Hinde was an English-descended colored schoolteacher, landowner, and town councillor and the leading colored politician on the island between 1837 and 1845. The petition expressed concern over statements in the press to the effect that a loan of £250,000 was to be raised on the security of the Colonial Government for the purpose of initiating an East Indian immigration scheme, and that the Immigration and Agricultural Society was recommending a drastic cut in salaries and wages for sugar estate personnel and workers, as well as a general cutback on expenditure in sugar plantation operations.

The petitioners contended that it would require the imposition of additional taxation on the citizenry to repay the contemplated loan, and this would be even more burdensome if the proposed cuts in salaries and wages were to be implemented. With incomes going down and taxes going up, they argued, fewer "respectable" free immigrants would be likely to come to Trinidad from the other West India islands, America, and Sierra Leone, and the labor market would be flooded with cheap labor from India. As "immoral heathens," the Indians themselves might not make the best immigrants. Immigration, they felt, should only be permitted if it did not involve the colony in debt or increased taxation. Loans acquired should be spent on roads and construction rather than on immigration. They accused the government of placing emphasis purely on immigration, rather than on the broader question of the improvement of agriculture.[3]

When the first Indians arrived in 1845, the *Trinidad Spectator*, a colored Creole weekly, speculated that they would not make efficient field laborers, as they were not "of robust make." The newspaper criticized the immigration for its low female ratio; for specific early abuses which surfaced in the working of the system, such as inadequate medical care arrangements; and for irregularities in the payment of wages (late payments, substitution of food for money payments, etc.).[4]

After three years of the experiment, an editorial of April 26, 1848, talked about the "inhuman manner in which they have been treated by some of the very men for whose especial benefit they were brought here, at the public cost." It commented also on the widespread vagrancy and high mortality rate among the early arrivals, lamenting the spectacle of the "pitiable figures wandering about our streets, our country roads, and the evidences of death having done its work among them, far from the ken of man." It complained of the "mad" policies of the government in introducing so many immigrants onto the island, when the consequences were so foreseeable.

The same editorial also drew attention to what it described as a potentially dangerous new element in the opposition to the immigration: mass hostility towards the immigrants among the Black labor force. Reporting on an incident in April 1848, when a number of Black laborers from Nevis broke into the house of an Indian laborer resident on the same estate and ransacked it of everything it contained, the *Trinidad Spectator* declared that this was only one of a series of similar incidents, that "an active spirit of opposition to the coolie" was springing up in various parts of the island among the Creoles and others "to drive the coolie out of the labor market." When the immigration was suspended in 1848, the newspaper welcomed the decision, in anticipation of an abandonment of the scheme altogether.[5]

The abuses of this 1845–48 period were highlighted even more dramatically by the zealous partisanship of the newly appointed "Coolie Magistrate," Major James Fagan, who took up his post in 1846. Major Fagan, a retired Indian army officer, was brought to Trinidad to fill a need for someone with a knowledge of Indian languages and customs to supervise the whole immigration and look after the welfare of the newcomers. He was partly a magistrate and partly a welfare officer and investigator into the social conditions of plantations utilizing Indian labor. Together with Governor Harris, it was Major Fagan who was responsible for formulating the first pass-law regulations, aimed at curbing the widespread vagrancy among the early immigrants. These regulations were disallowed by the Colonial Office after an uproar from antislavery elements in London and Trinidad, though they were later to become an integral part of the regular indenture system in the 1850s.

Major Fagan's term of office was brief and stormy, partly because of his zealous defense of the Indian laborers against employer abuse and irregularity, thereby incurring the wrath of the planter class, but partly also because his modus operandi and personality, somewhat abrasive and grandiose, brought him finally into conflict with Governor Harris as well. During his short term of two years, he articulated a number of complaints about the maltreatment of the immigrants, including their forcible ejection from some estates by planters when too ill or disabled to perform their functions, and their being left to wander aimlessly over the country-side, often "to die like dogs on the roadside."

This was done even to women, who were driven from their estates "naked, penniless and in every way helpless, to starve or to become the victims of loathsome disease from prostitution." He described the indenture system between 1845 and 1848 as "more recklessly cruel than what obtained in the times of slavery when the Negro, if unable to work from age or sickness, had a right to be maintained by his owner, and could not, like the coolie, be driven to perish on the roadside."[6]

Major Fagan also helped to uncover and investigate several cases of physical brutality against immigrants by estate managers. There was the celebrated case of Mr. Walkinshaw of Clydesdale Cottage estate in South Naparima in 1846, who was investigated for three separate cases of brutality: one Beechook, whom he beat and kicked for sitting down in the field to rest during work, after a week of inactivity due to illness, and whom he then offered $20 not to report the incident to the magistrate; one Kundappa, who died in the estate hospital from ulcerated feet left untended until it was too late; and one Jhandoo, who complained of being left in a sick condition for five days without food or a visit from the doctor or any estate official. Major Fagan also revealed that Mr. Walkinshaw was in the habit of doubling the size of the normal task, forcing laborers to work from 6 A.M. to 5:30 P.M. and denying them rations until the task was completed, often a two-day affair. After an official enquiry, the decision was taken to deny the Clydesdale Cottage estate any further Indian laborers, and the ones already there were removed.[7]

There was also the case in 1847 of Mr. Justice Anderson, proprietor of the Carolina estate, who assaulted one Bhodu with a riding whip in the course of a dispute over wages, cutting his head in the process. As late as May 1848, shortly before his own dismissal from office, Major Fagan was complaining that justice had yet to be done about that matter and that Bhodu's arrears of wages were still unpaid. Mr. Anderson had accused Major Fagan in his statement on the incident in 1847 of attempting to force a wage raise for the Indians from 30 to 40 cents a day.[8]

That Major Fagan's unrelenting activism on behalf of the Indians did not endear him to many of the planters goes without saying. However, he was highly regarded by the Indians themselves. A group of return immigrants to Calcutta from Trinidad in 1851, when questioned about conditions in Trinidad, spoke well of Major Fagan, whom they said was a good man whom "all coolies know." They praised his understanding of their language and customs: "If a line was drawn on the ground, and milk thrown on one side and water on the other, he could tell which was which, and the other gentlemen could not tell so much in our matters."[9]

He was also highly regarded by the colored Creole weekly the *Trinidad Spectator*, which also lauded his intimate knowledge of Indian languages and customs and praised his "sterling qualities as a man." The newspaper considered him well fitted for the post he held, stating, "The people have confidence in appealing to him, and . . . from him only can they be certain of obtaining redress for their wrongs."[10]

Two incidents in 1848 seem to have decisively turned official opinion against Major Fagan, climaxing in his dismissal by the Governor in June. In April there appeared in the London-based *Colonial Magazine* a letter sent anonymously to Lord George Bentinck and the Committee of the House of Commons then investigating the West India question, making wide-ranging suggestions about systematizing the indenture system, and the management of plantations in the West Indies generally.

Major Fagan was widely understood to be the author of that letter, and he never denied it in the controversy that surrounded it subsequently. In it he proposed an elaborate quasi-military hierarchy of officials headed by a General Superintendent of Immigration and Colonization, with powers of direct communication with the Colonial Office in London and the Governors of the West India islands.[11] What offended the plantocracy was not this somewhat grandiose and fanciful master plan for immigration, but the slanderous descriptions of the plantation system and its personnel in Trinidad contained in the document. It lamented that oriental barbarism, in its darkest day, was civilization in comparison with the moral destitution prevalent in the West India colonies. It claimed that the manner in which the absentee organization of the plantation was conducted by the attorneys, managers, and overseers led to a "gigantic scheme of spoliation of proprietors," with attorney-merchants making an immense profit out of the intermediary relation that they held, at the expense of the proprietors resident in Europe.

> As a result of this system, men of straw, on becoming appointed attorneys, rapidly rise to affluence and apparent consequence, living at the same time in princely style, while the absent proprietor gradually sinks into comparative poverty.
>
> The low, demoralised and illiterate managers, for such they generally are, naturally work at the grosser frauds of their superintending "100 pound attorneys", and thus they mutually further their personal fortunes to the serious detriment, and probable ruin, of the absent struggling proprietor. It is obvious that, to carry out such a system of plunder and corruption, the overseer must be selected from a low and demoralised class, to whom a license is thus unavoidably conceded, to practise frauds to any extent for which his situation may afford opportunity. In time this worthy aspires to, and actually acquires, the management of an estate.

Managers were described as persons who often "lived in a state of concubinage" with women, whom they placed in charge of estate shops which they stocked from the illegal sale of estate products such as sugar and syrup. They often bought lands for their partners, building houses constructed from estate materials and supplies. What is more, many of them had several mistresses, thus multiplying the described activities.

The *Colonial Magazine* itself was somewhat skeptical of the charges in the document quoted. Major Fagan, it stated, had not been in Trinidad or the West Indies long enough to enable him to make such sweeping condemnations about the West Indian plantation system. It described Major Fagan as "an active and zealous officer, anxious to carry out the duties assigned to him, but somewhat vain of his abilities, self-opinionated, and greedy of praise."[12]

The official voice of the Trinidad plantocracy, the *Port-of-Spain Gazette*, in an editorial on May 26, was less restrained in its response to the document. It thundered as follows:

> for the sake of our adopted country, of our own self-respect, we protest against the truth of the villainous picture which he has drawn of the inhabitants of this colony. If Major Fagan, in his capacity of Magistrate, has met with instances of "fraud", "extortionate deductions", "illicit gains and underhand advantages", which, as a Magistrate, anywhere—even in his native city of Cork—he must meet, it is to be supposed that he has dealt with such cases as they deserved; but such instances no more sanction his stigmatising the inhabitants of Trinidad as rogues and swindlers, than his own conduct as a public officer, his present foul libels, or his becoming demeanour and genteel breeding, would authorise us in asserting that all natives of Cork were malicious, boastful, violent and low.
>
> If Major Fagan can defend his report by facts, he had better do so, or he may consign himself to whatever party will receive him; for henceforth, from the public at large, he will meet only with the contempt and indignation due to the author of such foul libels.

The incident that led directly to Major Fagan's dismissal took place sometime in early May. A number of Indians employed on the Ganteaume sugar estate in Mayaro, about thirty-five in all, walked to the Governor's house in Port-of-Spain to stage a sit-down protest over the issue of their unpaid wages, held up for seven months. Major Fagan, acting on the side of the delegation, went into the Governor's house to see him. He was followed inside by a few of the Indians, who were promptly and somewhat roughly ejected by the Acting Colonial Secretary, Thomas Johnston.

The incident outraged Major Fagan. It seems that Major Fagan himself had been ejected by the Governor in the melee. In a letter to Johnston dated May 6, he complained,

> my treatment at the hands of Lord Harris in having been so publicly and ignominiously insulted by him at the Government House, and forbidden . . . to appear there again, virtually suspending me from office, I feel to be so galling and humiliating that death would be preferable to my present mental suffering under the consciousness of the indignity offerred to me. . . . I passed thirty years of my life in India, and in almost constant contact with its great men, civil and military. I never experienced indignity

or discouragement in any high quarter till I came to Trinidad, where the same principles of action that influenced my career in India govern me.[13]

A charge of assault was laid against Mr. Johnston. Major Fagan himself tried the case and found Johnston guilty, fining him twenty pounds for the offense. An exchange of letters with Governor Harris over the affair was then subsequently published in the *Trinidad Spectator*, leaked no doubt by Major Fagan himself. He was dismissed from his post and left the island in August.[14] The *Port-of-Spain Gazette* editorialized that he had brought his misfortune upon himself.[15]

The critique against the new immigration and its operative abuses in Trinidad during the 1845–48 period had been spearheaded by colored politicians and journalists, a segment of the Black labor force, and colonial officials like Major Fagan. Their agendas were not necessarily the same, as we have seen. Some, like Thomas Hinde and his supporters, wanted to arrest the policy altogether. Some, like the *Trinidad Spectator* and its supporters, were ambivalent about the new immigration, suggesting that it was not necessarily the best policy at that point in the island's history, yet also adopting a humanitarian approach towards the unfortunate immigrants themselves, anxious that they should receive some kind of protection from the authorities against planter abuse and maltreatment.

Major Fagan was not for the abandonment of immigration, but for its regularization and systematization under stringent and honest supervision and for the elimination of employer abuse in all its forms. The larger society, especially the Black peasantry, seemed not to have developed any generalized social response to the newcomers or the policies that brought them there. Antagonisms arising from direct competition on specific estates there undoubtedly were, but given the overall labor shortage in Trinidad, and perhaps the ease with which Black ex-slaves could find themselves lands to occupy or squat upon for their own livelihood, no sense of threat from the newcomers seems to have overwhelmed them, despite the warnings from the *Trinidad Spectator.*

This was not the case in British Guiana, where relations between the plantocracy and the Black ex-slaves in the years immediately after Emancipation had been marked by a sense of social conflict and class tension not paralleled in Trinidad. The Black withdrawal from the plantations between 1838 and 1845 had had a more drastic impact on Guianese than on Trinidad sugar production. Similarly, planter attempts to keep labor on the plantations had been more extreme, ranging from the use of violence and coercion, on the one hand, to elaborate material and financial enticements, on the other, by the more affluent planters. Black collective action had also assumed a more organized expression in this context than in Trinidad, whether in the form of the roving task-gang, vigorously bargaining for the appropriate wage and working conditions, or in the form of strike action, like the successful 1842 strike in Demerara and Essequibo against the attempted wage cuts of that year.

When, therefore, the decision was taken to introduce Indian immigrant labor in 1844, and the legislature (the Court of Policy) passed ordinances to raise a loan of £500,000 to facilitate the importation of labor, it was seen by the Black ex-slaves as an attempt to achieve by immigration what could not be achieved by other means: the undermining of their newfound social leverage in the plantation society. Immigration policy was thus seen to be not simply economically but politically motivated.

This interpretation was encouraged by their main advisers and public spokesmen, the English members of the London Missionary Society, who campaigned against the new immigration scheme from their pulpits, at mass public meetings, and through their newspapers. When the Annual Tax Ordinance of 1846 raised import duties on a variety of consumer items and imposed heavy licenses on shops, carts, porters, and boats, they pointed out to their followers that it was they who were being taxed exorbitantly to pay for an immigration scheme whose long-range purpose was to reduce their own wages and their social leverage in the labor market. Thus they were being forced to subsidize their own eventual retrenchment from the sugar industry.

The year 1846 saw an intensification of general public dissatisfaction. There were work stoppages on East Coast Demerara and a further exodus from the estates to the villages, an ugly riot and attack upon an estate manager on Leguan Island in the Essequibo River against a 20 percent wage reduction, plus large meetings organized by the missionaries to condemn the new immigration. The Governor spoke ominously about "evil-disposed persons" influencing the crowds against the immigration scheme. An attempt to silence the Reverend Wallbridge of the London Missionary Society with a libel suit had the opposite effect, as large crowds of Black supporters chanted outside the court for the dismissal of the Governor instead.[16]

The missionaries, surprisingly, went so far as to level their attacks not only at the planters and the government, but even at the immigrants themselves. Reverend Wallbridge lamented the introduction of "hordes of ignorant, idolatrous and sensual immigrants" into the society. He and his colleagues were worried about the impact the new immigration would have upon the financial viability of the Mission Churches themselves, supported as these were by the financial contributions from the Black congregations. The heavy taxation imposed upon the people to pay for the immigration scheme was leading to a drying up of these contributions, as workers struggled to cope with the rising cost of living. Reverend Wallbridge did not distinguish between the policymakers and the immigrants in his anguish over the decline of the Mission stations.

"A tide of ungodliness and immorality has set in," he lamented, "which threatens to sweep away the work of years, and the missionaries laboring in British Guiana need at the present time most peculiarly the sympathy, the prayers, and in many cases the pecuniary contributions of the friends of Missions in the Mother Country."[17]

Black laborers could hardly be indifferent to the newcomers in this kind of social and political atmosphere. Interestingly, their responses towards the initial arrivals of 1838, the "Gladstone Coolies," had been more sympathetic. When the hearings on the abuses on Plantation Vreed-en-Hoop had been held, Black laborers had come forward to testify that the Indians had been flogged and physically abused. By 1845, however, the Indians were being seen not as fellow victims of planter abuse, but as instruments of planter politics directed against Black workers and as threats to their newly won bargaining power in the labor market, evidenced by the successful 1842 strike. As the *Creole* newspaper would phrase it much later, immigration was intended to punish the Black population for having left the estates after Emancipation.[18]

That this view of the new immigrants was not entirely unfounded was clearly demonstrated by the crisis that arose after the passing of the Sugar Duties Act of 1846 and the financial crisis in the metropolis in 1846–48, which had a negative impact on the West Indian plantation economy. The decision to reduce wages by 25 percent in early 1848 as a way of coping with the crisis, and the general strike which erupted in January in response—the second since 1842—led to a very different denouement.

The presence of the immigrants (Portuguese as well as Indian) and their refusal to join the strike, preferring to accept the reduced wages, proved decisive in ending the resistance of the Black workers to the new planter imposition. On some estates, Black workers had even resorted to intimidation and violence against some of the immigrants in the attempt to get them to join the strike. But by March they had to accept defeat.[19] So effectively indeed had the planters regained the upper hand that the

Black workers never resorted to this form of general strike action again for the rest of the century.

The third and decisive phase of the Indian immigration began in 1851 and continued without interruption every year up to 1917. (Jamaica, as we have said, recommenced in 1860, and immigration was interrupted again several times thereafter.) Opposition to the immigration continued unabated throughout the entire period, the vocal spokesmen of the colored and Black middle classes dominating the discussions, often against an unresponsive or largely deaf officialdom. One period was dominated by journalists and their minority newspapers, and a later one saw that opposition being taken up by political spokesmen, as entree into legislative councils for coloreds and Blacks became easier. The second period began in the 1890s, with Black and colored representatives entering the local legislature in Trinidad before British Guiana.

The role of other social critics—colonial officials, judges, missionaries—tended to be uneven, and far more pronounced in pre-1870 British Guiana. The roles played by critics like Des Voeux and Beaumont in British Guiana had no counterparts in the post-1870 period, when the flagrant injustices against the Indians had been more or less brought under control. Missionary campaigning against the system tended to be more low-keyed after the 1840s in British Guiana, not completely dying out but lacking the earlier militancy. Trinidad had no tradition of anti-immigration missionary activity at all, almost all of this element being supportive of the indenture experiment. Jamaican missionaries, foreign and native, were more active on that score than their Trinidadian counterparts.

Towards the end of the nineteenth century, even a few planters in Trinidad began to critique the system and question its desirability. And as for overt mass self-organization on the immigration issue, this continued to be more a feature of the British Guiana than the Trinidad agitation, although even here there was less collective militancy than during the 1840s, at least until the renewed political agitations at the turn of the century. The main burden of the anti-immigration campaign after the 1850s, therefore, was carried by the Black and colored professional classes.

Trinidad after 1850

The main colored and Black newspapers in Trinidad were the *San Fernando Gazette* (1850–96) and the *New Era* (1869–91). There were several others that had relatively short life spans, but these two articulated most of the social positions on immigration and other matters to which the small Afro middle class subscribed in the nineteenth century.

The earliest statement on immigration by the *San Fernando Gazette* was in fact a protest on the ordinance (No. 9 of 1850) passed by the legislative council entitled "An Ordinance for the Encouragement into This Colony of Chinese Immigration." Criticizing the haste with which the measure had been passed (it was all done in one day), the newspaper went on to express the view that the Chinese would not make good agricultural laborers for Trinidad. It reminded its readers that the previous experiment in 1806 had not been a success, since most of the immigrants soon returned home, and the few who remained "never in any manner whatever proved themselves any great acquisition to the country."

It went on to describe a more recent failure in Mauritius in the 1840s and protested against draining the Exchequer "for the purpose of calling useless immigrants from the distant shores of the Pacific." It insisted that it was not against immigration for the purpose of developing the colony, but it was in favor of free spontaneous immigration based on rational inducements to the prospective immigrant.[20]

As the Indian immigration resumed its momentum, the newspapers (including many small ones) kept up their attacks upon the new dualistic labor system, utilizing public revenues as it did to fuel its growth. All the major arguments against such a labor system and its social consequences were articulated in the pre-1890 period. Receiving no response, however, from the planter–Colonial Office alliance, or indeed from metropolitan social activist organizations such as the Anti-Slavery Society, whose energies were channeled in other directions after the 1850s, they remained no more than powerless protestations from a noncohesive middle-class group. The official correspondence between the Governor and the Colonial Office hardly contained any reference to these elements.

Nor is it certain exactly how wide was the readership of these newspapers, as there were no quoted circulation figures to give us any indication of the size of their audience. Certainly there was never any attempt in Trinidad—in contrast with British Guiana—at mass mobilization or even petitioning the authorities on these issues before the 1890s, even though it is virtually certain that the colored and Afro-Creole educated sector would have shared most of the sentiments on indentured immigration expressed in these newspapers.

The *San Fernando Gazette* branded it a "Coolie Slave Trade" that was more "dangerous and degrading" than the old one. Capitalists and absentee proprietors were using it in order to drain the colony of its wealth. It was a disruption of the normal laws of the free labor market and was actually used not simply to cut labor costs, but also to keep the wage levels of the free laborer permanently depressed at the levels at which the immigrants were being paid. Moreover, it was subsidized through general taxation for the sole benefit of the plantocracy: If sugar or cocoa planters wanted to bring in indentured immigrants, they should do so at their own expense, not at the expense of a work force that the immigration system was designed to undermine. Black workers were available and willing to work on the estates, as were free immigrants from places like Barbados.

The indenture system was morally degrading to both indentured laborer and planter, existing as it did on a foundation of coercive regulations, violations of which were punishable by imprisonment—an arrangement morally reminiscent of slavery. It was also expensive beyond its ultimate worth, as it necessitated a large apparatus of courts, police, jails, and hospitals supported by public funds to keep it in regular working order.[21]

Inevitably, the newcomers themselves, with their strange new customs, came in for attack from the critics. Some of the derogatory descriptions were the inevitable result of the frictions generated by the attempt to juxtapose two races unfamiliar with each other in a competitive labor situation. Some were inspired by an artificial affectation of cultural superiority, a favorite posture of Westernized colonial middle-class elements towards alien races and cultures in their midst. The derogatory stereotypes were shared not only by those who felt threatened by their influx, but also by those who introduced them into the society in the first place.

Indians were an alien, non-Christian entity in a Western, Christian environment, "immoral heathens" as Thomas Hinde had called them as early as 1845. The small *Trinidad Free Press* lamented in 1851 that the "Emerald Isle of the West" was about to be converted into "a den for the naked heathens of the East."[22] The *San Fernando Gazette* thought that Asiatic paganism was infesting Christian Trinidad with "a virus" that later might be "impossible to eradicate" and which might one day "become fatal to us as a Christian people."[23] The establishment *Port-of-Spain Gazette* talked of the "heathenish rites and barbarous processions" associated with Hinduism.[24]

Associated with the notion of their alienness was their potential as a dangerous element in the society, capable of rebellion and disorder.[25] With every increase in their numbers in the society, these anxieties were fueled by the newspapers. The *Trinidad Chronicle* noted in 1871 that ten years before, only four wards had contained more than one thousand Indians; the new census had revealed that there were now ten such wards. It advised a reduction in the annual importation of immigrants and in the 1880s advocated an end to the immigration altogether, by which time the Indians were about 31 percent of the population.[26]

The attacks extended to the Indians' ability to contribute to the advancement of the colony. The *San Fernando Gazette* declared that the Indian could "hardly be said to colonize the place of his temporary abode, for his dream and his ambition are to drain it as much as possible of its coins to return to his home and there to circulate the treasures he has with such infinite sacrifice hoarded here."[27] The majority of the immigrants belonged to "the dregs of India, rotten with the most degrading and unnatural vices, thieves and liars, to whom the idea of duty is unknown, who regard an oath as nothing but a device to cheat their neighbours."[28]

Occasionally, amidst this barrage of anti-immigration and anti-Indian criticisms, there were rare glimpses of a critique of the indenture system from the kind of perspective which Major Fagan, in his own brash manner, had tried to introduce into the society, that is, from the standpoint of the harm that it was inflicting on the Indian immigrants themselves. Robert Lechmere Guppy, Mayor of San Fernando, an Englishman who had been resident in Trinidad for about fifty years, gave a graphic description of the degrading conditions under which Indian immigrant workers lived in the 1880s, in a memorandum to the Royal Franchise Commission of 1888:

> As first in the list of evils which afflict the Colony, I look upon the system of housing Indian immigrants in barracks. It was not introduced until after Major Fagan had been dismissed and the subjugation of the coolie to five years' indenture to a master imposed upon him by the government had become complete. At the outset barracks were only built for the Indians who came unaccompanied by women, and free laborers were lodged as before in separate cottages. The first in Naparima was erected at Palmyra estate, and I think that one was the first in the island. But as the estates got fully supplied with coolies the cheapness of the barrack caused it to be adopted universally.
>
> The barrack is a long wooden building eleven or twelve feet wide, containing perhaps eight or ten small rooms divided from each other by wooden partitions not reaching to the roof. The roof is of galvanised iron,

without any ceiling; and the heat of the sun by day and the cold by night take full effect upon the occupants. By standing on a box the occupant of one room can look over the partition into the adjoining one, and can easily climb over. A family has a single room in which to bring up their boys and girls if they have children. All noises and talking and smells pass through the open space from one end of the barrack to the other. There are no places for cooking, no latrines. The men and women, boys and girls, go together into the canes or bush when nature requires. Comfort, privacy and decency are impossible under such conditions.

A number of these barracks are grouped together close to the dwelling house of the overseers, in order that they may with the least trouble put them out to work before daylight in crop time, which they do by entering their room, and, if necessary, pulling them off their beds where they are lying with their wives.

If a man is sick he is not allowed to be nursed by his wife, he must perforce go to the hospital far away, leaving his wife, perhaps without the means of subsistence, in such a room as I have described, to her own devices, amid the temptations surrounding her. With all this, can anyone wonder at the frequent wife murders and general demoralisation amongst the Indian immigrants? In fact the barrack life is one approaching promiscuous intercourse. And the evil is not confined to the coolies. No decent Black laborer can take his wife to live amongst such surroundings. . . .

The absentee proprietor is not there to witness the scandals. The overseers will tell you, as I have often been told by them, that they are put there to make sugar and not to look after the morals of coolies.[29]

Certain elements within the magistracy were clearly sympathetic to the immigrants, often to the frustration of pro-planter partisans. A letter to the *San Fernando Gazette* in 1868 had complained—as mentioned already in chapter 5—about the decisions of Stipendiary Magistrate Thomas Shirley Warner, with their alleged favoritism towards the working classes.

By and large, however, Trinidad plantation society remained scandal free in the post-1850s period. Wise leadership from the Governors involved, tactful and humane supervision from Major Fagan's successor, Dr. Henry Mitchell, and a less cohesive and therefore less intransigent planter class helped to insulate Trinidad from the kind of scandals which rocked its sister colony right up to the early 1870s. William Des Voeux considered the Trinidad administration of the 1860s to be enlightened, practicing many of the ideas that Des Voeux considered British Guiana badly in need of introducing.[30]

The 1890s saw new developments in the anti-immigration lobby, raising the issue to a higher level of public awareness. The background to these developments was the crisis caused after 1884 by the fall in international sugar prices, itself the result of the competition from European beet sugar. From £22–£24 a ton—a relatively steady price level held for decades after the earlier drop in the mid-1840s—there was a sudden decrease to £12–£14 a ton after 1884, reaching an all-time low of £9 12s. per ton in 1896. Prices did not return above £20 until after the First World War.

The planters' response was to reduce the wage levels of the more specialized and skilled estate labor force, mainly Blacks and free Indians (resident and nonresident), and to reduce the number of daily tasks performed by individual laborers. This led to a general reduction of earnings to the level of the indentured Indians. (The unintended result of this policy was the hastening of the exodus of Blacks and free Indians from the sugar sector.) Immigration policies in the meantime were kept intact, and new indentured labor flooded the sugar estates as part of planter policy to keep the free wage levels permanently depressed. Often there was even a surplus of indentured labor on individual estates, with a consequent drop in their own earnings below the level required by the law.[31]

In this context, a number of voices in the 1890s began to question the need for further immigration inflows and recommended a gradual reduction of the numbers involved. These included the Protector of Immigrants himself, Charles Mitchell, in 1892, and legislators such as Lechmere Guppy. But these men ran up against a stubborn opposition in the sugar planter–dominated Legislative Council.

Even the establishment *Port-of-Spain Gazette* began in 1895 to support the call for a reduced immigration, thus making the entire press in the late 1890s unanimous in its opposition to the selfish policies being perpetuated by the planters in a period of depression. The *Port-of-Spain Gazette* even adopted the position that indentured labor had become more expensive than free labor.[32]

The plantocracy itself, moreover, had become divided on the issue. A number of the planters from the rising new cocoa sector were also adding their voices to the chorus of objectors to current immigration policy. In 1890, no more than fifteen of the more than one hundred cocoa estates were utilizing indentured labor. Dr. Comins had estimated that in 1891, out of ten thousand indentured laborers in the colony, no more than six hundred were employed on cocoa and coconut estates. Since the early 1880s, however, the Legislative Council under the sugar planters had raised the contribution of the cocoa sector to the Immigration Fund from 20 to 37 percent of the total export duty collected on local produce.

A memorandum from Alfred Tracey, an expatriate cocoa planter, to the West India Royal Commission in 1897 appeared to voice the concerns of at least some of his fellow planters.[33] He was opposed not to immigration generally, but to the exclusive system of state-aided Indian immigration. The system, he maintained, was too costly, entailing as it did the upkeep of a large immigration staff and a large and expensive medical staff, besides a considerable increase in jail and hospital accommodations. The wages of the indentured immigrants did not contribute to the permanent wealth of the colony, because of the considerable annual remittances to India and the large amounts taken back to India by those availing themselves of the return passage.

Moreover, it was usually the strong and the thrifty who returned to India, leaving behind the "incapables and beggars." Tracey felt that sugar planters should gradually reduce the numbers of those imported, with a view to an eventual end to the system. More stress should be placed on encouraging free immigrants from the other islands, principally Barbados, and a labor bureau established in the Immigration Department to furnish newcomers with information about employers' needs in Trinidad.[34]

With the increasing antagonism being expressed publicly against the high-handedness and stubborn domination of the Legislative Council by the sugar interest, newspapers like the San Fernando Gazette, speaking for the colored and Black middle class (and presumably Black masses), became even more strident in their denunciations of the immigration system and its benefactors. They made no moderate requests for reductions in importations, but called instead for an immediate end to the system; they made, moreover, no distinction between what might be an objectionable system and what they considered to be the objectionable nature of the immigrants themselves.

> When it is considered that the 70,000 coolies now in the colony have cost us £2,225,000 of money, equal to about £32 per head, one can then realize what a dreadful evil, what a crushing drawback coolie immigration has been to us.

There is not a single branch of our administration that is not tainted because of coolie immigration.

Coolie immigration is still a millstone around our necks, and until the planters are made to pay the entire cost of the indentured laborers they may require, real immigration will not exist, and the population of this country will be impossible.

The great majority of petty convictions in the Lower Courts are against Creoles. The real crimes—highway robbery, robbery with violence, rape, sodomy and other unnatural crimes, in fine, most of the heaviest part of the Calendar of the Assizes—is supplied by coolies.

What matters it to them [the planters] that the taxpayers be made to pay to demoralise and pauperise the colony by the introduction of a class of people not amenable to Christian civilization? What matters it to them that the population is brutalised by being made familiar with crimes hitherto unknown among them, by the most savage murders followed by hangings? What matters it to them that the general expenditure of the colony has increased threefold on account of these people? They pay no taxes. Trinidad is their milch cow, its population their beasts of burden. They, their wives and children, run no risks of being contaminated by the atmosphere of vice and degradation engendered by this foul blot with which it suits their interests to afflict the country.[35]

The most important development between 1894 and 1904 was the nomination of important members of the anti-immigration lobby from the colored and Black middle class to the Legislative Council. From this elevated platform, spokesmen like Henry Alcazar, Stephen Laurence, Vincent Brown, and Cyrus Prudhomme David carried their agitation to bring an end to state-subsidized indentured immigration both to London and to a wider public in the colony.

New working-class formations like the Trinidad Working Men's Association (T.W.A.) also made their appearance on the social scene, adding their voices to the chorus of dissenters. Allies were even recruited in the British Parliament, from the Labour Party, to help them press their case on this (and other issues) in the metropolis: Thomas Summerbell and Joseph Pointer, the latter of whom visited Trinidad in 1912.

Henry Alcazar, in voting against the annual quota for immigrants proposed in the Legislative Council in 1896, made the point that the small cane farmer class was also being adversely affected by the immigration system and was capable, if given the opportunity, of supplying the factories with most of the canes required at a lower cost than the current system permitted.[36] The racial ratio of the 6,150 cane farmers in 1898 was 62.2 percent Blacks (3,824) of local or West Indian immigrant descent, and 37.8 percent Indians (2,326). (By 1907 this had become a total of 12,334, of whom 46.8 percent, or 5,777, were Black, and 53 percent, or 6,557, were Indian.)[37]

In his memorandum to the West India Royal Commission in 1897, Alcazar also conceded, surprisingly, that Indian indentured immigration had indeed been necessary and vital in saving the sugar industry in Trinidad, given the unsteady work habits of the Black work force, at least up to about 1877, in his view. "Had it ceased some twenty years ago," he stated, "there would have been little to say against it." After that date, the system became "no longer required to fill a void which could not otherwise be filled," but became instead a weapon in the hands of the planter to control the labor market. The Black labor force since the late 1870s was "a new generation more numerous, bred in freedom, and much more willing and able to work steadily and efficiently" than the generation of liberated slaves had been.

The decline in the sugar industry in the smaller islands with the exception of Barbados, in his view, had also released much surplus labor that would be available to Trinidad and elsewhere. (Note that Tracey in his memorandum had advocated free immigration *especially* from Barbados, revealing some inconsistencies in the calls for immigration from this source among the anti-indenture lobbyists.)

To be allocating an annual sum of £20,000 from the general revenue towards the upkeep of the system was wasteful; the real allocation in fact included an extra £5,000 to £10,000 of export duties contributed by farmers and small farmers who received no benefit from Indian immigration.

Alcazar also critiqued the system on moral grounds, arguing that the planters were reduced to the moral level of slave owners:

On the employer . . . the effect is . . . similar to that of slavery, for if one-fifth of his bondsmen are set free every year, a fresh fifth at once take their place, and he has thus permanently about him a large number of his fellowmen bound to do his bidding under penalty of imprisonment. In fact, with regard to its effect on the employer, the system is not very different from slavery, with the gaol substituted for the whip. And one of the worst consequences of Indian immigration in Trinidad has been to keep its educated classes at the moral level of slave owners.[38]

The West India Royal Commission of 1897 also received a brief memorandum from representatives of a small section of the Black working class (boatmen, droghermen, and ships' laborers) on the issue of Indian immigration. A somewhat inarticulate document signed by one Charles Phillips, Secretary of the Working Men's Reform Club, complained about "coolie immigrants starving us" and the "unofficial members [i.e., Black Legislative Council representatives] nominally representing us." It stated that Blacks received little or no encouragement "in agricultural or any industrious exhibitions" and that Crown lands were not open to them. It characterized the Indians, inter alia, as contributing nothing "to city improvements."[39]

The high point of this anti-immigration lobbying came in 1909, when the Sanderson Commission of Enquiry into the Indian immigration system held its exhaustive investigations and interviews in London. This was the first comprehensive investigation by the Colonial Office, in collaboration with the India Office, into the whole indentured immigration experiment in the Crown Colonies and Protectorates of the British Empire. The Trinidad delegation from the anti-immigration lobby consisted of Cyrus Prudhomme David and Alfred Richards (the Afro-Chinese leader of the Trinidad Working Men's Association), backed up by Mr. Summerbell of the Labour Party.

The Sanderson Commission took evidence from a variety of interest groups and spokesmen in Trinidad: the plantocracy, members and ex-members of the Immigration Department, government officials, missionaries, independent social observers and writers, Indian community leaders such as F. E. M. Hosein and George Fitzpatrick, in addition to the anti-immigration spokesmen from the colored and Black middle class.

Their conclusions were not in favor of the anti-immigrationists. They rejected claims of widespread pauperization and unemployment caused by the system (a claim made by Alfred Richards). They were skeptical of some of the figures provided by the anti-immigrationists on decreasing wage levels in the sugar industry. But they noted the fluctuations in wage levels for sugar workers since the 1880s and noted as well that a special committee in Trinidad had recommended in 1906 that free laborers' daily wages be raised by law by fifteen cents to make up for the indentured laborers' advantage of free housing and medical care.

They concluded that any attempt to put an end to the immigration either suddenly or within a short term of years would inevitably have a most serious effect on the sugar industry and on the colony generally, as its prosperity still depended to so considerable an extent on sugar. But they recommended that the efforts of the government be directed towards restricting the importation "within the limits absolutely required to meet the needs of the estates" and towards "its gradual reduction as those needs diminish or can be met by other sources of supply."[40] In this respect their recommendations were similar to those of the 1897 West India Royal Commission.[41]

On the issue of financial contributions to immigration expenses, they concluded that the arrangement as it stood was not in fact unjust, agreeing with the finding of the special committee appointed to enquire into the labor question in Trinidad in 1905. The West India Royal Commission of 1897 had actually recommended that sugar planters be made to pay the entire cost of importation. The Sanderson Commission took into account, in addition to the 1905–6 Trinidad report, evidence from the Chairman of the West India Committee, Sir Neville Lubbock, to the effect that nonimporters of labor were also major beneficiaries of that labor. Sir Neville stated,

> We found that some years ago cunning employers of labor preferred not to import coolie labor at all, but let their neighbours have the whole expense of importing the immigration labor, and then when those people bought themselves off at the end of two or three years, could give them a slightly higher wage, and so tempt them away from the people who had been through the expense of importing them. The result was that it was agreed all around that the fair thing was to make everybody pay something towards the immigration, i.e. everybody who employed it.[42]

Also,

> the largest employer of coolie labor in Trinidad pays nothing at all, that is, the government. This government of Trinidad is far and away the largest employer of coolie labor. They do not import any coolies themselves at all, but they trust to getting the work of time-expired coolies who have been imported by the estates. It is very often argued . . . that we who want the coolie labor should pay for it. That would be perfectly just if we got it, but if you will look at the figures in Trinidad you will see that we do not get a quarter of it. If you take the total number of coolies, not indentured coolies but all coolies in Trinidad, and see how many are on

the estates, I think you will be rather surprised. Somebody is getting the benefit of the work of those who are off the estates, and the largest benefactor is unquestionably the government of Trinidad.[43]

The Sanderson Commission noted that the immigrants themselves contributed substantially to the general revenues, since various articles consumed specially by the Indian population were subject to customs duties. It quoted a memorandum from the West India Committee to the effect that the average annual revenue received during the previous five years from customs duties on ghee, opium, ganja (marijuana), and rice was £30,486, nearly double the amount contributed from the general revenue towards the expenses of immigration.[44]

The Commission also addressed itself to the issue of the harshness of the penal provisions of the labor law and the frequency with which they were applied in Trinidad (as elsewhere). The Indian spokesmen George Fitzpatrick and F. E. M. Hosein had also raised these criticisms and concerns on behalf of those whom they represented. They recommended an enquiry with a view to its possible mitigation in application.[45]

Despite the apparent setback to the anti-indenture cause in 1909–10, the Creole political lobby continued to raise its objections in the Legislative Council. Just two years after, in 1912, new hope began to appear, this time from within India itself. Stephen Laurence called the Council's attention the following year to the Indian National Congress leader G. K. Gokhale's motion to abolish indentured immigration from India.

> Little did I think when, a year ago, I addressed this Council . . . on the subject of immigration, and put forward objections to that system from a West Indian standpoint, just a week after, on the other side of the world, an Honourable Member of the Imperial Legislative Council of India would have upheld the same objection, but from an entirely different standpoint, that of the East Indian.[46]

Quoting excerpts from Gokhale's speech, he noted that the sentiment of enlightened nationalist India was building against immigration, and he expressed optimism that in a very short time, immigration would come to a sudden end.

> the sentiment of all India was against immigration. That same member [Mr. Gokhale] assured the [Indian Legislative] Council that, on the day before, at a meeting of the Moslem League, a unanimous vote was arrived at against the continuance of indentured Indian immigration to these colonies, and that there was also a united vote from the Hindoo population

through the National Congress to the same effect, and thus the whole of
India had united to oppose the [system] and held that a legitimate conse-
quence of that combined sentiment was that the Indian Government
should give expression by law to the opinion thus expressed by united
India.

Laurence quoted again from Gokhale's speech:

"This motion, the Council may rest assured, will be brought forward again
and again until we carry it to a successful issue. It affects our national
self-respect, and therefore the sooner the Government recognise the necessity of stopping it, the better it will be for all parties."

Laurence concluded:

This is undoubtedly what enlightened national India thinks with respect
to immigration to this colony. . . . If the views of these gentlemen in
India are corroborated, we may take it that there is no such intention of
gradually decreasing immigration, and I have no doubt that in a very short
time, we shall witness a sudden stoppage of immigration.

As it turned out, he was right. Indian nationalism, emanating from
the source of emigration, had succeeded in doing what years of colored
and Black pressure group agitation in the West Indies had not been able
to do.[47] The development was sudden and decisive and totally unrelated
to West Indian circumstances. But it ushered in a new era, for it meant
not only that immigration from India had ended, but also that the free
labor market had finally been established in the West Indian plantation
system.

British Guiana after 1850

British Guiana in the peak years of the indenture system went through
a similar experience as the one described for Trinidad: the stabilization
and "Indianization" of the sugar plantation, the upward swing in production output, and the crisis in international prices after 1884–85, steady-
ing somewhat after 1903. The opposition to the indenture system was
just as vocal and came from the same social elements. But there were
important differences unique to British Guiana.

Chief among these was the highly politicized atmosphere of class/
race conflict which permeated the debates about immigration and which
persisted throughout the century. This was a legacy of the 1845–48 agita-

tion encouraged by the missionaries and the confrontational setting between planters and Black ex-slaves which formed the background to the immigrants' arrival in the colony. But there were other factors that kept this atmosphere of antagonism alive.

These included the failure of the new Black peasantry to develop any real autonomy outside the plantation framework, despite its early vigor; the absence of substantial alternative production sectors outside of sugar which could provide employment for the Black village population, and the consequent marginalization and pauperization of the Black labor force by a plantocracy determined to supplant Black labor with Indian immigrant labor; and the continuation of the class-biased fiscal policies of the planter-controlled regime, imposing exorbitant taxation on the Black population to finance the very immigration experiment that was reducing them to relative marginality within the system.

The peculiar problems posed by the Guianese coastal terrain, requiring expensive drainage and irrigation to prevent constant inundation of fields and villages, which often became uninhabitable and disease infested, proved in the final analysis to be too much for the Black villagers. The vigorous cooperative efforts at collective purchases of large properties which distinguished the early post-Emancipation Black Guianese village movement were not sustained at the level that really mattered, the level of collective maintenance of village lands in the peculiar Guianese coastland environment and collective productive efforts aimed at creating economic alternatives to sugar. Life outside the sugar plantation embrace proved more expensive and less easy to achieve than in neighboring Trinidad or Jamaica, and the Black peasantry found itself in the late 1850s and 1860s increasingly pauperized by a sugar plantocracy which did not wish to find itself repeating the social conflicts of the 1840s, and many sections of which kept trying to dispense with Black labor altogether.

The grievances of the Black laborers were aired by their Black and colored spokesmen in the small independent newspapers. The missionaries of the London Missionary Society had reduced their open activism after the conflicts of the 1840s, although individuals did continue that tradition at a lower level of public agitation. Until the 1891 constitutional reforms which paved the way for minimal Black representation on the legislature by the 1900s, the anti-immigration voice remained, as in Trinidad, on that level of articulation.

The Creole (1856–82) was one of the main champions of the displaced Black worker, and after the 1860s there was a proliferation of small papers, most with short life spans: the *Liberator* (1868–69), the *Penny Weekly* (1869), the *Workingman* (1872), the *Watchman* (1871–79), the *Echo* (1887–99), the *Reflector* (1889–92), the *Liberal* (1891–94). (The *Colonist* and the *Argosy* were the main planter voices, with the *Royal Gazette* and the *Chronicle* taking a somewhat more liberal stance.)

Many of the basic lines of criticism paralleled the general tone of the campaign in Trinidad. There was the same mixture of attacks upon the principle of indenture, the economic and political motivations of the importers of immigrant labor, and the immigrants themselves. There was also the special tone of class/race resentment bred by the Guianese situation. In 1857, the *Creole* labeled the new immigration "the enemy, instead of the auxiliary, of freedom."[48] The *Liberator* reported in 1869 that the managers of some estates on East Coast Demerara were abusive towards the Black workers beyond words. One discharged all his Blacks and applied for more immigrants. A letter to the *Creole* in 1868 pleaded to the planters to "accept" the Black workers and to employ them more extensively on the sugar plantations; it called on them to forget old scores, thirty years after Emancipation.

There was a constant complaint about favoritism being meted out to the Indian at the expense of the Black population, with nothing being done to restore mutual confidence between Black workers and the plantocracy. The *Workingman* declared in 1872 that the Indians had been granted a Royal Commission in 1870–71 to investigate their own grievances against the plantation system but that the plight of Blacks had not merited the same sympathetic official response. A letter to the *Watchman* also pointed out that, as a result of the Commission's recommendations, the Indians had been given a voice on the legislature (the Court of Policy) with the grant of a permanent seat to the Immigration Agent-General, while Blacks continued to have no such representative voice. A petition in 1871 for constitutional reform with this end in view had been rejected.

The continuation of the discriminatory taxation, which levied high taxes on consumer items used by the general population and much lower taxes on items required for plantation operations, remained throughout the century as a symbol of oppression against the Black community. By the late 1860s, no less than 94 percent of the general revenue was being raised by taxes on consumption, and about 3 percent on plantation supplies.[49] The view was also widely held—including, it would seem, by many small merchants—that the Indians themselves, with their hoarding propensities and extremely frugal lifestyle, were not as contributory to the general revenues as others were.

Newspapers and commentators called attention to the growing marginalization and pauperization of the Black community in the 1870s. Blacks who wanted to work in the sugar industry were not being allowed to, and many were forced to migrate to next-door Surinam in search of employment. There was alarm that the unsanitary state of the villages, the absence of adequate medical facilities for Blacks, and the escalating cost of living in the midst of steady pauperization were all leading to disturbing levels of crime and vagrancy among the young, to heavy mortality (infant and adult), and perhaps to an extinction of the Black race.

Public meetings protested the conditions of widespread poverty in the Black community, attributing this poverty to immigration; among these were the meetings convened in 1881 by Reverend Joseph Ketley at Victoria and Strick-en-Heuvel. In that year there was a formal investigation into poverty within the Black community. Details were published in the *Colonist*.

Formal petitions presented to government at various times during the post-1850 period, invariably after some form of public agitation, also distinguished the Guianese anti-immigration protest from its milder Trinidad counterpart. There were petitions in 1868, 1874, 1880, and 1903, in addition to a comprehensive memorandum submitted by the anti-immigration lobby to the Sanderson Commission in 1909.[50]

The 1868 petition tried to argue that a proper and sensible labor policy towards Blacks in the sugar industry would actually be less expensive to the colony than the existing immigration system. The 1874 petition was signed by some twenty-two leading merchants, and it argued a commonly held view that the Indians' "rude, unconsuming manner of living" made them bad for business, and for the economy in general. This petition called for more Chinese immigrants, deeming the latter to be better consumers.

The 1880 petition, which the Governor refused to entertain, insisted that if a fiftieth part of the money spent on immigration had been spent on Black labor, there would have been no labor problem on the plantations. It claimed that the Indians were being pampered at the expense of the taxpayers and were actually a burden to the colony. It called again for free voluntary immigration rather than state-subsidized indentured immigration.

Under the constitutional reforms introduced in 1891, a certain measure of direct election of representatives to the legislature was made possible for the first time, under a slightly widened franchise, and these reforms brought a number of Creole professional spokesmen into the public arena. By 1901 the anti-immigration lobby had acquired a national platform, and through leaders such as Patrick Dargan, A. A. Thorne, and A. B. Brown, as well as other elected representatives belonging to the new People's Association of British Guiana (no less than seven out of fourteen elected representatives in 1909), the campaign again picked up momentum.

A petition with 3,952 signatures was sent to the Secretary of State for the Colonies, J. Chamberlain, in 1903 after a number of public meetings on the issue. And in 1909, the People's Association sent a comprehensive memorandum to the Sanderson Commission, outlining all the classic arguments against the continuation of Indian indentured immigration which had become standard throughout the anti-immigration campaign.[51]

> Handled sympathetically, the emancipated race might have given such service in the cane-fields as would have rendered recourse to indentured immigration unnecessary. But the planters had made up their minds that the sugar industry could only be carried on through the agency of a labor supply working under the penal conditions attaching to indenture. . . .
>
> . . . indentured immigration from the East was designed merely as a temporary expedient and as complementary to the labor already available to the colony. . . . The system, however, as might have been expected, has ended by virtually displacing the native laborer in the cane-fields, except in respect to certain forms of work, such as cane cutting, which the East Indian, because of his feeble physique, is ill fitted to undertake.

The major complaints revolved around the following:

—the injustice involved in taxing the Black population for the benefit of an immigration meant to displace the Blacks in the economic order;

—the discriminatory imbalances in the taxation policies themselves, weighted as they were towards taxation on mass consumer items;

—the marginalization of the Black population, leaving them to become "a class without guidance—neglected by the Government and left to sink or swim in the battle of life";

—the absence of a stable Black peasant class and the government's failure to help the Black peasantry overcome the special challenges imposed by the Guianese terrain;

—the unfairness involved in reducing Westernized modern creatures such as the Black Guianese workers to wage levels that only the frugal, non-Western immigrant could survive on;

—the determination of the wage levels for the free laborers by the wage paid to the indentured worker, rather than the other way around, as the legislation intended;

—the distressing levels of mortality, poverty, and unemployment, especially as the opportunities in the gold mining industry had been lately reduced by about 75 percent;

—the burden of the public subsidy on the indenture experiment, which should have been financed totally by the planters themselves, who alone benefited from it; and

—the inefficient and wasteful utilization of labor in the sugar industry, detrimental to even the free Indian laborer.

As in the Trinidad case, the Sanderson Commission did not agree with the Guianese anti-immigration lobbyists. It pointed out:

> even if regular negro labor were available for the ordinary light agricultural work on estates, which is very doubtful, it is certain that the industry could not afford to pay the high wages demanded and would disappear.

It also insisted:

> There is no lack of land available for negroes who really desire agricultural work, and small holdings are provided for them on the same terms as for East Indians. Few of them, however, take up new land, and of the land they formerly held much has been sold to the East Indians. The production of coffee, for which agricultural conditions in the colony are suitable, is in the hands of the Blacks, but the Governor reported in 1908 that in spite of an import duty of 4½ cents per pound a considerable proportion of the coffee consumed had to be imported, "while coffee in full bearing could be found growing neglected inland."[52]

A similar point had been made by the Colonial Secretary of State in his reply to the 1903 petition.

> The failure of the coloured population . . . to develop or maintain the coffee or cotton industries, makes it impossible for me to approve a policy which would make these extensive territories a close preserve for those who have not yet shown that they are able or desire to make use of them.[53]

There the matter rested for another decade. There were some renewed polemics in the pages of the *Chronicle* and the planter-controlled *Argosy* in 1913 about the desirability of further state-aided immigration, but the debate subsided before the outbreak of the First World War. For the Creole critics of indenture, their persistent failures were a testimony less to the weakness of their intellectual arguments than to the weakness of their political influence in the colonial order. It was finally left to forces outside the West Indies to determine the fate of the Indian indenture experiment.

Anti-immigration Agitation in Jamaica

The Jamaican anti-immigration lobby was not activated in the first period of the Indian entry, 1845–48. Not until 1858, when the second immigration was about to begin and the legislature had passed an Immigration Bill with a view to facilitating the process, was there an organized public outcry against the proposed scheme. Religious organizations like the London Missionary Society and the Jamaica Baptist Union, and anti-slavery citizen bodies like the "Friends of Freedom" and the "Friends of the People," organized mass public meetings at Faimouth and Vere and called for support against the bill.

Petitions were sent to London claiming that there was no labor shortage, that workers were prepared to work for adequate wages under proper treatment, and that the bill was a blow to the emancipation process. A number of workers' strikes against the bill also took place in places like St. Thomas-in-the-East, St. Thomas-in-the-Vale, and Clarendon. Newspapers like the *Watchman* also opposed the bill. But the immigration experiment was allowed to recommence, amid this mild furor of opposition.

A major spokesman against the new immigration in the 1860s was the Reverend Henry Clarke, who protested, "This system is more unjust and inhuman than slavery and the slave trade. Under the old system planters imported slaves at their own expense, but now [they do so] at the expense of the public. Under the old system they had to pay people to catch them; now this is done for them by ordinary police."[54]

Reverend Clarke remained a thorn in the side of the authorities throughout the pre-1870 period, and at one point legal proceedings were initiated against him by the Governor for some of his allegations on the state of the indenture experiment, but these proceedings were eventually dropped on the instructions of the Secretary of State for the Colonies.

Revelations in a newspaper article about oppressive conditions among the Indians in 1867 led to the appointment by the Governor, Sir John Peter Grant, of a local committee of enquiry, but the report did not endorse these charges, though it did recommend a number of changes in the law.[55] Not much was achieved by way of arresting the immigration, which was nowhere near the scale of the Trinidad or Guianese immigration and was certainly less concretely disruptive to Black Jamaican society than it was to the Black laborer elsewhere, despite the claims of the opposition.

Even government officials, including many governors of the island, had been somewhat lukewarm on the desirability of continued immigration, although they did not do much about the issue. Former Governor Sir Sydney Olivier told the Sanderson Commission in 1909 that he had never been a strong advocate, although he recognized that some planters felt the need for its continuance, based on their own individual needs.

There was a decline in Indian arrivals in the 1880s and a fitful revival in the 1890s, picking up after 1899. By this time most of the indentured labor was being employed by the large banana plantations, including those of the United Fruit Company and the wealthy banana planter Sir John Pringle.

Agitation against the influx was carried on in the latter period by the Jamaica Baptist Union. The missionaries wrote constantly to the Governor and the Colonial Secretary, in addition to organizing public meetings on the issue.[56] They claimed that it did not make sense to be importing foreign labor at public expense when at the same time Jamaicans themselves were migrating in search of employment to Central America (Panama and Costa Rica) at the rate of about 25,000 a year. They also made the point about the Indians not contributing much to the local economy by way of consumer spending, given their frugal lifestyles and meager dietary traditions. In support of their agitation, they sought and received solidarity from fellow religionists, the Negro Baptists of America and the Baptist Union of Wales.

A colored medical doctor, Josiah Edwards, appeared before the Sanderson Commission in 1909 to make the case for the anti-immigration lobby in Jamaica.[57] Edwards was himself a banana planter from St. Catherine whose 80 to 150 workers were always about 20 to 25 percent free Indians, but he was on principle opposed to the immigration. He quoted from a recent resolution passed by an influential local club, known as the National Club, to the effect that the presence of Indian immigrants tended to depress the wages of the Jamaican worker to less than one shilling a day, to get away from which competition many had to forge permits to steal across to Panama in search of work.

He was uncertain whether "the immigration of the coolie brings about the emigration of the native, or whether the emigration of the native brings about the immigration of the coolie," but he did concede that both tended to equalize each other and suggested that were it not for the Central American option, things might have been more serious in Jamaica. He also offered some additional observations of his own:

> all their moneys are sent over to India, or nearly all, and none spent for the benefit of the island, except what they cannot help. And in addition to that they do not improve, to a certain extent, the manners of the natives. What I mean is, they improve themselves; they come up to a certain standard, and in that they are benefited; but there are certain habits which they do bring to the island. For instance, this drug, ganga—they call it Leaf of Friendship—is now universally smoked by the native laborer, and it is very bad. I do not say that there are not bad habits that the coolies get from the natives, but that is one thing that I had in my mind's eye when I spoke.

The position of the Sanderson Commissioners in their final report was very much influenced by the views of former Governor Sir Sydney Olivier, who testified before the Commission and also submitted documents in support of his arguments. Sir Sydney criticized the Jamaica Baptist Union for constantly confining itself to the broad generalization which nobody contested, that there was an abundant supply of labor on the island. The problem, he insisted, was that the laborers, except in certain districts where land was scarce and the people comparatively poor, did not care to work on the estates for the wages offered, and under the conditions they found on some of them.

Planters would have preferred if the industries involved could be carried on solely with the aid of Creole labor, and they had made repeated and unsuccessful efforts to attract local labor in preference to immigrant labor over the years. But this was just not available in many places.

> The fact is that the Jamaican who has land or stock, or is in any way exempt from the necessity of working regularly as a common laborer, can almost invariably, when the banana trade is active, do better for himself . . . by growing, higgling, carting, or as a stevedore shipping bananas for two or three days in the week than he can as an estate laborer. This will give him all the pocket money he needs, and if he has a ground he

will want to attend to it in the balance of the week. Where, as is not generally the case, or only the case in periods of drought and scarcity, he is under the necessity of working regularly as a common laborer, or of starving, he can get higher pay and a more congenial existence for conveniently intermittent periods by emigrating to work in Central America.[58]

Under these circumstances, it appeared to the planters, and to the government of the colony, that estate industries should not be allowed to collapse so long as Indian immigrants could be obtained for them on terms advantageous both to themselves and to their employers. The arrangement did not operate to the disadvantage of the Creole laborer, since there was no real competition involved in their usage.

A letter from the Colonial Secretary to the Jamaica Baptist Union dated February 3, 1910, also stressed the same point. Banana planters in Portland and St. Mary were simply not able to attract Black labor from the other parishes on a steady basis. They could not compete with the higher wages offered in Colon and Port Limon. Moreover,

> The climate of the fruit-growing districts is new to them and affects their health; their housing is unhomely, and they miss their friends and families; the work is new and sometimes irksome to them, and the pay is not high enough, as it sounds in Colon and Costa Rica, to balance these discomforts. And as there is no difficulty in leaving their job whenever the inclination takes them they do so, and drift elsewhere.[59]

There were eighty-three estates employing only 4,000 Indian indentured laborers in 1912–13, when the McNeill-Lal delegation visited the island, and a total Indian population of just over 17,000, on an island of roughly 800,000 people.[60] Given this numerical smallness, and the fact that the financial burdens of the immigration in Jamaica by the turn of the century were being borne mainly by the planters themselves, quite unlike the other West Indian territories, the anti-immigration lobby did not appear to have as strong a case here as they seemed to in the other plantation colonies.

CHAPTER 7

Beyond Indenture: Chinese Mobility and Assimilation Patterns

The process by which the immigrants came to terms with their new societies after the end of their five-year terms of indenture was complex and multifaceted, with each group exploring its own range of limited options in its own fashion, depending on time, place, and subjective aspiration and capacity. The Chinese were not entitled to free return passages after ten years' residence in the colony, and this influenced their movement out of the plantation milieu at a quicker pace than the Indians (who indeed never totally abandoned that milieu, even into the late twentieth century). Like the Madeiran Portuguese before them, they showed no lasting affinity for life as plantation laborers on the sugar estates of their new environment and seized the opportunity to move into occupations that gave them a fuller measure of independence and control over their own destinies.

The movement away from wage labor, however, was clearly dependent on the nature of the alternatives open to them at any given moment. In British Guiana that movement was manifestly less speedy than it was in Trinidad, and when the 1870–71 Commission of Enquiry wrote its report, that fact was something on which the Commissioners commented. Small-scale farming, growing a variety of old and new crops for the domestic market, and retail trading, mainly of foodstuffs and liquor, constituted the primary early options open to them; the latter option eventually predominated and grew in the more mature stages into a large-scale urban import and wholesale distributive sector, among the more successful. The eventual movement away from agriculture—whether as small-scale or large-scale traders—distinguished the Chinese mobility and assimilation trends from those of their Indian immigrant counterparts, who remained overwhelmingly agriculturists into the twentieth century.

A significant number, mainly in British Guiana, prolonged their plantation lives by reindenturing for additional five-year terms, attracted by the offer of the $50 bounty, representing almost ten months' wages. In 1870, there were still 6,369 Chinese—5,210 indentured, 1,159 free—on the Guianese plantations, in a community of approximately 7,000 to 8,000. More than half of the indentureds were in their second term.[1] When reindenture became too expensive for the planters to continue in the mid-1870s, the movement away from the plantations quickened. By 1879, the Chinese population on the sugar estates had fallen to about 50 percent (3,129 of 6,322), 90 percent of whom were unindentured.

Reindenture in Trinidad was confined to one-year periods, at bounties of $10, and the number and percentage of those who availed themselves of this option was quite small. The tendency in Trinidad was actually in the other direction, that is, to try to commute the original five-year term of service after accumulating some savings and strike out on their own. This was the case even before 1858—with the earliest arrivals. The phenomenon of flight from the estates, as we have mentioned in chapter 4, was also more marked in Trinidad, with the result that in 1870 a mere handful of Chinese were still engaged as plantation workers, in contrast with their compatriots in British Guiana. In a total Chinese community of 1,400 in 1871, a mere 303 were still officially registered as estate workers, and 175 of these were absentees.[2] By 1875 there were none.

The Chinese in Trinidad

The crops that attracted the Trinidad Chinese small farmers (or market gardeners, as they were sometimes called) were unusually diverse for such a tiny community of agricultural producers. Some of the 1853 contingent went into corn and potato growing, which the Immigration Report of 1862 reported as having assumed "large dimensions" by that year. One writer recorded that one grower realized as much as $900 from his potato crop in 1859.[3] Mostly, they concentrated on growing local root crops ("ground provisions") to replace the imports of these staples from the smaller West Indian islands. The cultivation of sweet potatoes was apparently a Chinese specialty, and one farmer was held to have realized $1,000 from his 1865 crop.[4]

Many pioneered in popularizing the cultivation of certain vegetables—for instance, carrots, turnips, cabbages—in addition to the standard vegetable fare. Underhill voiced the opinion that "they understand tillage better than any other class of laborers."[5] De Verteuil, a White Creole historian, described them as "the best gardeners in the colony," responsible for supplying the local markets with most of their vegetables in the 1850s.[6] Some supplied the markets directly; others grew on a large scale and sold the produce to smaller suppliers, often Indian. There were Chinese pork butchers and, according to one writer in the 1860s, a thriving Chinese oyster trade in San Fernando.[7] A handful went into cocoa cultivation; still more acted as intermediaries (cocoa dealers) between the small rural producers and the exporters in the city.

Their main economic activity, however, was in the retail trades. The village shopkeeper in Trinidad by the late 1850s was, more often than not, a Chinese. A memorandum of 1857 by Charles Warner, Chairman of the Legislative Council Committee on Immigration, stated, "A large portion of the retail trade of the rural districts is in their hands."[8] The Chinese trader in the sugar districts often had reciprocal relations with the managers or overseers of neighboring estates, by which the latter would deduct from workers' wage payments money owed to the Chinese trader by immigrants who had taken goods on credit, in exchange for a small commission for their services.[9]

The Warner memorandum cited the specific case of one Chinese who had been indentured to the Jordan Hill estate in 1853 and who had become within four years after his arrival an affluent shopkeeper: he had a capital of at least $3,000 and commanded a mercantile credit to the extent of $5,000. The Immigration Report for 1863 commented on the success of the 1853 contingent of Chinese immigrants:

> in Trinidad, many of [the Chinese] who originally landed as contract laborers have now, by patient industry, attained a fair position in life, acquired houses, land and commercial influence. The Agent [in China] may point to those who have returned to China after ten years' residence here with comparative wealth, and these men, five of whom left Trinidad this month for Hong Kong, may tell their compatriots there, that having overcome the earlier difficulties inseparable from expatriation, they not only managed to live with comfort, but to carry back with them from $3,000 to $4,000 each, and that the same good fortune awaits those who unflinchingly pursue the same career.[10]

When the Reverend Charles Kingsley wrote At Last: A Christmas in the West Indies, based on his visit to the region in 1869, he also had cause to remark on the relative affluence of some of the Chinese whom he saw in the villages and the local churches in Trinidad.[11]

In the 1870s, the arrivals of 1862 began to follow in the footsteps of their successful predecessors. An article in the *Trinidad Chronicle* in January 1877 made mention of one Atteck, a shopkeeper and property holder, considered to be worth about £12,000, as well as one Soui (who had apparently adopted the Christian name of Daniel O'Connell), reported to be worth half that amount.[12] Even the previously undisciplined elements began to carve out niches for themselves in the larger society. Prison statistics for the 1870s and 1880s demonstrated that this element had slowly settled down to stable lives. The number of Chinese imprisoned for small and large offenses decreased from 143 in 1871 to 35 in 1873, 25 in 1874, 44 in 1875, and 30 in 1876.[13] By the 1880s the figures were 17 in 1886, 6 in 1887, 7 in 1888, 15 in 1889, and 8 in 1890.[14]

By the mid-1880s, and certainly by the time of the census of 1891, the vast majority of the small Chinese community in Trinidad had gravitated out of its early duality of occupation (part agriculturist, part small trader). Most found themselves in the latter occupation, jostling side by side with their Portuguese, Indian, and Black counterparts, but having—at least in Trinidad—an image of being the most successful of these groups in this field.

The geographical spread of the community had also increased, with a more pronounced urban orientation taking root by this time. The percentage of Chinese living in the northern urbanizing sections of the island (Port-of-Spain, and the county of St. George stretching from east to west) had moved from 39.3 percent (181) in 1861, to 41.5 percent (581) in 1871, to 57.8 percent (732) by 1881, and 61.3 percent (617) by 1891.[15] Those living in the primarily sugar districts of Central and South Trinidad (Caroni, Victoria, St. Patrick counties, and the town of San Fernando) had declined accordingly, from a high of 58.2 percent (815) in 1871, to 40 percent (507) in 1881, to 32 percent (324) in 1891.

Until the twentieth century, there was hardly any significant Chinese presence in the East Trinidad counties of Nariva and Mayaro, these being relatively depressed agricultural areas. By far the largest number lived in the capital city, Port-of-Spain (285), followed by various small towns and villages within the northern county of St. George, especially the cocoa-growing wards of Tacarigua and Arima (272).[16]

After the turn of the century, Central and South Trinidad again saw a slight percentage increase in Chinese, who were perhaps drawn again to these areas by the early oil prosperity there: 38.7 percent (322) in 1901, 42.8 percent (476) in 1911, 44.6 percent (596) in 1921. The North registered correspondingly mild declines (more Tacarigua and Arima wards than Port-of-Spain proper): 51.3 percent (427) in 1901, 39 percent (440) in 1911, 38 percent (510) in 1921.[17]

Despite this shift again towards the South, however, Port-of-Spain proper remained the major single center of residential concentration of the Chinese community, increasing steadily in numbers with each decade (from 200 in 1901 to 252 in 1911, 409 in 1921, and 670 by 1931). Some of the areas in the South to which they were drawn were themselves new urbanizing centers, such as La Brea and Siparia, in addition to the older Princes Town.

Whether based in the North, Central Trinidad, or the South, in the towns or the villages, the Chinese had become by the late 1880s, and certainly by 1891, an overwhelmingly small-trader community. This is confirmed by the 1891 census, which recorded that the largest single occupational category was that of shopkeeper (341, or 33.9 percent), followed by "salesman, shopman, clerk," that is, people employed in shop establishments (259, or 25.7 percent). These figures combined would make those involved in small-trading activities amount to 600, or 59.6 percent of the China-born community.[18] The census also recorded the existence of 23 big merchants and traders, presumably wholesalers and importers (13 of them based in Port-of-Spain), as well as 6 hotel keepers (3 in Arima, 1 in Port-of-Spain, 1 in San Fernando, 1 in Oro-pouche).[19]

By contrast, those involved in agriculture, mainly as small producers, had dwindled to a mere 45–47 by 1891. About half of these were residents of the northern ward of Diego Martin. There were 5 cocoa and coconut estate owners. Other occupations in which the Chinese were engaged in 1891 involved "indoor domestic servants" (100), hucksters and peddlers (43), general laborers and porters (32), "mechanics and handicraftsmen" (29), and charcoal sellers (6).[20] There was 1 person functioning as an interpreter and 1 as a bailiff, both based in San Fernando in the south. There were 3 bookkeepers. The census also recorded the existence of 6 paupers (mendicants), 5 of whom were female. In 1891 there were just 3 Chinese males in the Trinidad prisons, 2 in the Royal Gaol in Port-of-Spain, and 1 in Carrera Island convict depot.[21]

The Chinese community underwent a steady decline in size after the last arrivals of 1866 until the first decade of the new century, when it was augmented by the new immigration, this time free and voluntary.

The censuses for the years between 1861 and 1931 placed the Chinese at 461 in 1861, 1,400 in 1871, 1,266 in 1881, 1,006 in 1891, 832 in 1901, then upwards to 1,113 in 1911, 1,334 in 1921, and 2,027 in 1931.[22]

There were some areas of unreliability in these figures. The 1861 count, for example, was clearly an underestimate, and it is possible that either the census enumerators were inaccurate or there were many Chinese who did not wish to face these strangers with their questionable motivations during the taking of the census. This uncertainty would also surround many of the other head counts, but we can take them to be rough indicators of the state of the China-born community.

The other area of uncertainty surrounds the methodology of the head count. In some censuses, "Chinese" also meant "pure Chinese of local birth," although it is clear that in some later ones, such as 1921 and possibly even before, "Chinese" meant strictly "China-born." Mixed Chinese (offspring of one Chinese parent) were generally classified as "native Trinidadian," and only after 1931 were they specifically enumerated as a distinct group.[23]

This having been said, the fact remains that towards the end of the nineteenth century the Chinese community had not been reinvigorated by fresh arrivals from China in any significant manner, since the 1860s. The 1891 census revealed that a full 810, or 80.5 percent, of the 1,006 Chinese on the island were over forty years old, and that there was just 1 person under twenty, a twelve-year-old boy. However, small interisland movements had been a regular feature of life since the 1860s. A few Trinidad and Guianese Chinese had remigrated to work on Jamaican estates in the 1860s, and Guianese ex-indentured Chinese were constantly remigrating to Trinidad and Surinam. There was even one unusual case of a Chinese man who found his way to Trinidad in 1866 all the way from Cardenas in Cuba, after having escaped an attempt to reindenture him on that island for an additional four-year term beyond his eight-year service. He had escaped from Cuba in 1862 with another Chinese aboard an American ship and had lived in Halifax, Canada, for four years before attempting to relocate to Trinidad.[24]

The census of 1891 made mention of two or three wealthy Chinese "from California and elsewhere" who had established mercantile houses in Port-of-Spain. It stated also, "During the past ten or fifteen years there has been a considerable migration of Chinese between Trinidad and the neighboring colonies, with an evident excess of immigration over emigration and a consequent gain to this colony." No effort was made to quantify this increase, but the British Guiana immigration reports for the twenty-year period between 1885 and 1904 recorded the grants of legal passports to 223 Chinese for travel to Trinidad. The 1880 report recorded 197 traveling to Trinidad in that year alone. (The traffic was not all one-way: 89 Chinese between 1875 and 1878, and 45 between 1882 and 1889, were recorded as coming from the neighboring colonies, most presumably from Trinidad.)

Efforts to encourage free migration of Chinese settlers from China had never really borne fruit. The British Guiana exercise of 1879 had been the only successful example of this effort. As early as 1862 Reverend Lobscheid had suggested it in relation to both colonies, but nothing had materialized. In 1883–84 the proposed experiment of the Chinese shipping agent and entrepreneur Mr. Tong King Sing (described in chapter 4) had not borne fruit either. Migrations by individual family members had added to the stock of Chinese during the late nineteenth century. But it was not until the revolutionary years just before and after the collapse of the Ch'ing dynasty in 1911 that the free migration flow slowly began to augment the numbers already residing on the island. Mostly, they came from Hong Kong or from the same Cantonese districts as the earlier migrants (via Hong Kong). Moreover, they usually came on the basis of some family or clan relationship or contact on the island, or through the efforts of island-based business intermediaries with connections in the China districts or villages from which the new migrants came. More often than not, the main districts were those from which the earlier migrants had originated. More often than not also, those who left China in this period also had relatives or friends or neighbors from the same or nearby districts who were simultaneously migrating to other destinations in the Western Hemisphere: the United States, Peru, Surinam, British Guiana, Jamaica, and even Cuba.[25] Many would try several destinations before settling in one. By 1931, the China-born community had reached 2,027, an increase of 1,195, or almost 150 percent, in thirty years, while the local-born Chinese stood at 2,054, plus 1,158 of mixed parentage (one Chinese parent).[26] The Guiana-derived element would also have added a few hundred more to this amalgam.

Already, by the close of the nineteenth century, there were a number of prominent and well-known names among the Chinese mercantile class: Kang Lee, trading as Lee Kang and Company, importers of Chinese goods, tea, silk, and mattings, on Queen Street in Port-of-Spain; E. Lee, manager of the Orinoco line of steamers, on King Street; Lee Lum and Company and Kwong Lee and Company, both on Charlotte Street, large merchant houses dealing in foodstuffs, liquor, household consumer goods, Chinese merchandise, and also in cocoa. Other major licensed cocoa dealers listed in the business directories around 1910 included Marlay and Company, William Scott, William Akow, and Thomas Twong Sing. Major licensed pharmacists included Cornelius Henry Tywang and Alfred Richards.

The Trinidad Almanack for 1910 also listed a number of Chinese cocoa estate owners: E. B. Acham (later known as Eugene Chen), owner of San Isidore in Sangre Grande; Amelia Akow, owner of St. Amelia in Carenage; Eliza Hosang, owner of Adventure in Toco; Jacob Lee Aping, owner of La Horquetta in Tacarigua; J. R. Tom, owner of Pays Perdu and St. Madeleine in Chaguanas. The list is not exhaustive. The Marlay firm had large holdings in the Sangre Grande–Manzanilla region. John Lee Lum, a multifaceted immigrant businessman who also invested in the fledgling oil industry (the only Chinese to do so), owned several large cocoa estates, mainly in the Manzanilla and Montserrat regions, and a number of coconut estates in the southeast region of Mayaro. Both Kwong Lee and Company and Lee Lum and Company dated from the 1880s, and the latter seems to have been an offshoot of the former around 1885.[27] Lee Lum also owned a large number of retail shops throughout the island—about twenty—involved in selling foodstuffs and hardware from the 1890s. Up to his death in 1921, he was the acknowledged head of the Chinese community in Trinidad. (He settled in Hong Kong in 1908.) He also played a prominent role in the social affairs of the wider colonial society and was a member of the West India Committee.

The Chinese in British Guiana

In marked contrast with Trinidad, the early British Guiana Chinese experienced great initial difficulties in moving away from the plantation environment. The dubious attractions of reindenture—with its $50 bounty—apart, there was simply none of the easy mobility within the colony of the kind that enabled their Trinidad counterparts to find a quick niche outside the sugar estates. When the Commissioners conducted their investigations in 1870–71, that complaint from the Chinese was one which they felt obliged to record. In paragraph 328 of their report, this is how they phrased it:

> One of the complaints made to us here by the Chinese was that there was no other employment open to them but estates' work; and when it is

considered that the Portuguese, from their prior introduction, have a complete monopoly of the retail trade of the colony, that Crown lands cannot be purchased in blocks of less than 100 acres, and that it is very difficult to find private lands for sale, their complaints seem to be well founded.

The land question, and the Portuguese retail trade monopoly, did not exist in Trinidad to the same degree, and the relative absence of these obstacles had enabled the 1853 contingent to gain a head start as a small-farmer and small-trader community over its Guianese counterpart. Some small-scale farming had taken place in British Guiana, but in a style typical to that colony: on the estate lands themselves, that is, portions of idle land granted to some of the laborers by the planters themselves as an incentive to keep them wedded to plantation labor. On these small plots the Chinese would grow food for themselves, plus vegetables and root staples for a limited domestic market; they would also mind pigs and poultry.

However, the levels of land grant and consequently the levels of production were far below what would be required to enable the Chinese to develop into an economically viable community on their own. The allocations were very uneven. Of 248 acres so distributed, 110 were on two plantations alone. Moreover, about 2,000 of the 6,369 Chinese in 1870 had no land allocations at all. The 1871 report felt that most of the plots of land designated as gardens were not worthy of the name. However, they commented favorably on those they saw among the Chinese at Windsor Forest and Leonora.[28] Thus, as we have seen, most of them were still plantation laborers well into the late 1870s, although the decline of reindenture encouraged more of them to strike out on their own into the larger society.

One option that they did exercise quite frequently was that of migration to other West Indian territories. Trinidad and next-door Surinam (Dutch Guiana) were favorite destinations; some went to Jamaica. During the 1870s there was even an organized migration flow to St. Lucia, which it would seem was handled for a time by influential elements within the two local administrations until it was officially discouraged in British Guiana. Several indentured Chinese illegally broke their contracts and participated clandestinely in this scheme, until in 1876 passports were withheld from those who had not yet served out their full terms of service, unless they could repay the full cost of their passage money from China.

The records of Chinese departing from the colony in these years were very unreliable. Former magistrate Des Voeux claimed in his letter to the Colonial Office in 1869 that these departures were very few because of the strict supervision kept on outgoing vessels, yet he could not account for the great decline in numbers as reflected in the official statistics, a decline that was not explicable by the informal emigration returns and the death returns. There were no formal emigration statistics before 1881, but the Annual Immigration Report for 1882 recorded 2,143 Chinese departures between 1872 and 1882 (destinations unrecorded).

It is clear that clandestine emigration, similar to the Trinidad-Venezuela connection in the case of the Indians, was the only explanation for the severe decline in the Chinese community in the 1870s and 1880s. A community that stood at a maximum of 10,022 in 1866 was a mere 6,880 in 1871, and 5,234 in 1881.[29] It was reported that Chinese middlemen got bounties of $80 a head for Chinese introduced into Surinam, and bounties of $20 for those introduced into Trinidad. There was also a widespread passport racket, in which those who migrated to Trinidad and Surinam with legal passports would sell them for reuse by other Chinese inside British Guiana.[30]

Up to 1870, the Chinese who had acquired property in British Guiana were a mere fraction of the total community. Des Voeux stated that these were mainly gambling house owners, drivers, and no more than a dozen shopkeepers. A small handful took to illicit rum distillation, rum smuggling, and brothel keeping, as mentioned before. The 1871 report reiterated, "The Chinese, in other colonies, have monopolised the retail trade, and the raising of vegetables for the market, but in British Guiana, the Portuguese who came before them have got possession of the retail trade, and most of the market gardening, and show no signs of being extruded from it."[31]

The same point about the relative disadvantages faced by the Guianese Chinese was made in a petition by members of the Chinese community to the Governor in 1865, applying for a grant of Crown land to enable some of them to establish a small agricultural settlement of free Chinese. The petitioner, a Chinese missionary named Wu Tai Kam (O Tye Kim), stated as follows:

> Your petitioner on his arrival in this colony remarked with surprise, that his people were not as prosperous here as those who had been an equal time in other countries; the few exceptions having for the most part become such by gambling and other disreputable means; and he has become aware in the course of his labors, that a large proportion of the immigrants are in consequence dissatisfied with their condition and prospects, and are contemplating emigration at the end of their indentures. They have heard

that their countrymen in the neighboring colony of Trinidad are in a comparatively flourishing condition; that many there are growing rich in the pursuit of trade and in the cultivation of the soil; and this knowledge has added to their discontent, and confirmed their determination to go elsewhere.[32]

In supporting the petition for a grant of land for a free Chinese settlement, the Governor conceded that the social positions of the Chinese communities of Trinidad and British Guiana in the mid-1860s were strikingly different, that "the Portuguese element of our population occupies the same position as the Chinese in Trinidad," and that something must be done, or else "the Chinese will be found to emigrate from this colony en masse." A few members of the Court of Policy objected to the idea of a special settlement on the ground that it might afford an asylum for discontented indentured Chinese laborers "who might take refuge there and defy all the police in the colony to capture them."[33]

The personal influence of the main petitioner was largely responsible for getting the project endorsed by the government. Wu Tai Kam had been a Christian convert and a lay preacher in Singapore for about thirteen years before his arrival in the colony in 1864. He had traveled to London and met influential figures in the Society for the Propagation of the Gospel in Foreign Parts, who had been instrumental in getting him sent to British Guiana, where he met the Immigration Agent-General and the Governor. He also became very influential among the Chinese, forming a congregation of about 120 Chinese Christians soon after his arrival. The petition for lands to found a Chinese settlement, plus a £600 government loan, was approved in early 1865, and Hopetown Settlement, named after Vice-Admiral Sir James Hope after a visit there, was founded at Kamuni Creek, in the county of Demerara, 30 miles from Georgetown.

By the end of the year, Hopetown Settlement had 170 Chinese settlers, most of them drawn from the Christian Chinese converts at Plantation Skeldon in Berbice, mainly men who had previously come to British Guiana together in 1860. The settlement was initially very successful, and the close-knit Chinese community there grew a variety of crops for the domestic market (potatoes, cassava, plantains, bananas, ginger, vegetables of all kinds, and rice). They also reared livestock (cattle, pigs, poultry) and excelled in the manufacture and sale of charcoal and shingles, even breaking the Portuguese monopoly in this industry within a few short years. The community had a shop at Hopetown and one in the capital, Georgetown, where farming supplies and the products grown by the settlers were distributed.

So pleased were the authorities with the success of this experiment that the Governor agreed to the proposal that free immigrants be encouraged to come from China specifically to Hopetown, on voluntary two-year terms of service (no wages, but free food and clothing and free passage to British Guiana) after which they could set themselves up as independent settlers. The proposal was supported by the Emigration Commissioners in London and by Sampson, the emigration agent in China in 1866. Wu Tai Kam was even appointed as the official missionary to the Chinese at a salary of £300 per annum in August 1866.

The proposal never got off the ground, however. Early in 1867, Wu Tai Kam found himself in the middle of a personal scandal, having got a colored woman pregnant. He was himself a married man, with a wife and three children in Singapore. He was forced to flee in disgrace in July, with three of his close followers, and it was assumed that he was headed for Trinidad. He was never heard from again but was reported to have settled in China after a short sojourn in the United States.

Hopetown Settlement continued to exist as a viable enterprise, and when the Commissioners made their investigations in 1870, they paid it a visit. They commented unfavorably on the poor drainage system, which they said rendered most of the land not near the stream useless for cultivation. They also felt that the settlement was too far from Georgetown and from "the support of civilising associations and rules." However, they thought the experiment to be worthwhile and an example on which other settlements could improve.[34]

There were in fact other smaller Chinese land settlements which were established with government help in the 1870s and 1880s: along the Demerara River, on the west coast of Demerara, as well as on the Corentyne coast in Berbice. One village in Upper Corentyne (No. 72) with a thriving rice cultivation was actually known as "Hong Kong" or "Chinaland" because of its sizeable Chinese community.[35] In 1881 there were 161 Chinese in the Upper Corentyne District. Most had established settlements there around the mid-1870s, having terminated their indentures at Plantation Skeldon nearby.

Hopetown itself continued to decline from an estimated population of 567 (311 men, 123 women, 133 children) in 1871 to about 240 in 1891, 198 in 1901, and a mere 73 by 1911. Its exclusively Chinese character had also disappeared by the 1890s, and it became a racially heterogeneous and amorphous farming settlement, not bound by either ethnicity or religion as the original community was designed to be. An official who visited the settlement in 1914 estimated it to have twenty-three houses with a total population of 76 souls, broken down as follows: 26 males and 20 females of pure Chinese descent, 1 male and 6 females of mixed Chinese and Negro race, 7 females of mixed Chinese and mulatto race, 2 males of mixed Chinese and Portuguese race, and 14 with no Chinese blood at all, being 2 males and 5 females of Negro stock, 1 male and 3 female East Indians, and 3 female mulattoes.[36]

Whatever the initial difficulties experienced by the Chinese in moving out of the plantation milieu, by the late 1880s they had succeeded in overcoming most of them. The emergence of a vibrant small-trader community, large enough to challenge the Portuguese domination of this sector, was reflected in the immigration report statistics for 1891: 50.6 percent of the 784 food shop licenses held by Asians were Chinese, as were 89.3 percent of the 320 licenses for the sale of liquor (spirits, wines, and malts). By the 1890s, Chinese shopkeepers were not only widespread throughout the villages of the colony, but also dominant in several urban areas: Lombard Street in Georgetown, Main Street in New Amsterdam. The *Colonist* newspaper had commented as early as August 1877: "In Lombard Street it will soon be the exception to meet men of any other race."[37]

The large import and wholesale traders had also emerged by the 1880s: Kwong-San-Lung and Company was importing merchandise directly from China by then. Chinese were also druggists, butchers, hucksters, cart and boat cab owners, barbers, laundrymen, and legal sellers of opium and ganja (marijuana) by the 1890s.

Cecil Clementi, in his 1915 study, *The Chinese in British Guiana*, provided portraits of a number of individual Chinese families who had achieved prominence by the last quarter of the nineteenth century, most of them not only merchants but also large plantation owners. Among them was the family of John Ho-a-Shoo (1852–1906), who came with the *Corona* in 1874 and ten to fifteen years later was a sugar estate owner and prominent merchant (Ho-a-Shoo Ltd.) with several businesses in both the sugar-bearing and gold-mining areas of the colony. Three of his children studied at the University of Edinburgh in the 1900s and 1910s, two of them medicine and a third agriculture. One—a girl, Asin—became a Fellow of the Royal College of Surgeons and eventually settled in Hong Kong in 1915. Another family of merchants and estate owners was that of David Ewing-Chow, whose father arrived on the *Dora* in 1860 and whose two sons were in 1915 studying in England, one a law student at Cambridge, the other a medical student at Edinburgh. One of George-town's leading jewelers, based on Lombard Street, was M. U. Hing, whose grandfather had lost all his possessions in China, a victim of the Taiping Rebellion, and whose father Wu A-Hing had migrated to British Guiana as a mere boy on the *Chapman* in 1861.

The most famous figure in 1915 was the Chinese empire builder Wong Yan-Sau (also known as Evan Wong), who came to British Guiana at the age of ten with his parents on the *Dartmouth* in 1879. By 1915 he was "one of the wealthiest colonists in British Guiana," owner of the Omai gold mines in Essequibo and several thousands of acres of planta-tions in East Coast Demerara and Essequibo, growing sugar, cocoa, coffee, rubber, coconuts, and timber; he was a merchant and landlord of several businesses and properties in Georgetown and in the rural areas. He was also "connected with the gold and diamond industries, . . . owner of several balata grants, and largely interested in the timber industry . . . possessor of several saw-mills, . . . shareholder in many companies in Georgetown, and owner of several racehorses as well as of a number of brood-mares." In 1915 one of his eight children was a student of civil engineering at Bristol University in England.[38]

Despite the successful mobility of the Chinese in British Guiana in the last portion of the nineteenth century, leading to the establishment of greater ties with the colony, there was no lessening of the large-scale downward trend in population numbers described earlier, far more sig-nificant than comparable trends in Trinidad during the same period. The census figures for the Chinese community since the 1870s were 6,880 in 1871, 5,234 in 1881, 3,714 in 1891, 2,622 in 1911, and 2,722 in 1921 (there was no census in 1901). These statistics included 841 locally born Chinese in 1881, 1,239 in 1891, 1,988 in 1911, and 2,346 in 1921. Thus in 1881 there were 4,393 China-born, 2,475 in 1891, a mere 634 in 1911, and 376 in 1921.[39]

Not all of this steep decline is explicable by the dying out of the older generation and lack of fresh immigrants until the 1910s (actually 1,718 came from China between 1879 and 1915). Emigration from British Guiana was a constant in the 1870s and 1880s. Clementi stated that formal emigration statistics recorded a net loss of 1,963 between 1881 and 1902, with 2,141 leaving and 178 arriving. The immigration reports even recorded the formal destinations of most of those who received passports between 1885 and 1904: 223 to Trinidad, 157 to Surinam (including Nickerie), 150 to Cayenne, 123 to China, 52 to Colon, 22 to Jamaica, 3 to St. Lucia, 2 to Mauritius, 1 each to England and Barbados.

Between 1903 and 1913, the departure total was 1,874 and the arrival figure 1,630, making a net loss of 244.[40]

Only after the 1911 census does the Chinese community in British Guiana (China born and locally born) begin to evidence an upward increase. In 1921 the numbers were 2,722, a net increase of 100 in ten years; in 1931, 2,951; and in 1946, 3,567. This not only reflected a natural increase in the local-born community, but also corresponded with the new postwar influx that also took place in Trinidad, as well as Jamaica.

The minuscule prewar Jamaican contingent of free Chinese, meanwhile, augmented by sporadic inflows from the other territories, had also evidenced the same trends towards small-scale retail shopkeeping and urbanization. By 1891, 61.3 percent of that community were Kingston residents, as we saw in chapter 4, a mere seven years after their arrival on the island. The real development of the Jamaican Chinese community began with the twentieth-century postwar influx. Jamaica and Trinidad were the main recipients of the new migration, and Jamaica's tiny Chinese community escalated from virtual insignificance in the nineteenth century to the position of being the largest and most vibrant in the twentieth (not counting Cuba). By 1943 the community numbered 6,879 (2,818, or 41 percent, of them China-born immigrants), compared with Trinidad's 5,641 (2,366, or 42 percent, China born), and British Guiana's 3,567 (548, or 15.4 percent, China born).[41]

Assimilation Trends

Chinese assimilation patterns in West Indian plantation society evolved against the background of the society's uniqueness—its colonial historical context, its Euro-African-Amerindian heterogeneity, its New World social environment. Compared with their contemporary counterparts who were migrating—often from the same districts in the Cantonese region—to North America, the Chinese who went to the West Indies remigrated to China less easily and frequently, distance and cost of passage being prohibitive factors, as well as the fact that they were not entitled like their Indian indentured counterparts to a free return passage. Return trips to China, whether permanently or for a short visit, were definitely only for the affluent, those who had achieved a certain measure of economic success after their years of indenture were over.

Whatever they had been led to believe before they had embarked for the West Indies (or Latin America generally), that success was not automatic or easily attainable. There was no local equivalent of a gold rush, only the most difficult and backbreaking plantation labor, under conditions that were hardly designed to facilitate their accumulation of wealth. Some planters had even objected in the 1860s to the continuation of Chinese immigration on the ground that their frequent tendency to leave the plantations at the earliest opportunity was detrimental to the purpose of the immigration experiment.

It was a waste of public funds, they felt, to be encouraging the immigration of "future shopkeepers" rather than a group of natural agriculturists.[42] No official mobility mythology, no "West Indian dream," entered this indenture experiment to mystify its main purpose. If social advancement was always possible, it was achievable only after the contractual period was over, hardly ever during that period itself.

Sampson, the emigration agent in China after Austin's departure in 1862–63, was complaining in 1865 that the emigration effort was being hampered by the failure of the West Indies–bound Chinese to return to China to demonstrate to their compatriots the concrete benefits of this experiment. He stated that none had returned by 1865, compared with the few from Cuba and Peru. In fact, this was not true. Whatever the difficulties of the West Indian environment, there was always the vigorous minority who succeeded early in triumphing over the environmental odds. About seven of the 1853 Trinidad batch had returned to Canton by 1862, and a further five to Hong Kong by 1864.[43] Some of them went for brief visits before returning to Trinidad, where they had become successful businessmen. Five more returned to China from Trinidad in 1869 on the *Arima*, intending to return. They took with them $7,500 (£1,562 10s.)—£312 10s. each.[44]

Even in British Guiana, where conditions for self-improvement were admittedly difficult in the early years, a family of 8 (3 men, 4 women, 1 child) returned on the *Ganges* in 1869, a few years after Sampson's complaint, carrying with them savings totaling around £1,166 13s. 4d. The head of the family also had an £83 letter of credit to defray expenses from Calcutta to Canton. In the years following, others made the return trip to China. In September 1870, 10 Chinese returned on the *Ganges*. In 1871, a family of 15 (including 7 females) returned with $3,200 (£666 13s. 4d.) on the *Wellesley*.[45] In 1872, 138 returned on two ships, the *Rohilla* and the *Enmore*, with savings totaling £7,729 3s. 4d.[46] Thus about 175 returned from British Guiana alone between 1869 and 1872. Thirty-one more returned on the *Rohilla* in 1876.[47]

It is difficult to gauge the exact extent of the total return migration.

Of the 2,143 who left British Guiana between 1872 and 1882, only the 1880 Immigration Report recorded specific destinations, 29 for China. At least 123 returned between 1885 and 1904. There are no comparable figures for Trinidad. It is clear that it was confined to the successful (unlike the Indians) and that it involved the China born more than the local born. Local-born Chinese ties to the homeland diminished progressively with the generational factor, even though Chinese ethnicity as a binding factor within the community was retained, but varying a great deal with individual families and diluted over time by the process of creolization/Americanization, cultural and racial. However, the China link remained, and indeed never died, side by side with the assimilation and "creolization" process.

Factors contributing substantially to the assimilation of the Chinese community in the new environment were the gradual loss of the language as an active medium of communication, the frequency of interracial marriages and liaisons, and the emergence of sizeable mixed Chinese communities. Partly because of their smaller numbers, partly because of their own group attitudes, and partly because of the presence of another larger "non-Creole" immigrant group (the Indians), race relations between the Chinese newcomers and the larger society developed in a less frictional atmosphere than that existing between Blacks and Indians. The Chinese became an exotic and partially assimilated addendum to the melting pot tradition of the plantation societies of Trinidad and British Guiana.

The earliest encounters between the Chinese and the freed Blacks were not completely free from conflict. Some of the immigrants who arrived in 1853 found themselves, in both colonies, in miniconfrontations with Black laborers and villagers. We mentioned in chapter 4 the clash between the Plantation Blankenburg Chinese and the Black villagers from Den Amstel on West Coast Demerara in 1853. This is how the Governor described the scenario soon after:

> The conduct of the Chinese after the first dispute between one of their number and one of the villagers, which it seemed probable originated in their ignorance of each other's intention and language, had been marked by great violence and a formidable spirit of combination, which but for the presence of mind of the manager of the plantation and the firmness of three policemen whom he summoned to his aid from the nearest station must have led to bloodshed. The six ringleaders were sentenced to a month's hard labor each in Georgetown gaol.[48]

The Governor also commented on

> the great deference to constituted authority exhibited by the Chinese
> throughout these transactions, thirty or forty of them . . . laying down
> their weapons and allowing a part of their number to be arrested by a few
> unarmed policemen of the very race and colour for which they had previ-
> ously shown such extreme contempt as to attack at least 600 arrayed for
> the defence of the village.

Interestingly, after the incarceration of the six Chinese ringleaders,
the Blacks assured the authorities that they would henceforth be more
patient and forbearing towards the newcomers; indeed, they assured
them, they considered the Chinese more "respectable" than the Indian
coolies and would be glad to live on good terms with them.

A brawl on Friendship estate in South Trinidad between Black laborers
and the Chinese from the *Australia* resulted in three people, two Blacks
and one Chinese, nursing heads wounded by stick blows. The Immigration Agent-General described it as a "drunken affray," resulting from a
misunderstanding between the superintendent and the new laborers, and
the Chinese on Friendship were transferred to nearby Williamsville estate, where another group of their compatriots were already working
well.[49]

These clashes were arguably far less violent than those among the
Chinese themselves, discussed in chapter 4. Official reports on the first
Chinese in Trinidad in fact stated, "Not being clogged with the trammels
of caste, they mix more freely than the coolies with the creoles, who say
of them, they are not so 'cornful' as the coolies."[50] As time went on
and more Chinese arrived in the West Indies, this admixture of mutual
antipathy and mutual friendliness continued.

Other racial clashes did occur—for example, on Plantation Zeelandia
in British Guiana in 1863, over the discovery of a cache of stolen items
where some of the Chinese prone to nocturnal burglary had hidden their
spoils. Plantation Bel Air on East Coast Demerara was the scene of
another racial clash in 1866.[51] There were reports too that Blacks occasionally harassed the Chinese in British Guiana, sometimes seizing them
and cutting off their "pigtails."

However, one later account published in 1898 had this to say: "[The
Chinese] work hard and live well; [and] unlike the East Indian, mingled
freely with the Black and coloured races. . . . The Negro population,
who make a butt of the patient Hindoo and bully his life out of him, are
afraid of the Chinaman, and leave him alone."[52]

Contemporary accounts from Trinidad seemed to suggest a more relaxed relationship between the races generally. No major racial incidents
of the kind that had erupted in British Guiana were reported either
in the immigration reports or in the published accounts of the period.
Occasionally they got involved in interestate clashes, like the one between the laborers of Endeavour estate and Woodford Lodge estate in
Chaguanas in Central Trinidad in 1865, when one Chinese was killed,
but these conflicts were multiracial in nature—Indians and Chinese from
one estate versus Indians and Blacks from the other.[53] Sometimes these
incidents were the by-product of strike action; the strike by Chinese
workers on Perseverance estate in Couva in 1866, for example, led to
clashes between the Chinese strikers and the Black policemen and their
helpers. In this incident, thirty-nine Chinese were arrested and jailed,
but only six of the ringleaders were subsequently charged and sentenced
to two months' imprisonment with hard labor.[54]

The newspapers occasionally carried the odd letter or article expressing
resentment at the economic "exploitation" carried out by Chinese (and
Indian) small traders. One letter in the San Fernando Gazette in the 1880s
complained as follows:

> The Chinese do not raise agricultural products, they are not laborers; but
> reap the benefit of others' labor, and become prosperous, while the poor
> people, proprietors and others are gradually getting ruined. The Chinese
> are to be compared to horse leeches, or to a parasite which settles on a
> plant not vigorous enough to throw it off, and which it saps of its strength.
> They resort to all manners of devices to cheat the people even in the
> buying, selling, weighing and gambling.[55]

This attitude towards the shopkeeper class, however, while not uncommon or unusual, never seemed to erupt into any major expression of race
and class resentment against the Chinese. Racial hostility against the
small-trader class did express itself several times in British Guiana, but
primarily against the Portuguese, in 1848, 1856, and again in 1889.
Indeed, it was only in Jamaica, with its minuscule Chinese community,
that one such event of major proportions was recorded, in 1918, during
the whole period of this study.

The incident, which touched off a spate of rioting and violence against
the Chinese and their properties, not only in Kingston, but also in the
nearby parishes of St. Catherine, St. Mary, St. Ann, and Clarendon,
took place in July. A Chinese shopkeeper, Fong Sue, had apparently
caught   one of his female employees in the illicit embrace of a Black

neighborhood policeman. With some of his Chinese friends, he gave the seducer a solid beating, and the policeman went into hiding for about two days, during which rumors began to spread that he had been murdered by the Chinese for threatening to arrest Fong Sue for violating a law prohib-iting the sale of goods on Sundays.

A mob gathered and began to attack and loot several Chinese shops indiscriminately over a wide area, incensed at the alleged murder of the policeman. So large were the mobs involved that in St. Catherine parish alone, the police made more than 452 arrests, and 300 people were eventually convicted.[56]

The riots, which were directed only against the Chinese, were clearly a product of the same kind of social resentment reserved in British Guiana for the Portuguese. They were to occur twice again in modern Jamaican history, in 1938 and again in 1965. One analyst has suggested that the presence of significant competing elements from other racial groups among the small-trader class in Trinidad and British Guiana had suc-ceeded in shielding the Chinese in these territories from that kind of social outburst, whereas their conspicuous monopoly status in over-whelmingly Black Jamaica had deprived them of the sort of benign image they enjoyed elsewhere.[57] (There may be an element of truth in this observation, since this perception of popular racial attitudes towards the Chinese among the different West Indian territories tends to hold true well into the modern period.)

Chinese attitudes towards interracial marriages or common-law liai-sons may have contributed somewhat to the lesser degree of antipathy felt towards them on the part of the larger society. There is no question that they were far less racially exclusive than the Indians, who were constrained on matters of mating and family relations by their rigorous caste and religious prejudices, even among themselves. Chinese mating patterns in the West Indies (and indeed in Latin America) corresponded in fact very closely with their practices in other, more classic migrant destinations, for example, Southeast Asia. There, the habit of migrating in almost exclusively male communities, often leaving their womenfolk behind in their China villages, and often evolving a form of permanent dual family situation—one family in the new environment, one family back in China—was an established practice.

Several British officials, assessing the probable benefits of Chinese emigration to the West Indies, had commented in the 1850s on the Chinese practice of intermarrying with local inhabitants. On the prospect of this happening in the West Indies, where the majority of the population in the 1850s was Black, they appeared to be divided. Mr. White had written to Governor Barkly of British Guiana in 1851:

> In all the islands and countries where the Chinese have hitherto settled as emigrants, they have found branches of the Malay family and races cognate to their own; this would not be the case in the West Indies, and I have very great doubts whether they would form connexions of a permanent character with the Negro women, so as to become contented and resident colonists. If this difficulty can be got over, I have no doubt as to the successful result of Chinese emigration on the future destinies of the West India colonies.[58]

Other officials, however, expressed other views:

> I have no doubt the Chinese will readily amalgamate with the females they find in the country they are going to. They have no feelings of caste to restrain them in this direction, as the Hindoo coolies have. The natives of India in the Straits never intermarry with the Malays, whereas in three or four generations the Malay-Chinese females have become so numerous as to afford a sufficient supply for the Chinese population.[59]

Most of the unattached Chinese males who arrived in Trinidad in the 1850s and 1860s in fact remained permanent bachelors. This is borne out by the statistics recorded in the 1891 census (which remains the best single source of information on the progress and development of the immigrants thirty years after their arrival in the island). An equally significant minority of them formed liaisons with the local Black and mulatto women, whether in formal marriage or (more often) in informal common-law unions, and this is borne out equally by the same statistics. That a reasonably sizeable mixed Chinese community had arisen by the 1890s is borne out, if not by the census statistics (which did not begin to enumerate this group until 1931), by at least the statements of contemporary writers and observers.

The 1,006 Chinese enumerated by the 1891 census, all but 49 of whom were over the age of thirty, consisted of 838 men and 168 women. Of the total, 647 (580 men, 67 women) were unmarried; 298 (234 men, 64 women) were married; and 61 (24 men, 37 women) were widowed. Thus at least 170 of the married men had to be married to non-Chinese women, since only 64 Chinese women were married. This would not include those who were technically unmarried but who might well have been living in a common-law liaison with a local (or immigrant, i.e., Indian or Venezuelan mestiza) woman.

H. J. Clark, Chief Government Statistician, wrote a small book on Trinidad in 1893 in which he stated: "The Chinese, unlike the East Indians, have intermarried freely with the native women, and their descendants are thus being gradually merged in the general population."[60] Many other earlier accounts also testified to the same phenomenon, constantly contrasting this tendency with that of the more conservative and traditionalist Indians.

Even the official reports occasionally made note of this factor. Indeed, as early as 1853 an official report referred to one Chinese doctor who had come over on the *Lady Flora Hastings* marrying "a Creole of this island" and enjoying "a flourishing practice, much to the extreme disgust of the licentiates of less venerable institutions." Despite the envy and outrage of this doctor's less successful professional peers, the authorities seemed to have seen this union, consummated "contrary to the predictions of persons conversant with the Chinese character," as a welcome sign for the future of Chinese immigration.[61] By 1857 five Chinese immigrants had married local women, and another three were said to be contemplating marriage to Portuguese Blacks from the Cape Verde islands.[62]

Later official reports in the 1860s continued in the same vein. The Immigration Agent-General stated in a letter of March 1861, "Not less than thirty have married Creoles, and seventeen have families."[63] The Immigration Report for 1863 referred to the fact that many of the 1853 arrivals had found wives among the local women, and suggested that this was preferable to their bringing to Trinidad Chinese women who were not bona fide wives, since the number of women who had arrived on the *Wanata* and had been subsequently deserted by their alleged husbands was presenting a social problem.

Daniel Hart affirmed in 1866: "They freely marry creole women, and are careful in selecting those that are handsome."[64] Henry Kirke said much the same thing in 1898 about the Chinese in British Guiana: "As Chinese women are scarce, the Chinaman has always a coloured woman as a concubine, and they generally manage to get the best looking girls in the place."[65] Chinese women were always more numerous among the Guianese immigrants, but the 1871 report still confirmed the relative frequency of mixed marriages and liaisons before 1870.

They have not the same objection to living with females of a different race from themselves that the Indians have. This may be owing in some degree to the small proportion of women who have emigrated from China, but the principal reason for it is that the Chinese have not the difficulty of caste to get over that the Indian has, and are more cosmopolitan in their habits.[66]

Not all the social commentators on British Guiana seemed to be agreed on the extent of the phenomenon, however. The evidence was sufficiently contradictory for the Reverend H. V. P. Bronkhurst to write in 1883:

> between the Black Creoles and Chinese there has existed a strong, bitter, prejudicial feeling towards each other, and so far as I have been able to ascertain there is no likelihood of a Chinaman ever marrying a Black woman, or a Black man ever marrying a Chinese woman. A similar feeling exists among the East Indian coolies also towards the Black race. Of course I do not refer to the isolated cases of such marriages which have taken place in the Colony, nor do I refer to the illicit intercourse between the Chinese, East Indian immigrants, and Black women: but I speak of the immigrants as a whole.[67]

The 1871 report also recorded a rare instance of a Chinese man living on Adelphi estate in East Coast Berbice with a Madrasi woman.[68] Gradually, as the newcomers acclimatized to their new surroundings and to one another, Chinese-Indian unions increased, although probably more slowly than Chinese-Creole unions. By 1891, Dr. Comins was saying, "It is not an uncommon thing to find a cooly woman living with a Chinaman as his wife, and in one or two instances the woman has accompanied her reputed husband to China."[69] The Immigration Report for 1892 reported six marriages between Chinese men and Indian women in British Guiana.

All of this having been said, it remains equally true that the extent of the phenomenon of mixed unions among the early Chinese can be exaggerated. It is clear from the Trinidad census figures of 1891 that a full 60 percent or more of the indentureds who arrived in the 1850s and 1860s died without families, even allowing for the existence of uncounted common-law unions.[70] And although it was numerically larger than Chinese male–Chinese female marriages or unions, the percentage of those who did enter into mixed unions was not more than 17 or 20 percent (again allowing for the unquantifiable common-law unions).

It is clear also that a significant minority kept up the China connection, side by side with the simultaneous trends towards cultural and racial creolization/Westernization. The prominent businessman Kang Lee left

Trinidad with his entire family in 1896 to settle in Hong Kong. The equally prominent Lee Lum family spent more than two years in China before returning to Trinidad in 1895.[71] The China connection kept up by some of the leading Chinese families in British Guiana around 1915 has already been mentioned.

With the influx of new immigrants in the twentieth century, this tendency would have been reinforced, at least among the affluent. There was also the tendency among many of the older China-born elements to save money in order to return to China to die in their home villages, although this trend would be clearly difficult to quantify. In addition, the practice among a minority of the affluent of sending their sons to China (or Hong Kong) to return with Chinese wives existed then, as it still exists today (though much diminished) among a much later immigrant community.

The existence of Chinese district associations in the new environment, catering to those who came from particular areas of the Cantonese region around the Pearl River delta, testified to the continuing vibrancy of the immigrants and their traditional lifestyles in the larger "American" milieu. Even when, as was inevitable with all migrant groups to the Americas, the local-born second and third generations evolved away from the native tongue as a primary medium of communication among themselves, adopting the English language and Western styles of dress and values, the fact of Chinese ethnicity as a binding factor continued, making the members of the community a distinctive marginal element within the larger melting pot tradition.

Even the children of mixed unions (then as well as now), testimony as they were to the broader creolization process, would generally develop the dual identities and loyalties of their parents, with the self-identification process varying considerably from one individual to another, according to personal temperament and choice. The process of assimilation/creolization was thus not a process of *absorption* by the larger culture, but more a subtle process of *hybridization*, a blend of the Old World and the New, the New World here meaning the Euro-African melting pot tradition that was unique to the Americas.

Apart from the decline of the Chinese language as an active medium of communication among the local born, other early indicators of assimilation included the adoption of Christianity, even by the China born. The 1891 Trinidad census indicated that a full 914 of the 1,006 Chinese had converted to various kinds of Christian religions by that decade; 606 belonged to the Church of England (Anglican), 285 to the Roman Catholic church, 13 were Presbyterians, 3 Wesleyans, and 7 belonged to various other Christian denominations. There were 71 self-defined non-Christians: 52 Buddhists, 6 who identified themselves as Hindu, and 5 as Mahometans, with 8 "other non-Christians"; 21 were "not described." How many of these conversions represented the creation of an active practicing Christian community, and how many were simply symbolic or cosmetic conversions for the purpose of acknowledging the customs of the new society—like the equally prevalent practice of adopting Westernized first names, and often also surnames—remains difficult to say.

A few became preachers, mainly in British Guiana. In that colony, the tradition of a Chinese Christian community was established through the influence of immigrants converted in China by the Reverend Lobscheid, as well as the influence of Wu Tai Kam between 1864 and 1867. It survived throughout the century. Several Chinese ethnic Christian churches were built in British Guiana in the 1870s and 1880s, mainly in Georgetown and New Amsterdam. The Trinidad newspaper, the *San Fernando Gazette,* recorded the delivery in 1878 of a Christian sermon in the Chinese language by a visiting British Guiana–based Chinese preacher to a Trinidad Chinese congregation.[72]

Chinese curiosity about Christian worship was demonstrated as early as the first arrivals from Amoy in 1853. An official report described some of those who had arrived on the *Glentanner* and the *Lord Elgin:* "They display their imitative tendencies in a most extraordinary way—several of them having attended a neighboring missionary chapel on the Sabbath and gone through the whole service as if they understood it, kneeling, sitting or standing with the rest of the congregation."[73] As many as 100 of the 383 who arrived from Hong Kong on the *Dora* in 1860 had been converted to Christianity in China.[74]

By the end of the 1850s, there were already fifteen Catholic and two Anglican converts among the Trinidad Chinese. By early 1862, there were fifty Anglicans.[75] The Reverend John Morton, founder of the Canadian Presbyterian Mission in Trinidad in 1868, recorded the presence of Chinese worshipers in his congregation (his San Fernando church founded in 1872).[76] One even became a preacher and adopted the Western name of Jacob Corsbie in the late 1870s.[77] Canon Charles Kingsley described a Christian church service he attended in Trinidad in 1869, at which many affluent Chinese women were present, dressed in European attire.[78]

However, a large number of them also paid no attention to the new faith, especially in the early years. The Reverend W. H. Gamble of the

London Baptist Missionary Society, who wrote a small book in 1866 based on nine years of residence on the island, declared,

> The Chinese do not celebrate any religious festival that I have ever heard, and the only symbol of their religion is a small bracket fixed up against the side of the house, on which is placed a burning lamp, a few Chinese characters being written on red paper, and pasted above the lamp. Ask anything about this matter, and the general answer given is, "This is for me religion."[79]

Chinese styles of dress also jostled side by side with Western styles in the early years. Reverend Gamble's descriptions went on:

> The Celestials are a peculiar people in their own country; and though much of their peculiarity is lost by their residence here, still some of their peculiarities remain. The long plait of hair growing from the crown of the head is as sacredly preserved, and as carefully coiled around the head in Trinidad by the well-to-do Chinaman, as by his brother Chinaman in the Celestial Empire. It is difficult to find out why this appendage is so carefully guarded—but carefully preserved it is: and distressing indeed is it to the poor unfortunate Chinese who is sent to gaol, and has to submit to the indignity of having his head shaved. Not that they are not accustomed to shaving their heads, for most of them shave the whole of their heads clean, with the exception of the sacred plait. They are, as a people, devoid of whiskers, and very few have either beard or moustache. Some of the higher class have the very long, thin moustache which is to be seen represented in the images of mandarins on view in tea-shop windows.
>
> The native dress of the Chinese has nothing picturesque about it; short wide trousers of blue cotton, with a kind of short smock-frock of the same material, from the whole of the dress, crowned, however, by a circular and conically-shaped hat, which puzzles you to say whether it is most like one of Bruce's soldiers' targets, or a part of a beehive. They are in shape like a target, and in material similar to that of which beehives are made, and withal they are serviceable. They extend wide, and throw a considerable circle of shade around the wearer, effectually shielding him from the sun.

A number of the immigrants also chose to adopt Western names— sometimes a first name, often an entire name—partly as a concession to their new environment, often under the influence of over-zealous Christian missionaries. Names like Jacob Corsbie and Daniel O'Connell have already been mentioned. Others included Thomas Wilson, John William, Henry Pantin, and John William Hendrickson![80] This was, however, a minority phenomenon, although children of immigrants would generally be christened with Western names, which were then appended to their Chinese family names (or a version of them). The children of the China born would also be given a Chinese first name, in addition to their Western one.

The continuation of this blend of Eastern and Western customs could be seen in other areas. In British Guiana—though not in Trinidad— Chinese New Year street parades continued late into the nineteenth century, side by side with newly acquired cultural pastimes.[81] Henry Kirke was witness to an amusing cricket match in British Guiana with an all-Chinese cricket team in the 1870s.[82] The Chinese also popularized their own cuisine throughout the Creole society, while simultaneously adopting and incorporating many aspects of the local cuisine into their own culinary practices. They popularized many of their own gambling games among the Creole masses (whe-whe in Trinidad, cheefa in British Guiana), while retaining their own eccentric attachments to the pastime. Henry Kirke told the story of a man whose passion for gambling led him to lose most of his worldly possessions:

> I know of one case where a man lost all his money, then his house and furniture, then his wife, and then he staked himself as a slave for six months and lost that, and strange to say, he faithfully worked out his debt of honour, toiling for his master without wages for the allotted time, and then began life afresh, a saddened, and let us hope, a wiser man.[83]

Another Westernization agency that would have had an impact on Chinese social development in the West Indies was the Western (specifically Anglo-) colonial education system, which affected all races by the last quarter of the century. The school became the major socializing agency of the larger colonial society, since it was in this environment that the children of immigrants would have the most intimate contact with others from another race. In the period up to the First World War, a very select minority would also have sent their children on to British universities—not a widespread practice during this period in the colonial West Indies.

This trend would increase significantly in the 1920s. By 1929, a Chinese journalist visiting the West Indies would say, in a magazine addressed to China readers, "There are few Chinese in the West Indies who have not had the advantage of a high school education, and an increasing number attend Oxford, London and Edinburgh universities in search of professional training."[84]

Eugene Chen of Trinidad (1878–1944).
Courtesy Brian Chen and family.

One unusual product of the tiny Chinese professional stratum in Trinidad went on to become perhaps the most distinguished Chinese American of his time. This was Eugene Chen, the lawyer who left the island
to become an integral part of the Chinese nationalist movement after
1912, becoming Sun Yat-sen's foreign affairs adviser and personal secretary (his "English" secretary) up to Dr. Sun's death in 1925. A member
of the Central Executive Committee of the Kuomintang, he was a Foreign
Minister of the short-lived Canton and Wuhan-based progressive Kuomintang government until the Chiang-Kai-Shek coup of 1927, and after
that a major Left Kuomintang and anti-Chiang figure until his death. He
died in Japanese-occupied Shanghai in 1944, at the age of 66, under
house arrest. The Chinese Communists who came to power in 1949 later

removed his ashes to the Cemetery of the Heroes of the Revolution in Peking and erected a memorial in his honor there.[85]

Another mixed Chinese person, Alfred Richards, was a major figure in the leadership of the early labor movement in Trinidad and a founder of the Trinidad Workingmen's Association (T.W.A.). He was also one of the local witnesses who testified before the Sanderson Commission in London in 1909.[86] A vigorous elected official in Port-of-Spain city council politics in the 1920s and 1930s, he was eventually elected Mayor of Port-of-Spain twice between 1936 and 1941. Two other Chinese elected officials in Port-of-Spain progressive city politics in the 1930s were Dr. Tito Achong and a young lawyer, J. Edward Lai-Fook, the former eventually becoming Mayor of Port-of-Spain himself in 1941, after Alfred Richards. An interesting but lesser-known figure was the businessman-journalist Aldric Lee Lum, son of businessman John, who published and edited the progressive newspaper *Argos*, which played a key role in the early post-1918 labor movement. (It was even attacked by the colonial authorities for its anticolonial journalism.)

British Guiana too, by the late thirties, had produced two elected members of the local legislature who were Chinese, R. V. Evan Wong and the lawyer Theophilus Lee, the latter also holding the portfolio of President of the British Guiana Labour Union (B.G.L.U.). (The younger brother of R. V. Evan Wong, Dr. Basil Evan Wong, also distinguished himself, like his Trinidad counterpart Eugene Chen, in China affairs, serving as a colonel in Chiang Kai-shek's military forces during World War II.)

By and large, however, participation in public life was the exception rather than the rule for the professionals of this small community, living as they did in colonial countries still very far from any national cohesion in the early decades of the century.

CHAPTER 8

Sojourners to Settlers: West Indian East Indians, and East Indian West Indians

The philosophy underlying the entire Indian indenture system envisaged the immigrant contract laborers as transients within the plantation system, persons who would spend five years as indentured laborers and five additional years at labor of their own choosing before returning to India, courtesy of the state. The safeguard of the free return passage as an indispensable element of the indenture contract was insisted upon by the government of India and concerned liberal-humanitarian elements, and the Indians themselves might not have embarked on the long journey to the West Indies without its inclusion. Thus the notion of the Indian immigrant as transient, rather than as potential citizen, as sojourner rather than settler, arose out of the special circumstances surrounding the birth of the indenture system.

A combination of factors led to a change of perception (official and unofficial) on the status of the Indian in the new society. Among them were the spontaneous inclinations of a large number of the Indians themselves, as well as, ironically, the attitudes of the planter class as it sought ways of easing the burdens of having to pay for the return passage.

A substantial number of the immigrants, despite all the trials and tribulations of their indenture experience, chose to remain in the new environment, which they began to see as adopted homes rather than as places of temporary compulsory labor, as lands of possible new opportunities for self-expansion and creative growth and mobility rather than as societies constricted by planter exploitation. The statistics of repatriation trends confirmed that this attitude was quite widespread. In the total period of the migration, the percentage of those who did eventually take up their return passage rights was 30 percent, the rest voluntarily opting for a Caribbean relocation.

Even the minority who did return to India clearly demonstrated, by the collective wealth they had accumulated in the New World, that for many—if not necessarily all—the voyage to, and temporary sojourn in, the West Indies had been worth it and had made a material difference in their lives. Up to December 1868, about 3,201 immigrants had returned from Trinidad, carrying an average of nearly twenty pounds each.

In December 1865, 514 (441 adults) returned from Trinidad on the *British Trident* with £9,700 in cash and £2,701 in jewelry and other valuables. Among the returnees were a man and his wife who had originally emigrated to Trinidad in 1846, returned to Calcutta after five years, came back in 1858 at their own expense, and returned to Calcutta a second time with £199 in specie and £20 16s. 8d. in the Treasury. There was also another man who had served two terms of indenture, one in Mauritius and another in British Guiana, had been robbed of his savings at Calcutta, had indentured himself a third time in Trinidad, and was now returning home once more with significant savings. Forty of these 514 passengers were paupers, invalids, and vagrants sent back at the expense of the colony.[1]

In 1869, 372 (289 adults) returned with £16,087 14s., an average of £55 13s. 4d. each. In 1870, 408 (313 adults) returned with £12,736 12s., an average of £40 13s. 10d.[2] Dr. Comins pointed out in 1893 that in forty-one years (1850–91), 12,082 migrants returning from Trinidad, "including women, children, infants in arms, the lame, the halt and the blind," took back with them over a quarter of a million in solid cash, "to say nothing of the gold and silver ornaments with which women are laden, and the large sums of money, generally of gold, concealed in belts around their persons and in their boxes."[3]

The same average applied to the 6,281 who returned from British Guiana even before 1870. The *Clarence* returned in 1865 for Calcutta and Madras with 469 Indians (389 adults) with savings amounting to approximately £31 each for Calcutta adults and £10 14s. each for Madrasis.[4] The *Ganges* returned in 1867 with 451 Indians (366 adults) with an average savings of £30 each.[5] Between 1861 and 1869 alone, a total of 2,166 (1,779 adults), with deposited savings of £64,020 14s. 9d. (equal to £35 19s. 9d. on each adult), had left from British Guiana.[6]

In 1871 two ships returned from Jamaica, one with 487 (362 adults) with £13,986 (an average of £38 13s. per adult), the other with 438 (314 adults) with £3,274 16s. (£10 8s. 7d. average, minus jewelry).[7]

Critics of the indenture system have pointed out, first, that almost all of this wealth was only acquired after indenture, and not during the indenture period itself (or in any case via plantation wages alone); second, that there were often major differences between the richest of the returning migrants and the average, so that the average savings of £20 was not truly reflective of the real savings of many returnees. Moreover, there was always a significant number of paupers and invalids sent back at the expense of the state among the returnees.

Those who had remained in the West Indies had done so for a variety of different reasons. Some had contracted intercaste marriages that would not be accepted in their home villages on their return. Some had not acquired the wealth required to buy them back into caste favor, after having "lost caste" by the very act of migration itself (crossing the *kala pani*, or black waters). Many had returned to India, found reintegration into traditional village life impossible after their "modernizing" influences in the West Indies, and returned by either reindenturing or paying their passages back.

The broad post-indenture alternatives open to the Indians in the West Indies were the same as for the other ethnic immigrants who had preceded them on the plantations. They could choose to remain on the estates, availing themselves of the relative security afforded by the sugar milieu (free housing, free health care, regular wages, and other benefits such as free garden plots or pasturelands for cattle). They could acquire and move off onto their own lands, living a life of independent peasant proprietorship with or without occasional work for wages on nearby plantations. They could become independent artisans or self-employed workers of one kind or another, working either within their own communities or within the broader multiracial Creole society. They could become small or medium traders, stationary shopkeepers, or itinerant hucksters, hawking their wares over the countryside. They could become town dwellers or remain country dwellers. They could even migrate to other lands within the Western Hemisphere in search of new opportunities elsewhere, temporarily or permanently.

Indians were free to choose their own lifestyles after their indenture terms were over, and they became all of these things. Certain trends, however, were dominant among them, distinguishing them from the other ethnic groups, and certainly from their fellow Asians, the Chinese, who shared life on the plantations with them during the 1860s and early 1870s. Unlike the Chinese, whose involvement in small-scale farming generally acted as a temporary base before they became overwhelmingly

Indian Commissioner welcomed by East Indian National Association at Princes
Town, 1913. Standing (*left to right*): Mr. David Mahabir, Mr. Jules Mahabir,
Master Ramcharan, Mr. Peter Ramcharan; seated (*left to right*): Mr. Chimanlal
(Indian commissioner), the Honorable George Fitzpatrick, and Abdul Aziz.
From *Indian Centenary Review, 1845–1945* (Trinidad).

involved in trading activities (rural and urban), the Indians became primarily agriculturists and remained overwhelmingly so into the twentieth
century. Their social backgrounds in India, their innate love for and
knowledge of the land and its cultivation, made them over time the
classic farmers and food producers of Trinidad and British Guiana, dominating the Black population in most key areas of rural production. (Tobago island, joined to Trinidad in 1889, and untouched by Asian immigration before or after, remained a Black peasant enclave throughout).

Free Indian Communities before 1870

The period before 1870 saw the Indians in British Guiana, like their
Chinese fellow workers, making frequent use of the first option of re-
indenture to remain largely on the estates for a second five-year term.
When the Commission of Enquiry reported in 1871, a full 76.8 percent

of the Indians (33,143) were still under indenture. The majority (20,039) were on their first five-year term of service, about a quarter (8,557) on their second five-year term. A significant number were serving third (2,952) and fourth and further (1,595) terms of five years.[8]

The free or ex-indentured Indian population was divided into those who continued to remain resident on the estates (7,262) and a small number who had decided to launch new lives off the estates, in the villages and nearby rural settlements. According to the 1871 British Guiana census, about 8.4 percent of the Asians (Indians and Chinese) were living off the estates in that year, 3,215 in the villages and settlements and 1,466 in the urban areas of Georgetown and New Amsterdam. One study estimated 2,736 of these to be Indians (1,562 in Demerara, 721 in Essequibo, 453 in Berbice).[9] Thus 6.3 percent of the Indians lived off the estates, 23.2 percent were free, and 76.8 percent were indentured in 1871. They made up less than 4 percent of the Guianese village population.

Trinidad, by contrast, which only allowed one-year reindentures in the 1860s and which had greater and easier access to off-estate settlement possibilities (legal and illegal), developed a different pattern before the 1870s. The number and percentage of Indians who reindentured were decidedly smaller, and the movement out of the estates was more rapid. A small number even commuted their original five-year terms in order to leave the estates more quickly. Sixty, for example, did so in 1861, 241 in 1862, and 224 in 1863.[10]

Unlike the Chinese, though, a substantial number of these continued to maintain a close relationship with the estates, combining a few days work for the sugar plantations with independent peasant cultivation on their own account. A large number, though much less than their counterparts in British Guiana, continued to live physically on the estates, preferring to maintain a close connection with plantation wage labor, despite their free status. The percentage of indentured to free Indians, and free estate residents to free off-estate residents, revealed a quite different pattern in Trinidad.

As early as 1855, an official estimate suggested that there were as many as 2,000 free Indians (31.3 percent) living largely independently off the estates, in a total Indian population of 6,385, with 509 more resident and working voluntarily on the estates. The indentured population amounted to 3,195, plus a further 681 who had reindentured in 1851 for a second five-year term (five-year reindentures ended in Trinidad around 1854, with the repeal of the 1851 law permitting them). Thus the percentage of total indentureds was 61 percent, and the total free population already 39 percent by the end of 1855.[11]

By 1862 the free Indian numbers had reached even higher. The Annual Immigration Report for 1863 stated that 4,520 had officially received certificates of termination of industrial residence (free certificates). The report also went on to say that the number of free Indians out of that 4,520 who then resided in the urban areas of Port-of-Spain and San Fernando and in the rural hamlets had become too great, and they had become "too unsettled in their habits" for anything like a statistically accurate description of their activities. Moreover, "the women and children belonging to this class are naturally more numerous than among those indentured to, or resident on, estates, but their exact proportion can scarcely be estimated until the next general Census." The number of indentureds for 1863 was recorded at 10,072, and the numbers of free on-estate resident adult workers at 2,046.[12]

The rapid expansion of the free Indian class in Trinidad, compared with their Guianese counterparts, who remained largely estate resident and reindentured, is reflected in the 1871 census figures. The census recorded an Indian population of 27,425. Of these, 10,616 were indentured, according to the 1871 Immigration Report. Thus 38.7 percent were indentured, and 61.3 percent free, by 1871. Roughly 29 percent (7,940, i.e., 4,271 adults and 3,669 children) were free on-estate residents. This meant that the off-estate residents were 8,869, or 32.3 percent, more than three times their Guianese counterparts numerically, and more than four times percentage-wise.

Up to 1869, the free off-estate Indians in Trinidad, despite formal obstacles to land acquisition, were an enterprising peasant proprietor class. The 1863 Immigration Report stated: "They have exhibited a new feature during the last year or 18 months, and imitated the Chinese in cultivating gardens in the vicinity of town and elsewhere, sometimes on an extensive scale, while the numerous huts erected in these gardens shew that to a certain extent they are becoming identified with the creole population." They cultivated a variety of vegetables and Creole root staples ("ground provisions" such as cassava, yams, sweet potatoes, and tannias). Peas, corn, and rice seemed to dominate over the other produce. They also owned a large number of cows and were major milk suppliers, especially to Port-of-Spain, by the early 1870s. The 1863 Immigration Report also talked of those who "flock to the small cocoa and provision holdings, or squat on Crown lands."

Hindu musical group.
Courtesy University of the West Indies (Trinidad) Library.

It is clear that by 1870, when official policy towards land acquisition and settlement among free Indians underwent a conscious change, the incipient small-scale peasant producer class was already fairly well developed. The extent of their landholdings, and the legitimacy of their acquisitions up to this point, remain somewhat obscure and undocumented, but what is obvious is that this class was not the creation of post-1869 policies on land grants to Indians, as is often suggested, but an existing and vibrant element within Trinidad society well before official policies took notice of them and tried to encourage their further and more orderly expansion.[13]

On an island as underdeveloped as Trinidad was in the 1860s, illegal occupation of land was more normal than not, and free Indians helped themselves like most others. Most of the island's squatters, including the Indians, were in central and southern Trinidad, in areas like Montserrat Ward, Couva, and the South Naparimas. A large number of squatters (but an unknown number of Indians) could also be found in Tacarigua in the north. Some were close to the plantations themselves, but a good many were also in deep and inaccessible inland territory. Up to 1868, responding to a government initiative, at least thirty-five Indian squatters out of roughly seventy-seven had already purchased and paid up fully for their lands from the government in the ward of Montserrat in Central Trinidad. In that year, there were apparently hundreds of total squatter applications for regularization still under review, involving about 8,000 acres, in the ward of Montserrat alone.[14]

A large number of the free Indians also worked for wages, either part-time on the sugar estates or on the estates of other local cultivators (often themselves illegal occupiers of Crown lands). A large unspecified number flocked to Venezuela, to work for high wages on the cocoa estates there. Many were free Indians who had not completed their ten-year residency period on the island, though they might have served their five-year term. Technically they were not permitted to migrate, but they went illegally anyway. They also encouraged many of their indentured compatriots, as we saw in chapter 5, to desert their plantations and migrate to Venezuela with them.

The 1864 Immigration Report stated about this phenomenon: "The island squatter, like the Spanish Main cocoa planter, pays high wages to the unindentured or free immigrant, who thus acts as a perpetual decoy to those under contract or newly arrived."

A few migrated elsewhere. Thirty-two Indians went to Martinique in 1853–54 in what must have been a highly isolated example of that kind of movement.[15]

Many became shopkeepers, like the Chinese, and a still larger number became hucksters or itinerant traders. The affluent minority among them emerged from this small-trader class, many of whom also became money-lenders to their own countrymen. A small number of the shops might have even been owned indirectly by Indian plantation officials (usually drivers or foremen), who themselves had often dubious ways of accumulating initial capital from their perches of quasi influence in the estate hierarchy.

The 1859 Immigration Report referred to a small minority who were well off enough to return a second time from India with their wives, paying their own passages and returning to their adopted home as free immigrants. Some even paid their own fares back to India. Records indicated that this took place in 1862 in British Guiana, and in 1865 as many as 77 did the same from Trinidad.[16] Dr. Comins also stated in his report, written much later, "In addition to the returning immigrants, there are always a certain number of well-to-do immigrants going to and from India, who despise the immigrant ships in which they could get a passage for a very moderate payment, and prefer to travel by the mail steamers, paying about £50 as passage money."[17]

This small affluent minority existed even in hard-pressed pre-1870 British Guiana. It seems that as many as 464 Indians had returned to the colony up to 1870 after a trip to India, paying their own passages back.[18] A further 180 (including 44 women and 5 children) had paid their own passages back to India on the regular immigrant ships, 87 of them in 1862, 51 in 1864, 28 in 1865, and 14 in 1867.[19]

The pre-1870 off-estate Indian community in British Guiana, small in relation to the larger body of Indians who were voluntarily reindenturing themselves for a second term, lived mainly in the villages and settlements close to the plantations. Most villages, in fact, like many of the African villages formed in the 1840s and 1850s, were carved out on the front lands of the plantations themselves, and the individual lots bought or rented from the planters.

Their economic activities were not as vigorous as those of their Trinidad counterparts, but many did reasonably well in their newfound independence. Without distinguishing between the Indians and the Chinese, the 1871 report stated that in 1870 both groups had 235 licenses for provision shops, 91 for horses, mules or donkeys, 77 for carriages and carts (private and for hire), 14 for the retailing of coconut toddy, an alcoholic beverage made from the coconut flower, 2 for the retailing of opium, 1 for a butcher shop, and 1 for a store.[20] (The Portuguese, however, continued to be the dominant group in the licensed trading and transportation sector.) A small number of Indians kept lodging houses. Some joined the police, and "a few sepoys have been admitted into the West India regiments, in which many more are anxious to enlist."[21]

A large number continued to be dependent on estate labor, although cattle farming (and its related milk selling) and rice and plantain cultivation—all on a relatively small scale—were the main occupations. Indians in British Guiana—on estate and off estate, indentured and free—had a large number of cows and sheep in their possession.

Squatting on Crown lands in the interior, while it did take place, was not widespread, most people preferring to live in the coastland areas. The phenomenon of the "prosperous squatter-farmer"—indentured and free—which was widespread in the Trinidad of the 1860s, was less of a feature of the Guianese setting. The Trinidad Immigration Report for 1876 explained it this way:

> In Trinidad the facilities for evasion not only abound but are especially tempting; small settlers swarm in every direction, creole as well as coolie. . . . In Demerara the situation is totally different. . . . The coolie will not rashly betake himself either to the swamp behind or the sea in front, while on either side the estates are ruled on the same principles as that to which he is indentured.

Free Indians after 1870

The period after the 1870s generally began a new, more complex stage in the relationship of the immigrants to the new society. Immigration continued apace and indeed assumed larger dimensions. Indians also continued to return to India in large numbers.[22] But the factors making for a greater sense of attachment to the new environment also multiplied in this period, emphasizing still further some of the options exercised by many of the pre-1870 arrivals.

These new factors included a substantial increase in the number of locally born Indians, with the consequent hybridization of place loyalties often created by that process. Already, by the 1871 census, locally born Indians had risen to approximately 16.5 percent of the total Indian communities of both Trinidad and British Guiana. By 1881 this percentage had risen to 26 to 27 percent in each territory.[23]

The immigrants themselves showed a strong partiality towards remaining in the new environment, including very many who actually returned to India and subsequently decided to come back to the West Indies for one reason or another. One official report from Trinidad stated: "Every year a number of people who have been repatriated return to this colony in the ships, paying their own passages. They invariably say that after their life in Trinidad, they do not care to remain in India."[24]

Dr. Comins confirmed that every year, large numbers of Indians wishing to return to Trinidad as indentured laborers had to be rejected on grounds of age. The lucky ones with the money to pay their own fares made it over in that way, but a large number were always rejected: "Having spent or lost all their savings [they] have to remain in India, and regret the day they left the colony to which they are unable to return."[25]

A former Assistant Protector of Immigrants in Trinidad told the Sanderson Commission in 1909 that many people who actually applied to return to India often did not exercise that option when the time came and that the practice was so common that the Immigration Department often waited until it received about 1,500 applicants before it obtained a 500-passenger ship, because it knew that not more than one-third would really leave.[26]

The number of so-called return migrants to the West Indies grew increasingly larger as the years progressed. These return migrants might reindenture from India for a second term of service or return as free immigrants (the latter were described in the reports as "casuals" or simply "passengers"). Not all returned to their original colony of indenture, choosing to try their luck with a new territory. Many indeed might even have served their first terms in sugar colonies elsewhere, like Mauritius or Fiji.

No less than 287 people paid their own passages to Trinidad in the decade between 1881–82 and 1892. The numbers of second-indenture return migrants who arrived in Trinidad between 1877 and 1892 amounted to 2,358. Of these, 757 had originally been indentured in Trinidad. The others came via British Guiana (591), Surinam (232), Jamaica (182), Natal (149), Mauritius (148), Bourbon, Martinique, and Guadeloupe (129), St. Vincent (88), Fiji (45), St. Lucia (24), Rangoon (6), Grenada (4), Assam (2), and Cayenne (1).[27]

These numbers kept up a steady momentum right up to the last years of the indenture system. In the decade between 1901 and 1910–11, 280 paid their own passages to Trinidad, and there were 789 return migrants under indenture, 188 originally from the island itself. The others came via Natal (283), British Guiana (133), Fiji (72), Jamaica (52), Surinam (38), Mauritius (18), St. Lucia (2), New Caledonia (2), and Straits Settlements (1).[28]

The statistics for British Guiana reflected the same general pattern. In the twenty-year period between 1871 and 1890, a total of 1,725 Indians arrived in British Guiana as "casuals," paying their own fares. The number of return migrants under indenture was 3,837.[29] About 2,841 were originally in the colony before remigrating from India. One witness before the Sanderson Commission reported that in the two previous seasons, there had been 226 return migrants to British Guiana (154 in 1906–7, 72 in 1907–8).[30]

Central to the attractions of the new environment were the opportunities for occupational mobility, and particularly for land ownership, which became more regularized and widespread in the last quarter of the nineteenth century. The orderly creation and encouragement of a settled Indian peasantry with a stake in the land, and a consequent attachment to the new society, became desirable in the eyes of officialdom from around 1869 in Trinidad and 1880 in British Guiana. Many Indians in Trinidad, as we have seen, had already begun to make these choices on their own initiative, albeit somewhat clandestinely in most cases.

The new government initiatives resulted from a mixture of motives. Sporadic suggestions about the desirability of encouraging the formation of a small landowning segment among the immigrants had been made since the 1850s and 1860s. Some wanted the Indians to settle as citizens of the new society, but many were simply preoccupied with reducing the financial burdens connected with the free return passage, as well as with the simultaneous problem of keeping labor tied to the estates. Partially satisfying some of the immigrants' land hunger was a concession some of the planters were willing to make in pursuit of this less altruistic end.

The first suggestion, that Indians should be legally allowed to commute the value of their return passage in exchange for a grant of Crown land of equivalent worth, came in an ordinance drafted in Trinidad in 1847 (No. 9 of 1847). This provision fell by the wayside, however, without any attempt to translate it into practice. The Immigration Agent of British Guiana, James Crosby, also raised a similar suggestion in 1863, with the same results. It seems also that the Colonial Office had been inclined on principle to accept the idea around 1859, but again there had been no follow-through.[31]

It was not until the late 1860s that the question of Indian landownership was raised again in Trinidad, as part of the general preoccupation with the high cost of a potential return of all the immigrants who were then entitled to a free passage to India. It was raised too as part of the larger policy initiative then in progress of dealing with the issue of widespread squatting. In trying to regularize the tenure of this multiracial community of illegal occupiers of public lands by persuading them to purchase their lands, the Trinidad government made it possible for the small squatter community of Indians already in existence to stabilize their situation along with others, as we saw earlier. In addition, the easing of restrictions on the sale of Crown lands also made it possible for at least ninety-six Indians to purchase 910 acres at £1 an acre by 1871.[32]

TRINIDAD

Most of the lands acquired by Indians in the initial post-1870 years came via the land-for-return-passage commutation program, under which free grants of 10 acres (or alternatively, after 1873, 5 acres and £5 in cash) were made in exchange for the return passage rights of the grantees. Under this program, which effectively lasted from 1869 to 1880, the Indian small peasantry crystallized formally into a distinct and vibrant segment of Trinidad society, giving the thrust towards post-indenture landownership a legitimacy that it did not have in the pre-1870 period.

The land commutation program actually went through two phases: from 1879 there was another decade during which the grant became a £5 cash exchange for the return passage rights, instead of a pure land grant (or land plus cash grant).[33] With this cash grant, the grantees could purchase their own land in an area that they wished (at least in theory). When the whole commutation program came to an end in 1889, about 3,979 grants had been made in all, involving about 11,933 people (including 5,591 children). Those who received actual land grants in the first decade (of 10 or 5 acres) amounted to 2,643. The total land acreage alienated in the commutation program was 19,055 acres, with the 10-acre grants accounting for about 61 percent of the total.[34]

A whole host of new village settlements arose out of this program. Most of them were located in central and south Trinidad, close to the functioniong sugar plantations in the counties of Caroni, Victoria, and St. Patrick, but a significant number of settlements also sprang up in the north as well, in the northeastern wards of Arima, Tacarigua, and Toco, and even Diego Martin and Maracas in the northwest. The total number of settlements was about twenty-seven, with about 44 percent located in the Montserrat Ward in central Trinidad.

The consensus seems to have been that the settlements were only partially successful, and indeed, in many instances, a complete failure. A Canadian missionary, the Reverend John Morton, gave perhaps the best analysis and judgment of the whole effort. Where the land was good, where some interest was taken in the settlers and they were "in touch with cocoa cultivators," he told a Labor Commission in 1905, the settlements prospered, but on the whole the settlement scheme was a failure.[35]

He suggested a number of reasons for this outcome. The first was the "inexperience and improvidence" of many of the grantees. They had never owned land before, and they had no experience in dealing with woodland. They "attacked the forest with axe and fire," and the result of this slash-and-burn approach to the land was a temporary "magnificent" first crop, followed by destruction of the soil. A second reason was the absence of control on the part of the government and the general lack of interest in the success of the settlements. The people were left in their inexperience to fail and were then blamed.

Third, the absence of a sense of real community among the settlers ensured a failure of some of the settlements. "In the blocks they could learn little from one another, and when asleep in the villages their gardens were pillaged." Giving the settlements an Indian name and re-creating an Indian village milieu were not sufficient where the real social relations were not harmonious, especially where the location of some settlements was severely defective in some respect. "Whitelands village was located on pure sand, Chandernagore in a swamp, and Chin-Chin west of a lagoon."

Reverend Morton told the commission that in 1905 "only one petty hamlet" remained to show where one of these three villages stood. Other examples of badly chosen lands existed. The land at Chin Chin was available only because no one would buy it. That at Malabar and Mausica, only 2 or 3 miles from the town of Arima, was available only because "no intelligent man would have it at almost any price."

Finally, the whole settlement scheme came to an end because it had lost the confidence of the respectable intelligent Indians. They "gave an odious name to the land and turned their tribal opinion against it." As a result, very few grants were taken up for three or four years prior to 1890. Cash grants were eventually also considered not "in good form" to accept as commutation for the return passage. Only "the poor and shiftless" would accept the £5 grant on its own, and more often than not, the money passed into the hands of their creditors.

Despite these failures, there were examples of real successes, according to Reverend Morton. Where the land was good, or where there was good land in the neighborhood, these settlements led to a large influx of private purchasers of Crown lands nearby, thereby enlivening and enriching the village communities involved. Sometimes the purchasers were the grantees themselves, expanding their holdings. This happened near Fyzabad, Rousillac, Calcutta, Coromandel, Caratal, and Las Lomas.

The Sub-Intendant of Crown Lands reported in 1876 that the functioning settlements were doing very well: 3,147 acres had produced 18,983 bags of rice, 2,931 barrels of peas, and 7,925 barrels of maize, besides large quantities of ground provisions in 1875. The settlements in

Montserrat Ward in particular dominated over the other wards.[36] Produce supplied the domestic markets in town and country, in some cases helping to cut down on foreign imports—for example, provisions and vegetables from next-door Venezuela and the smaller West Indian islands immediately to the north.

A large number of the settlers had continued to work for wages on the nearby sugar estates, leaving their families to tend to the lands. A minority chose to rent or sell the lands to other Indians, instead of settling down on the lands themselves. As early as 1875, out of fourteen settlements with a population of 3,756 Indians, 7.5 percent (284) were renting their own allotments from grantees.[37] A significant minority took advantage of the rising fortunes of the cocoa industry to enter into the cultivation of this crop. Reverend Morton singled these out as perhaps the most successful of the grantees.

After 1891, no further money was voted for the commutation of return passages, and the land distribution program's chances of being revived began to dwindle. The Immigration Report for 1890 commented that official opinion on the program was divided, some still supporting the idea as a good one needing better management, some supporting money grants alone, and others opposed to its continuation altogether.

The Protector of Immigrants, Charles Mitchell, believed that the continuation of the program was not advisable. His reasoning was that all the experience of the Immigration Department had shown that immigrants who had made up their minds to return to India would not accept any kind of grant in exchange for their return passage rights, while those who did accept such grants were generally people who had no intention of returning anyway. All that did happen was that revenues from potential land sales were being decreased by these free offers. Moreover, most of the lands adjacent to the large agricultural centers had already been taken up, and to place any new allotments at a distance from these centers would only withdraw from them a large number of the free Indians, to the detriment of the estates.

The land commutation settlements, with their mixed fortunes, had merely been the catalyst for the expansion of an Indian peasantry. Most of the real expansion in the last quarter of the nineteenth century came from those who purchased lands, public and private, with their own savings (or with loans from moneylenders). Unlike British Guiana next door, most of these purchases were of public (i.e., Crown) lands, which were plentiful in Trinidad and had been made easy to acquire by the post-1869 liberalization of the Crown lands purchases regulations. With

no minimum acreage purchase requirement, and the purchase price at
one pound per acre, the government made it possible for large numbers
of people to venture into land ownership and small farming.[38]

The Indians seized the opportunity to expand on their economic foundations, though without abandoning wage labor on the estates in large
numbers as the Black ex-slaves had done before them, in the 1840s and
1850s, and as the Chinese too were doing in the 1870s. Despite the
inevitable complaints from many of the planters, the evidence was that
many of the free Indian laborers continued not only to give their labor
to the sugar estates, especially during crop time, but even to remain in
some numbers as residents on the estates themselves, living alongside the
new indentured arrivals in estate-provided housing.

In 1876, the estate-resident Indian work force was equally divided
between the indentureds (10,057) and the free (10,062). In 1890, the
indentureds were even in the minority (9,960 vs. 12,413), and twenty
years later, in 1910, the position was still the same (11,551 vs. 13,516).[39]
Those who lived off the estates in their newly acquired lands—46,164,
or 67 percent, in 1890; 82,366, or 76.6 percent in 1910—continued to
divide their time between their own properties and the sugar estates, in
numbers that were always difficult to quantify precisely but which were
always significant. The 1884 Immigration Report stated, "Except from a
regular census it would be impossible to ascertain what the number of
immigrants not under indenture working on estates really is, even on
estates which make returns, as many of these laborers reside in villages
in their own or hired houses, and work on one estate or another just as
suits their convenience." Dr. Comins commented on this element as
follows:

> He is quite willing during crop time, when high wages are given and when
> he can spare the time from his own lands, to come and work at cutting
> canes, etc. for a few weeks, and this he will do whenever he has nothing
> much to do on his own farm; but as a regular worker he is lost to the sugar
> estate, nor can he be depended on to work regularly on the cocoa estates.
> He will come and offer his services, and if his wages are good he will work
> in a desultory way, but his heart is in his own lands, and he is off to them
> directly they need his attention. I have seen a man working on a sugar
> field, and a few hours afterwards I have met him scampering on ponyback
> many miles up the mountains to his home and farm in some distant gorge.[40]

The actual amount of Crown lands purchased annually by the Indians progressed slowly during the commutation years (1869–80). Official reports, quoted earlier, showed 96 buying 910 acres by 1871. Between 1870 and 1880 there were 356 purchases, while 2,614 were receiving free land grants. In 1881, there were 47, and by 1884 there were 134.[41] Then, as the land grants ended, and as the crisis years of the sugar industry hit in 1884–85, there was a sudden escalation in land buying. By 1890, official reports show the Indian community in ownership or occupation of 35,844 acres.[42]

An average of 2,000 acres a year was bought during the 1890s, and about 3,500–4,000 a year in the next decade. Land sales slowed down somewhat after 1910 as the government reserved key lands for oil exploration, but the average stayed around 300–400 acres a year until the end of indentured immigration in 1917.[43] More than 9,000 Indians became landowners by purchase of Crown lands between 1885 and 1920, with land sales to Indians being generally about one-third of total sales.

The total amount of land owned and cultivated by Indians in 1920 was reported to be around 95,306 acres.[44] This figure—which was not completely accurate, as the reported figures tended to fluctuate each year—would also include a certain amount purchased from private owners. It would be fair to state that in Trinidad—in contrast with British Guiana—the percentage of land bought from private owners would have been relatively small compared with that bought from the Crown, the latter always being so much more convenient and accessible in post-1870 Trinidad, and the terrain being generally much more favorable and manageable than the problematic Guianese terrain.

A significant amount of land was also rented from Indian and non-Indian owners, and this added to the total amount of land under active cultivation by the Indian peasantry. Much of the land cultivated in the northern county of St. George was rented land, including the vibrant Peru Village (later St. James) on the western outskirts of Port-of-Spain. This was how Dr. Comins described the northern scene in the 1890s:

> The number of those who have left sugar estates and have settled in villages or on plots of ground either leased or bought is very great. From beyond Peru Village, which is a large Indian settlement, to Arima, a distance of perhaps 19 miles, the road, omitting some long blanks where estates intervene, is thickly lined with Indian huts, and the people met on the road, though often strangely habited, are undoubtedly from the East.

Describing a typical scene along the main road from Port-of-Spain to Arima in the east, Dr. Comins continued:

> A very common custom is for a family to rent a piece of land facing the road, 130 feet deep by 70 broad, for 9 or 10 dollars a year. On this they soon run up a hut something in the Indian style, thatched with *gotahul* grass, though often the roof is of corrugated zinc. There is always a wide verandah to sleep in, if too warm inside, and to sit in during the day, and there is generally a little outhouse attached for a cow or donkey, very often both, also a goat or two and half a dozen fowls.
>
> The prejudice as to Hindus keeping fowls and eating eggs seems in a great measure to have disappeared. Many of these people keep little shops at which the usual food, grains, and other commodities are sold. Some take out spirit licenses, and a few of the shops are of large size and do a thriving trade.[45]

The 1891 census reported a total of 720 "peasant proprietors," but this was surely grossly inaccurate and probably due to the fact that most of them must have described themselves as "agricultural laborers," which indeed most of them still were.[46]

Also to be included in the lands cultivated by the Indians were those belonging to the plantations themselves, allotted to resident workers in parcels of varying sizes as an incentive for them to remain on the sugar estates after indenture. This practice was not as widespread as it was in British Guiana, where the plantations actually monopolized most of the best lands in the colony, but it was significant enough to be mentioned in the Comins Report of 1893. The lands were used for growing crops on a limited scale and very often as pasturelands for grazing cattle owned by the resident workers.[47]

According to the Immigration Report for 1920, the lands owned by the Indian small- and large-farmer class in that year—about one-fifth of the total lands owned and cultivated on the island—were cultivated as follows:

Cocoa	58,078 acres
Sugar cane	13,010
Rice	7,662
Peas	5,724
Ground provisions	5,268
Corn (maize)	3,677
Coconuts	929

Coffee	703
Fruits	255
Total:	95,306 acres

The average size of the individual landholdings tended to be between 5 and 20 acres, but there were major social differentiations between the landholders. A few of them were major large-scale proprietors with several hundred acres. In 1914, the McNeill-Lal delegation reported that one of them owned more than 500 acres and actually employed indentured laborers himself, sixty of them.[48] This was the ex-indentured immigrant Boodoosingh, who owned Patna cocoa estate at La Brea in Victoria County.

This was not the first instance of such a phenomenon. In the 1880s another ex-indentured immigrant, Barathsingh, owned the sugar- and rice-growing Corial estate, also in Victoria County, and the records show this 200-acre estate as employing several indentured laborers: nine in 1879, eight in 1880, twenty-three in 1881, and thirty-five in 1882.[49]

Messrs. McNeill and Lal commented that in 1913 there were several Indians with more than 100 acres each, and with annual incomes ranging from £500 to £1,250 from land, house property, and trade. Boodoosingh himself had an annual income exceeding £2,000.

Three new crops cultivated extensively by the Indians after the 1870s were cocoa, sugar cane, and rice. The involvement in cocoa actually began modestly before 1870, but with the steady upward expansion of this industry after the 1880s, particularly after the sugar depression beginning in 1884–85, it was inevitable that large numbers of free Indians would participate in the general turn towards this crop. They worked on the cocoa estates of other planters, both as wage laborers and as cocoa contractors (people who contracted to grow new cocoa trees for a fixed time period, usually five years, on the estates of others and received payment at the end of that contractual period for each cocoa-bearing tree). They also grew cocoa on their own lands and sold the produce to the larger dealers. As cocoa production came to rival sugar production in importance in the 1890s, the Indians who grew their own crops also contributed vigorously to this expansion.[50] In the northeastern area considered the "gateway to the cocoa country" (Arima, Sangre Grande), it was estimated that about five-hundred Indians owned small cocoa properties in 1891.[51]

Sugar cane small farmers, growing canes to be sold to the sugar factories, also became an integral part of the sugar industry in the years of crisis, as the plantations sought different ways of cutting down on production costs. "Decentralizing" sugar production and encouraging the growth of independent cane farmers was one policy adopted in the 1880s, and Indians became part of a swelling multiracial cane-farmer class, which included both Creole and immigrant Blacks. The percentage of canes grown by small farmers at the turn of the century stood at roughly 23 percent. The number of cane farmers stood at 6,696 in 1899, with 2,826, or 42 percent, being Indians. From about 1908 onwards, Indians became a majority of this class (5,922 vs. 5,619).[52] By 1916 they stood at 11,014 versus 8,214 Blacks.[53]

Rice cultivation, so dear to the Indian peasant, also became an important activity after the 1880s. Dr. Comins remarked in 1891: "They have recently discovered that the lagoon lands, which have been considered worthless and can be bought for a nominal price, are capital places for growing rice, and they are eagerly buying up all they can get, for, owing to the scarcity of rice and the high import duty, rice growing is a most profitable business."[54]

By 1896 the imports of rice had fallen to five-sixths of local needs. Despite this development, however, the level of rice production in Trinidad remained far below that in British Guiana, where this industry soared after the turn of the century, becoming a major export industry. In 1920, Trinidad had 9,500 acres under rice cultivation, compared with British Guiana's 55,200 acres. Import substitution for the domestic market was the best the Trinidad farmers could manage, and even on that level, the challenge was not fully met, since Trinidad continued to remain a net importer of rice. Still, it engaged the energies of hundreds of free Indian farmers, most of the producing units being less than 5 acres in size, and indeed often less than 1 acre.

Agricultural labor (both estate labor and independent cultivation) was the primary activity of the vast majority of the Indians, about 78.3 percent in 1891, 75 percent in 1911, and 67 percent in 1921.[55] But a sizeable number had become involved in a wide range of other occupations by the 1880s. Based on conversations with the Reverend John Morton, Dr. Comins gave a list of the main occupations in 1891, in descending order of priority (priority being defined as status giving and/or of profit-making value):

Usury
Proprietors of Rum Shops
Proprietors of Cocoa Estates, and Provision Shops

Cab Proprietors and Carting

Proprietors of Coconut Estates

Rice Cultivation on own lands, combined with Cattle-rearing and Milk-selling

Market Gardeners

Goldsmiths and Silversmiths

Hucksters or Pedlars

Grass Sellers

Fishermen

Lodging House Keepers

Charcoal Burning, Rice Growing and Corn Growing in forest clearings

Contracts for growing Cocoa trees, usually five years, with right to all crops grown

Contracts for "farming" i.e. taking entire charge of an area of sugarcane cultivation during the growing of the crop

Skilled labor in sugar factories, driving engines, etc.

Skilled labor on the sugar estate, draining, forking, etc.

Grooms, Coachmen, Laundresses, Domestic Servants

Scavenging (all the roads in Port-of-Spain are cleared daily by free coolies employed as scavengers)

Roadmaking, and on the Railroad as laborers, pointsmen, gatekeepers, and in the Botanical Gardens[56]

A headman or driver on an estate was a person of influence, often owning a shop in the neighboring village, "seldom in his own name." Through this activity, and moneylending especially to new immigrants, he acquired substantial wealth. There were also other status occupations held by an educated minority: teachers, lawyers, clerks. There were also priests, preachers, ministers, catechists, salesmen, agents, druggists, dispensers, railway guards; women were employed as midwives, seamstresses, and domestic servants. And there were always the legal and illegal movements to and from eastern Venezuela, where Indians worked in the gold fields and on the cocoa estates, the wages of the former being "40 cents a day higher than ordinary day labor on [Trinidad] estates."

The 1891 census enumerated 109 teachers (15 of them women), 23 "planter-proprietors," 30 "merchants, agents, dealers," 605 shopkeepers, and 223 "overseers, overlookers, drivers." As mentioned earlier, the estimate of 720 "peasant proprietors" had to be vastly undercounted, most of these people probably being enumerated under the title of agricultural laborers.

According to the census analysis, the Indians formed 42.5 percent of the 1,425 shopkeepers on the island, larger than any other group (the Chinese were next with 23.9 percent, followed by 15.3 percent Trinidadians). Of the 1,008 overseers and drivers, Indians were 24.8 percent, compared with 40 percent Trinidadians and 24.4 percent British West Indians. Of the 3,452 peasant proprietors, Indians were 20.9 percent, compared with 60.2 percent Trinidadians. Of the agricultural laborer class (58,534), Indians were 67.6 percent, with 18.3 percent Trinidadians and 11.2 percent British West Indians.[57]

Thirty years later, the 1921 census, taken four years after the end of indentured immigration, enumerated 1,075 shopkeepers and hucksters, 1,394 "proprietors," 237 "managers, submanagers and overseers," 4,254 peasant proprietors, and 49,380 agricultural laborers. There were also 284 teachers (61 of them women), 93 "ministers of religion," 5 lawyers, and 1 doctor.[58]

Indians in 1921 were still overwhelmingly rural (and would remain so well into the modern period), largely based in the sugar-growing areas of Caroni and Victoria counties, but spread over most of the island, with Tacarigua Ward in the northern county of St. George and the various wards of St. Patrick in the southwest responsible for significant segments of the population. In 1921 they formed 33.18 percent (121,407) of the Trinidad-Tobago population, 31 percent of these (37,341) being India born.[59]

One interesting factor usually left undiscussed by analysts was the small overseas migration from Trinidad among the free Indians. Every year a small minority applied for passports to travel overseas, whether for temporary or permanent reasons (the statistics do not differentiate). Their destinations give us some idea of their orbit of movement in the new environment, the social and physical "action space" of the free Indian resident. The most popular overseas destination was Venezuela, followed by British Guiana. The annual immigration reports did not begin to record these departures systematically until around 1890. In the twenty-four-year period between 1897 and 1920, the number of passports issued to free Indians in Trinidad for travel overseas was as given in Table 8.1.

The Venezuelan traffic was of course much larger than these legal trips indicate, since most of the Indian laborers who traveled to and from

TABLE 8.1

Venezuela	999	Tobago	11
British Guiana	437	Barbados	7
Grenada	155	South Africa	7
St. Vincent	94	Guadeloupe	4
Surinam	42	United States	4 (3 in 1897, 1 in 1901–2)
India	41*	Martinique	3
St. Lucia	30	Haiti	3 (in 1912–13)
Jamaica	25	St. Kitts	2
Colon	19	Arabia	2 (in 1908–9)
Cayenne	16	Cuba	1 (in 1911–12)
Puerto Colombia	13	Italy	1 (in 1918)
		Total:	1,916

*These were people not traveling via the normal return vessels to India.

the mainland were not automatically entitled to passports, being either deserters or people who had completed less than ten years in Trinidad. Free Indians living on the island more than five but less than ten years were not supposed to travel, if they wanted to retain their rights to a free return passage to India. For most of these free Indians, clandestine travel to Venezuela was easier and more frequent.

Noticeable too in these travel statistics were the departures for Windward island destinations such as Grenada, St. Vincent, and St. Lucia. These islands had had their own brief experiences with Indian indentured labor. Grenada had received 3,200 up to the 1880s, and St. Vincent, 2,472 up to the late 1870s. St. Lucia had received 4,354 up to as late as the 1890s.[60] Officially, 278 had repatriated to India from Grenada, 1,050 from St. Vincent, and 2,446 from St. Lucia.[61] No doubt a certain number had relocated to the larger territories of Trinidad and British Guiana, but a small community of free Indians had remained on these islands, in a minority situation similar to that of their counterparts in Jamaica and the French islands of Martinique and Guadeloupe.

The travel statistics quoted above showed that the interisland movements were not all one-way, that free Indians from Trinidad (and indeed British Guiana) occasionally went to the Windwards in search of work. One witness before the Sanderson Commission in 1909, a cocoa proprietor from Grenada, recorded that he had about forty such immigrants on his own estate, some of whom had been with him for eighteen years. He confirmed that such migrations from the larger territories were quite regular.[62]

BRITISH GUIANA

The growth of the off-estate free Indian community was much slower, after as well as before 1870. Up to the mid-1870s, one major factor responsible for this was the persistence of five-year reindentures, a practice that had been discontinued in Trinidad since the 1850s. The planters had insisted on its retention to the 1870–71 Commission, but in its final report the Commission had recommended its reduction to one-year periods, criticizing some of the abuses connected with its operation. This took effect with Law No. 7 of 1873, the legislation resulting from the report.

Despite the abuses, however, a large number of the Indians had not seemed to object too strenuously to the practice. With their $50 bounty, they often bought a cow which they were usually allowed to graze freely on estate pasturelands and which helped them to supplement their estate wages through their informal monopoly on milk supplies to the neighborhood. Ironically, it was the planters themselves who brought the whole reindenture system to an end around 1875, when they collectively raised the official reindenture fee to a prohibitive level (two hundred dollars) in order to protect those planters who were importing labor directly from India.

As the institution waned, the free Indians began to move off the estates more quickly and in greater numbers. By the 1890s, the ratio of off-estate to estate-resident Indians (indentured and free) assumed the dimensions that it had reached in Trinidad since the late 1850s: 33 percent (35,668) of a total of 108,484 in 1891. Twenty years later, in 1911, it was 50 percent (62,893) out of 126,838. The ratio of indentureds to total free (on and off the estates) also lowered dramatically: in 1881, indentureds were 25 percent (22,752) of the total; by 1891, they were 16 percent (16,710), with 84 percent free.[63]

Despite the growth in the size of the free communities both on and off the estates, a noticeable feature of the Guianese situation was the large number of Indians who continued to remain resident on the estates, voluntarily opting for wage labor and the life of the plantation after the end of indenture. This continued right up to the end of the system in 1920. The number of Indians voluntarily resident on the estates in 1921, after the cancellation of all indentures, was 54,088, or 43.3 percent of the total community of 124,939, the off-estate population being 63,139 in the villages and 7,712 in the towns, that is, 56.7 percent.[64]

The main reason for this had to do with the difficult nature of the Guianese terrain, mentioned before, and the monopoly of the best coast-lands by the plantations. The readiness of the planter class to keep labor tied to the estates by several kinds of inducements (free garden plots, pasturelands, plus the free housing and health care facilities normal to indenture) also paid off more fully in a geographical environment where independent cultivation beyond the estate lands always had a less attractive, less promising general outlook than in next-door Trinidad, with its spacious and fertile virgin territory.

Even the lands that eventually became the main small holdings of the independent peasantry were primarily bought from private, rather than public (Crown), lands, portions of existing plantations sold out to the Indians in small allotments for both residential and cultivation purposes (as had been done in the 1840s and 1850s with Black ex-slaves) or abandoned estates bought individually or collectively from their owners.

State encouragement of independent landownership came, as in Trinidad, in two stages. But both occurred here later in time, and both options were always overshadowed in British Guiana by the purchases from private landowners undertaken by the Indians themselves. Free land grants in commutation of the return passage right were officially sanctioned in 1880, stalled in 1882, and then revived in 1897–1902. Liberalization of the regulations surrounding purchases of Crown lands came in 1898.

A recent study on the growth of the independent Guianese peasantry distinguished three separate strategies adopted by the planter class over time towards the ex-indentured immigrants, in the effort to keep labor closely wedded to the needs of the sugar plantation.[65] The first strategy entailed encouraging the free Indians to remain on the estate, where their labor would be easily accessible. The second strategy involved encouraging them to remain in the neighborhood (i.e., largely on front land villages carved out of the plantation lands themselves). The third involved encouraging them to remain in the colony. All involved the assumption that the location of the new landowning class was important, and also that the continued availability of labor to the estates was the main *reason* for the encouragement of small peasant cultivation.

Reluctance to concede the potential for an independent producer class beyond the plantation regimen, and strenuous efforts to block that possibility whenever it could be blocked, were the main planks of planter policy throughout most of the century. The West India Royal Commission of 1897 had cause to remark on this fact and to stress the need to bring an end to the multiple restrictions placed in the path of the free immigrants in their efforts to become a landowning and food-producing class beyond the confines of the plantation system.

In the years immediately following the end of five-year reindentures, 1873 to 1876, about 12,000 Indians were said to have left the plantations, in search of alternative livelihoods in the towns and countryside.[66] Estimates of their numbers vary widely, but one study suggested that by 1881 there were 14,470 living off the estates—6,908 in Demerara, 4,673 in Essequibo, 2,889 in Berbice.[67] Most were to be found in the "straggling, unorganized settlements dotted all along the coastal strip."[68] About 2,500 lived in and on the outskirts of Georgetown and New Amsterdam.

There were no exclusively East Indian villages in the beginning, although Indians tended to move into the unoccupied spaces between and on the outskirts of Black villages. In the eastern and largely uninhabited Upper Corentyne district, however, they tended to predominate, exercising their independence from the plantation syndrome with their two main activities, cattle rearing and rice growing. The Immigration Report for 1876 described them as diffused all over the country, employed as woodcutters, cattle minders, cart drivers, domestic servants, and agricultural laborers, with many of them owning cabs, donkey and mule carts, many employed in the police force, some cultivating their own farms on rented or purchased lands, and some engaged as shopkeepers.

Recorded immigrant land purchases between 1872 and 1882 were a mere 615. About 45 percent of the purchases in the decade of the 1870s were of small front land estate lots of 1 acre, carved out by the planters in an effort to entice the laborers to stay in close proximity to the estates.[69]

It was the prolonged sugar depression that began in 1884–85 which accelerated the movement out of the estates (as in Trinidad) and which partly prompted the attempt by the government to create a land commutation program of the kind that Trinidad had been experimenting with in the 1870s. There had been one attempt to commence such a program in 1871 with the government purchase of an abandoned plantation, Nooten Zuill, in East Coast Demerara.[70] But the program was stillborn, as no Indians applied for land grants, considering the lands too far away and too unstable for settlement. The property was subsequently sold to a neighboring estate owner.

Small groups of Indians had also applied for such land grants on plantations of their own choosing in 1877 and 1879, but the state had turned down their requests. Only in 1880, with the purchase of Huist Dieren, an abandoned sugar estate in Essequibo, could the program be said to have tentatively begun in British Guiana. It was divided into 350 cultivation lots of 2 acres each, and 270 residential lots of a quarter acre each. The adults of a family were allotted 1 cultivation lot and 1 residential lot each (2¼ acres). Children between ten and fifteen years of age received a further 2 acres each, and children under ten, half an acre each.

Up to 1882, 49 residential lots and 69 cultivation lots were granted in exchange for the grantees' rights to their return passages. The program was then arrested by the new Governor, Sir Henry Irving, transferred from Trinidad. In his view, free land grants were not the answer to the problem of the accumulating backlog of free return passages. What was required was to enable the immigrants to buy land for themselves in localities of their own choosing. While technically such people would still retain their return passage rights, in practice they were unlikely to claim these rights once they had settled down as landowners and cultivators in the colony.

After 1882 this became official policy, and attempts were made to sell lands to immigrants from state-held estates (or colony lands, as they were called) which had been seized from their owners for one reason or another (failure to pay taxes or to maintain the property). The remainder of the lots at Huist Dieren were also put up for sale at $24 an acre. No Indians bought land there at that price, however, as they claimed that land could be purchased in other areas of Essequibo for about $5 an acre. A number of those who had bought lots (about sixty-seven) also defaulted on their payments, leaving their allotments to be repossessed by the state.

The Huist Dieren experiment struggled along with a number of the kinds of problems which would later affect the other attempts at land commutation settlements after 1897: irrigation and drainage problems and the expenses of upkeep and general maintenance; inability of the settlers to live off their small allotments, plus a lack of access to steady labor on the estates nearby; multiple defaults on tax and purchase payments due; general inexperience on the part of many of the settlers in the business of small-scale independent cultivation; and the inhospitable nature of large portions of the soil. When Messrs. McNeill and Lal visited the colony in 1913, they found 354 inhabitants of this settlement still residing there, half of them non-Indians.[71]

One recent study described the government land commutation settlement program in British Guiana as "conceived in expediency, born in uncertainty, baptised in doubt, and living precariously for many years."[72] After a fifteen-year spell with no further free land grants in exchange for return passage rights, the program was renewed in 1897 under the pressure of the recession and the threat of large-scale repatriation which this created. Four new abandoned estates were bought and redistributed in the years between 1897 and 1902, when the program was again terminated, this time finally. The estates were Helena on East Coast Demerara (1897), Whim on the Corentyne (1898), Bush Lot on West Coast Berbice (1899), and Maria's Pleasure on Wakenaam Island in Essequibo (1902).

A total of 2,711 Indians received allotments on these properties: 1,206 on Helena, 574 on Whim, 755 on Bush Lot, and 176 on Maria's Pleasure. Many of the problems which had beset the Huist Dieren experiment were repeated here. Some of the grantees never moved into their allotments, having farms elsewhere and interested only in reselling their grants to others. Many who did relocate were not especially vigorous cultivators and neglected their lands in favor of wage labor on nearby estates. Added to this were the ravages of nature (a severe drought in 1899 which crippled many at Whim and Bush Lot) and the self-inflicted damages caused by collective negligence in keeping their drains and dams in order.

Still, many managed to do reasonably well, growing rice and other food crops and planting coconuts, coffee, and fruit trees in some settlements. At Whim, Bush Lot, and Huist Dieren, rice was the primary cash crop. On all of the settlements, cattle rearing and milk selling were important activities.

Messrs. McNeill and Lal concluded in 1914 that the land commutation settlement scheme was defective in its planning and execution, especially on the arrangements for supply of irrigation water and the maintenance of a proper drainage system. In 1913 there were 1,411 people on Helena, a quarter of them non-Indian. The other settlements, mainly of Indians, had 433 on Whim, 622 on Bush Lot, and 223 on Maria's Pleasure. Whim, which was close to two large plantations, Port Mourant and Albion, where regular work was available for the male settlers, was generally regarded as the most successful, and Bush Lot as the least successful, of the settlements.[73]

Public land sales to free Indians were divided into sales of "colony lands," that is, estates seized and held by the state for various tax and maintenance defaults, and sales of Crown lands proper, that is, the non-plantation interior or unoccupied coastlands. Governor Irving's suggestion in 1882 that Indians be allowed to purchase colony lands of their own choosing instead of being given free land grants in exchange for return passage rights was approved and acted upon in the first decade of the recession. Up to 1890, at least 214 buyers had combined to acquire

3,883 ¼ acres of state-held plantations, mainly in Berbice and Essequibo.[74] Many of these were then subdivided by the purchasers and
resold to others in smaller allotments.

The Irving initiative, however, ran into difficulties when the planter-
controlled Combined Court refused to allocate the necessary funds for
irrigation and drainage maintenance on many of the estates. A lull in
the sales of colony lands also accompanied the renewed efforts to revive
the land commutation settlement program between 1897 and 1902. After
1898, moreover, the sale of public properties became dramatically easier
with the easing of the Crown land sales restrictions in force since 1839.

Prompted more by the need to open up the interior for gold prospecting
and mining ventures than by the need to encourage the expansion of
the new peasantry, the restrictions on sales of Crown lands had been
progressively eased since 1887, soon after the gold industry had assumed
some importance in the colony's economic development. However, the
criticisms made by the West India Royal Commission in 1897 concerning
restrictions on the growth of a small peasantry added to the decision-
making momentum. After 1898, Crown lands could be bought at fifteen
cents an acre, and homesteads up to 25 acres at ten cents an acre could
be established.[75] Lands could also be leased at five cents an acre annually.

The new regulations, the imperatives of the depression years, and,
most significant, the increasing importance of rice cultivation in British
Guiana combined to encourage a major expansion of the off-estate Indian
population after 1900. From just under one-third of the total Indian
population in 1891, it was about one-half by 1911 and about 56 percent
by 1921. New areas of the interior along the rivers of Mahaica, Mahaicony, and Abary, as well as Corentyne and Berbice rivers, came into
Indian ownership and cultivation. The state also sold off newly acquired
properties on East Coast Demerara, in the Canals Polder, and on West
Bank Demerara, to farmers growing ground provisions and other local
food crops for the domestic market. Between 1890 and 1913, 844 purchases of Crown lands, up to 31,913 acres, were made by Indians.[76]

The vast majority of the lands taken up by the free Indians in British
Guiana, as mentioned before, were purchases and rentals of private lands.
This was so because these were the best lands in the colony and monopolized by the plantocracy. However, throughout the entire period of the
expansion of this new class, all the existing options for land acquisition were exercised simultaneously: small rentals or grants from existing
planter-employers, purchases of estate front lands from planter-employers
in small residential "villages," purchases (group or individual) of aban-

doned estates from planters anxious to sell, purchases of "colony lands," free land grants from the state in commutation of return passage rights, purchases of nonplantation Crown lands after 1898 under the relaxed regulations, and finally, occupancy leases of Crown property for varying terms of years. Rentals or small purchases from large landowning Indians themselves, who had acquired their properties in one or more of the above-mentioned ways, were also common. So too were purchases from Black villagers, mainly in East Coast Demerara and Essequibo.

Lesley Potter has broken down the districts where most of the land purchases took place in the years after 1870 as follows (see Table 8.2).[77]

Thus before 1900 the eastern and western extremes of the colony—Corentyne and Canje on the one hand, and Essequibo on the other—saw the most active land buying of private and public lands. After 1900 West Bank Demerara and East Coast Demerara became prominent destinations, with the availability of public lands especially in the former district. Corentyne continued to be a favorite destination, with the riverine Crown lands of sparsely populated Mahaica-Mahaicony-Abary becoming an important new area of settlement. Note too that the urban centers of Georgetown and New Amsterdam also saw some reasonably vigorous land buying before 1900 (mainly on the outskirts of both towns), with a decline in popularity after the interior districts were generally opened up to purchase.

Potter also pointed out that a significant portion of the land sales were sales of small 1-acre lots on the front lands of existing plantations, that is, by planters to their own laborers. Between 1870 and 1890, 32.6 percent of the land sales were of this nature; between 1891 and 1900,

TABLE 8.2

	1870–1900	1901–1920
Essequibo	16.4	5.9 percent
West Coast Demerara	5.4	6.6
West Bank Demerara	4.6	20.3
East Bank Demerara	3.5	2.6
Georgetown	11.7	3.8
East Coast Demerara	4.0	17.4
Mahaica-Abary	9.5	14.9
West Coast Berbice	3.4	2.7
Berbice River	1.0	4.2
New Amsterdam	5.0	1.0
Canje	14.4	4.7
Corentyne	21.0	16.0

25.9 percent; between 1901 and 1910, 17.3 percent; and between 1911 and 1920, 28.7 percent.[78]

Central to the expansion of the new Indian landholding and farming class were the activities of rice growing and cattle rearing. What cocoa cultivation did for the Trinidad Indians, rice cultivation did for the Guianese. In fact, it was they who developed the industry almost single-handedly into a major export industry by 1908 (cocoa in Trinidad, of course, was always a multiracial activity).

Walter Rodney has reminded us that the Indians were not the first to grow rice in British Guiana, that African slaves from the rice-growing areas of the Upper Guinea Coast in West Africa had brought these skills with them to the colony, as had the Timinis (Temnes) of Sierra Leone and Liberia in the early nineteenth century to Berbice.[79] Both Indians and Chinese had experimented with rice cultivation also in the 1860s, mainly on estate lands. But the imperatives of sugar production tended to clash with the rhythm of rice cultivation, and the planters discouraged its continuation and growth. A small number of free Indians managed to cultivate a few thousand acres off the estates in the district of Mahaica-Abary, and some of those who were involved in the first land commutation settlements even displayed their rice crops at a local exhibition in 1882. By 1879 there were also about three hundred to four hundred free Indians working about 1,500 acres at Plantation Success in Essequibo.

It was the sugar depression of the mid-1880s which changed the planters' attitudes and which also released much free Indian labor from the estates into new districts, where the cultivation of the crop became both an imperative and a challenge. In 1884, there were only about 2,500 acres under rice cultivation in British Guiana. By 1914, thirty years later, that acreage was about 47,000.[80] In 1884, British Guiana was an importer of rice, about 19,411 tons a year. By 1906, it had begun to export the product, in limited quantities. Ten years after, in 1916, the industry supplied all of domestic needs and had crossed the 10,000-ton mark in the amount it exported out of the colony, representing about 4 percent of total exports. The dollar value of rice exports also passed the one-million-dollar mark in that year.[81]

Up to 1898, when riverine Crown lands became more easily available for purchase, about half the total acreage of 6,000–7,000 acres in rice cultivation was located on sugar estate lands. By the 1910s, even lands on the estates normally reserved for cattle grazing were being brought under rice cultivation. William Morrison, an estate manager, told the Sanderson Commission in 1909 that 11,000 acres out of the 40,000 acres then under rice cultivation were located on sugar estate lands.[82] But most of the real expansion took place in the new districts, especially the Corentyne coast.

As with cocoa in Trinidad, the rice industry came to compete with sugar for the labor of the free Indians, and even many indentureds elected to desert the plantations to take up wage labor in remote rice settlements. So widespread had this practice become that the Planters' Association began to clamor for the nonsugar sector to be made to contribute to the Immigration Fund and for a corresponding decrease in their own contributions. In contrast with Trinidad, however, where cocoa planters were made to do just that, no such changes were introduced in British Guiana.[83]

By the 1900s many Blacks had begun to participate in rice cultivation once more on a reasonably significant scale, mainly in Berbice. Their overall numbers remained small, however. Even foreign and Euro-Guianese ventures into the rice industry were attempted in 1897, and again in 1909, but the ventures folded up without success. Rice cultivation remained an Indo-Guianese–dominated enterprise. European participation in the rice milling sector of the industry was more significant. British Guiana had four rice mills in 1902, forty-four in 1906, and eighty-six by 1917. In the early years, the European and Euro-Guianese segment dominated this activity, but within a decade or so, even this sector fell largely under Indian control and ownership. Messrs. McNeill and Lal came upon two rice mills in 1913 which were owned by Indians who had themselves been indentured immigrants at one point.[84]

Rice cultivation was generally combined either with casual wage labor for the sugar estates, where such estates were physically nearby (as in West Coast and West Bank Demerara, East Coast and East Bank Demerara), or, very often, with cattle farming in those districts far from the sugar estates (as in interior Mahaicony-Mahaica, parts of the Corentyne, or the North West District in Essequibo). Other crops were also grown: ground provisions, coffee, citrus, coconuts. Cattle rearing, with its related activity, milk selling, was the next major activity after rice cultivation. Major herds of cattle, sheep, and goats were held on both estate and off-estate lands. The most prominent of the cattle farmers were to be found in the Corentyne and West Berbice, in the Mahaica-Mahaicony district, and on the Essequibo coast and islands (Leguan, Wakenaam). About 80 percent of the milk-selling industry was in the hands of the new Indian peasantry by 1890.

Cattle farming could range from the farmer with hundreds of herds of cattle (seven hundred in one case recorded by Dr. Comins in 1893) to the humble plantation laborer with one or two cows, allowed to graze on estate pasturelands either for free or for a small rent. The latter practice had begun in the pre-1870 period, and the purchase of a cow with the $50 bounty money was always the primary investment of immigrants reindenturing for a second time. The earnings acquired from milk selling would be the main supplement to their wages earned from plantation labor.

When the Royal Commission into the West India Sugar Industry conducted its hearings in 1897, one question-and-answer exchange on the activities of the free Indians went as follows:

Q: How do immigrants, who are not on sugar estates, make a living as a rule?

A. They work on the estate two or three days a week; they have their cow and their little farm, and they make it up in that way.[85]

However, by the 1890s, cattle rearing was already big business on the Corentyne savannahs. Dr. Comins recounted that when he was in Surinam, he found an active trade in the export of cattle going on between the Indians of British Guiana and the inhabitants of Nickerie on the Dutch side of the Corentyne.[86] It was impossible to quantify the numbers of immigrants who owned cattle, or even the number of cattle in the colony. In 1891 Dr. Comins estimated the number of cattle owned by estate-resident laborers (indentured and free) at 20,631. This did not include cattle kept by them in pastures not connected with the estates, or the considerable numbers owned by free Indians living outside the estates altogether.[87] The total number on the estates declined slightly by 1911–12 to 13,384, owing largely to the shift of concentration to rice cultivation on many estate lands. The numbers kept by the non-estate cattle farmers remained unquantifiable, of course.[88]

Free Indians who were not landowners, lessees, or plantation laborers engaged in a variety of other occupations, many similar to those of their Trinidad counterparts, a few unique to British Guiana. The wealthiest was the shopkeeper and the moneylender. Dr. Comins had this to say about this class:

Contrary to my experience of Trinidad where the coolies are the principal shopkeepers of the island, I find the former industrial occupants of the soil—the Portuguese and the Chinese—have been able to hold their own with greater success, and often the estate is indebted to them for the provision of all ready money to meet the wages of laborers and current expenses of the estate. . . . There are often two or three shops on an estate, one or more of which may be owned by coolies. . . . In addition to selling provisions and an assortment of necessaries of all descriptions, they are always ready to lend money on the usual Indian terms of usury, and many become very wealthy men.[89]

In British Guiana most nonsugar occupations required the payment of annual licenses in order to operate legally, so a fairly accurate assessment of the numbers engaged in certain occupations can be obtained. Messrs. McNeill and Lal gave a breakdown on license holders for 1913 (see Table 8.3).[90] In 1913, free Indians were also mechanics, clerks, postmasters, male nurses or dispensers, government civil servants of secondary rank, interpreters, and police. There were a handful of professional men, 3 lawyers and 4 doctors. In contrast with Trinidad, there were few teachers: as late as 1937, Indians had succeeded in producing just 94 teachers (79 male, 15 female) out of a total of 1,181 in the colony. There were many day laborers in the towns and many in the public works sector.[91]

The census data from 1891 to 1921 give us some idea of the percentage of Indians in various sectors of Guianese society over the years (see Table 8.4).[92]

At the end of indenture, in 1921, Indians lived in all districts of the colony, but the largest numerical concentrations were to be found in Corentyne and the East Coast (21,221), East Coast Demerara (19,867), West Coast Demerara (11,765), Essequibo Coast (11,461), and Mahaica-Abary (9,016). By that year, they were 124,938 in number, 42 percent of the colony's population.[93]

The small migration or overseas travel factor among the free Indians in British Guiana was recorded officially much earlier than in Trinidad. Figures for the twenty-year period from 1871 to 1890 (see page 251)

TABLE 8.3

Provision Shops	542	Hucksters	1,529
Spirit Shops	9	Pawnbrokers	15
Druggists' Shops	47	Horse and Mule Carts	68
Wine and Liquor Shops	120	Donkey Carts	1,609
Opium and Ganja Shops	23	River and Sea Craft	833
Tobacco and Liquor Shops	535	Carriages, 4 wheels, for hire	107
Butchers' Shops	66	Carriages, 2 wheels, for hire	9
Stores	82	Horses or Mules, for hire	298
Cook Shops	43		

TABLE 8.4

	1891	1911	1921
Professional (incl. public service)	5.8	8.2	6.8 percent
Commercial	10.6	24.3	23.6
Industrial	4.3	5.4	4.9
Agricultural	75.9	81.6	91.9
Domestic	7.6	7.8	4.7
Unoccupied	19.8	31.1	38.8
Total Indian Population:	37.9	42.7	42.0 percent

give us a picture of their favorite overseas destinations, permanent or temporary (see Table 8.5). Trinidad and Surinam were the main destinations of Guianese Indians. Of these 1,267 travelers in twenty years, 307 were immigrants who had completed five but not ten years in the colony, and they forfeited their right to a free return passage to India by traveling (presumably permanently) before their ten-year residence was fulfilled. The travel statistics for the years 1891 to 1904 also revealed the same destination preferences, but with a marked shift towards Surinam and Nickerie over Trinidad (about 63.5 percent to 22.3 percent, out of approximately 2,470).[94]

JAMAICA

The tiny free Indian community in Jamaica evolved in a more constricted economic terrain compared with the larger island patterns. The broad options were the same, although the mobility opportunities were

TABLE 8.5

Trinidad	695	Lisbon	5 (in 1876)
Surinam	274	Tobago	3
Nickerie		Grenada	2
(also Surinam)	80	Mauritius	2
St. Lucia	51	British Honduras	1
Cayenne	37	Antigua	1
Barbados	35	St. Eustatius	1
Martinique	23	Panama	1 (in 1881)
Jamaica	20	Madeira	1 (in 1881)
St. Vincent	17	United States	1 (in 1876)
England	16	China	1 (in 1889)
		Total:	1,267

clearly not as plentiful, despite the great wealth apparently acquired by a minority of them. Free Indians were already more than 80 percent of the small community of 14,889 by 1879.[95] A sizeable number continued to live on the estates, and most Indians were plantation laborers when Dr. Comins visited in 1891.

His breakdown of the occupations among the Indians at that time is given in Table 8.6.

Noticeable in this list was the large number of shopkeepers (415), the largest of the nonagricultural occupations. In fact, Dr. Comins noted that the shops on or near the plantations were usually owned by Indians or Afro-Jamaicans, and that unlike the other territories, there were no Chinese or Portuguese shopkeepers in these areas.[96] (Twenty years later, though, this situation had changed. The Jamaica Immigration Report for 1910 spoke of the "invasion of the Chinese who control practically all the retail.")

The vast majority, as elsewhere, continued to remain wedded to agriculture. Most of these were laborers on the banana and sugar estates, with the former being more plentiful, given the rise of that industry in the 1880s and the relative decline of the sugar industry in the Jamaican industry. The 1911 census recorded 5,323 banana workers, as compared with 2,854 sugar workers.[97]

The small peasantry had also risen, both landowners and renters, and they cultivated the usual variety of vegetables and provisions for the local market. Much of this activity was small scale, and there was nothing comparable to the cocoa cultivators and cane farmers of Trinidad, or the

TABLE 8.6

Sailors	5	Washers	26
Peasant Proprietors	62	Priests and Mendicants	36
Agricultural Laborers	6,241	Teachers	5
Tending Stock on Pasture	10	Midwives	3
General Laborers	861	Goldsmiths and Jewellers	23
Railway, Road or Street		Bakers and Cake Makers	32
Laborers	27	Fishermen	2
Merchant, Agent, Dealer	10	House Proprietors	383
Shopkeepers	415	Living on Private Means	1
Shopmen, Salesmen, Clerks	85	Females attending Domestic	
Market Gardeners	110	Duties	74
Indoor Domestic Servants	74	Watchmen	32
Domestic Groom, Coachman,		Woodcutters	2
Gardener	51	Persons of No Occupation	2,145

rice growers and cattle rearers of British Guiana. The 1911 census recorded 122 market gardeners, 140 banana "planters," 18 cane farmers,
265 provision planters, 138 rice planters, 15 coffee planters, and 22
cassava planters, as well as 45 "cattlemen." A Colonial Office dispatch
recorded that in 1915–16 there were approximately 11,049 acres of land
valued at £59,733 owned by Indians. Much of this land was widely
dispersed over the fifteen parishes, but there were significant concentrations in St. Mary, St. Thomas, St. Catherine, Trelawny, and
Clarendon.[98]

Land had been acquired over time through purchases of private and
Crown lands, and an unquantifiable amount had been bought with
bounty moneys received in exchange for return passage rights. The commutation program in Jamaica had had since its inception in 1869 an
on-again, off-again history resulting from the internal vicissitudes of
Jamaican fiscal politics, but a large number of Indians had received cash
grants of £10 to £12 over the years when the program was fully operative,
and they had used the grants to buy lands in areas of their own choosing.
The pure land grants of 10 acres were less frequent, and the Indians
themselves had preferred the cash option. The whole scheme was finally
ended in 1906, after a brief three-year revival following an earlier termination in 1897.

Messrs. McNeill and Lal stated that up to 1910 the land commutation
allotments had amounted to 284, involving 3,214 acres, but that a large
number (188) had not been taken up by the grantees, while many others
had been resold.[99] Most lands held by Indians in Jamaica, however, were
acquired through purchases rather than through free state grants.

Assimilation and Creolization

In any discussion on the complex processes by which the Indians made
their cultural and spiritual adjustments to the new society, it should be
remembered that such adjustments had to be made in interaction with
different and often separable elements at work in the total environment.
To reduce the discussion of assimilation and creolization (i.e., Americanization, Caribbean-style) to a mere discussion on race relations with the
larger African society, as many analysts are prone to doing, would be to
distort the realities of their inner encounter with the new society, an
encounter that often had no direct bearing on the issue of Indian-African
race relations as such.

Because of their special legal status, the largely isolated nature of their existence on the plantation, and the tendency towards rural residential and often occupational isolation even after indenture, the problematic encounter with the forces of modernization (economic and cultural), colonialism, and racial dominance embodied by the planter-colonial government alliance was often experienced alone, without direct reference to the quite separate but equally important matter of adjustment to other sectors within the colonial labor force.

Sometimes the dynamics of both adjustment processes overlapped, but quite often they were unrelated. The vertical encounter with Westernization and the horizontal encounter with Afro-Westernization were not identical, at least not as the inner experience was lived within the immigrant community itself. Often, the Indians found themselves resisting both processes, or resisting one more than the other, or partially accommodating with both, in a dialectical process dictated by their own internal development as a community or by external forces at large in the society at any given moment in time. The process was not simple, nor was it uniform or static. Walter Rodney's description of this process as one of "two semi-autonomous sets of working class struggles against the domination of capital" comes close to the point, although it may be argued that he underplayed the extent to which this dichotomy affected the cultural process.[100] Here, too, a dialectical pluralism was often at work.

The primary modernization (and Westernization) agency with which the Indian laborer had to deal was the mode of production itself, namely, the plantation, with its special manner of organizing people collectively for the purpose of producing a modern export commodity. The hierarchical and occupational divisions of village life in India crumbled before the roughshod equalization to which every immigrant was subjected, not just at the workplace, but also in the residential barracks which had been constructed for them. Sacrosanct notions of caste purity and separation, buttressed by religious ritual and practice, made no sense in the environment of the new mode of production, where new social and occupational divisions imposed their own imperatives on the immigrants.

To be sure, the notion of caste as an abstract form of social differentiation did not die, since ways of seeing always have a habit of altering more slowly than the supporting structures which created them in the first place. But as the external environment and the material foundations changed, these factors in themselves created and compelled new forms of inner interaction between the members of the new community of plantation wage laborers. In an environment where a *chamar* or a Madrasi of low caste could conceivably exercise more authority than a *chattri* or

Rajput, or indeed even acquire more wealth after indenture than the latter, traditional notions of superiority were often severely challenged for their material irrelevance as time went by.

Moreover, despite the general constriction of mobility opportunities which confronted all the immigrants after they left the plantation, the fact was that there was a widening of the range of available occupations for many caste members traditionally relegated to narrow specific fields in village India. Indian shopkeepers did not have to be *bunnias*, and they were usually not. The accumulation of wealth after indenture was open-ended and dependent on factors unrelated to birth and hereditary status. While many immigrants did revert to their traditional caste occupations after plantation life was over, even more found themselves entering into fields that would have been unthinkable in India given their caste backgrounds.

Caste endogamy was also a casualty of the modernizing force of the plantation system. In addition to the problems caused by the low female-male ratio, it was inevitable that changing notions and visible indicators of status in the new environment would alter the intercaste relation at the level of marriage and family life. While this phenomenon was frequent among the immigrants themselves, the erosion of the traditional criteria for choosing a mate was hastened by the generational factor and the increase in the numbers of locally born Indians. The notion of caste differentiation continued to influence the process, but the necessities and concrete perceptions of the new social environment often dictated otherwise.

If the rigid barriers of caste could not stand up against the necessities of the New World environment, the Indians nevertheless found a new application of the notion of caste superiority in their attitudes towards the Black population, whom they incorporated into their traditional worldview at the lowest caste levels, partly out of an inner cultural judgment on the mores and culture of the Black strangers, partly as a result of the racially charged setting into which they had been deliberately placed in the politics and economics of post-Emancipation plantation society.

The two races never clashed on a significant level, simply because the labor competition on the sugar plantation was not as acute as it might have been, given the racial division of labor in the field and the factory and the existence of alternative options for the Black population outside of sugar (more so Trinidad than British Guiana). But it was the common perception among nineteenth-century observers of the racial scenario that they shared an aloofness towards, and a mutual contempt for, one another which became the basis for their twentieth-century mode of interaction on many levels.

The issue was not made any simpler by the attitude of the Indians on interracial male-female relations. The *San Fernando Gazette* described the Indian male as "betraying a natural aversion to forming connections with strange women."[101] Given their rural isolation from mainstream Creole society, the matter was clearly of socially marginal importance in the conduct of everyday affairs, but Creole society often commented on the topic and constantly contrasted the Indians with the other ethnic immigrants without seeking explanations in the very hierarchical inhibitions of the Hindu caste system itself. It was accordingly oblivious to the internal social discriminations within the Hindu community itself, and to the knowledge that the Caribbean was not the only society where the cultural inhibitions of the Hindu peasants had prevented them from practicing any form of racial exogamy on any but the most insignificant level. (In chapter 7, we have already referred to the issue of interracial unions in Malaya.)

All of this having been said, it would have been a miracle if there had been no interracial liaisons between the newcomers and the natives at all. Indeed, as early as the first inflow of Indian immigrants in 1838 in British Guiana, the records indicated that a number of interracial unions had taken place between Indian men and Black women. About eight to ten on Waterloo and Highbury estates were singled out for mention, and a child of one of these unions was said to have died around 1842 on an estate next to Highbury estate.[102] Dr. Bunyun, in his 1848 report to the Governor of British Guiana, had even remarked on the features of the children of some of these unions: "The two of most advanced age are on Plantation Lochaber, Berbice. They are remarkable looking children, of very symmetrical forms, with handsome intelligent countenances, and glossy black hair in long wavy locks."[103]

That these unions continued throughout the indenture period, that they were more often than not the product of illicit relations not sanctioned by the Indian community, arising out of the dynamics of plantation day-to-day life and occasionally from interracial interaction at the village level—all of these things are well established. That the whole issue of racial gender mixing between Indian and African never succeeded in getting past the taboo stage of consciousness during the whole period of this study (and indeed for long afterwards), quite in contrast with the situation with the other ethnic immigrants, is also well known. Towards the close of the indenture system, after several decades of low-level racial interaction, the Trinidad census of 1911 could record that in that year there were 1,514 people of mixed Indian origin on the island, 975 with an Indian father and 539 with an Indian mother. In 1921, there were 2,229, 1,580 with an Indian father and 649 with an Indian mother. Even here, however, the census does not tell us much about the nature of the racial mixture involved.

The Indian community developed and transformed itself in the new environment, as we have said, largely on its own internal dynamic, with the race relations issue rendered marginal by the occupational and residential segregation that was a factor of nineteenth-century life. The issues of the erosion or retention of their traditions in the New World environment in the context of creeping Westernization was of greater immediate import than that of building cultural bridges with the non-Indian colonial labor force.

For the broad majority, the loss of certain aspects of their traditional lifestyle did not mean the loss of tradition altogether. The constantly increasing influx of new immigrants over the years, the sheer size of the community in Trinidad and British Guiana, the relative spatial separation from other races in the society, clustered as they were in largely Indian villages not far from the plantations proper—all ensured that while old customs were being transformed (and some partially eliminated, such as the practice of cremation and the male-oriented marriage dowry) in the new environment, new forms of intraethnic interaction were evolving, perhaps a blend of the Old World and the New, the traditional and the "modern," but always within the life of the group itself, as it responded and adjusted to life in a New World village environment.

The fact that most Indians continued to remain agriculturists of one kind or another (laborers or independent cultivators) encouraged the continuation of a rural community cohesiveness with strong identity bases of its own—as non-Western immigrants, as Indians, as Hindus and Muslims, as immigrants or descendants of immigrants from particular provinces or districts in North or South India. Language, and more so, religion, were not made to feel redundant in the everyday interaction of village life but were indispensable protective tools of survival in a strange new world, the main forms of insulation from the world of the Other, whoever that Other might be. The Bhojpuri dialect of the majority quickly gained ascendancy over the other regional dialects of Hindi brought to the New World, and a creolized version of this speech became the inner language of the villages vis-à-vis the larger Creole society.

Hinduism as it was practiced in the Caribbean reflected the somewhat elastic character that it possessed even within India itself. Possessing no central hierarchy of prophet-interpreters, no central core of dogma or belief, and remarkably diversified in its various expressions at the village level, ranging from low-caste cults involving animal sacrifice to classical metaphysical discourses on the natural and spiritual order (as reflected within the popular religious epics the *Ramayana* and the *Mahabharata*), the religion evolved as an extension of the eclectic belief systems and practices of the Hindu peasants who had migrated to the New World.

It survived through the collective wisdom and memory of the immigrants who were constantly replenishing the labor force until 1917 and through the varying interpretive capacities of the community holy men or pundits, with their often ambiguous claims to Brahmin status. It survived also through the occasional visits of more learned religious dignitaries from India itself, bringing with them their own brands of Hindu worldview and emphasis and seeking converts and followers in the New World Hindu communities.

Both Hinduism and Islam (the latter a more organized and international religion) remained intact and vibrant among the majority of the immigrants and their children, in spite of prejudice and often derision from the larger colonial society, with its Western Christian emphasis. Nineteenth-century racist perceptions on the legitimacy of non-Western cultures pervaded upper-class colonial society, and these were echoed by the Westernized Black Creole elements at the professional and mass levels. The low social status of the Indians also encouraged the popular misconception that these religions were unsophisticated and lower-class religions, in addition to being alien and impenetrable. Even the well-meaning Christian missionaries who proselytized among the Indians seeking converts to Presbyterianism, Roman Catholicism, and Anglicanism were not free from the derogatory view of Eastern religions then in vogue among imperialist thinkers.

Unlike the Africans who had preceded them on the West Indian plantations, however, or even the Chinese, whose nonreligious pragmatism and secular Confucianism rendered them more open to persuasion from Western religious preaching, the majority of the Indian immigrants persevered in their beliefs and religious loyalties, unconvinced that they were in need of religious upliftment and secure in their own unsophisticated way with their own eclectic traditions, which they knew had been tested over the centuries. As late as 1931, after more than seventy-five years of Christian missionary effort, 91 percent of the Indians in British

Guiana and 83 percent of those in Trinidad were still adherents of their traditional religions. In Trinidad, the following statement by Governor Sir William Robinson in the 1890s best summed up their attitudes: "The Hindus seem to be highly indifferent in matters of religion, and from sheer habit probably, steadily adhere to their pagan tenets and practices. Only an imperceptible minority have become converts, and I say with regret that little reliance can be placed on these converts."[104]

In the Caribbean historical context, the cultural tenacity of the Indian immigrants represented simultaneously a form of confident self-assertion against the forces of Westernization and the colonialist order (an expression of themselves as Subjects, rather than Objects, in the private and cultural sphere), and an umbrella of self-protection against the social derision which plantation society and the larger Creole value system had reserved for them.

The humblest villagers were versed in the knowledge of the Hindu scriptures. J. H. Collens wrote in the 1880s that after work in the evenings, immigrants could often be seen gathered together in small groups, crouching down in a semicircle, chanting whole stanzas of the epic poems, like the *Ramayana*, among themselves.[105] The Hindus worshiped their deities in their homes and in their temples, the Muslims prayed in their mosques, and both groups celebrated their religious festivals.

These tended to multiply after the 1870s, when the social expansion out into the independent village settlements allowed them a greater measure of cultural autonomy than they had been allowed on the plantations. By the 1880s, in addition to festivals like the Shiite Muslim festival of Muharrum (Tadjah or Hosein) and the South Indian Fire-Walking ceremony, the traditional celebrations like Divali, Ramleela, Phagwa (Holi), and Shiva-Ratri had resurfaced in the New World environment.[106] The Muslims restored the festival of Eid-ul-Fitr, and the orthodox frowned somewhat on the rowdy and bacchanalian direction which the annual Muharrum festival had taken.

To be sure, not all members of the Indian community were as culturally impervious as the majority clearly were to the Westernizing forces in their new society, and gradually, as the transition from sojourner to settler, from immigrant to citizen, progressed, a growing minority expressed their preferences for Westernization in various ways. A combination of modernizing factors continued to hasten the transformation of their Old World outlook on life: materialist notions of wealth, new occupational snobbisms, the gradual adoption of English (or Creolese) as the main language of communication, new religions (Christianity), Western education. The thrust towards upward social mobility in a Creole environment which did not officially see itself as culturally or religiously pluralistic, but rather as a Westernized melting pot, also hastened the minority trend towards some form of assimilation.

Religious conversion and primary education in Christian missionary ethnic schools provided the main early entrees into the world of the West, in a society where urbanization and significant interracial encounter remained at a minimal level until late into the century (perhaps later for British Guiana). By 1891, the Indian community in Trinidad had 2,258 Roman Catholics, 1,712 Anglicans, 1,622 Presbyterians, and 122 "other Christians" in addition to its 55,180 Hindus, 8,619 Muslims, and 436 "other non-Christians." Still, even among the Trinidad-born Indians, the Hindu and Muslim element predominated by far (17,498 Hindus and 2,990 Muslims). Among the Christianized elements, however, it was noticeable that locally born elements outnumbered the converted India-born elements (3,856 vs. 1,858).[107]

Forty years later (and one decade after the end of the indenture system), the 1931 census recorded the existence of 8,469 Roman Catholics, 3,946 Anglicans, and 10,335 Presbyterians in an Indian community of 138,201. The British Guiana census recorded just 9,045 Christians (6.9 percent) in 1931, as against 96,342 Hindus (73.8 percent), 21,789 Muslims (16.7 percent), 1,214 "other non-Christians," and 2,150 "not stated" in a community of 130,540.

In the long run, it was the educational effort of the Canadian Presbyterian Mission, commenced in 1868 by the Reverend John Morton in Trinidad, and in 1896 by the Reverend J. B. Cropper in British Guiana, which played the major roles in this Westernization process.[108] Denominational schools had existed before the efforts of the Canadian Presbyterians: the Anglicans had started in Trinidad as early as 1856, at Tacarigua in the north, and by the late 1860s had 6 other Anglican primary schools catering to the education of East Indian and other children. The Roman Catholics built 3 schools in north Trinidad in the 1870s especially for East Indian children, 2 in Port-of-Spain and 1 in San Juan. In British Guiana before 1896 the number of denominational schools for students of all races was as follows: Church of England 72, Church of Scotland 36, Congregationalists 30, Wesleyans 29, Roman Catholics 27, Moravians 2, Lutherans 1.

But the Indian attendance at these schools was always quite low, owing to a combination of factors. Among these were parental suspicion of the combination of education and religious conversion; their dislike of the policy of catering to a mixed student population, unable as many were to rid themselves of their castelike dislike (and possibly tribal fear) of the Africans; and the language barrier (there being no special provision for Hindi or Hindustani speakers). Another factor was the general indifference to the value of education for children among immigrants whose intentions of remaining in the society were not always final and who were usually compelled by economic necessity to give preference to keeping their chidren working on the estates, rather than having them in schools for long periods of the day.

The Canadian Presbyterian schools differed from the other denominational schools in that they catered specially to rural Indian community education; provided instruction and published materials in English, Hindi, and Hindustani; and tended to be largely Indian in student composition. In Trinidad, the mission had opened seven schools by 1871 with a total of 331 students (270 of them Indian). By 1890, there were forty-nine schools with 2,884 students; by 1917, seventy schools with 11,375 students. British Guiana in the last year of indentured immigration had twenty-eight Canadian mission schools. Ninety percent of the Indian children who received a primary school education did so in the Canadian mission schools.

In addition to these primary schools, the mission in Trinidad had established a college for training preachers in 1892, a teacher training school in 1894, a secondary school for boys in 1900, and a secondary school for girls in 1912 (Naparima), all in the southern town of San Fernando. In British Guiana, secondary schools for boys and for girls were established at New Amsterdam in Berbice. The training of native teachers, preachers, and catechists, especially in Trinidad, produced a vigorous middle layer of Christian Indians, who carried on the work of the mission with dedication and sacrifice. Trinidad Indians in 1921 had 223 male teachers and 61 female teachers. Most of these would have been products of the Canadian Presbyterian effort.

However, the extent of the overall success of Western missionary education efforts within the Indian community remained very low up to 1917, when indentured immigration ended, and indeed well into the twentieth century, despite the existence of the educated Christian minority. School attendance among the young generally ranged from one-third to one-half of those actually enrolled at any given moment. Overall literacy rates remained extremely low among the Indians as a whole. In 1931 Indians were one-third of the Trinidad population, but 60 percent of the 177,760 illiterates, with a 23 percent literacy level. The literacy level in 1931 in British Guiana was just 25 percent among the Indians, contrasting with 72 percent among the Chinese and 81 percent among the Blacks.[109]

The rise of a well-to-do middle-class stratum within the Indian community might have created new social divisions and new stratification patterns by the last quarter of the century, but on the issue of familiarity or affinity with Western culture or religion, there would have been less innovation. The majority of the nouveaux riches continued to share the traditional loyalties of the villagers. This would apply particularly to the new commercial class, whose accumulation of wealth and social status in the colonial society would not have been dependent on their mastery of the norms and educational standards required by the larger Christian Creole society.

The tiny professional and bureaucratic strata were the ones who would have been most affected by Western culture and religion, although even among these there would have been a tendency towards an Indian cultural nationalism among a sensitive few, reacting against the colonial Western intellectual and religious embrace (and often also against what many would have considered Afro-Western pretensions about their own cultural superiority).

Urban residence, with its attendant cosmopolitanism of outlook, continued to remain quite low for the Indians, in comparison with other immigrant groups such as the Chinese and the Portuguese. Where it did exist, as in San Fernando or Georgetown and New Amsterdam, the Westernized Indian middle classes at the turn of the century tended, despite their Western outlook, to live separate social lives. Occupationally still rooted in service to their own communities as lawyers, doctors, and teachers, they were culturally suspended between their more traditional brethren and the Westernized but still alien melting pot of Creole society.

The expansion of their occupational clientele and their own occupational base into the more integrated sectors of socioeconomic activity, indispensable to the development of a broader cosmopolitan New World outlook, would have to await several more decades. In this context, it would be fair to describe their state of development at the end of indentureship in 1920 (and long after) as a highly transitional, incipient creolization, if by creolization is meant the development of a quasi-Westernized mode of rootedness in the new environment.

While culturally distinct from the traditional India which all still respected (barring a colonially minded few), and which was often still alive and vibrant in the villages of Trinidad and British Guiana, while distinct also even from the new Westernized middle class of India itself (going through a similar hybridization of sensibility), they nevertheless stood— often by choice, given the luxury of their occupational segregation—on the margins of the Western Creole melting pot and its inner political and cultural concerns.

One recent study suggested that there were in fact two "creole" societies in the Caribbean (again using the term "creole" in the larger sense of the Americanization of each ethnic group, with its own ways of experiencing the new rootedness, or indeed even the new alienation).[110] Another analyst described this as an unresolved ongoing tension between "being" and "belonging," posed by the new society.[111] These were, however, very incipient concerns at the beginning of the twentieth century and were not to become important in a larger societal sense until much later into the modern period. In 1920, the India-born element of the new community of "East Indian West Indians" was still around one-third of the total community. A visiting Royal Commission in 1921–22 (the Wood Commission) described the community then as "largely illiterate, speaking some five or six different languages, and living a life of its own."[112]

The marginality of the Indians up to the beginning of the new century was reflected in the manner of their intervention and participation in public life. Despite the fact that their presence had been generating the most intense internal debates within Creole plantation society throughout the period of immigration, they themselves had remained on the outside of these debates, expressing their autonomy against colonialism in their own work environment, utilizing their own inner resources of wit and grit in the battle for survival, and relying on their traditional communal wisdom to resolve their own inner problems among themselves. Their links with the world of official society had generally never extended beyond the authority of the Immigration Department.

When an occasional spokesman sought to voice his sentiments on public matters, it was always with a view to defending the ethnic group's right to be there and to be accorded more humane treatment by the larger society. This was done sometimes in the press, through the writing of letters to the editors of the small newspapers. By the 1880s and 1890s, it was being done through community petitions to officialdom (the governor, or local and visiting commissions of enquiry) and the formation of

communal organizations such as the East Indian National Association
(1897; 1916 in British Guiana) and later the East Indian National Congress (1909).

They mobilized communal opinion on issues affecting their own welfare, among them the legal recognition of marriages conducted under
their own religious auspices, problems arising out of the pass-law requirements as they affected free Indian movements, free return passage rights,
and the severity of the discipline imposed on indentured laborers by the
law as well as by the plantation officials. They agitated also for communal
representation on the local legislature. Two members of the Indian community of Trinidad, lawyers George Fitzpatrick and Francis Evelyn Mo-
hammed Hosein, also appeared before the Sanderson Commission hearings in London in 1909, the former a formal representative of the East
Indian National Association sent from Trinidad.[113]

Indians participated in electoral politics at the local government level,
despite the widespread voter registration apathy among the few Indians
who did qualify to vote in the early twentieth century. By 1920, when
indentureship came to an end, they had already succeeded in getting
elected two Indian mayors, one in each colony, in New Amsterdam and
San Fernando.[114] Even on the national legislatures, their presence came
to be felt before the end of indentureship, with the nomination in 1912
of George Fitzpatrick to the Trinidad Legislative Council and the election
in 1916 of J. A. Luckhoo to the British Guiana Combined Court.

However, the general quality of Indian participation in public life up
to 1920 never gravitated much beyond the stage of ethnic pressure group
agitation, despite the electoral successes just mentioned.[115] Even Mr.
McNeill of the McNeill-Lal delegation had dismissed the Trinidad East
Indian National Congress as an organization "for airing the views of a
few conceited people."[116] The creative tensions of an interracial solidarity
against colonialism, or the evolution of a cosmopolitan political
worldview appropriate to a mature New World commitment, would constitute challenges for a later period, when the "creolization" or Americanization process was more developed.

CHAPTER 9

Conclusion: Asian Indenture
in Comparative Perspective

From a comparative standpoint, the Asian immigration experiment to the British West Indies can be seen as analytically valuable from any of several angles of vision: as a distinct form of labor system and labor control to be compared with other semifree (or unfree) labor systems of the same period (or before); as another human immigration episode in an age of unprecedented large-scale international immigration, especially to the Americas; and as a distinct and unique nineteenth-century example of Asian overseas migration and adjustment to a largely non-Asian and nonmetropolitan environment, with its attendant relocation and assimilation problems.

From the angle of Caribbean post-Emancipation history, its unfolding was important as embodying a unique form of the transition from slavery to free labor, a process that was hemispheric in nature but quite diverse in its particular expressions.[1] It was also important because the pluralist and cosmopolitan shape of modern society in Trinidad and British Guiana (also Dutch Surinam), as well as many of their modern political and ethnic problems, owed their origin to this experiment begun in 1838, the year of Emancipation.

Stanley Engerman has contrasted the nineteenth-century forms of indentured or contract labor with their seventeenth- and eighteenth-century precursors.[2] Reminding us that the institution of indenture preceded that of slavery in the evolution of plantation (and nonplantation) America, he contrasted the dynamics of the preslavery stream of contract labor (largely European) with that of the postslavery (largely Asian) stream. They differed not only in their racial aspects, the areas of out-migration as well as of in-migration, but often also in the contractual terms and conditions of employment, the numbers repatriating versus those settling in the New World environment, and the mobility opportunities available after indenture.

Engerman did not sufficiently stress that the processes that "pushed" the contract migrants overseas were probably identifiable as early and later versions of the same historical process (incipient Western industrialization, first domestic, later overseas, and its impact on internal social relations within the countries of out-migration). He chose instead to highlight the differences in the abstract wealth of each sending region (indentured migration from "rich" nations vs. indentured migration from "poor" nations), without further elaboration.

This is a comparison that does not take into account the real trade relations between India and China on the one hand and early modern Europe on the other prior to the late eighteenth- and nineteenth-century encounter between these civilizations. In addition, by ignoring the historical processes responsible for this very "poverty" in the nineteenth century (the beginnings of the global division of labor required by expanding Western industrialization), such an analysis is in danger of obscuring the real structural *interconnection* between these "rich" and "poor" entities in the nineteenth century.

This useful comparative discussion on different forms of the indentured labor system needs to be extended and amplified beyond the framework set by Engerman. There were considerable differences in the contractual terms and conditions under which even the second (Asian) stream entered into the hemispheric plantation systems. One form of contract migration (e.g., the Latin American Chinese "coolie trade") was handled mainly by private enterprise speculators at the recruiting, transportation, and purchasing ends of the spectrum, with minimal state involvement except for legal and bureaucratic supervision during the employment of the laborer (often quite inadequate and always open to the worst kinds of bribery and corruption). Another form of contract migration was state initiated, regulated, and supervised from the countries of out-migration to the countries of in-migration (as was the British nineteenth-century experiment). The crucial distinction between the two involved major differences in the philosophy and practice of indenture during this period which cannot be glossed over analytically.[3] It also raises serious questions (which cannot be discussed here) about whether the Latin American Chinese indentured servants were in practice significantly different from slaves, regardless of what the law (Cuban or Peruvian) deemed them to be.[4]

Moreover, the discussion on the voluntary versus involuntary nature of contract migration cannot ignore the deep contradictions in the laws themselves (British and Spanish), which authorized a range of automatic criminal penalties (including imprisonment) for violations of contractual obligations of a civil nature, and which authorized recruitment *that did not inform the intending emigrants of the existence of these laws in the receiving countries.* How "voluntary" were migrants who were not told that if they did not do their work properly in the new environment, they would end up in jail, especially if their own experience of labor migration within their own country or within Asia generally did not prepare them for quite the same levels of coercion?

It should be noted also that the first type of contract migration (Europeans to the New World) did not die out in the eighteenth century but continued in a somewhat muted form even during the period of Asian indenture. The Reverend John Morton of the Canadian Presbyterian Mission in Trinidad often had to remind critics of the Indian indenture system that English and Scottish young men working as overseers and clerks in the Trinidad and Guianese plantations were often themselves under some form of three-year indenture (much like some of the earlier arrangements that preceded slavery in the Americas or existed in non-plantation regions of North America).[5] The qualitative and racially preferential differences between these two distinct forms of contract arrangement existing in the same century need to be analyzed in any comparative discussion.

What is more, the frequently horrendous conditions under which many of the earlier white indentured servants worked in the New World—not at all always an easy rite of passage into the new society—need also to be emphasized, as Eric Williams did in his discussion of the fate of the contract servants in the French West Indies in the seventeenth century.[6] Contract labor was not always as easily distinguishable from other coercive labor systems after arrival in the New World as the formal laws would have had it seem, whether in the seventeenth century or the nineteenth, and in many cases, the very fluidity of the laws themselves were reflections of the ambivalence of the receiving countries' perceptions.

A more minute attention has to be paid to the differences between the formal laws of the countries involved, as well as the differences in the *lived experiences* of the contract laborers themselves. Societal traditions which mediated the relationship between the laws and the actual application of the laws cannot be ignored in any meaningful comparative discussion.

Asian immigration to the Caribbean region, as we have pointed out in chapter 2, was part of a larger dispersal of Asian labor in that period, partly a continuation of preimperialist traditions of overseas movement (as in the case of the Chinese to Southeast Asia, and the Indians to Ceylon), partly a direct result of the imperialist impact on nineteenth-century Asia and the larger changes taking place in the global economy. The role played by the evolution of world sugar production as a catalyst in these movements needs to be stressed, but the Chinese diaspora cannot be explained simply in relation to sugar: the occupational roles they played in Peru were diverse, while the simultaneous migrations to California and Australia (from the same districts in southern China) were part (and a small part) of a vast multiracial and multinational exodus toward these countries.

Within the Caribbean region, major distinctions are evident between those plantation systems making the transition from slavery to free labor directly and fully and those that resorted to indenture as an intermediary transitional option, to control the untrammeled spread of the free wage labor system. What evolved in societies like Trinidad and British Guiana was in fact a hybrid labor system, with semifree labor utilized in the main sector of the plantation system, and a nominally free labor system in the peripheral areas of economic activity.[7] In some societies like Cuba, the vigor of sugar expansion permitted a unique coexistence of all forms of labor—slave, indentured, and free—at the same time, until the 1880s.

Distinctions are also to be made between those societies (e.g., Trinidad and British Guiana) which were dependent wholly on the indenture system (or its hybridization with free labor) and those (e.g., Jamaica, the Windward islands, and the French West Indies) which did utilize indenture, but as a purely peripheral (and ultimately noneffective) post-Emancipation option.

The ethnic challenges and frictions that followed in the wake of these experiments also reflected different levels of intensity in the evolution of these historically related but distinct plantation systems. Wherever the Asians (particularly the Indians) arrived, in large or small numbers, their very presence and mode of introduction generated complaints, and frequently fierce hostility, from those affected by their arrival.

There was a level at which the responses they attracted, and the dialectical tensions arising from their incorporation into the plantation work force, reflected an inevitable "native"-immigrant dialectic which was (and is) fairly common in most countries: the phenomenon of immigrant cheap labor being introduced to undermine the perceived gains and social strength of the preexisting labor force.

Where the level of diversification of the economy involved is low or structurally difficult; where options for the native work force are accordingly constricted, either by structural conditions or by political design; where the numbers of immigrants seem to be far in excess of actual labor requirements; and where the initial cultural and communication estrangement between immigrant and native is not conducive to softening the effect of the de facto competition on the labor market—these conditions inevitably generate social resentments (and often small-scale and large-scale clashes) between newcomers and citizens, strangers and natives. This might (and does) occur between immigrants and natives of the same race (White or Black, even Asian Indians or Asian Orientals), and the history of international immigration movements is full of such examples, but the existence of racial and racial-cultural differences always exacerbates the larger dilemma.

The African–Asian Indian tensions which grew out of the indentured immigration experiment in Trinidad and British Guiana reflected basic human responses to a common phenomenon, but they received concrete life and expression in a specific plantation milieu. Analysts are divided on the extent and importance of this frictional relation, some (like Walter Rodney) emphasizing the larger class-unifying factors simultaneously at work in the society during the nineteenth century (work experience, cultural convergences, colonialism, the time factor), others pointing out that the racial segregation of experience and culture were real factors which cannot be conceptually glossed over.[8] Others have noted that the de facto residential and occupational segregation that existed for most of the period of this study (up to 1920) actually deemphasized the friction in real terms, despite the mutual and distanced dislike for each other.[9]

Distinctions must clearly be drawn, however, between those societies where the Indian presence was large enough to make these issues important and those where their presence might have acted as an added but not central factor in the life of the society. Pluralism and pluralist processes become more complex only where the sheer force of numbers imposes itself upon the larger societal consciousness.

Ironically, it is only with the progressive growth of the society in the modern period, and the deepening commitment of the newcomers to

their new homes, that these pluralist issues have become critical. All of
this, however, falls outside the scope of our discussion. For much of the
period of our study, the framework for the future dialectic between the
main races of the Trinidad and British Guiana working class had just
barely been laid, and much of real life continued to be lived in residential
and occupational compartments, and within the embrace of mutually
unintelligible lifestyles.[10] Neither "creolised from below nor anglicised
from above," as one analyst put it,[11] the Indians were very much a tribe
apart up to 1920 and beyond. But fundamental processes—new social
differentiations, new worldviews, new place loyalties—were already at
work inside the sheltered life of these immigrant communities themselves
which would make a difference, for better or worse, only in a later period.

APPENDIX I

Tables of Statistics

21. Property Owned by Indians in Jamaica (Including Numbers of Shopkeepers and Spirit License Dealers) in 1915–1916, by Parish
22. Occupations of Free Indians in Jamaica in 1911
23. Chinese Migration to the British West Indies, 1806–1884
24. Female Emigration from China to the British West Indies, 1860–1884
25. Plantations and Districts in Trinidad Employing Chinese Indentured Labor, 1853–1871
26. Sugar Plantations in Trinidad Employing Chinese Indentured Labor on 31 December 1866
27. Plantations and Districts in British Guiana Employing Chinese Indentured Labor, 1853–1880
28. List of Offenses Committed by Chinese Immigrants in 1866 in Trinidad
29. Area Distribution of China-Born Chinese Residents of Trinidad, 1861–1931
30. Occupational Distribution of Chinese in Trinidad in 1891
31. Natives of China in the British Caribbean, 1861–1946
32. Composition of Population of Trinidad, by Nationality and Birthplace, 1851–1931
33. Composition of Population of British Guiana, by Racial and Ethnic Origin, 1841–1931

TABLE 1. Average Annual Sugar Production in the British West Indies,
1814–1916 (in Tons)

Year	B. Guiana	Trinidad	Jamaica	Barbados	St. Kitts	Antigua	B. W. I. Total	World Cane Sugar Total
1814–23	23,237	7,629	78,518	11,622	6,051	8,346	176,027	—
1824–33	55,936	12,322	68,465	14,838	4,819	8,215	204,699	—
1834–38	51,278	15,227	54,225	20,309	4,246	8,328	184,060	—
1839–46	31,865	15,000	33,431	15,652	5,002	8,927	131,177	891,089
1847–56	41,790	22,061	27,474	28,622	5,347	9,858	167,665	1,156,400
1857–66	61,284	26,564	25,168	36,367	7,978	10,011	190,690	1,393,800
1867–76	81,894	44,611	25,666	40,358	9,418	9,516	240,221	1,748,900
1877–86	88,728	54,094	21,571	46,260	11,641	10,627	254,815	2,045,400
1887–96	109,718	52,490	20,891	54,667	17,245	13,147	278,559	2,895,100
1897–1906	108,110	44,352	16,263	46,675	12,911	10,473	—	5,175,766
1907–16	100,968	48,290	17,515	32,179	11,246	13,441	—	8,910,033

Source: Noel Deerr, The History of Sugar (London: Chapman & Hall, 1949–50), vol. 1, pp. 193–203; vol. 2, pp. 377, 490–91.

TABLE 2. Values of Sugar Exports of Trinidad and British Guiana, 1831–1910
(in Pounds Sterling)

Year	Sugar Exported	Value	Value of Total Exports
	Trinidad:		
1831	14,997 tons	204,029	244,392
1841	13,103	409,416	510,113
1851	19,899	294,248	390,009
1861	30,147	376,865	645,561
1871	53,592	938,000	1,492,811
1881	43,608	668,153	2,099,101
1891	45,357	662,789	2,058,761
1901–2	45,254	453,304	2,445,651
1906–7	45,004	430,182	2,872,325
	British Guiana:		
1831	58,757	—	1,879,979
1841	30,657	953,113	1,463,719
1851	38,577	643,134	865,133
1861	64,854	1,121,378	1,583,649
1871	93,506	2,190,510	2,748,720
1881	91,942	2,019,257	2,597,291
1891	116,109	1,662,741	2,532,554
1901–2	105,695	1,038,163	1,833,623
1906–7	114,951	1,059,503	1,843,107

Source: Gt. Britain, Parliamentary Papers 1910, XXVII (Cd. 5194), Report of the Committee on Emigration from India to the Crown Colonies and Protectorates (Sanderson Commission Report), pt. 3, p. 170.

TABLE 3. Values of the Annual Exports of Products of Trinidad, British Guiana, and Jamaica, 1882–1896 (in Thousands of Pounds Sterling)

Year	Sugar	Cocoa	Trinidad: Other	Total	Transit Trade	Total
1882	982	317	141	1,440	1,012	2,452
1883	993	373	152	1,518	1,168	2,686
1884	734	381	160	1,275	1,494	2,769
1885	769	386	152	1,307	940	2,247
1886	630	521	141	1,292	1,217	2,509
1887	895	354	150	1,399	472	1,871
1888	818	612	128	1,558	575	2,133
1889	969	411	147	1,527	782	2,309
1890	739	531	143	1,413	766	2,179
1891	735	440	182	1,357	702	2,059
1892	775	648	164	1,587	669	2,256
1893	841	535	140	1,516	804	2,320
1894	675	509	154	1,338	663	2,001
1895	689	621	126	1,436	629	2,065
1896	773	452	138	1,363	803	2,166

Year	Sugar	Gold	British Guiana: Other	Total	Transit Trade	Total
1882	2,955	3	60	3,018	191	3,209
1883	2,968	4	31	3,003	169	3,172
1884	2,122	1	42	2,165	157	2,322
1885	1,626	3	49	1,678	123	1,801
1886	1,667	24	40	1,731	111	1,842
1887	1,982	44	37	2,063	127	2,190
1888	1,773	64	40	1,877	148	2,025
1889	2,140	110	60	2,310	161	2,471
1890	1,737	235	51	2,023	139	2,162
1891	1,974	376	45	2,395	137	2,532
1892–93	1,803	494	51	2,348	85	2,433
1893–94	1,723	511	42	2,276	83	2,359
1894–95	1,365	500	46	1,911	129	2,040
1895–96	1,183	450	35	1,668	102	1,770
1896	1,280	461	73	1,814	109	1,923

Year	Sugar	Coffee	Jamaica: Bananas	Logwood	Total*	Transit	Total
1882	910	134	89	92	1,472	37	1,509
1883	777	161	94	89	1,366	103	1,469
1884	649	99	192	135	1,351	132	1,483
1885	541	157	130	153	1,181	272	1,453
1886	387	120	166	181	1,078	202	1,280
1887	556	209	146	192	1,334	175	1,509
1888	490	322	271	353	1,662	166	1,828
1889	382	292	252	375	1,502	112	1,614
1890–91	435	284	444	382	1,807	96	1,903
1891–92	511	337	263	303	1,629	93	1,722
1892–93	432	341	340	336	1,690	70	1,760
1893–94	428	342	473	449	1,983	93	2,076
1894–95	426	357	429	344	1,829	94	1,923
1895–96	360	285	317	359	1,775	98	1,873

Source: Gt. Britain, Parliamentary Papers 1898, L (C. 8655–57), Report of the Royal Commission on the West Indian Sugar Industry (Norman Commission), app. B.
*Other export products included in the totals were oranges, pimento, ginger, coconuts, and miscellaneous products like cocoa, tobacco, grapefruit, lime juice, annatto, pineapples, and kola nuts.

TABLE 4. Area under Sugar Cane Cultivation in Trinidad, British Guiana, and Jamaica, 1841–1921

Year	Trinidad: Total Acreage under Cultivation	Acreage under Sugar	Acreage under Cocoa
1845	54,413	28,507	8,764
1855	52,807	29,059	9,967*
1861–62	68,592	36,739	14,238*
1871	83,841	47,319	18,935
1881	98,171	52,163	25,188*
1891	194,000	58,500	94,500
1901	318,000	52,000	190,000
1911	423,600	62,600	290,200
1921	670,188	43,265	200,252

Year	British Guiana: Total Acreage under Cultivation	Acreage under Sugar	Acreage under Rice
1841	n/a	24,850	—
1851	n/a	31,354	—
1861	n/a	52,726	—
1871	n/a	75,944	—
1881	142,635	77,379	—
1891	169,920	78,307	2,500
1901	157,644	67,884	15,020
1913	152,072	72,685	33,888
1921	172,151	63,420	55,911

Year	Jamaica: Total Acreage under Cultivation	Acreage under Sugar	Acreage under Other Cultivation
1841	n/a		
1851	n/a		
1861	n/a		
1871	516,924	47,559	469,365
1881	539,039	39,712	499,327
1891	640,249	32,487	607,762
1901	695,807	25,257	670,550
1908	870,840	31,178	839,662†

Sources: Trinidad: Blue Books of Statistics, Annual Immigration Reports, Census Reports of Trinidad; British Guiana: Dwarka Nath, A History of Indians in Guyana (London, 1970), pp. 249, 260; Jamaica: Gt. Britain, Parliamentary Papers 1910, XXVII (Cd. 5194), Report of the Committee on Emigration from India to the Crown Colonies and Protectorates (Sanderson Commission Report), pt. 3, p. 76.
* Includes approximately 200–300 acres in coffee.
†Includes 62,164 acres in bananas, 25,547 in coffee, 8,200 in cocoa.

TABLE 5. Migrants Introduced into the British Caribbean,
Mainly under Indenture, 1834–1918

	India (1838–1918)	Madeira (1835–81)	China (1853–84)	Africa (1834–67)	Europe (1834–45)	Other (1835–67)	Total Migrants
B. Guiana	238,909	32,216	13,533	14,060	381	1,868	300,967
Trinidad	143,939	897	2,645	8,854	—	1,333	157,668
Jamaica	36,412	379	1,152	11,391	4,087	519	53,940
Grenada	3,200	601	—	2,406	—	—	6,207
St. Vincent	2,472	2,102	—	1,036	—	—	5,610
St. Lucia	4,354	—	—	730	114	—	5,198
St. Kitts	337	2,085	—	455	—	—	2,877
Antigua	—	2,527	100*	—	—	—	2,627
B. Honduras	—	—	474	—	—	178	652
Dominica	—	164	—	400	—	—	564
Total	429,623	40,971	17,904	39,332	4,582	3,898	536,310

Source: George Roberts and Joycelyn Byrne, "Summary Statistics on Indenture and Associated Migration Affecting the West Indies, 1834–1918," Population Studies 20, no. 1 (1966), p. 127.
*One hundred Chinese were landed on Antigua in 1863 from a French vessel stranded off the island of Barbuda.

TABLE 6. Migration from India to the British West Indies, 1838–1918
(Numbers Arriving)

Year	B. Guiana	Trinidad	Jamaica	St. Lucia	Grenada	St. Vincent	St. Kitts	Total
1838	396	—	—	—	—	—	—	396
1845–50	12,374	5,568	4,551	—	—	—	—	22,493
1851–55	9,981	5,054	—	—	—	—	—	15,035
1856–60	16,206	11,208	2,121	1,215	944	260	—	31,954
1861–65	15,654	7,474	2,524	320	1,357	521	337	28,187
1866–70	22,436	11,836	5,279	—	269	1,145	—	40,965
1871–75	24,355	11,868	6,079	—	—	333	—	42,635
1876–80	27,374	12,763	2,313	1,184	458	213	—	44,305
1881–85	20,500	11,551	966	925	172	—	—	34,114
1886–90	20,471	13,988	2,135	554	—	—	—	37,148
1891–95	21,397	13,565	1,651	156	—	—	—	36,769
1896–1900	14,780	7,414	1,276	—	—	—	—	23,470
1901–5	13,177	12,433	1,471	—	—	—	—	27,081
1906–10	10,592	12,547	2,955	—	—	—	—	26,094
1911–15	7,304	4,051	3,091	—	—	—	—	14,446
1916–18	1,912	2,619	—	—	—	—	—	4,531
Total	238,909	143,939	36,412	4,354	3,200	2,472	337	429,623

Source: George Roberts and Joycelyn Byrne, "Summary Statistics on Indenture and Associated Migration Affecting the West Indies, 1834–1918," Population Studies 20, no. 1 (1966), p. 129.

TABLE 7. Emigration from Calcutta and Madras to the Sugar Colonies, 1842–1870

Destination	Port of Embarkation	Men	Women	Children	Total Departing
Trinidad	Calcutta	25,059	8,023	4,445	37,527
	Madras	2,971	1,257	764	4,992
Total		28,030	9,280	5,209	42,519
B. Guiana	Calcutta	46,081	14,497	7,654	68,232
	Madras	7,242	2,486	1,731	11,459
Total		53,323	16,983	9,385	79,691
Jamaica	Calcutta	8,180	2,671	1,526	12,377
	Madras	1,842	562	388	2,792
Total		10,022	3,233	1,914	15,169
Mauritius	Calcutta	148,669	35,650	24,496	208,815
	Madras	72,230	22,066	16,529	110,825
	Bombay	22,954	5,743	3,064	31,761
Total		243,853	63,459	44,089	351,401
Natal	Calcutta	695	194	122	1,011
	Madras	3,421	1,269	747	5,437
Total		4,116	1,463	869	6,448
Minor B. W. I.	Calcutta	4,281	1,471	746	6,498
Colonies &	Madras	306	124	93	523
St. Croix					
Total		4,587	1,595	839	7,021
French W. I.					
(Inc. F. Guiana)	Calcutta	—	—	—	—
	Madras*	219	72	39	330
	French Ports (Pondicherry, Karikal)	10,581	4,046	1,384	16,011
Total		10,800	4,118	1,423	16,341
Reunion	Calcutta	6,076	1,359	680	8,115
	Madras	1,410	491	230	2,131
	French Ports	3,265	1,089	405	4,759
Total		10,751	2,939	1,315	15,005
Total Emigration (1842–70):					
	Calcutta	239,041	63,865	39,669	342,575
	Madras & French Ports	103,487	33,462	22,310	159,259
	Bombay	22,954	5,743	3,064	31,761
Total		365,482	103,070	65,043	533,595

Source: Gt. Britain, Parliamentary Papers 1874, XLVII (314), Report by J. Geoghegan on Emigration from India, p. 70.
*Only to Guadeloupe.

TABLE 8. Total Number of Emigrants from India to the Sugar Colonies in Each Year (1842–1870) and Their Destinations

Year	Total Emigrants	Destinations
1842	459	Mauritius
1843	39,755	Mauritius
1844	8,242	Mauritius
1845	12,511	Mauritius, British Guiana, Trinidad, Jamaica
1846	16,735	Mauritius, British Guiana, Trinidad, Jamaica
1847	10,719	Mauritius, British Guiana, Trinidad, Jamaica
1848	9,671	Mauritius, British Guiana, Trinidad
1849	7,670	Mauritius
1850	9,800	Mauritius
1851	14,266	Mauritius, British Guiana, Trinidad
1852	22,674	Mauritius, British Guiana, Trinidad
1853	19,781	Mauritius, British Guiana, Trinidad
1854	19,327	Mauritius, British Guiana, Trinidad
1855	16,629	Mauritius, British Guiana, Trinidad
1856	14,555	Mauritius, British Guiana, Trinidad, Grenada
1857	20,805	Mauritius, British Guiana, Trinidad, Grenada
1858	45,838	Mauritius, British Guiana, Trinidad, Grenada, St. Lucia
1859	43,057	Mauritius, British Guiana, Trinidad, St. Lucia, Jamaica
1860	22,838	Mauritius, British Guiana, Trinidad, Jamaica, St. Kitts, Natal
1861	31,493	Mauritius, British Guiana, Trinidad, Jamaica, St. Vincent, St. Lucia, Grenada, Natal, Reunion
1862	14,766	Mauritius, British Guiana, Trinidad, Jamaica, St. Croix, Reunion
1863	11,731	Mauritius, British Guiana, Trinidad, Reunion, Natal
1864	22,084	Mauritius, British Guiana, Trinidad, Reunion, Natal, Guadeloupe, Cayenne
1865	27,589	Mauritius, British Guiana, Trinidad, Reunion, Natal, Cayenne, Martinique, St. Vincent, Grenada
1866	21,347	Mauritius, British Guiana, Trinidad, Jamaica, Reunion, Natal, Guadeloupe, Martinique, Cayenne, St. Vincent
1867	7,614	Mauritius, British Guiana, Trinidad, Guadeloupe, Martinique, Cayenne
1868	13,379	Mauritius, British Guiana, Trinidad, Jamaica, Guadeloupe, Martinique, St. Vincent
1869	15,827	Mauritius, British Guiana, Trinidad, Jamaica, Reunion, Guadeloupe, Martinique
1870	12,433	Mauritius, British Guiana, Trinidad, Jamaica, Guadeloupe, Martinique, St. Lucia, Grenada
Total	533,595	

Source: Gt. Britain, Parliamentary Papers 1874, XLVII (314), Report by J. Geoghegan on Emigration from India, p. 84.

TABLE 9. Provincial and District Origins of Indian Emigrants to the Sugar Colonies, 1842–1870 (Emigrating from Calcutta Alone)

Destination	Orissa	Bengal Western	Bengal Central	Bengal Eastern	Bihar	North-West Provinces, Oudh, and Central India	Elsewhere
Mauritius	3,116	33,131	8,951	1,118	108,156	47,286	3,619
B. Guiana	719	14,028	2,166	238	24,681	25,551	1,164
Trinidad	378	8,396	1,305	176	11,278	16,027	853
Jamaica	147	3,214	341	106	4,496	4,654	377
Minor B. W. I.	28	1,461	266	46	2,405	2,076	100
Natal	2	216	24	—	356	370	16
Reunion	19	1,667	171	29	4,027	4,469	262
Total	4,409	62,113	13,224	1,713	155,399	100,433	6,391

Total: 343,682

Source: Gt. Britain, Parliamentary Papers 1874, XLVII (314), Report by J. Geoghegan on Emigration from India, p. 71.

TABLE 10. Indentured Immigrants Known to Have Returned to India up to 1916

Period	B. Guiana	Trinidad	Jamaica	St. Lucia	St. Vincent	Grenada	St. Kitts–Nevis	Total
1843–50	482	—	—	—	—	—	—	482
1851–55	1,908	1,395	1,520	—	—	—	—	4,823
1856–60	1,975	982	126	—	—	—	—	3,083
1861–65	1,316	817	—	—	—	—	—	2,133
1866–70	1,265	772	—	749	—	76	—	2,862
1871–75	3,620	970	1,952	162	—	—	—	6,704
1876–80	5,269	1,875	1,345	—	165	—	—	8,654
1881–85	7,335	2,265	1,815	95	559	29	—	12,098
1886–90	9,414	2,924	1,281	463	326	95	61	14,564
1891–95	10,082	3,775	834	604	—	78	—	15,373
1896–1900	6,988	3,638	—	—	—	—	—	10,626
1901–5	7,671	3,838	2,124	373	—	—	—	14,006
1906–10	5,838	3,471	111	—	—	—	—	9,420
1911–16	2,977	2,726	772	—	—	—	—	6,475
Total	66,140	29,448	11,880	2,446	1,050	278	61	111,303

Source: George Roberts and Joycelyn Byrne, "Summary Statistics on Indenture and Associated Migration Affecting the West Indies, 1834–1918," Population Studies 20, no. 1 (1966), p. 132.

TABLE II. Area Distribution of Indians in Trinidad, 1861–1911

	1861	1891	1911
Borough of Port-of-Spain	250	1,088	2,533
St. Ann's Ward Union	781	2,617	2,989
Diego Martin Ward Union	394	3,678	4,909
Tacarigua Ward Union	1,971	11,820	14,266
Borough of Arima	—	257	386
Arima Ward Union	292	3,395	3,127
Mayaro Ward Union	8	251	850
Manzanilla Ward	—	—	5,857
Toco Ward Union	16	83	207
Blanchisseuse Ward	1	20	37
Chaguanas Ward Union	962	5,748	9,632
Couva Ward Union	1,527	8,567	8,797
Montserrat Ward	—	3,920	8,110
Savanna Grande Ward Union	1,575	7,398	14,198
Borough of San Fernando	195	996	1,426
Naparima Ward Union	4,856	17,794	22,046
Oropouche Ward	—	—	7,879
Cedros Ward Union	660	2,586	2,795
Tobago	—	—	73
Waters of the Colony (Port-of-Spain, San Fernando, Brighton, La Brea, Tobago)	—	—	3
Total	13,488	70,218	110,120

Source: Census Reports of Trinidad and Tobago.

TABLE 12. Distribution of Indian Resident Estate Labor in Trinidad,
by Counties, 1862–1910

County	No. of Estates	Indentureds			Unindentureds					Sugar Produced
		M.	W.	Total	M.	W.	B.	G.	Total	
				1862						
St. George	37	1,890	644	2,534	288	98	362	312	1,060	—
Caroni	32	1,492	516	2,008	274	104	247	226	851	—
Victoria	66	3,166	1,133	4,299	561	164	510	419	1,654	—
St. Patrick	18	583	205	788	185	64	101	100	450	—
Total	153	7,131	2,498	9,629	1,308	430	1,220	1,057	4,015	
				1876						(hogsheads)*
St. George	30(S)† 3(C)	1,519	582	2,101	762	339	505	337	1,943	15,131
Caroni	25	1,827	701	2,528	870	397	527	430	2,224	14,201
Victoria	48	3,206	1,347	4,553	2,144	1,022	1,137	980	5,263	23,910
St. Patrick	11(S) 1(cc)	600	275	875	281	100	137	114	632	4,544
Total	118	7,152	2,905	10,057	4,057	1,858	2,306	1,861	10,062	57,786
				1890						
St. George	16(S) 8(C)	1,461	568	2,029	1,077	584	549	390	2,600	12,948
Caroni	22(S) 7(C)	2,483	911	3,394	1,592	783	819	706	3,900	23,653
Victoria	34	2,832	1,062	3,894	2,205	1,190	1,075	798	5,268	28,968
St. Patrick	6(S) 1(cc)	459	160	619	271	151	110	84	616	2,372
Mayaro	1(cc)	17	7	24	15	10	3	1	29	—
Total	78(S) 15(C) 2(cc)	7,252	2,708	9,960	5,160	2,718	2,556	1,979	12,413	67,941
				1910						(tons)
St. George	2(S) 18(C)	936	331	1,267	499	292	109	97	997	1,884
Caroni	12(S) 30(C)	3,247	1,308	4,555	2,549	1,297	646	559	5,051	22,343
Victoria	16(S) 9(C)	3,364	1,378	4,742	3,677	1,962	757	622	7,018	27,723
St. Patrick	8(C) 2(cc)	319	126	445	141	66	39	36	282	—
St. Andrew	15(C)	352	153	505	73	33	26	14	146	—
Nariva	1(cc)	28	9	37	14	7	0	1	22	—
Total	30(S) 80(C) 3(cc)	8,246	3,305	11,551	6,953	3,657	1,577	1,329	13,516	51,950

Source: Annual Immigration Reports (Trinidad).
* 1 Hogshead = 15–16 Cwt. (or approximately 1,800 lbs.).
† (S) = Sugar; (C) = Cocoa; (cc) = Coconut. No Symbol indicates Sugar.

TABLE 13. Distribution of Indian Resident Estate Labor in Trinidad, by Products (Cocoa, Coconut, Sugar), 1896–1904

Year		Cocoa			Coconut			Sugar		
		M.	W.	C.	M.	W.	C.	M.	W.	C.
1896	(ind.)	376	163	—	83	44	—	6,707	2,258	—
	(unind.)	96	57	140	55	32	84	4,883	2,397	4,248
1898	(ind.)	310	141	—	35	17	—	5,905	3,418	—
	(unind.)	57	41	135	8	4	8	4,427	2,142	3,291
1900	(ind.)	350	141	—	29	13	—	4,020	1,828	—
	(unind.)	220	85	143	7	3	15	4,616	2,433	2,722
1902	(ind.)	485	216	—	41	15	—	4,603	2,298	—
	(unind.)	272	116	155	9	5	12	3,792	1,875	2,173
1904	(ind.)	887	382	—	23	10	—	5,729	2,521	—
	(unind.)	235	132	198	8	3	16	3,415	1,842	2,276

Source: Trinidad Legislative Council Paper 13 of 1906, app. 1 (adapted): Report of the Special Committee appointed to consider matters relating to the Labour Question in Trinidad, 1906.

TABLE 14. Area Distribution of Indians in British Guiana, 1871–1911

	1871		1891		1911	
District*	Total ASIAN	Non-Estate ASIAN	Total E. Indian	Non-Estate E. Indian	Total E. Indian	Non-Estate E. Indian
Essequibo Coast	8,182	488 (5.9%)	13,651	5,165 (37.8%)	12,808	7,484 (58.4%)
Wakenaam	2,432	121 (5.0%)	3,902	720 (18.4%)	2,741	1,761 (64.3%)
Leguan	2,026	168 (8.3%)	3,910	1,031 (26.4%)	2,231	2,231 (100%)
East Bank Essequibo	1,691	21 (1.2%)	4,100	936 (22.9%)	3,101	1,965 (63.4%)
West Coast Demerara	7,571	470 (6.2%)	12,866	2,381 (18.5%)	12,809	4,628 (36.0%)
West Bank Demerara	4,026	554 (13.8%)	6,436	2,430 (37.7%)	7,721	4,335 (58.8%)
East Bank Demerara	4,983	123 (2.5%)	8,690	2,715 (31.2%)	11,242	4,203 (37.2%)
East Coast Demerara	10,278	462 (4.5%)	22,830	4,274 (18.7%)	22,178	6,727 (30.4%)
Mahaica-Abary	2,580	204 (7.9%)	4,011	1,366 (34.0%)	8,220	6,625 (76.0%)
Berbice (W)	1,140	174 (15.3%)	1,705	260 (15.3%)	3,652	2,190 (60.0%)
Berbice River	2,127	12 (0.6%)	4,429	894 (20.2%)	5,389	1,656 (30.7%)
Canje	2,601	69 (2.7%)	5,052	2,407 (42.7%)	4,984	2,507 (50.5%)
Corentyne & E. Coast Berbice	3,146	207 (6.6%)	7,827	2,943 (37.6%)	19,354	9,279 (47.9%)
Georgetown	1,264	1,264 (100.0%)	3,976	3,976 (100.0%)	6,018	6,018 (100%)
New Amsterdam	202	202 (100.0%)	1,262	1,262 (100.0%)	1,292	1,292 (100%)
Total	54,249	4,539 (8.4%)	104,647	32,760 (31.3%)	123,740	62,901 (50.7%)

Source: Lesley Key-Potter, "The Post-Indenture Experience of East Indians in Guyana, 1873–1921," in B. Brereton and W. Dookeran, eds., East Indians in the Caribbean (New York: Kraus, 1982), p. 84 (amended and corrected).
*Not included: Pomeroon River and North-West Districts and "other interior."

TABLE 15. Indentured and Free Indian Immigrants in British Guiana, 1881–1911

| | Estate Residents | | | | Non-Estate | |
Year	Adults (ind.)	Adults (unind.)	Children	Total	Residents	Total
1881	22,752	26,979	12,500	62,231	25,757	87,988
1891	16,710	38,356	17,750	72,816	35,668	108,484
1901	14,609	39,565	18,518	72,692	57,649	130,341
1911	9,141	54,804 (Inc. Children)		63,945	62,893	126,838

Source: Annual Immigration Reports (British Guiana).
Note: These figures are usually higher than the census figures.

TABLE 16. Indentured and Free Indian Immigrants in Jamaica, 1879–1908

Year	Indentured	Unindentured (on and off estates)	Total E. Indians
1879	2,741	12,148	14,889
1889	461	12,580	13,041
1899	1,683	12,973	14,656
1908	2,833	10,988	13,821

Source: Gt. Britain, Parliamentary Papers 1910, XXVII (Cd. 5194), Report of the Committee on Emigration from India to the Crown Colonies and Protectorates (Sanderson Commission Report), pt. 3, p. 73.

TABLE 17. Crown Lands Purchased by East Indians in Trinidad, 1885–1921

Year	No. of Grants to Total Population	Acreage*	No. of Grants to Indians	Acreage*
1885	599	8,171	164	2,150
1886	661	11,123	142	2,051
1887	739	10,800	198	2,736
1888	585	9,115	144	1,811
1889	434	5,391	149	1,816
1890	489	6,165	162	1,865
1891	517	6,925	n/a	1,482
1892	528	5,622	n/a	1,778
1893	684	7,222	n/a	2,462
1894	699	7,072	n/a	2,028
1895	630	6,894	256	2,742
1896	407	4,390	n/a	1,205
1897	432	4,690	171	1,869
1898	706	8,002	217	2,699
1899	1,299	14,630	445	4,087
1900	1,422	13,856	492	4,474
1901 (to 3/31)	331	3,764	112	1,067
1901–2	1,303	11,509	605	4,518
1902–3	1,141	9,882	346	2,797
1903–4	1,233	12,407	532	4,166
1904–5	1,539	16,208	646	4,898
1905–6	1,232	12,780	544	4,103
1906–7	991	8,004	493	3,306
1907–8	1,157	9,494	475	3,186
1908–9	1,369	13,402	651	4,802
1909–10	992	8,123	430	2,977
1910–11	543	3,466	232	1,283
1911–12	342	1,425	101	253
1912–13	274	1,638	80	478
1913–14	411	3,319	134	626
1914–15	405	2,508	120	627
1915–16	281	867	65	159
1916–17	379	1,625	65	141
1917–18	586	3,188	160	296
1918–19	938	7,099	491	3,359
1919–20	485	2,536	129	612
1920–21	689	4,166	145	767
Total	27,452	267,478	9,096	81,676

Sources: 1885 to 1908–9: Gt. Britain, Parliamentary Papers 1910, XXVII (Cd. 5194), Report of the Committee on Emigration from India to the Crown Colonies and Protectorates (Sanderson Commission Report), pt. 3, p. 130; 1908–9 to 1920–21: Annual Reports of the Sub-Intendant for Crown Lands (Trinidad), in Trinidad Legislative Council Papers.
* Acreages given in round figures.

TABLE 18. Indian Occupations in Trinidad in 1891 and 1921

Census of 1891	Natives of India		Indian Natives of Trinidad	
	Male	Female	Male	Female
Official and Professional				
Catechist, Local Preacher	15	0	1	0
Civil Service Officer, Clerk	5	(4 Anglo-Indians)	2	0
Court Officer, Interpreter	8	0	4	0
Druggist, Dispenser, Midwife	1	13	3	0
Engineer, Civil	1	(Anglo-Indian)	0	0
Hospital Wardsman, Nurse	1	4	0	0
Messenger, Porter, Gov't. Office	1	0	0	0
Lawyer's Clerk	0	0	3	0
Minister, Christian	1	0	1	0
Police	1	0	0	0
Postman	1	0	0	0
Priest, Hindu, Mahometan	40	0	1	0
Teacher	43	1	51	14
Total	118	18	66	14
Domestic				
Domestic Indoor Servant	190	357	57	254
Groom, Coachman, Gardener	230	10	62	3
Laundress	0	43	0	36
Total	420	410	119	293
Commercial				
Accountant, Clerk, Bank, Commerce	4	(2 Anglo-Indians)	0	0
Bookkeeper, Clerk	0	0	1	0
Merchant, Agent, Dealer	25*	2	3	0
	*(1 Anglo-Indian)			
Salesman, Clerk—Undefined	95	15	99	12
Shopkeeper	398	115	42	50
Total	522	132	145	62
Agricultural				
Contractor	103	4	14	2
Farmer	2	1	0	0
Laborer, Agricultural	22,547	11,051	3,098	2,893
Manager, Submanager	1	0	1	0
Market Gardener	98	59	14	21
Overseer, Overlooker, Driver	220	0	3	0
Planter (Cocoa)	2	0	1	0
Planter, Undefined	12	0	0	0
Proprietor (Cocoa Estate)	6	1	0	1
Proprietor, Peasant	541	80	81	18
Total	23,532	11,196	3,212	2,935
Industrial				
Cab Proprietor, Driver	8	0	4	0
Carter	126	0	76	0
Charcoal Burner, Seller	52	13	4	0
Engine Driver	2	0	0	0
Fisherman, Fish Seller	14	4	3	1
Grass Seller	54	8	43	5

continued

TABLE 18. *continued*

	Natives of India		Indian Natives of Trinidad	
Census of 1891 (cont'd.)	Male	Female	Male	Female
Huckster, Pedlar	157	119	12	32
Laborer, General Undefined	3,088	1,448	566	483
Laborer, railroad, etc.	198	29	21	5
Lodging House Keeper	7	3	0	1
Mechanic, Handicraftsman	247	6	79	2
Milk Seller	27	32	1	8
Other Occupations	7 (1 Anglo-Indian)		2	0
Railway Guard, Gateman, Pointsman, etc.	6	0	1	0
Seamstress	0	42	0	57
Total	3,993	1,704	812	594
Indefinite and Unoccupied				
Household Duties	0	676 (4 Anglo-Indian)	0	405
Living on Private Means	80	102	11	35
Occupation Not Described	127	187	32	50
Pauper, Mendicant	95	34	0	3
Proprietor, House	15	10	3	1
Proprietor, Undefined	21	4	0	0
Children Attending Gov't. School	76	25	699	218
Children Attending Assisted School	151	54	1,495	650
Children Attending Private School	14	5	87	51
Children Not Attending School	977	879	6,056	6,566
Total	1,556	1,976	8,383	7,979

	Natives of India and Indian Natives of Trinidad	
Census of 1921	Male	Female
Official		
Public Officers	54	3
Messengers, Porters in Gov't. Offices	12	1
Professional		
Police	8	0
Military	4	0
Members of Legal Profession	5	0
Members of Medical Profession	1	0
Ministers of Religion	93	0
Civil Engineers and Surveyors	6	0
Teachers	223	61
Mercantile, Agricultural, and General		
Merchants, Agents, and Dealers	61	9
Clerks, Shopmen, etc.	720	117
Domestic Servants	572	1,532
Managers, Submanagers, and Overseers	237	0
Mechanics and Handicraftsmen*	992	5
Shopkeepers and Hucksters	582	493
Peasant Proprietors	3,214	1,040
Métayers and Cane Farmers	682	175
Agricultural Laborers	30,235	19,145
General Laborers, Porters, etc.	7,199	2,375
Boatmen and Fishermen	94	0

(continued)

TABLE 18. *continued*

Census of 1921 (cont.)	Natives of India and Indian Natives of Trinidad	
	Male	Female
Mariners	3	0
Hotel Keepers	6	8
Retail Spirit Dealers	1	0
Proprietors	1,008	386
Living on Private Means	208	259
Laundresses	3	92
Seamstresses	0	327
Wives and Daughters Engaged in Domestic Duties	—	9,241
Educational		
Children Attending Gov't. School	1,436	531
Children Attending Assisted School	4,562	1,895
Children Attending Private School	210	171
Children Not Attending School	14,633	16,477

Source: Census Reports of Trinidad and Tobago.
*Mechanics and Handicraftsmen: Fitters, Molders, Blacksmiths, Gun- and Locksmiths, Carpenters, Wheelwrights, Tailors, Shoemakers, Saddlers, Goldsmiths, Watchmakers, Plumbers, Masons, Painters.

TABLE 19. Crown Lands Purchased and Leased by Indians in British Guiana, 1891–1913

	Grants and Homesteads		Licenses of Occupancy	
Year	Number	Acres	Number	Acres
1891–92	2	150	4	200
1892–93	3	300	1	35
1893–94	2	350	3	250
1894–95	4	310	7	493.50
1895–96	4	350	1	100
1896–97	4	284.42	—	—
1897–98	10	850	—	—
1898–99	63	5,992.63	1	93
1899–1900	18	1,440	44	501.12
1900–1901	72	5,800.71	28	231.72
1901–2	39	2,171.70	3	155
1902–3	80	1,990	—	—
1903–4	95	3,370.50	7	421.41
1904–5	29	494	17	248.42
1905–6	82	1,743.27	17	3,091.08
1906–7	30	598.21	17	900.10
1907–8	59	1,361.42	11	283.43
1908–9	63	1,188	17	2,140.75
1909–10	23	535	4	328.55
1910–11	59	1,152.03	5	1,140.08
1911–12	36	525.44	4	10.93
1912–13	67	960.38	10	333.66

Source: Gt. Britain, Parliamentary Papers 1915, XLVII (Cd. 7744), Report to the Government of India on the Condition of Indian Immigrants in the Four British Colonies and Surinam (McNeill-Lal Report), app. 16, p. 148.
Notes: Financial year = 1 April to 31 March. Grants are practically absolute transfers. Homestead grants are limited to 5 acres, with restrictions on alienation for a period of ten years. Licenses to Occupy are leases for a term.

TABLE 20. Indian Occupations in British Guiana in 1891 and 1921

Census of 1891	Male	Female	Census of 1891	Male	Female
Professional			*Industrial*		
Priests	67	—	Goldsmiths	96	—
Teachers	9	—	Grass Sellers	397	100
Interpreters and			Hucksters	197	80
Messengers	39	—	Milk Sellers	96	273
Police	66		Mechanics	298	173
Domestic			Market Gardeners	0	0
Domestics, Indoor	539	546	Fishermen	189	0
Domestics, Outdoor	157	213	Bakers and Cake Makers	104	93
Washers	—	75	Barbers	153	0
Commercial			Chemists and Druggists		
Merchant, Agent, Dealer	88	5	and Midwives	21	25
Employed on Railway	2	—	Charcoal Burners	11	0
Cab Owners	23	—	Gold Seekers	18	0
Agricultural			*Not Earning*		
Agricultural Laborers	49,258	30,746	Females engaged in		
Attending Machinery	63	—	Domestic Duties	—	629
Attending Stock, etc.	608	39	"Scholars"	3,897	2,992
Overseers, etc.	204	38			
Watchmen, etc.	458	—			
General Laborers	687	11			

Census of 1921		Total	Census of 1921		Total
Service			*Agricultural*		
Government Officers			Proprietors and Farmers		12,465
and Interpreters		47	Laborers, etc.		65,280
Police, Prisons, and			Total		77,745
Militia		20			(out of 84,970)
Total		67	*Domestics*		1,403
		(out of 2,210)	*Fishermen*		303
Learned Professions			*Miscellaneous*		22
Clergy, Teachers, and			*Not Earning*		
Other Professions		283	"Scholars"		7,459
		(out of 2,937)			(out of 37,696)
Commercial			Children and Persons		
Merchants, Agents,			Not Employed		27,806
Dealers		331	Females Attending		
Shopkeepers		445	Domestic Duties		5,121
Clerks, Shop Assistants		627	Total		124,938
Hucksters and Peddlars		845			
Industrial		2,481			

Sources: 1891 Census: D. W. D. Comins, Note on Emigration from India to British Guiana (Calcutta, 1893), app. A; 1921 Census: J. D. Tyson, Memorandum of Evidence for the Royal Commission to the West Indies presented on behalf of the Government of India (New Delhi, 1939), pp. 33–34.

TABLE 21. Property Owned by Indians in Jamaica (Including Numbers of Shopkeepers and Spirit License Dealers) in 1915–1916, by Parish

Parish	Acreage Owned	Value of Property (in Pounds Sterling)	No. of Shopkeepers*	No. of Spirit License Dealers*
Kingston	94	5,110	6	2
St. Andrew	29½	1,234	3	1
St. Thomas	2,002½	12,775	102	28
Portland	747½	5,522	23	4
St. Mary	2,275¾	13,375	47	21
St. Ann	36¼	172	1	—
Trelawny	1,624	2,390	14	1
St. James	150½	838	10	1
Hanover	509¾	2,520	14	—
Westmoreland	393¼	4,223	28	3
St. Elizabeth	501¾	1,360	6	2
Manchester	84¼	362	2	—
Clarendon	996¾	4,477	48	9
St. Catherine	1,697½	5,375	26	10
Total	11,143¼	59,733	330	82

Sources: Trinidad Legislative Council Paper 86 of 1918: Correspondence published by the Government of India relative to East Indian Emigration, Despatch from Colonial Office to India Office, 7 June 1917; Gt. Britain, Parliamentary Papers 1910, XXVII (Cd. 5194), Report of the Committee on Emigration from India to the Crown Colonies and Protectorates (Sanderson Commission Report), pt. 3, p. 76.
* 1909 figures.

TABLE 22. Occupations of Free Indians in Jamaica in 1911

	Male	Female	Total
Professional			
Chemists	1	—	1
Dispensers and Druggists	2	—	2
Fakirs	2	—	2
Interpreters	5	—	5
Medical Practitioners	1	—	1
Ministers of Religion, Evangelists, and Religious Workers	16	1	17
Nurses (Accoucheuse)	—	3	3
School Teachers	5	3	8
Students	2	4	6
Vergers	1	—	1
Total	35	11	46
Domestic			
Domestic Servants	54	134	188
Gardeners (Domestic)	37	6	43
Housekeepers	—	4	4
Nurses (Sick and Domestic)	—	8	8
Total	91	152	243
Commercial			
Barkeepers	—	4	4
Clerks, Mercantile and General	8	1	9

continued

TABLE 22. *continued*

	Male	Female	Total
Cab Drivers and Coachmen	11	—	11
Commercial Travelers	1	—	1
Draymen	12	—	12
Fruit and Vegetable Sellers	—	7	7
Hawkers and Pedlars	11	1	12
Higglers	—	4	4
Livery Stable Keepers	1	—	1
Merchants	2	1	3
Motormen	2	—	2
Office Messengers	4	—	4
Oil Sellers	—	3	3
Produce Dealers	1	—	1
Seamen (Merchant)	4	—	4
Shopkeepers	245	130	375
Speculators and Traders	6	1	7
Stationers and Booksellers	1	—	1
Store Servers and Storemen	21	49	70
Watchmen and Watchwomen	56	3	59
Total	386	204	590
Agricultural			
Bee Keepers	4	—	4
Cart and Wagon Drivers	78	—	78
Cattlemen	45	—	45
Engine Drivers	2	—	2
Firemen	2	—	2
Fishermen	24	—	24
Gardeners (Market)	92	30	122
Grooms	4	—	4
Jockeys	1	—	1
Laborers, Banana	3,446	1,877	5,323
Laborers, Pen	98	50	148
Laborers, Sugar	1,677	1,177	2,854
Laborers, Other	512	326	838
Overseers	2	—	2
Pen Keepers and Proprietors	8	1	9
Planters, Banana	110	30	140
Planters, Cane	13	4	17
Planters, Cassava	20	2	22
Planters, Coffee	14	1	15
Planters, Provision	194	71	265
Planters, Rice	94	44	138
Planters, Sugar	1	—	1
Planters, Tobacco	12	1	13
Ploughmen	24	—	24
Pruners	4	—	4
Persons Assisting in Cultivation	56	120	176
Rangers and Headmen	106	—	106
Stablemen	6	—	6
Total	6,649	3,734	10,383
Industrial			
Apprentices (Trades)	12	2	14
Bakers	3	1	4

continued

TABLE 22. *continued*

	Male	Female	Total
Basket Makers	—	1	1
Blacksmiths	4	—	4
Bricklayers and Masons	4	—	4
Butchers	5	—	5
Carpenters	14	—	14
Cigar Makers and Workers	1	2	3
Coal Burners	2	—	2
Coopers	1	—	1
Distillers	1	—	1
Fish Sellers	—	3	3
Goldsmiths and Jewelers	57	—	57
Hairdressers	9	—	9
Hatmakers	—	2	2
Machinists and Mechanics	1	—	1
Milliners and Seamstresses	—	46	46
Milk Sellers	1	2	3
Oil Boilers	1	—	1
Painters	3	—	3
Plate Layers	1	—	1
Printers and Compositors	2	—	2
Rope Makers	1	—	1
Saddlers and Harness Makers	2	—	2
Ship Chandlers	1	1	2
Shoe Makers	7	—	7
Street Cleaners	1	—	1
Sugar Boilers	2	—	2
Tailors and Tailoresses	26	1	27
Tinsmiths	1	—	1
Tobacconists	2	—	2
Washerwomen and Laundresses	—	17	17
Total	165	78	243
Indefinite and Unproductive			
Paupers	8	2	10
Private Means	43	70	113
Children and Persons of No Occupation	2,551	3,201	5,752
Total	2,602	3,273	5,875

Source: Census of Jamaica 1911, quoted in Gt. Britain, Parliamentary Papers 1915, XLVII (Cd. 7744), Report to the Government of India on the Condition of Indian Immigrants in the Four British Colonies and Surinam (McNeill-Lal Report), app. 34 (a), p. 243.

TABLE 23. Chinese Migration to the British West Indies, 1806–1884

Year	No. of Vessels	Destination	Embarked	Landed	Died at Sea	Born at Sea
1806	1	Trinidad	200	192	8	—
1853	3	B. Guiana	811	647	164	—
	3	Trinidad	1,013	988	25	—
1854	1	Jamaica	310	267	43	—
	2	Jamaica (via Panama)	205	205	—	—
1859	2	B. Guiana	761	699	62	—
1860	6	B. Guiana	1,964	1,942	23	1
1861	10	B. Guiana	3,501	3,371	133	3
1862	7	B. Guiana	2,690	2,592	102	4
	1	Trinidad	549	467	83	1
1863	1	B. Guiana	413	396	17	—
1864	1	B. Guiana	517	509	10	2
1865	5	B. Guiana	1,768	1,691	82	5
	2	Trinidad	609	593	22	6
	1	B. Honduras	480	474	6	—
1866	2	B. Guiana	798	789	9	—
	2	Trinidad	613	597	16	—
1874	1	B. Guiana	388	388	1	1
1879	1	B. Guiana	516	515	1	—
1884	1	Jamaica	681	680	1	—
Total	53		18,787	18,002	808	23
Summary:						
British Guiana			14,127	13,539	604	16
Trinidad			2,984	2,837	154	7
Jamaica			1,196	1,152	44	0
British Honduras			480	474	6	0
Total			18,787	18,002	808	23

Sources: Annual Reports of the Colonial Land and Emigration Commission (1853–73); Gt. Britain, Colonial Office Records, C.O. 295 Series (Trinidad); Cecil Clementi, The Chinese in British Guiana, table 1 (Georgetown: Argosy, 1915).

TABLE 24. Female Emigration from China to the British West Indies, 1860–1884

Year	Vessel	Destination	Port of Embarkation	Depart	Arrive	Females Embarked W.	G.	Females Arrived W.	G.	Total Arrived
1860	Whirlwind	B. G.	H. Kong	24.12.59	11.3.60	56	4	56	4	372
	Dora	B. G.	H. Kong	9.1.60	3.4.60	120	16	117	16	383
	Red Riding Hood	B. G.	Canton	22.1.60	8.4.60	12	0	10	0	311
	Minerva	B. G.	H. Kong	9.2.60	23.5.60	65	2	65	2	307
	Norwood	B. G.	H. Kong	10.3.60	23.7.60	52	4	48	4	317
Total						305	26	296	26	
1861	Sebastopol	B. G.	Canton	23.12.60	28.3.61	45	1	42	1	329
	Red Riding Hood	B. G.	Canton	19.1.61	13.4.61	48	0	47	0	310
	Claramont	B. G.	H. Kong	1.1.61	13.4.61	87	1	86	1	282
	Saldanha	B. G.	H. Kong	4.2.61	4.5.61	69	0	67	0	492
	Chapman	B. G.	Canton	27.2.61	9.6.61	57	0	53	0	290
	Mystery	B. G.	H. Kong	3.3.61	9.6.61	41	1	39	1	337
	Montmorency	B. G.	H. Kong	14.3.61	27.6.61	18	0	17	0	283
	Sea Park	B. G.	Canton	18.3.61	7.7.61	52	1	40	0	263
	Whirlwind	B. G.	H. Kong	9.4.61	31.7.61	51	4	47	4	352
	Lancashire Witch	B. G.	H. Kong	26.3.61	5.8.61	28	0	26	0	433
Total						496	8	464	7	
1862	Agra	B. G.	Canton	26.11.61	15.2.62	36	0	35	0	287
	Earl of Windsor	B. G.	H. Kong	4.12.61	17.3.62	141	3	124	2	303
	Red Riding Hood	B. G.	Canton	19.1.62	11.4.62	47	1	45	1	324
	Maggie Miller/ Wanata	T'dad.	H. Kong	13.2.62	3.7.62	170	4	124	1	467
	Persia	B. G.	H. Kong	19.3.62	10.7.62	112	5	107	5	525
	Lady Elma Bruce	B. G.	Amoy & Swatow	29.4.62	15.8.62	33	0	32	0	384
	Sir George Seymour	B. G.	H. Kong, Canton & Swatow	1.4.62	20.8.62	38	0	29	0	289
	Genghis Khan	B. G.	H. Kong, Canton & Swatow	2.5.62	20.8.62	97	2	86	2	480
Total						674	15	582	11	
1863	Ganges	B. G.	Canton	4.4.63	29.6.63	100	4	92	4	396
1864	Zouave	B. G.	Canton	19.12.63	28.2.64	157	3	151	1	509
1865	Brechin Castle	B. G.	Canton	18.10.64	26.1.65	78	0	76	0	269
	Montrose	T'dad.	Canton	17.11.64	18.2.65	104	1	100	1	313
	Queen of the East	B. G.	Canton	5.1.65	18.4.65	112	2	107	2	481
	Paria	T'dad.	Canton	11.2.65	25.5.65	81	0	76	0	280
	Light of the Age	B. Honduras	Amoy	8.3.65	12.6.65	14	2	14	2	474
	Sevilla	B. G.	Canton	8.3.65	22.6.65	93	0	91	0	305
	Arima	B. G.	Canton	31.3.65	18.7.65	59	0	50	0	311
	Bucton Castle	B. G.	Canton	30.4.65	28.8.65	74	0	60	0	325
Total						615	5	574	5	
1866	Dudbrook	T'dad.	Amoy	23.10.65	12.2.66	1	0	1	0	272
	Red Riding Hood	T'dad.	Amoy	4.12.65	24.2.66	5	1	5	1	325
	Light Brigade	B. G.	Amoy	18.1.66	14.4.66	4	1	4	1	487
	Pride of the Ganges	B. G.	Canton	31.3.66	31.7.66	29	1	29	1	302
Total						39	3	39	3	

continued

TABLE 24. *continued*

Year	Vessel	Destination	Port of Embarkation	Depart	Arrive	Females Embarked W.	G.	Females Arrived W.	G.	Total Arrived
1874	*Corona*	B. G.	Canton	23.12.73	23.2.74	40	5	40	5	388
1879	*Dartmouth*	B. G.	H. Kong	24.12.78	17.3.79	47	5	47	5	515
1884	*Diamond/ Prince Alexander*	Jamaica	Macao, H. Kong	8.5.84	12.7.84	105	17	105	17	680

Summary: Female Emigration, 1860–1884

	Embarked W.	G.	Total	Arrived W.	G.	Total
British Guiana	2,098	66	2,164	1,965	62	2,027
Trinidad	361	6	367	306	3	309
Jamaica	105	17	122	105	17	122
British Honduras	14	2	16	14	2	16
Total	2,578	91	2,669	2,390	84	2,474

Sources: Annual Reports of the Colonial Land and Emigration Commission (1853–73); Gt. Britain, Colonial Office Records, C.O. 295 Series (Trinidad); Cecil Clementi, *The Chinese in British Guiana* (Georgetown: Argosy, 1915).

TABLE 25. Plantations and Districts in Trinidad Employing Chinese Indentured Labor, 1853–1871

Plantation	County	Ward	Vessels
Aranguez	St. George	Aricagua	*Wanata, Paria*
Aripero	St. Patrick	Oropouche	*Lady Flora Hastings*
Barataria	St. George	Cimaronero	*Australia, Clarendon*
Belle Vue	St. Patrick	Oropouche	*Lady Flora Hastings*
Birkinhill	n/a	n/a	*Lady Flora Hastings*
Bon Accord	Victoria	Pointe-a-Pierre	*Clarendon*
Bon Air	St. George	Arouca	*Red Riding Hood*
Bonne Aventure	Victoria	Pointe-a-Pierre	*Lady Flora Hastings*
Bronte	Victoria	Naparima	*Paria*
Broomage	Victoria	Savanna Grande	*Australia, Wanata, Paria*
Brothers	Victoria	Savanna Grande	*Paria*
Buen Intento	Victoria	Savanna Grande	*Australia, Wanata, Paria*
Camden	Caroni	Couva	*Australia, Montrose*
Canaan	Victoria	Naparima	*Lady Flora Hastings*
Caraccas & Susannah	Caroni	Couva	*Paria*
Cedar Hill & Forres Park	Caroni	Savonetta	*Paria*
Columbia	St. Patrick	Cedros	*Dudbrook*
Concord (North & South)	Victoria	Naparima	*Australia, Wanata, Paria, Dudbrook, Red Riding Hood*
Corinth	Victoria	Naparima	*Montrose*

continued

TABLE 25. *continued*

Plantation	County	Ward	Vessels
Cornish	n/a	n/a	*Clarendon*
Craignish	Victoria	Savanna Grande	*Australia, Lady Flora Hastings*
Curepe	St. George	St. Joseph	*Australia, Lady Flora Hastings*
Densley	St. George	Tacarigua	*Clarendon*
Edinburgh	Caroni	Chaguanas	*Lady Flora Hastings*
El Dorado	St. George	Tacarigua	*Wanata*
Endeavour	Caroni	Chaguanas	*Clarendon, Wanata, Paria, Dudbrook*
Esperanza	Caroni	Savonetta	*Wanata, Paria, Dudbrook*
Exchange	Caroni	Couva	*Clarendon, Paria, Dudbrook, Red Riding Hood*
Fairfield	Victoria	Savanna Grande	*Clarendon, Paria*
Felicity	Caroni	Chaguanas	· *Lady Flora Hastings*
Friendship	Victoria	Naparima	*Australia, Montrose, Dudbrook, Red Riding Hood*
Garden	St. George	Arouca	*Red Riding Hood*
Garth	Victoria	Savanna Grande	*Australia*
Glenroy	Victoria	Savanna Grande	*Montrose*
Golconda	Victoria	Naparima	*Montrose*
Harmony Hall	Victoria	Savanna Grande	*Red Riding Hood*
Jordan Hill	Victoria	Naparima	*Australia, Wanata*
La Romain	Victoria	Naparima	*Australia*
L'Envieuse	St. Patrick	Cedros	*Paria*
Les Efforts & Mon Repos	Victoria	Naparima	*Clarendon, Wanata, Red Riding Hood*
Lochmaben	St. Patrick	Cedros	*Montrose*
Lower Caroni	Caroni	Caroni	*Australia*
Macoya	St. George	Tacarigua	*Australia, Dudbrook, Red Riding Hood*
Matilda	Victoria	Savanna Grande	*Lady Flora Hastings*
Mt. Pleasant	Caroni	Savonetta	*Wanata, Montrose, Dudbrook, Red Riding Hood*
Ne Plus Ultra	Victoria	Naparima	*Wanata*
Orange Grove	St. George	Tacarigua	*Australia, Montrose, Dudbrook, Red Riding Hood*
Otaheite	St. Patrick	Oropouche	*Clarendon, Dudbrook, Red Riding Hood*
Paradise	Victoria	Naparima	*Wanata*
Perseverance	Caroni	Couva	*Dudbrook, Red Riding Hood*
Perseverance	St. Patrick	Cedros	*Wanata, Paria*
Petersfield	Caroni	Chaguanas	*Dudbrook*
Phillipine	Victoria	Naparima	*Wanata, Dudbrook, Red Riding Hood*

continued

TABLE 25. *continued*

Plantation	County	Ward	Vessels
Phoenix Park	Caroni	Savonetta	*Wanata, Dudbrook, Red Riding Hood*
Plein Palais	Victoria	Pointe-a-Pierre	*Wanata, Clarendon, Paria*
Providence	Caroni	Savonetta	*Wanata, Red Riding Hood*
Retrench	Victoria	Naparima	*Wanata, Paria*
River	St. George	Diego Martin	*Clarendon*
Rivulet	Caroni	Couva	*Montrose*
St. Clair	St. George	Arouca	*Dudbrook, Red Riding Hood*
St. Clair	St. George	Mucurapo	*Dudbrook*
St. Ellena & Ben Lomond	Victoria	Savanna Grande	*Montrose, Dudbrook*
St. François	Caroni	Caroni	*Lady Flora Hastings*
St. John	St. Patrick	Oropouche	*Paria*
St. John's	St. Patrick	Cedros	*Australia, Wanata, Paria*
St. Marie	St. Patrick	Cedros	*Australia, Montrose, Dudbrook*
Tarouba	Victoria	Naparima	*Wanata, Red Riding Hood*
Union Hall	Victoria	Naparima	*Clarendon*
Upper Caroni	Caroni	Caroni	*Australia*
Wellington	Victoria	Naparima	*Wanata*
Williamsville	Victoria	Savanna Grande	*Australia, Montrose, Red Riding Hood*

Arrival Dates of Vessels to Trinidad:	
Fortitude	12 October 1806 (no record of plantation distribution)
Australia	4 March 1853
Clarendon	23 April 1853
Lady Flora Hastings	28 June 1853
Maggie Miller/Wanata	3 July 1862
Montrose	18 February 1865
Paria	25 May 1865
Dudbrook	12 February 1866
Red Riding Hood	24 February 1866

Sources: Annual Reports of the Colonial Land and Emigration Commission (1853–73); Annual Immigration Reports (Trinidad); Gt. Britain, Colonial Office Records, C.O. 295 Series (Trinidad); Chinese Indenture Contracts, Trinidad National Archives.

TABLE 26. Sugar Plantations in Trinidad Employing Chinese Indentured Labor
on 31 December 1866

Plantation	Proprietor	Chinese on Estate	Chinese Absentees	Indians on Estate
St. George County:				
Mucurapo				
St. Clair	A. R. Gray	9	0	43
Aricagua				
Aranguez	A. Blasini	10	3	203
Arouca				
Bon Air	H. Watts & Co.	14	2	101
Garden	A. R. Gray	10	0	45
St. Clair	E. de Montalembert	10	6	19
Tacarigua				
Macoya	A. McLean	20	1	136
Orange Grove	A. Cumming & Co.	55 (inc. 12 F.)	13	205
Caroni County:				
Couva				
Exchange/ Camden	A. Cumming & Co.	157	27	249
Caraccas/ Susannah	L. Preau	11	2	77
Perseverance	J. Spiers & Co.	53	12	118
Rivulet	H. Watts & Co.	29	2	65
Savonetta				
Mt. Pleasant/ Cedar Hill/ Forres Park	L. Leroy	70	20	157
Esperanza	A. Cumming & Co.	31	17	106
Providence	A. Cumming & Co.	19	11	122
Phoenix Park	A. Cumming & Co.	43	14	68
Chaguanas				
Endeavour	H. Bernard & Co.	43	9	62
Petersfield	H. Bernard & Co.	13	3	110
Victoria County:				
Pointe-a-Pierre				
Plein Palais	H. Bernard & Co.	7	5	34
Savanna Grande				
Buen Intento	H. Watts & Co.	7	4	94
Brothers	H. Bernard & Co.	14 (inc. 3 F.)	1	90
Broomage	H. Watts & Co.	22	10	94
Fairfield	Turnbull, Stewart & Co.	9	0	11
Glenroy	H. Watts & Co.	9	9	90
St. Ellena & Ben Lomond	H. Watts & Co.	26	0	21
Harmony Hall	H. Bernard & Co.	18	1	75
Williamsville	H. Bernard & Co.	33	0	59

continued

TABLE 26. *continued*

Plantation	Proprietor	Chinese on Estate	Chinese Absentees	Indians on Estate
Naparimas				
Bronte	Turnbull,			
	Stewart & Co.	9	0	52
Concord (S)	J. R. Harris	29	5	113
Corinth	A. T. Bertete	26	19	32
Friendship	J. Rowbottom	14	2	60
Golconda	J. Spiers & Co.	16	0	114
Les Efforts/				
Mon Repos	H. Bernard & Co.	35	14	97
Philippine	G. P. McKenzie	38	4	48
Retrench	R. Wilson	3	0	19
Tarouba	H. Bernard & Co.	5	4	72
St. Patrick County:				
Cedros				
Columbia	H. Bernard & Co.	13	0	33
Lochmaben	E. C. Johnstone	7	2	41
L'Envieuse	A. Cumming & Co.	6	0	86
Perseverance	H. Watts & Co.	3	3	76
St. John's	H. Watts & Co.	6	3	58
St. Marie	H. Bernard & Co.	16	0	43
Oropouche				
St. John	E. Lange	8	2	7
Otaheite	J. W. Gambal	11	1	22

Total Estates Employing Chinese Labor in 1866: 43–49

Total Estates Employing Indentured Labor in 1866: 153

Sources: Trinidad Royal Gazette 35, No. 10 (6 March 1867), pp. 7–11: Return of Estates inspected by the Agent-General of Immigrants during the Half-Year ending 31 December 1866; The Trinidad Official and Commercial Register and Almanack for 1867.

TABLE 27. Plantations and Districts in British Guiana Employing Chinese
Indentured Labor, 1853–1880

Districts	Plantations
Essequibo Mainland (22 estates— 1,334 males, 256 females)	Aurora, Anna Regina, Better Hope, Coffee Grove, Columbia, Golden Fleece, Hampton Court, Henrietta, Hoff van Holland, Huis't Dieren, Johanna Cecilia, La Belle Alliance, Land of Plenty, Lima, Mainstay, Union, Perseverance, Richmond, Sparta, Spring Garden, Windsor Castle, Zorg
Essequibo Islands (13 estates— 945 males, 211 females)	Bankhall, Caledonia, Endeavour, Friendship and Sarah, Hamburg, Maryville, Moorfarm, Palmyra, Retrieve, Sophienburg, Success, Waterloo, Zeelandia
West Coast Demerara (16 estates— 2,295 males, 375 females)	Anna Catherina, Blankenburg, Cornelia Ida, de Kinderen, Groenveldt, Hague, La Jalousie, Leonora, Met-en-Meerzorg, Nouvelle Flanders, Stewartville, Tuschen, Uitvlugt, Vergenoegen, Windsor Forest, Zeelugt
Demerara River (17 estates— 1,985 males, 345 females)	Belle Vue, Diamond, Farm, Haags Bosche, Haarlem, Herstelling, Houston, La Grange, Malgre Tout, Pouderoyen, Peter's Hall, Ruimveld, Schoon Ord, Versailles, Vive-la-Force, Wales, Vriesland
East Coast Demerara (27 estates— 3,118 males, 446 females)	Annandale, Bel Air, Bee Hive, Cane Grove, Chateau Margot, Cove & John, Cuming's Lodge, Enterprise, Enmore, Goedverwagting, Good Hope, Greenfield, Helena, Hope, Industry, Le Ressouvenir, La Bonne Intention, La Bonne Mere, Lusignan, Melville, Montrose, Mon Repos, Non Pareil, Ogle, Spring Hall, Success, Turkeyen
West Coast Berbice (3 estates— 225 males, 17 females)	Bath, Cotton Tree, Hope & Experiment
Berbice River (7 estates— 374 males, 78 females)	Blairmont, Everton, Friends, Highbury, Mara, Ma Retraite, Providence
East Coast Berbice (8 estates— 565 males, 123 females)	Adelphi, Albion, Canefield, Goldstone Hall, Port Mourant, Rose Hall, Smythfield, Smithson's Place
Corentyne River (2 estates— 424 males, 147 females)	Eliza, Mary Skeldon
Total Chinese Allotted:	13,293
Total Chinese Unallotted:	113 (74 M., 39 F.)
Deaths, etc.:	135
Total	13,541

Source: Cecil Clementi, *The Chinese in British Guiana* (Georgetown: Argosy, 1915), tables 4 and 6.

TABLE 28. List of Offenses Committed by Chinese Immigrants
in 1866 in Trinidad

Larceny	110	Obscene Language	1
Breach of Contract	220	Exposure of Person	2
Debt	2	Violent Language	1
Obstructing Street	2	Plying without License	6
Want of Certificate	502	Introducing Tobacco in Prison	2
Menaces	6	Removing Spirits without Permit	2
Resisting Police Constable	7	Selling Opium without Licence	2
Having Stolen Property	6	Receiving Stolen Property	1
Trespass	6	Harbouring Immigrants	1
Assault	8	Ill-treating Animals	5
Damage with Intent to Steal	13		
		Total	905

Source: Gt. Britain, Colonial Office Records, C.O.295 Series (Trinidad), vol. 239 (1867): Report of
the Superintendent of Prisons and Returns of the Royal Gaol for 1866.

TABLE 29. Area Distribution of China-Born Chinese Residents of Trinidad,
1861–1931

	1861	1871	1881	1891	1901	1911	1921	1931
Districts:								
Port-of-Spain	84	220	333	285	200	252	409	670
San Fernando	94	146	138	68	33	17	57	155
Arima	—	—	—	105	83	41	25	44
Counties:								
St. George	97	361	399	227	144	147	76	170
St. David	—	—	7	13	12	34	41	32
St. Andrew	1	—	18	44	58	117	110	95
Nariva	—	—	—	—	—	—	35	55
Mayaro	—	4	2	8	13	36	41	46
Caroni	42	203	175	137	150	148	132	140
Victoria	124	375	144	88	112	214	233	266
St. Patrick	19	91	50	31	27	97	174	317
Ward of Tobago	—	—	—	—	—	—	—	—
Waters of the Colony	—	—	—	—	—	10	1	35
Stragglers	—	—	—	—	—	—	—	2
Total	461	1,400	1,266	1,006	832	1,113	1,334	2,027

Source: Census Report of Trinidad and Tobago, 1931.

TABLE 30. Occupational Distribution of Chinese in Trinidad in 1891

Official			*Agricultural**	
Interpreter	1		Agricultural Laborer	41 (29 M., 12 F.)
Bailiff	1		Market Gardener	2
Domestic			Overlooker, Watchman	3
Indoor Domestic Servant	101 (92 M., 9 F.)		Peasant Proprietor	5 (4 M., 1 F.)
Groom, Gardener	6		Proprietor	7 (6 M., 1 F.)
Industrial			*Indefinite and Unoccupied*	
Charcoal Seller	6 (5 M., 1 F.)		Household Duties	38 (all F.)
Huckster, Peddler	43 (34 M., 9 F.)		Living on Private Means	29 (7 M., 22 F.)
General Laborer, Porter	32 (26 M., 6 F.)		Occupation not Described	19 (8 M., 11 F.)
Mechanics &			Pauper, Mendicant	6 (1 M., 5 F.)
Handicraftsmen	29 (27 M., 2 F.)			
Hotel Keeper	6			
Other Occupations	5			
Commercial				
Bookkeeper, Clerk	3			
Merchant, Agent, Dealer	23			
Salesman, Shopman, Clerk	259 (245 M., 14 F.)			
Shopkeeper	341 (304 M., 37 F.)			

*The census comments as follows: "Of the 12 proprietors appearing in this Table, 5 are returned in the Schedules as 'proprietors of cocoa and coconut estates', and 2 as 'proprietors'. Of the 43 other persons comprising the agricultural class, 29 males and 12 females are returned as 'agricultural laborers', and 2 males as 'market gardeners'. From the other facts recorded in the Schedules, it is, however, evident that the majority of those described as 'agricultural laborers' belong to the latter class—being chiefly persons engaged in cultivating small provision grounds or 'gardens'. Only 7 Natives of China are returned as resident on sugar estates viz. 3 agricultural laborers, 2 overlookers, a shopkeeper and a gardener."

Location of Shopkeepers (341):	M.	F.	Location of Shopkeepers (341):	M.	F.	Location of Shopkeepers (341):	M.	F.
Borough of Port-of-Spain	74	13	Borough of Arima	29	1	Montserrat Ward	27	2
St. Ann's Ward Union			Arima Ward Union			Savanna Grande Ward		
St. Ann's Ward	—	—	Arima Ward	2	—	Union	22	2
Laventille Ward	2	1	Guanapo Ward	4	—	Borough of San Fernando	17	—
Cimaronero Ward	1	—	Turure Ward	2	—	Cedros Ward Union		
Aricagua Ward	1	—	Manzanilla Ward	7	—	Cedros Ward	2	—
Santa Cruz Ward	5	1	Upper Caroni Ward	9	—	Erin Ward	5	—
Total	9	2	Total	24	0	Total	7	—
Diego Martin Ward Union			Mayaro Ward Union	4	—	Naparima Ward Union		
Diego Martin Ward	6	1	Toco Ward Union	5	1	N. Naparima Ward	1	—
Mucurapo Ward	6	—	Blanchisseuse Ward	1	—	S. Naparima Ward	2	1
Maraval Ward	—	—	Chaguanas Ward Union			Pointe-a-Pierre Ward	4	—
Carenage Ward	4	1	Chaguanas Ward	10	3	Oropouche Ward	4	—
Chaguaramas Ward	1	—	Carapichaima Ward	3	1	La Brea Ward	1	—
Total	17	2	Total	13	4	Guapo Ward	1	—
Tacarigua Ward Union			Couva Ward Union			Total	13	1
Tacarigua Ward	19	4	Couva Ward	4	1			
St. Joseph Ward	5	—	Savonetta Ward	3	1			
Maracas Ward	1	1	Total	7	2			
Caura Ward	5	1						
Lower Caroni Ward	5	1						
Total	35	7						

Source: Census Report of Trinidad and Tobago, 1891.

TABLE 31. Natives of China in the British Caribbean, 1861–1946

Territory	1861	1871	1881	1891	1911	1921	1931	1946
B. Guiana*	2,629	6,295	4,393	2,475	634	376	423	548
B. Honduras	1	133	68	52	27	12	n/a	42
Antigua	—	—	—	111	13	4	n/a	—
Trinidad	461	1,400	1,266	1,006	1,113	1,334	2,027	2,366
Jamaica*	—	—	140	347	1,646	2,413	n/a	2,818
All Others	—	—	—	—	—	—	—	—
Total	3,091	7,828	5,867	3,991	3,433	4,139	n/a	5,774

TABLE 32. Composition of Population of Trinidad, by Nationality and Birthplace, 1851–1931

Year	Colony	B. W. I.	Colony Indian Parents	India	U.K.	Other British	China	Africa	Other Foreign*	Not Described	Total Population
1851	40,627	10,800	—	4,169	729	12	—	8,097	4,915	260	69,609
1861	46,936	11,716	—	13,488	1,040	—	461	6,035	4,301	461	84,438
1871	56,692	13,707	4,545	22,880	954	—	1,400	4,256	4,779	425	109,638
1881	69,307	24,047	12,800	36,020	1,062	—	1,266	3,035	5,150	441	153,128
1891	107,376	30,689	24,648	45,594	990	113	1,006	2,259	5,671	35	218,381
1901	134,639	42,373	38,714	47,677	1,385	152	832	1,212	6,745	170	273,899
1911	165,529	47,802	59,535	50,585	1,020	287	1,113	475	7,109	97	333,552
1921	186,287	47,044	84,066	37,341	1,389	983	1,334	177	7,094	198	365,913
1931	216,138	45,762	114,946	23,255	1,454	688	2,027	164	8,349	—	412,783

Sources: Census Reports of Trinidad (Trinidad and Tobago after 1889); R. R. Kuczynski, *Demographic Survey of the British Colonial Empire*, vol. 3 (London: Oxford University Press, 1953).
*"Other foreign" included the largest of this category, the Venezuelans: 2,195 (1871), 2,277 (1881), 2,955 (1891), 3,537 (1901), 3,708 (1911), 4,127 (1921), 4,236 (1931). They included also natives of Portugal and Madeira: 605 (1871), 709 (1881), 701 (1891), 731 (1901), 708 (1911), 517 (1921), 365 (1931). Also Indians born in the foreign (non-British) West Indies: 129 (1911), 77 (1921), 130 (1931).

TABLE 33. Composition of Population of British Guiana, by Racial and Ethnic Origin, 1841–1931

Year	Whites	Blacks	Coloreds/ Mixed	Portuguese	Indians	Chinese	Amerindians	Others	Total Population
1841	2,776	91,074		2,619	343	—	n/a	1,321	98,133
1851	3,630	108,438*		7,928	7,682†	—	7,000	1,316	135,994
1861	2,881	110,216		9,859	22,081	2,629	7,000	1,241	155,907
1871	2,903	122,862		12,029	48,363	6,880	n/a	454	193,491
1881	3,225	143,319		11,926	79,929	5,234	7,656	1,829	253,118
1891	4,558	115,588	29,029	12,166	105,463	3,714	7,463	347	278,328
1911	3,937	115,486	30,251	10,084	126,517	2,622	6,901	243	296,041
1921	3,291	117,169	30,587	9,175	124,938	2,722	9,150	659	297,691
1931	2,127	124,203	33,800	8,612	130,540	2,951	8,348	352	310,933

Sources: Census Reports of British Guiana (no census in 1901); R.R. Kuczynski, *Demographic Survey of the British Colonial Empire*, vol. 3 (London: Oxford University Press 1953).
Notes: See Table 31 for China-born totals. Foreign-born Portuguese (Madeirans) numbered 7,925 (1871), 6,879 (1881), 5,378 (1891), 1,908 (1911), 1,170 (1921), 673 (1931). India-born immigrants numbered 42,681 (1871), 65,161 (1881), 73,031 (1891), 59,849 (1911), 39,965 (1921), 24,087 (1931). West Indian immigrants numbered 9,278 (1851), 8,309 (1861), 13,385 (1871), 18,318 (1881), 21,025 (1891), 12,268 (1911), 10,128 (1921), 9,677 (1931). African-born immigrants numbered 14,251 (1851), 9,299 (1861), 7,541 (1871), 5,077 (1881), 3,433 (1891), 706 (1911), 185 (1921), 67 (1931).
*Includes 7,168 African immigrants, 7,083 "Old Africans," 4,925 natives of Barbados, 4,353 natives of other West Indian Islands.
†Includes 3,665 Madras Coolies, 4,017 Calcutta Coolies.

Evolution of Laws on Immigration in Trinidad, British Guiana, and Jamaica

Trinidad Immigration Laws since 1870

Ordinance No. 13 of 1870 was a consolidating and amending Ordinance which established the law then relating to immigration and which from time to time has been amended in such manner as to form the present law as consolidated in 1899, now Ordinance No. 161 of the revised edition.

The former Ordinance contained most of the provisions now in force relating to the immigrant on arrival for indenture and his general welfare, and after his arrival for allotment to the employer, and the powers and duties of the Protector (then called the Agent-General) in his behalf during his five-year term of service.

Clauses were therein contained as to the feeding of immigrants and the hospital accommodation to be provided on the plantations, as well as their admission to public hospitals when necessary.

There was also provision for work to be performed and penalties for absence from work and vagrancy, and on completion of the contract of service the right to return passage and certificate of industrial residence.

Penalties were provided for unlawfully aiding immigrants to leave the Colony and for employment of those under indenture to others.

In 1875 there was introduced the provision for computing the *mean* death rate as at present existing, and the consequences of an excessive death rate.

The minimum wage of 1s 1d was established at a time of depression when it became possible that the laborers not under indenture might have been paid less than that sum per day or for the task. The previous system was that the indentured immigrant was to be paid at the same rate as free laborers.

In 1878 foreign enlistment was provided against in respect of indentured immigrants and their descendants as it now exists.

In 1881 the present law relating to the marriage and divorce of immigrants not professing the Christian religion was introduced and immigrants were able to legalize their marriages and divorces according to their personal law, by a system of registration.

Indian festivals were also regulated by law in 1882, before which time there had been much disorder and obstruction of the public highways in certain districts.

In 1885 the law was extended as to days lost by reason of absence from work or periods of imprisonment, in such cases such lost days were indorsed and the period of indenture was extended to cover the time so lost. This provision has since been repealed and no lost days are taken into account, but desertion was punished and further provisions for arresting and detaining immigrants were introduced, but the immigrant was given the right to absent himself to lay complaints or to visit the Protector and Inspectors.

In 1894, on the completion of the term of five years' service, the immigrant acquired a right to a free return passage, and at one time at his option he was granted land in lieu of return passage, but this was abolished and the male and female immigrants were made to pay a proportion of the return passage money, now one-half for the male adult immigrant and one-third for the female. Children with their parents and dependents and the destitute and disabled receive free return passages.

In 1902 the repatriation fund was created and the planters now contribute £1 11s.6d. for each immigrant indentured to them, payable by instalments during the five years of service.

In 1902 it was also provided that every employer should make a quarterly return to the Protector of every immigrant whether indentured or not who resides and works on his plantation.

In 1908 it was realised that it had become necessary, in the computation of the rate of wages for task work payable to Creole and other non-indentured laborers to take into account the cost of an indentured immigrant to an employer in respect of indenture fees, hospitals, dwelling, etc. on a scale to be fixed by the Governor in Executive Council from time to time (fixed at 40 cents). This provision now allows of a money payment of 40 cents per day to free laborers instead of 25 cents as was then the law.

The above are the main changes in the amending Ordinances since 1870, but many small amendments were introduced in respect of working detail affecting no principle.

The comfort and well-being of the immigrant is fully provided for, and the powers and control of the immigration department are a guarantee against any abuse of the system.

27th May 1909.   Edgar Agostini, Attorney-General.

Source: Gt. Britain, Parliamentary Papers 1910, XXVII (Cd.5194), Report of the Committee on Emigration from India to the Crown Colonies and Protectorates (Sanderson Commission Report), vol. 3, app. (Trinidad), p. 127.

British Guiana Immigration Laws since 1870

After the very searching investigation of the commissioners appointed by Sir John Scott in 1870 to inquire into the treatment of immigrants in this Colony, the Immigration Ordinance, afterwards passed with amendments as No. 7 of 1873, was drawn up by Sir George Young, one of the commissioners, embodying the recommendations which the members of the commission had made in their report.

This Ordinance was subsequently either added to or amended by the following:

No. 1 of 1875, repealing sections 139, 140, 141, 142, determined the duration of the compulsory issue of rations by estates authorities to newly arrived immigrants to be for a definite term of three months.

No. 4 of 1876 repealed sections 84, 86, 87, 105, 107, 109, 111, 145, and introduced amendments relating principally to the duration and determination of the term of indenture, which was rendered subject to extensions, equivalent to the duration of the immigrant's absences from his estate, on account of imprisonment, desertion, and from work without lawful excuse. To record these absences the register of defaulters was provided for. Section 145, relating to the issue of passports, was amended by provision that no passport should be granted to an immigrant under indenture, or, without the special sanction of the Governor, to any immigrant who had been introduced at the expense of the Colony, and who had not resided in the Colony for five years, unless such immigrant paid the entire cost of his introduction.

Ordinance No. 9 of 1878 repealed sections 19 and 20 of Ordinance 7 of 1873, relating to the fiscal provisions in regard to the charge against the general revenue of the Immigration Department, the medical officer to the Immigration Department, and of the District Medical Officers, and the charge against the Immigration Fund of the whole cost of immigration. After this the general revenue contributed to the Immigration Fund one-third of the total amount of all charges connected with immigration.

Ordinance No. 1 of 1883, repealing a portion of section 41 of Ordinance 7 of 1873, fixing the rate of interest on promissory notes given for indenture fees, and enacting that the Governor and Court of Policy should determine the rate of interest.

Ordinance No. 9 of 1886 repealed section 10 of No. 7 of 1873, and provided for the appointment of District Medical Officers, and established a Government Medical Service.

Ordinance No. 2 of 1887 provided for the protection of female immigrants from violence caused by jealousy, for the punishment of persons who enticed away the wives or reputed wives of immigrants, for division of property in case of separation of man and wife or male and female immigrants who have cohabited, and for divorce for misconduct.

Ordinance No. 7 of 1887 repealed section 167 of Ordinance No. 7 of 1873, substituting, in the case of immigrants, "inquiry" by district magistrate for the ordinary coroner's inquest regarding "unnatural death."

Ordinance No. 10 of 1887 repealed sections 144, 146, 147, and 166 of Ordinance No. 7 of 1873, and substituted amendments relating to the right of an immigrant to a return passage to India, to imprisonment with hard labor, and in connection with the system of computing the terms of imprisonment by the number of tasks finished.

No. 10 of 1887 also provided for the administration of intestate estates of indentured immigrants, the coming under indenture of minors who attain the age of 10 years within five years of their allotment to plantations, and giving magistrates power to remand to the estate's hospital indentured immigrants charged before them, should the immigrant appear in need of medical care or examination.

Ordinance 15 of 1887 (Administrator-General's Ordinance) provided for the administration of small intestate estates of unindentured immigrants.

Ordinance 23 of 1890 made provision for the introduction of immigrants other than Asiatic.

Ordinance 18 of 1891, consolidating the before-mentioned Ordinances, together with the amendments and additions that had been made from time to time, was passed, but was suspended by Ordinance 29 of 1891 pending the report of the Commissioner appointed by the Government of India to enquire into the condition and treatment of East Indian immigrants in British Guiana and other Colonies. This Ordinance, 18 of 1891, came into operation, with additions and amendments, on the 1st November 1894.

Ordinance 4 of 1893 extended the provisions of Ordinance 10 of 1887 with reference to the administration of intestate estates under $10 in value, of unindentured immigrants dying in public institutions.

Ordinance 16 of 1894 makes the following additions and amendments to Ordinance 18 of 1891:

The Immigration Agent-General not to be responsible for the performance of the duties of the medical officers.

The term of indenture of female immigrants for purposes of labor was altered from five to three years.

The procedure in regard to requisitions for ensuring the sanitary fitness of dwellings on plantations was amended in certain particulars.

The making of regulations for the management and arrangement of certified hospitals and the framing of the hospital dietary was vested in the Surgeon-General alone.

Appeals made by employers against requisitions by medical officers were required to be made to the Surgeon-General.

Male immigrants only to be held liable to punishment as habitual idlers.

A slight modification was made in the definition of obstacles to the recognition of marriages "on arrival."

The Immigration Agent-General was given the additional power in dealing with intestate estates to assign a share of the property (not exceeding one half) to the person with whom such immigrant may have cohabited at the time of death.

Conditions as to right of return passage to India amended in certain respects and contribution of a portion of the cost required of the immigrant, such condition affecting only those recruited subsequent to the passing of the Ordinance.

The Immigration Agent-General, with express sanction of the Governor, to have power to relax the provisions of the section relating to return passage.

Government medical officers to send in to the Surgeon-General yearly instead of quarterly a return of the diseases entered in the hospital registers of their districts.

Ordinance 6 of 1895 made provision for extending the time for payment of indenture fees on allotment of immigrants.

Ordinance 11 of 1895 amended clauses of Ordinance 18 of 1891 in regard to the financial arrangements on the transfer of allotments from one employer to another, and extended the privilege of quitting the Colony under a passport.

Ordinance 27 of 1900 amended clauses of Ordinance 18 of 1891 relating to regulations for the construction, arrangement, drainage, and sanitary condition of the dwellings, etc., of indentured immigrants, and of unindentured immigrants living near indentured immigrants, and of the yards and grounds about such dwellings:—

To penalties in default of unindentured as well as indentured immigrants in respect of their dwellings and surroundings.

To the removal of immigrant patients from an estate's hospital to a public hospital at the discretion of the Surgeon-General.

To the division of property by magistrate of married immigrants or immigrants who have cohabited and wish to separate.

Made provision for the payment by employer of part of the cost of return passages of immigrants introduced during the season commencing in 1898 and subsequently.

Repealed section 199 of Ordinance 18 of 1891 in regard to the right to a return passage and providing for the payment by the immigrant introduced as above of a portion of the cost of return passage—one half in the case of males and one third in the case of females, giving the privilege of free passage to the wife, child, or dependent of an immigrant, providing they accompanied him in the return ship, but not conferring such right on immigrants engaged in India on the understanding that he or she should contribute part of the cost of return passage; or on immigrants who have surrendered their rights thereto, or in whose interest, being child or dependent under 12 years of age, the Governor deems it advisable that they should remain in the Colony, or on immigrants still under indenture in respect of whom commutation money has not been refunded to the employer.

The Ordinance provided further that immigrants forfeited claim to return passage if they quitted or attempted to quit the Colony except as provided under the law.

That immigrants who have previously resided in the Colony and been reintroduced from India have no right to return passage.

Authority to Immigration Agent-General to relax, with the express sanction of the Governor, the provisions relating to return passage.

That the right to return passage of immigrants introduced prior to 1898 should not be affected.

The Ordinance also made provision for the surrender of the right to return passage in consideration of a grant of land or of a money payment, no surrender of such right by a married woman being valid, however, without the consent of her husband.

For giving to the wife exclusive right to do as she pleased with such equivalent, should she receive one, as if she were not married.

For the delegating of the powers and duties of the Immigration Agent-General in regard to village settlements to any Immigration Agent or any person appointed by the Governor to be superintendent of such settlements.

This Ordinance also amended the form of indenture list in respect of the period of labor under indenture of female immigrants.

Ordinance 3 of 1903 imposed a tax on land of $1.50 per acre if under cane cultivation, and of 2 cents per acre if empoldered but not under cane cultivation—this tax to be exclusively applied in diminution of the amounts payable by employers of indentured immigrants to the Immigration Fund.

Under this Ordinance land belonging to plantations and leased to farmers for the cultivation of the sugar cane was not liable to acreage tax.

Ordinance 24 of 1905 repealed section 180 of No. 18 of 1891, and the power to remove from a plantation all or any of its indentured immigrants, if sufficient grounds were shown therefor, was vested in the Governor-in-Council instead of in the Governor alone.

A portion of section 86 of No. 18 of 1891 was repealed, and employers were held liable for the maintenance in public hospitals of deserters.

On account of the abolition of the Administrator General's Office

Provision was made for the administration of small intestate estates of unindentured immigrants, making it obligatory on an employer to report the death of unindentured immigrants as well as the indentured, together with an inventory of the goods of the deceased.

Ordinance 15 of 1906 made minor alterations in section 3 of Ordinance 24 of 1905 with reference to the removal of immigrants from a plantation for sufficient cause.

Ordinance 7 of 1907 gave power to Consolidated Immigration Loan Commissioners to obtain advances from the Crown Agents for the Colonies.

Ordinance 19 of 1907 enacted that the liability of an employer for maintenance of indentured immigrants in hospital should cease after 12 months on a certificate from the medical superintendent that said immigrant is unfit, by reason of leprosy or insanity, to return to labor, and for his burial in case of death.

Repealed part of section 117 of Ordinance 18 of 1891 and enacted that no hiring or contract of service of unindentured immigrants be taken to be a contract for more than one month, and gave power to Official Receiver to divide property of immigrants in certain cases.

Ordinance 9 of 1908 extended the period of service for which a contract is entered into with an unindentured immigrant from one to 12 months.

26th May 1909.   W. Crawford,
                                                    Acting Immigration
                                                    Agent-General.

Source: Gt. Britain, Parliamentary Papers 1910, XXVII (Cd.5194), Report of the Committee on Emigration from India to the Crown Colonies and Protectorates (Sanderson Commission Report), vol. 3, app. (British Guiana), pp. 7–9.

Jamaican Immigration Laws 1845–1910

The introduction of immigrants into Jamaica from the East Indies began in the year 1845, when the ship *Blundell* arrived with 261 souls from Calcutta. In 1846, 1,890 immigrants were introduced from India, and in 1847, 2,400. These people were regarded as free laborers, and were at liberty to enter into contract for periods not exceeding one year, with any planter in the island for whom they chose to work. Such employer was required to pay to the Government a capitation fee of 40 shillings for each immigrant of eight years old and upwards.

2. At first the immigrants promised to give great satisfaction, and Captain Darling, Agent-General of Immigration, reported on them as follows:

Of their general sobriety, good conduct, attention to their work, skill as laborers, contentment with their condition, and evident tendency to advance in civilised habits, I have heard but one opinion from those under whom they are employed.

Unfortunately, however, these immigrants did not turn out as well as was expected, owing to the lack of proper supervision, and it was not long before many of them had deserted their employers, or refused to enter into fresh contracts, with the result that a large number became vagrants and went about the country begging. So unsatisfactory was the condition of affairs existing, that, as early as 1847 (only two years after the commencement of the experiment) the Government of the island refused to receive any more immigrants from India.

3. In 1858 a law was passed (22 Vict. c. 1) placing immigration on a better basis.

Under this law there were stringent regulations with regard to the lodging and food of immigrants, and it was enacted that these people should be provided with proper diet, medicine, etc., when sick, at the expense of the employer.

This law also provided that, on arrival, the immigrants should be indentured to their employers for two years certain, and penalties were provided for breaches of contract, absence from work without sufficient cause, and desertion.

Immigration under this law was resumed in 1860.

The cessation of immigration between the years 1847 and 1860 seems to have had a disastrous effect on the industries of the colony.

Many estates with expensive machinery were abandoned, as there was not sufficient labor available to keep them in cultivation.

4. Notwithstanding the law passed in 1858, the condition of the immigrants on estates continued unsatisfactory, and in 1867 the Governor, Sir John Peter Grant, appointed a commission to enquire into the immigration system and to suggest improvements.

This commission presented its report in October 1867, and, in accordance with the recommendations made therein, Law 34 of 1869 was passed.

The most important provisions of this law were as follows:

(a) That each adult male coolie must receive 1 shilling a day, and each female of any age, lad under 16 years of age, nine pence per day; to be paid irrespective of labor performed, unless a complaint had been formerly made before the sub-agent of the district for insufficiency of work done.

(b) Part of the wages to be given in rations, the price to be charged being fixed by the Governor, and the rates published in the *Jamaica Gazette*. Any sum earned above the value of the rations to be paid in money.

(c) No task work to be allowed unless the rates for it have been sanctioned by the Agent-General of Immigration.

(d) The coolies may be put on money wages if they can show that they can earn one shilling per day, or that food can be obtained in the district at moderate rates, and without their losing time in procuring it.

(e) Union hospitals to be established for all sick and infirm indentured immigrants, and a daily rate of sixpence to be charged against the employers for the treatment of the sick when in hospital.

(For a full report on this law, see Sir John Peter Grant's despatch to the Secretary of State for the Colonies dated the 10th of October 1872.)

The good effect of this law was immediately apparent, and immigration was successfully continued until 1876, when the importation of the East Indian immigrants had to be held in abeyance, as the funds applicable for this purpose under the law were exhausted.

5. In 1875 a law had been passed which authorised the rate charged for the care and maintenance of sick coolies in the Union hospitals being increased to one shilling and sixpence (1s. 6d.) per day for every patient.

This alteration caused a great deal of dissatisfaction amongst employers, and a petition was presented to the Legislative Council praying that the General Revenues of the Colony should bear a portion of the expenses attending immigration. The petition was referred to a Select Committee, who recommended as follows:

(a) That immigration into Jamaica be continued on the basis of all the charges connected therewith being defrayed within the year in which they are incurred, and that no addition be made after the present year to the debt for this service.

(b) That the annual expenditure in connection with immigration be defrayed in the proportion of one third from General Revenues, and the remaining two thirds from employers of coolie labor, and the export duties.

(c) That the repayment of the present immigration debt be effected through a more gradual payment each year than is now required by the existing Loan Act.

The report was discussed in the Legislative Council, and the Governor was asked to transmit all the documents to the Secretary of State for the Colonies.

6. As a result of a despatch from the Secretary of State, a Bill entitled the Immigration Law was passed by the Legislative Council in 1878, but there was much opposition to this measure, and several petitions were addressed to the Secretary of State on the subject.

7. In the following year the matter was finally settled by the passing of the Immigration Finance Law, No. 18 of 1879, and the Immigration Protection and Regulation Law, No. 23 of 1879.

Under the first of these laws employers were relieved of the cost of maintaining sick immigrants in hospital, and it was enacted that these expenses should be borne by general revenue.

The export duties on coffee and dyewoods were applied to the purpose of general revenue.

The export duties on sugar and rum were applied to constitute an Immigration Fund.

It was enacted that the following expenses should be defrayed from the Immigration Fund:

(a) The cost of return passages of all immigrants indentured before the first day of January 1878, who may be entitled to such return passages, and pensions to Indian immigrants permanently incapacitated from work before the expiration of ten years' service;

(b) The salaries and pensions of all officers and persons employed on the fixed establishment of the immigration service of this island, either in this island or elsewhere; and

(c) All expenses incidental to the carrying of the immigration laws into effect not otherwise provided for.

It was further enacted that the entire cost of recruiting, depot expenses in India, and in other ports or places from which immigration is permitted (exclusive of salaries of officers and persons as mentioned in section 7) and all passage money of immigrants, and all amounts invested to provide back passages for immigrants, and all other charges incidental thereto should be borne by the employers of immigrants;

Provided that the balance to the credit of the Immigration Fund 1879, at the end of each financial year, shall be applied to diminish the charges payable by employers of immigrants under this section in respect of immigrants indentured in the year following to a minimum sum of fifteen pounds per immigrant, or as near thereto as may be.

The amount of such diminution shall be settled by the Protector, whose decision shall be final.

The amount payable by an employer of immigrants to the Protector of Immigrants for each immigrant was made payable as follows:

In the option of the employer, either wholly in cash, or

One tenth part of such expenses in cash on allotment, and the residue by promissory notes bearing the date of the allotment, and payable as follows:—

(a) One note for one-tenth part of such expenses, with interest thereon at the rate of six per cent per annum at the end of one year from date;

(b) Four notes, each for one-fifth of such costs, with interest thereon at the rate aforesaid, at the end respectively of two, three, four, and five years from date.

8. The Immigration Protection and Regulation Law 23 of 1879, consolidated the laws relating to immigration, and made complete provision for the protection of immigrants and the regulation of immigration.

9. Laws 1 of 1881 and 3 of 1883 were enacted for the purpose making certain minor amendments to Law 23 of 1879.

10. By Law 23 of 1879, section 97, it was enacted that every complaint against an immigrant for an offence against the Immigration Law, or against rules made under the law, should be tried and disposed of by an inspector or by the Protector, and not otherwise.

Law 4 of 1899.—Owing to the decreased number of immigrants being introduced at the time, it was considered advisable to reduce the number of inspectors in the island, and Law 4 of 1899 was passed, so as to make it lawful for the resident magistrate of any parish to try and dispose of any complaint against an immigrant for an offence committed within such parish against the Immigration laws, or against any rules made thereunder.

11. Immigration from India was discontinued in 1885, but so great was the difficulty experienced by the planters in obtaining the necessary labor on estates, that in 1889 and 1890 the question of the resumption of immigration was brought forward, and a Select Committee of the Legislative Council appointed to enquire into the subject.

As a result of their labors, Laws 14 and 20 of 1891 were passed.

The chief provisions of these laws were as follows:—

(a) The export duties on sugar and rum were abolished, also the duties on coffee and dyewoods.

(b) *Law 14 of 1891, section 1.* So much of Law 18 of 1879 as provided what expenses were chargeable against the Immigration Fund, what expenses were payable by employers of immigrants, and the manner in which these expenses were payable, was repealed.

(c) The salaries and pensions of all officers and persons employed on the fixed establishment of the Immigration Service of the island, either in the island or elsewhere, were to be borne by, and paid out of, the general revenues of the island.

(d) All other expenses connected with immigration, including the entire cost of recruiting, depot expenses in India, and all passage money of immigrants, whether coming or returning, were to be charged on, and paid through, the agency of the Immigration Fund 1879.

(e) The following payments were required to be made by employers to the Protector of Immigrants, in respect of each immigrant allotted:—

Either the sum of £15 10s. in cash on allotment, or the sum of £17 10s. in manner following (that is to say)—

£2 in cash on allotment, and the residue in promissory notes as follows: £1 10s. at one year after date; £3 10s. at two years after date; £3 10s. at three years after date; £3 10s. at four years after date; £3 10s. at five years after date.

(f) *Law 20 of 1891, sections 11–13.* With a view to meeting the expense of the repatriation of immigrants, it was enacted that any person employing an immigrant who had served his term of indenture, but had not completed a continuous residence of ten years in the island, should pay to the Protector of Immigrants the sum of one shilling for each week or part of a week such immigrant was employed by him—these payments to be placed to the credit of the Immigration Fund.

(g) *Law 14 of 1891, section 11.* It was provided that, should the Immigration Fund prove at any time unable to meet the claims upon it, the deficiency should be made good out of the General Revenues and Assets of the island.

(h) *Law 20 of 1891, sections 1–9.* It was considered expedient to extend the provisions of the Immigration Protection and Regulation Law 1879, so as to make the same available for the establishment of a system of indenturing native laborers, and it was enacted that any persons other than East Indian immigrants could be indentured to any employer for the period of one year, and that all the provisions of the Immigration Protection and Regulation Law 1879, and the several laws amending the same relating to indentured immigrants and their employers, excepting such portions as relate in terms to a person intro-duced into the island from parts beyond the seas, should apply to indentured laborers and their employers under the provision of this law.

Employers of such native laborers were required to give a promissory note, at nine months, for the sum of £2 10s., payable to the Protector of Immigrants, in respect of each indentured laborer engaged by him.

At the termination of the term of service of any indentured laborer, such laborer was entitled to receive from the Protector of Immigrants the sum of £2.

(*Note.* No laborer has taken advantage of these provisions of the law.)

12. In 1896 the Indian Immigrants' Marriage, Divorce and Succession Law was passed, Law 22 of 1896.

13. *Law 12 of 1897, section 1.* The provisions of Law 23 of 1879 relating to the return passages of immigrants were repealed by Law 12 of 1897, which enacted that every East Indian immigrant entitled to return to India would be provided with a passage back to the port from which such immigrant sailed for this island on payment

of one-fourth of the passage money in the case of males and one-sixth in the case of females. This law was subsequently amended by Law 2 of 1899, section 2, which increased the portion of passage money payable by immigrants to one half in the case of males and one third in the case of females.

Law 12 of 1897, section 1 (1). Law 12 of 1897 provided that every immigrant entitled to a return passage should give notice to the Protector of Immigrants at least three months immediately preceding the expiration of his residence of 10 years in the island, or of the like residence of any other Indian immigrants entitled to be provided with passage. This was repealed by Law 13 of 1903, section 6 (1), which provided that the immigrant should claim such back passage within two years after the date of which it becomes due and claimable.

Law 12 of 1897, section 1 (2). Under Law 12 of 1897 immigrants who are destitute or disabled are entitled to free return passage.

14. *Law 13 of 1903.* Law 13 of 1903 gave to immigrants who have completed a continuous residence of 10 years in the island the right to commute their claim to back passage for a grant of land, and it was provided that each immigrant who so wished to commute his claim should receive 10 acres of land.

This provision was repealed by Law 29 of 1906, which enacted that no Indian immigrant engaged after the coming into operation of this law should be entitled to commute his claim to a back passage for a grant of land.

15. Laws 13 of 1903 and 13 of 1905 enacted minor amendments to the previous Immigration laws.

16. Under Law 20 of 1905 it was provided that:—

If the financial condition of the Immigration Fund requires such action, it shall be lawful for the Governor, with the advice and consent of the Privy Council, to increase or reduce from time to time the payments to be made under section 6 of Law 14 of 1891 by employers of immigrants upon the allotment to them of such immigrants.

Note. With regard to this provision the following resolution was passed by the Legislative Council on the 20th March 1907:—

> "That in view of the decline in the number of East Indian immigrants imported into the Colony since the increase to the employers of the rate per head it is desirable in the agricultural interests of the colony that the importation of such immigrants should be encouraged, by reducing the cost to the employer of the same per head to £17 10s., the amount previously fixed."

27th May 1909.   Chas. W. Doorly,
                                                      Protector of Immigrants.

Source: Gt. Britain, Parliamentary Papers 1910, XXVII (Cd.5194), Report of the Committee on Emigration from India to the Crown Colonies and Protectorates (Sanderson Commission Report), vol. 3, app. (Jamaica), pp. 73–75.

Samples of Contracts of Indenture

Chinese Contract of Indenture (1862 version)

Articles of Agreement, made this third day of April in the year of the Christian era 1862, being the fifth day of the third month of the first year of the reign of Jeungtey, according to the Chinese Imperial Calendar, between _____, native of China, of the one or first part, and J. Gardiner Austin, Esq., Special Agent of the British Government for the regulating and encouragement of emigration from China to the British West Indies, of the other or second part, as follows:—

The said party of the first part in consideration of the covenants, agreements, and stipulations hereinafter entered into by the said party of the second part, doth hereby promise and agree to and with the said party of the second part in manner and form following, that is to say:—

1. That he the said party of the first part shall and will, so soon as he shall be required by the said party of the second part, embark on board the British ship _____, now lying at anchor in the harbour of Hong Kong, and bound for the colony of _____, and remain on board the said ship henceforward until she proceeds to sea, and shall then proceed as a passenger on board the said ship, to _____ aforesaid, for the purpose of carrying out the stipulations hereinafter contained on the part of the said party of the first part.

2. That the said party of the first part shall and will from time to time, and at all times during the term of five years, to be computed from the day of the arrival of the said ship _____ in the said colony of _____, serve such persons, his heirs, executors, administrators or assigns, and on such plantation in _____ as the Governor may appoint, in the growing or manufacturing of articles, the produce of such plantation, according to the provisions hereinafter contained.

3. That the said party of the first part shall and will work as such labourer as aforesaid, for the space of seven hours and a half of each day during the aforesaid term of five years, and on such plantation as aforesaid, with a reservation of not less than five days to be set apart during each year as holidays at the China New Year by the said Governor, and of every Sabbath day. And in consideration of the agreement herein contained on the part of the said party of the first part, the said party of the

second part hereby promises and agrees to and with the said party of the first part in manner following, that is to say:—

4. That the said party of the second part shall provide the said party of the first part with a free passage to the said colony of _____, and shall supply him gratuitously with such food and clothing as may be necessary for the voyage.

5. That so long as the said party of the first part shall continue and be employed as such labourer, as aforesaid, and perform the agreements on his part hereinbefore contained, he the said party of the second part shall cause to be paid weekly to the said party of the first part the same rate of wages for the same proportionate quantity of work as may from time to time be paid to unindentured labourers working on the same plantation, and shall cause to be provided for the said party of the first part during the same service, house, garden-ground and medical attendance, all free of expense to the said party of the first part.

6. That the said party of the second part shall, on demand of the said party of the first part, so soon as he shall embark on board the said ship _____ for the purpose of carrying out the terms of its agreement, make an advance on account of wages to the said party of the first part to the extent of $20, shall pay or cause to be paid monthly to the assigns or nominees of the said party of the first part in China $____ of the wages to be earned by the said party of the first part in the said colony of _____, the first payment to be made on the day of the date of embarkation of the said party of the first part on board the said ship _____, provided always, and it is hereby agreed, that any sum so advanced to the said party of the first part as aforesaid shall be stopped or deducted out of the wages to be earned by the said party of the first part, at the rate of $1 per month, and that any payments so made as aforesaid monthly to the assigns or nominees of the said party of the first part in China, shall be stopped or deducted in equal amounts monthly from the wages to be earned by the said party of the first part.

7. That the said party of the first part shall be at liberty to terminate this agreement, at the end of any one of the said five years, by paying for each year then unexpired a sum equal to one fifth of the amount paid for his introduction, namely, $75, and shall further be at liberty to change his employer at the end of the third or fourth year.

8. That the said party of the second part shall provide or cause to be provided for the said party of the first part during such period as he continues to serve under the terms of this agreement, with the means of corresponding monthly, free of expense, with his relations in China, and of remitting money to them.

(signed)

J. G. Austin.

This done in duplicate, each of the parties aforesaid retaining one copy, at _____, on the 3rd day of April, in the year of our Lord 1862, in the presence of the undersigned, who declares that this contract has been signed willingly, and with full knowledge of its contents, by the said _____.

G. W. Caine,
Acting Emigration Officer.

Received an advance of $20 on account of wages, and a gratuity of $_____ for wife and _____ children.

I agree to employ _____ upon the terms stated above.   (_____)
I certify that the labourer whose name appears above has been allotted by His Excellency the Governor of _____ to plantation _____; and that the signature of the employer was made in my presence.

(_____)
Immigration Agent-General of _____.

Note: Resolution of the Governor and Court of Policy of British Guiana [found only in British Guiana contracts]
"That the immigrants should be guaranteed full employment on adequate wages, paid weekly, with a house rent free, with medical attendance, medicines, food, and hospital accommodation when sick, and that it should be explained to them that a man can earn easily from two to four shillings, women from one to two shillings, and children eight pence per diem, and that a full supply of food for a man can be bought for eight pence per diem."

Author's note: In the contract version authorized by section 45 of the British Guiana Consolidated Immigration Ordinance, No. 4 of 1864, sections 6 and 7 of the version above are omitted, and section 8 becomes section 6. The references at the end to advances and gratuities are omitted. However, section 44 permits the Emigration Agent in China (if authorized by the Governor and Court of Policy) to make special provision for commutation rights and right to change employers, as well as to pay advances to the intending emigrants, in the form allowed in the contract version above. Under section 122, however, repayments on advances were subject to a 6 percent per annum interest rate.

Contract of Residence of Chinese Female Emigrant
(specimen authorized by British Guiana Ordinance No. 4 of 1864, section 48).

No. _____, Ship _____.

Contract made this _____ day of _____ in the year 186___, between _____ as Proprietor (or Attorney of the Proprietor, or Lessee, etc.) of the Plantation _____ in the county of _____ in the colony of British Guiana, of the one or first part, and _____ Chinese female immigrant of the other or second part, witnesseth as follows:—

That the said female Chinese immigrant shall reside on the said plantation for the term of five years from date; and that the party of the first part shall supply her, free of cost, with suitable lodging and with such medicine, nourishment, and medical attendance, and hospital accommodation, as she may need when sick.

Signature of Employer.
Signature of Chinese Female Emigrant.

I hereby declare that the Female Chinese Emigrant, party to this contract, signed the same voluntarily and with a due understanding of its effect.

Immigration Agent-General.

Indian Contract of Indenture (made in 1900s)

Conditions of Service and Terms of Agreement which the Recruiter is authorized to offer on behalf of the Agent to Intending Emigrants.

1. *Period of Service.* For male emigrants five years from the date of allotment; for female emigrants three years from the date of allotment.

2. *Nature of Labour.* Work in connection with the cultivation of the soil or the manufacture of the produce on any plantation.

3. *Number of Days on which the Emigrant is required to labour in each week.* Every day, excepting Sundays and authorised holidays.

4. *Number of Hours in Each Day during which the Emigrant is required to labour without extra remuneration.* Nine, inclusive of half an hour for rest and refreshment. [British Guiana contracts: Seven hours in the fields or ten hours in the factory buildings.]

5. *Monthly or Daily Wages or Task Work Rates.* Able-bodied adults of and above 16 years of age, shall be paid 1 shilling halfpence (1s. 0 1/2d.), which is at present equivalent to 12 annas and 6 pie for each days' work. Adults not able-bodied, or minors of and above 10 years and under 16 years of age, shall be paid eight pence, which is at present equivalent to 8 annas for each day's work, and when performing extra work shall be paid in proportion for every extra hour of work. Wages earned will be paid fortnightly. If the emigrant be required to work by task instead of by time, the same wages shall be paid as to unindentured labourers on the same or other neighbouring plantations, or to indentured labourers on the neighbouring plantations, and such wages may be more, but shall not be less than the minimum wages payable for time work.

6. *Conditions as to Return Passage.* The emigrant on completing a continuous residence of 10 years in Trinidad, and holding or becoming entitled to a certificate of exemption from labour shall, with family, if any, should they not be under indenture, or, if under indenture, should commutation money have been paid to their employer, be provided with a return passage back to Calcutta on payment of one-half of the passage money in the case of men, and one third in the case of women. Provided that every such emigrant who is destitute or disabled shall, with dependents, be entitled to a free return passage. Persons who have previously proceeded to the colony and returned to India shall not be entitled to return passages. After completing a continuous residence of five years and holding or becoming entitled to a certificate of exemption from labour, the emigrant may return to India at his own cost. Blankets and warm clothing are supplied gratis on leaving India but not for the return voyage.

7. *Other Conditions.* Full rations will be provided for adults and minors by the employer for 12 calendar months following the date of allotment, according to the scale sanctioned by the Government of Trinidad, at a cost of three pence, which is at present equivalent to three annas daily, and to each infant under 10 years of age one third of a ration free of cost. Suitable dwellings will be assigned to emigrants

free of rent, and such dwellings will be kept by the employer in good repair. Hospital accommodation with medical attendance, comforts, etc., will be provided free of charge to all emigrants under indenture and their families.

[Here follow the conditions printed in the native languages]

I agree to accept the person named on the face of this form as an emigrant on the above conditions.

Recruiter for Trinidad.

In my presence,
Registering Officer at _____.
Dated _____ 190____.

Government Emigration Agent for
Trinidad.

Protector of Emigrants.

Notes

Introduction
by Sidney W. Mintz

The writer thanks Rebecca Scott and Jacqueline Wehmueller for their valuable suggestions and advice. Persisting errors are his responsibility alone.

1. An anthropological specialist in overseas Chinese migration, Dr. Denise Helly, recently proposed a four-part chronology for classifying the movement of labor into the Caribbean region, from the mid-nineteenth century to the present (Introduction to *The Cuba Commission Report: A Hidden History of the Chinese in Cuba. The original English-language text of 1876* [Baltimore: Johns Hopkins University Press, 1993]). In Helly's chronology, the movement with which Dr. Look Lai is concerned in the present book figures as the first, and earliest, stage. But in the Caribbean region, that migration was instead the final chapter in a much longer story.

2. Philip Curtin's careful and conservative estimate is that Jamaica imported a total of 747,500 slaves, up to the end of the trade, and a total of 662,400 in the period 1701–1810 (*The Atlantic Slave Trade* [Madison: University of Wisconsin Press, 1969], 71, 268). In the case of French Saint Domingue, his figure for the period 1701–1810 (which, of course, really ends in 1791, with the outbreak of the revolution) is 789,700 (ibid., 268).

Chapter 1
British West Indian Society and Economy after Emancipation

1. Trinidad and British Guiana, both annexed into the British Empire during the French Revolutionary and Napoleonic Wars (1793–1815), were new sugar territories.

2. Bryan Edwards, *History, Civil and Commercial, of the British Colonies in the West Indies*, vol. 2, bk. 6, chap. 4 (New York 1966 reprint of 1819 edition), p. 523.

3. Eric Williams, *From Columbus to Castro: The History of the Caribbean, 1492–1969* (London: Andre Deutsch, 1970), pp. 237–38.

4. Ibid., p. 244.

5. Eric Williams, *Capitalism and Slavery* (London: Andre Deutsch, 1964), p. 146.

6. Ibid., p. 169. See chap. 9 generally.

7. William Sewell, *The Ordeal of Free Labor in the British West Indies* (New York: Harper & Bros., 1861), p. 311.

8. See Douglas Hall, "The Flight from the Estates Reconsidered: The British West Indies, 1838–1842," *Journal of Caribbean History* 10 (1978), pp. 7–24.

9. Parliamentary Papers (P.P.) 1842, XIII (479), Report of the Select Committee of the House of Commons on the Commercial State of the West India Colonies 1842 (hereafter the Lord Stanley Committee). See also K. N. Bell and W. P. Morrell, eds., *Select Documents on British Colonial Policy, 1830–1860* (Oxford: Clarendon Press, 1928).

10. Colonial Office (C.O.) 295/162, Harris to Grey, 19 June 1848.

11. William Emanuel Riviere, "Labour Shortage in the British West Indies after Emancipation," *Journal of Caribbean History* 4 (1972), p. 11.

12. Michael Moohr, "The Economic Impact of Slave Emancipation in British Guiana, 1832–1852," *Economic History Review* 25, no. 4 (1972), p. 590.

13. Sewell, *Ordeal of Free Labor*, p. 265.

14. P.P. 1851, XXII (1383), Eleventh General Report of the Colonial Land and Emigration Commissioners, app. no. 41: Report by the Superintendent of Immigrants (Trinidad), 16 January 1851.

15. P.P. 1842, XIII (479), Report of the Lord Stanley Committee 1842: Evidence of William Burnley, #715–16.

16. Riviere, "Labour Shortage," p. 29.

17. P.P. 1842, XIII (479), Report of the Lord Stanley Committee 1842: Evidence of William Burnley, #637–38.

18. P.P. 1843, XXIX (621), General Report of the Colonial Land and Emigration Commissioners, 24 August 1843, p. 28.

19. See Table 1, Appendix 1.

20. Good eyewitness accounts can be found in William Burnley, ed., *Observations on the Present Condition of the Island of Trinidad* (London: Longman's, 1842); Barton Premium, *Eight Years in British Guiana, 1840–1848* (London: Longman's, 1850); M. F. Milliroux, *Demerara: Transition from Slavery to Liberty* (London, 1877; translation of 1843 French edition).

21. John Davy, *The West Indies before and since Slave Emancipation* (London: W. & F. G. Cash, 1854), pp. 313–14.

22. Daniel Hart, *Historical and Statistical View of the Island of Trinidad* (Port-of-Spain: Chronicle, 1866), pp. 82–83.

23. Riviere, "Labour Shortage," p. 17; Brian Moore, *Race, Power and Social Segmentation in Colonial Society: Guyana after Slavery, 1838–1891* (New York: Gordon & Breach, 1987), p. 34 (hereafter cited as *Guyana after Slavery*).

24. See quote from U.S. Consul Report in D. W. D. Comins, Note on Emigration from India to British Guiana (hereafter Comins Report [British Guiana]) (Calcutta, 1893), p. 7.

25. See Table 1, Appendix 1.

26. Williams, *From Columbus to Castro*, p. 378.

27. See Table 2, Appendix 1.

28. See Table 3, Appendix 1.

29. P.P. 1847–48, XXIII, pt. 2, (184): Report of the Select Committee on Sugar and

Coffee Planting in Her Majesty's East and West Indian Possessions and the Mauritius, chaired by Lord Bentinck, 29 May 1848.

30. Donald Wood, *Trinidad in Transition: The Years after Slavery* (London: Oxford University Press, 1968), p. 66.

31. See quote from L. De Verteuil's *History of Trinidad* in D. W. D. Comins, Note on Emigration from India to Trinidad (hereafter Comins Report [Trinidad]) (Calcutta 1893), p. 3.

32. *Trinidad Royal Gazette*, 10 May 1855: "Return of Prisoners Committed to the Royal Gaol of Port-of-Spain during 1854."

33. See Tables 32 and 33, Appendix 1.

34. Annual Immigration Reports (Trinidad) for 1898–1910.

35. George Roberts and Joycelyn Byrne, "Summary Statistics on Indenture and Associated Migration Affecting the West Indies, 1834–1918," *Population Studies* 20, no. 1 (1966), p. 127, pp. 130–31.

36. Nathaniel Peck and Thomas Price, *Report of Messrs Peck and Price who were appointed at a Meeting of the Free Colored People of Baltimore, held on the 25th November 1839, delegates to visit British Guiana and the island of Trinidad for the purpose of ascertaining the advantages to be derived by Colored People migrating to these places* (Baltimore, 1840).

37. Wood, *Trinidad in Transition*, p. 68.

38. C.O.295/175, Ward to Grey, 27 November 1851.

39. C.O.295/98, Hill to Stanley, 1 August 1833.

40. Wood, *Trinidad in Transition*, pp. 78–79.

41. See Table 5, Appendix 1. Donald Wood gives accounts of 676 French and German immigrants who landed in Trinidad in 1839, as well as a British party of 203 bound for Venezuela in 1846, 70 of whom stayed on in Trinidad. Wood, *Trinidad in Transition*, pp. 85–91.

42. Roberts and Byrne, "Statistics on Indenture and Associated Migration," p. 127, have a lower estimate of 897 for Trinidad (see Table 5, Appendix 1). The estimate of 1,298 is taken from Wood, *Trinidad in Transition*, p. 106.

43. Moore, *Guyana after Slavery*, pp. 150–56.

44. For a discussion on the fate of the Protestant followers of Dr. Robert Kalley, ejected from Madeira in 1846, see C. B. Franklin, *After Many Days: A Memoir* (Port-of-Spain: Franklin's Electric Printery, 1910), pp. 51–54. See also Wood, *Trinidad in Transition*, pp. 104–6; Jo-Anne S. Ferreira, "The Portuguese of Trinidad," in Gerard Besson and Bridget Brereton, eds., *The Book of Trinidad* (Port-of-Spain: Paria, 1991), pp. 263–72.

45. For a discussion on the Portuguese in British Guiana, see Mary Noel Menezes, *Scenes from the History of the Portuguese in Guyana* (London, 1986); Moore, *Guyana after Slavery*, chap. 7; K. O. Laurence, "The Establishment of the Portuguese Community in British Guiana," *Jamaican Historical Review* 5, no. 2 (1965), pp. 50–74.

Chapter 2
Push Factors and Migration Trends in India and China

1. See Tables 5, 6, and 23, Appendix 1.

2. In 1752–54, total imports from East India generally amounted to £1,086,000, total exports to £748,000. In 1759–60, imports amounted to £1,785,680, exports to

£1,161,670. The principal imports were calicoes, silks, muslins, raw silk, tea, pepper, arrack, saltpeter, porcelainware, gold, and diamonds; the first three items were also re-exported to Europe. The principal exports were woolen manufactures and metalware. Sir Charles Whitworth, *State of the Trade of Great Britain in Its Imports and Exports, 1697–1774* (London: G. Robinson, J. Robson, et al., 1776), pp. xxii, 9.

3. The Muslim rulers of Bengal had collected £818,000 in land revenues in 1764–65. The British were collecting £3,235,259 by 1794–95. Romesh Dutt, *The Economic History of India under Early British Rule*, vol. 1 (New Delhi: Government of India, 1970), pp. 85, 450.

4. Rudolph von Albertini, *European Colonial Rule, 1880–1940* (London: Oxford University Press, 1982), pp. 27–33.

5. Quoted in Jawaharlal Nehru, *The Discovery of India* (Garden City, N.Y.: Anchor, 1960), p. 298. For a debate on the extent and impact of this deindustrialization or "re-ruralisation" process, see *Journal of Economic History* 23 (December 1963), articles by Morris D. Morris, Bipan Chandra, and Tapan Raychaudhuri.

6. Quoted in Panchanan Saha, *Emigration of Indian Labour, 1834–1900* (New Delhi: People's Publishing House, 1970), p. 58.

7. By 1837–40, India was the largest single market within the British Empire for British exports: £4,565,000 worth of products, equal to the combined imports of the White Settlement colonies of Australia–New Zealand, South Africa, and Canada–New-foundland (£4,504,000). This status as primary colonial market continued for another hundred years, with only Australia–New Zealand receiving a comparable level of British exports after 1925. The entire British Empire received just around one-third of total British overseas exports in the nineteenth century. India was also, until around 1898, the largest single colonial supplier of primary commodities to Britain, and after this date, second only to Australia–New Zealand right up to the Second World War. The Indian commodities included cotton, jute, rice, tea, indigo, wheat, hides, linseed, flax, sugar, silk goods and raw silk, wool. Britain received just under a quarter of its overseas imports from Empire sources in the nineteenth century. Werner Schlote, *British Overseas Trade from the 1700's to the 1930's* (London: Oxford University Press, 1952), pp. 168–69; *Cambridge History of the British Empire*, vol. 3, 1870–1919, chap. 6, p. 217.

8. Saha, *Emigration of Indian Labour*, pp. 42–47. As late as 1903, an Indian govern-ment organ, the *Calcutta Englishman*, described the status of the Indian peasant in his native land as follows:

> It is strange that these gentlemen who profess themselves so deeply interested in the poverty of India have never turned their attention to the hundreds of thousands of serfs in this country, real "adscripti glebae," as much bound to the land as were the serfs of feudal Europe. A man borrows from a *bunnia* a sum of money to celebrate a domestic festival. He finds thereafter that he is unable not only to repay the capital, but the interest. The *bunnia* then compels him to become his servant and laborer. He gets in return his food, one piece of cloth a year, and a present of a rupee or two on the occasion of a domestic event in his family. It is evident that under these conditions the original debt will never be paid off. Not only does the unfortunate borrower become a slave for life, but the debt is handed on to his children, so that we find in India, generations of people, all the slaves of *bunnias*. They are too ignorant to realise that the law will not uphold the scandalous contract made by the moneylender, who generally rents land from *zemindars* and is therefore

in a position to find regular employment for his slaves. It is among the serfs that the majority of the recruits for emigration are to be found. C.O. 114/99, Report of the Emigration Agent in India for British Guiana for 1902–3.

9. Hugh Tinker, A New System of Slavery: The Export of Indian Labour Overseas, 1830–1920 (London: Oxford University Press, 1974), p. 44.

10. Daniel and Alice Thorner, Land and Labour in India (Bombay: Asia Publishing House, 1962), pp. 52–53, 77.

11. George Grierson, Report on Colonial Emigration from the Bengal Presidency (hereafter Grierson Report) (Calcutta, 1883), paragraphs 71, 82, 168, 173. "In Shahabad . . . 12/16 [sic] of the recruits search for the recruiters, and voluntarily emigrate. I have known instances of men coming 40 miles to look for a sub-depot" (paragraph 71). "Emigration is most popular in Patna and Shahabad. It is also popular to a lesser extent in Saran. We can predicate this of no other district. The reason is easy to see . . . the fact of a large number of emigrants having returned who have given good accounts of the colonies" (paragraph 173).

12. Christopher Hibbert, The Great Mutiny: India 1857 (New York: Penguin, 1980).

13. P.P. 1874, XLVII (314), Report by J. Geoghegan on Emigration from India (hereafter the Geoghegan Report), tables A, B, C, pp. 78–80; J. C. Jha, "The Indian Mutiny-cum-Revolt of 1857 and Trinidad (West Indies)," Indian Studies: Past and Present 13, no. 4 (1972), pp. 419–30. See also Table 8, Appendix 1.

14. Grierson Report, paragraph 91. See also paragraph 88: "[From] Saran . . . thousands emigrate temporarily to Eastern Bengal and Calcutta. . . . Large numbers . . . who fail to find work, are recruited at Calcutta, Patna and other places, and thus it happens that while natives of Saran form a large portion of the colonial emigrants, very few are recruited in their own district."

15. Tinker, New System of Slavery, pp. 52, 388.

16. Annual Immigration Report (Trinidad) for 1899.

17. Tinker, New System of Slavery, p. 131. There was also the slightly dubious story related by Sir Neville Lubbock to the Sanderson Commission of Enquiry into Indian Emigration in 1909, of the prince who came as an indentured servant to Trinidad and actually worked as a laborer for ten years before returning to India. P.P. 1910, XXVII (Cd. 5193), Report of the Committee on Emigration from India to the Crown Colonies and Protectorates (hereafter the Sanderson Commission Report), Evidence of Sir Neville Lubbock, 5 May 1909, #2600.

18. Comins Report (British Guiana), p. 52.

19. See Tinker, New System of Slavery, chap. 5, for specific examples.

20. P.P. 1910, XXVII (Cd. 5193), Sanderson Commission Report, Evidence of William Morrison, 7 May 1909, #2923.

21. Annual Immigration Report (Trinidad) for 1905–6.

22. P.P. 1910, XXVII (Cd. 5193), Sanderson Commission Report, Evidence of Colonel Duncan Pitcher, 7 June 1909, #4742, discussing police attitudes to recruiters in Lucknow and Cawnpore. See also Grierson Report, paragraph 67, and diary entry for 27 December 1882; the latter states as follows:

"[Sub-Agent for Trinidad in Dinapur] complains bitterly of interference from the police. [He] says that, when he recruits men of respectable castes, the police find their way into the depot and turn them out, saying that Government is going to make Christians of them, and that they will be eaten up by maggots and leeches. When recruiters go along through the bazaar, the police and the people abuse the recruiters and tell the recruits not to go."

23. P.P. 1872, XVI (C.562), Thirty-second General Report of the Colonial Land and Emigration Commissioners, pp. 8–9.

24. P.P. 1910, XXVII (Cd.5193), Sanderson Commission Report, Evidence of William Heron Coombs, 12 July 1909, #9085–87.

25. P.P. 1874, XLVII (314), Geoghegan Report, p. 70. See also Basdeo Mangru, "Stifled at Birth: Private Emigration from Bombay to British Guiana in the Mid-Nineteenth Century," *Immigrants and Minorities* 6, no. 2 (1987), pp. 190–99.

26. They were known as the Gladstone Coolies, having been brought over by the planter John Gladstone, among others.

27. Tinker, *New System of Slavery*, p. 49.

28. Saha, *Emigration of Indian Labour*, p. 33.

29. From 1,000 acres devoted to tea plantations in 1850, the number grew to 207,600 acres by 1880, and 525,000 by 1900, about half of these in Assam. See Census Report of India, 1901, pp. 85–86.

30. P.P. 1874, XLVII (314), Geoghegan Report, p. 72. Most of these would have emigrated in the 1840s and 1850s. This estimate does not include the pre-1842 shipments to Mauritius and British Guiana. Geoghegan also estimated an exodus of 49,860 Muslims and 88 Christians by 1870, in addition to 218,973 Hindus, from Calcutta.

31. The Charter Act of 1853 united Bengal, Bihar, Orissa, and Chota Nagpur into a single province called Bengal. Bihar and Orissa later became separate provinces.

32. Saha, *Emigration of Indian Labour*, p. 70.

33. See Table 9, Appendix 1.

34. Tinker, *New System of Slavery*, p. 113.

35. P.P. 1874, XLVII (314), Geoghegan Report, p. 71. See also Table 9, Appendix 1.

36. Saha, *Emigration of Indian Labour*, p. 30.

37. P.P. 1910, XXVII (Cd.5192), Sanderson Commission Report, paragraph 35, quoting a Government of India document dated 3 May 1877.

38. Ibid., paragraphs 68 and 77.

39. Steven Vertovec, *Hindu Trinidad* (London: Macmillan, 1992), p. 90.

40. Government of India, Bengal Emigration Reports: Annual Report on Emigration to British and Foreign Colonies from the Port of Calcutta for 1908.

41. Raymond Smith, "Some Social Characteristics of Indian Immigrants to British Guiana," *Population Studies* 13, no. 1 (1959), p. 39.

42. Tinker, *New System of Slavery*, p. 57.

43. See Table 7, Appendix 1.

44. P.P. 1910, XXVII (Cd.5193), Sanderson Commission Report, Evidence of Robert Duff, 23 July 1909, #10,070–73.

45. Comins Report (Trinidad), p. 24.

46. Annual Immigration Reports (Trinidad) for 1906–17.

47. Government of India, Bengal Emigration Reports: Annual Report on Emigration to British and Foreign Colonies from the Port of Calcutta for 1877–78.

48. Wood, *Trinidad in Transition*, p. 145.

49. Comins Report (British Guiana), p. 20.

50. Annual Immigration Report (British Guiana) for 1905–6.

51. Wood, *Trinidad in Transition*, pp. 46–47.

52. P.P. 1910, XXVII (Cd.5193), Sanderson Commission Report, Evidence of Colonel Duncan Pitcher, 7 June 1909, #4807.

53. Comins Report (Trinidad), p. 50.

54. P.P. 1910, XXVII (Cd.5192), Sanderson Commission Report, paragraph 19; Basdeo Mangru, *Benevolent Neutrality: Indian Government Policy and Labour Migration to British Guiana, 1854–1884* (London: Hansib, 1987), p. 239.

55. K. O. Laurence, *Immigration into the West Indies in the Nineteenth Century* (Barbados: Caribbean University Press, 1971), p. 57; see also Table 10, Appendix 1.

56. A few hundred Indians (mainly Punjabi Sikhs) went to Canada and California at the turn of the century. But Indian large-scale migration to the Western world did not really begin until the post–World War II migrations to Britain.

57. In 1851 about 25 percent of the population of Amoy were reported to have died of hunger and disease. *The Friend of China and Hong Kong Gazette*, 25 December 1852.

58. Quoted in Leon Hellerman and Alan Stein, eds., *China: Readings on the Middle Kingdom* (New York: Simon & Schuster, 1971), p. 145.

59. In 1860, there were actually more Chinese in the Latin American region than in the United States. According to the national Census statistics, in Cuba alone there were 34,834 Chinese in 1861, compared with 34,933 in the United States. In that year too, there were already about 15,000 in Peru, and 4,000 in the British West Indies.

60. Evelyn Hu-De Hart, "Coolies, Shopkeepers, Pioneers: The Chinese of Mexico and Peru, 1849–1930," *Amerasia Journal* 15, no. 2 (1989), pp. 91–116; Evelyn Hu-De Hart, "Immigrants to a Developing Society: The Chinese in Northern Mexico, 1875–1932," *Journal of Arizona History* 21 (1980), pp. 49–86; Juan Perez de la Riva, "Demografía de los Culies Chinos en Cuba, 1853–1874," *Revista de la Biblioteca Nacional José Martí* 57, no. 4 (1966), pp. 3–31; Denise Helly, *Ideologie et Ethnicité: Les Chinois Macao à Cuba, 1847–1886* (Montreal: Les Presses de l'Université de Montréal, 1979); Arnold Meagher, "The Introduction of Chinese Laborers to Latin America: The Coolie Trade, 1847–1874," Ph.D. dissertation, University of California, Davis, 1975.

61. P.P. 1852–53, LXVIII (1686), Correspondence respecting Emigration from China: Report by Harry Parkes, September 1852, pp. 24–25.

62. Jack Chen, *The Chinese of America* (San Francisco: Harper & Row, 1980), p. 6.

63. P.P. 1854–55, XXII (1953), Fifteenth General Report of the Colonial Land and Emigration Commissioners, p. 50.

64. Barry Higman, "The Chinese in Trinidad, 1806–1838," *Caribbean Studies* 12, no. 3 (1972), pp. 21–44. This settlement of Chinese actually predates the settlement of tea growers in Brazil, usually cited as the earliest of the nineteenth-century Chinese settlements in the Americas, by several years. See, for example, Eugenio Chang-Rodriguez, "Chinese Labor Migration into Latin America in the Nineteenth Century," *Revista de Historia de America* 46 (December 1958), pp. 375–97.

65. E. L. Joseph, *History of Trinidad* (London 1970 reprint of 1838 edition), p. 233.

66. See Table 23, Appendix 1. Laurence, *Immigration into the West Indies*, p. 36; W. Look Lai, "Chinese Indentured Labor: Migrations to the British West Indies in the Nineteenth Century," *Amerasia Journal* 15, no. 2 (1989), p. 123, table 3 on Chinese emigration to Cuba, 1847–74 (adapted from Perez de la Riva, "Demografía de los Culies").

67. See Table 24, Appendix 1. P.P. 1867, XIX (3855), Twenty-seventh General Report of the Colonial Land and Emigration Commissioners, pp. 28–29.

68. C.O.295/218, Report by Agent-General of Immigrants Henry Mitchell on the arrival of the *Wanata* in Trinidad, 11 July 1862; Cecil Clementi, *The Chinese in British Guiana* (Georgetown: Argosy, 1915), pp. 126–33.

69. P.P. 1854–55, XXXIX (o.7), Despatches respecting Chinese immigrants introduced into British Guiana and Trinidad: Winchester to Bowring, 22 July 1854.

70. Chinese Indenture Contracts, Trinidad National Archives.

71. Meagher, "Introduction of Chinese Laborers," p. 105A, table 3.

72. Meagher himself gives a higher estimate of 1,200 in another section of his book, "Introduction of Chinese Laborers," on p. 68. The shipment to Martinique is recorded in the Twentieth General Report of the Colonial Land and Emigration Commissioners (1860): P.P. 1860, XXIX (2696), p. 53.

73. P.P. 1852–53, LXVIII (1686), Correspondence respecting Emigration from China: Report from Canton British Consul Adam Elmslie to Dr. Bowring, 25 August 1852. The Eleventh General Report of the Colonial Land and Emigration Commissioners (1851) recorded as follows:

> The island of Hong Kong was born as a British colony in 1842. Prior to British occupation the island population probably never exceeded 2,000, including those of Punti, Hakka and Hoklo origins. In 1849 the Chinese population was recorded as 28,297, of whom 18,763 were male, 4,673 female, and 4,861 children. British and foreign resident population were numbered at 1,210, occupying 349 houses.

P.P. 1851, XXII (1383).

74. P.P. 1852–53, LXVIII (986), Despatches respecting Chinese immigrants introduced into British Guiana and Trinidad: White to Barkly, 21 June 1851 and 19 July 1851.

75. See Table 24, Appendix 1. Meagher, "Introduction of Chinese Laborers," p. 96.

76. Persia Campbell, *Chinese Coolie Emigration to Countries within the British Empire* (London 1923) gives the following estimates on p. 142:

Comparative Cost of Importing Coolies from India and China

Passage of 100 Coolies from India at £16 a head	=	£1,600
Return of 15% to India at £13 a head	=	£195
		£1,795

[West Indian planters claimed that not more than 10% to 15% of Indians took advantage of return passage options.]

Under the proposed terms of the 1866 Chinese Convention:

Passage of 100 coolies from China at £25 a head	=	£2,500
Return of 80% (20% mortality) at £15 a head	=	£1,200
		£3,700

[Thus the cost of 100 Chinese laborers would exceed the cost of 100 laborers by nearly £2,000]

77. The arrivals of 1862 and 1866, more so than those of 1865. See chapter 4 for a discussion on these laborers.

Chapter 3
The Formal Organization of the British West Indian Indenture System

1. Ordinance No. 18 of 1891 (British Guiana), Section 42; Ordinance No. 19 of 1899 (Trinidad), Section 34.

2. See Table 3, Appendix 1.

3. For a discussion on the evolution of the five-year indenture contract, see P.P. 1871,

XX (C.393), Report of the Commissioners appointed to Enquire into the Treatment of Immigrants in British Guiana (hereafter the British Guiana Immigration Commission, 1870–71), sec. 4, paragraphs 86–106, and sec. 10, paragraphs 226–41. See also K. O. Laurence, "The Evolution of Long-Term Labour Contracts in Trinidad and British Guiana," *Jamaican Historical Review* 5, no. 1 (1965), pp. 9–27.

4. Specimens of Indian and Chinese indenture contracts can be found in Appendix 3.

5. P.P. 1871, XX (C.393), Report of the British Guiana Immigration Commission, 1870–71, paragraph 174.

6. Ibid., app. H, pt. 1, pp. 38–39. See also Clementi, *Chinese in British Guiana*, pp. 67–69.

7. Copies of the Trinidad Chinese indenture contracts are housed in the Trinidad National Archives. See Appendix 3 for specimens of the main forms.

8. P.P. 1852–53, LXVIII (986), Despatches respecting Chinese immigrants introduced into British Guiana and Trinidad, for accounts of the 1853 contract arrangements.

9. P.P. 1871, XX (C.393), Report of the British Guiana Immigration Commission, 1870–71, paragraph 175.

10. Ibid., paragraph 174.

11. Wood, *Trinidad in Transition*, pp. 119–20.

12. Ordinance No. 18 of 1891 (British Guiana), and No. 19 of 1899 (Trinidad), pt. 9, entitled *Leave and Desertion*.

13. Ibid., pt. 8, entitled *Labour and Wages*.

14. For the full text of this 1864 law, see P.P. 1865, XVIII (3526), Twenty-fifth General Report of the Colonial Land and Emigration Commissioners (1865), app. 35.

15. P.P. 1871, XX (C.393), Report of the British Guiana Immigration Commission, 1870–71, paragraph 253.

16. See Appendix 2 for a detailed survey of the main changes in the law in Trinidad, British Guiana, and Jamaica.

17. P.P. 1871, XX (C.393), Report of the British Guiana Immigration Commission, 1870–71, paragraph 181.

18. Meagher, "Introduction of Chinese Laborers," table 4.

19. Clementi, *Chinese in British Guiana*, pp. 138–39.

20. P.P. 1871, XX (C.393), Report of the British Guiana Immigration Commission, 1870–71, paragraph 176. See also Joseph Beaumont, *The New Slavery: An Account of the Indian and Chinese Immigrants in British Guiana* (London: W. Ridgway, 1871), p. 47, sec. 2, paragraph 4.

21. P.P. 1860, LXIX (2714), Correspondence respecting emigration from Canton: Parkes to Hammond, 13 November 1859, enclosure. See also Clementi, *Chinese in British Guiana*, p. 84.

22. Ibid., pp. 78–79.

23. Ibid., p. 138.

24. C.O.295/234, Manners-Sutton to Cardwell, 12 April 1866.

25. For a complete discussion of the 1864 Act, see P.P. 1874, XLVII (314), Geoghegan Report, pp. 39–46.

26. M. Kirpalani et al., eds., *Indian Centenary Review, 1845–1945* (Trinidad: Guardian, 1945), pp. 31–33.

27. P.P. 1910, XXVII (Cd.5192), Sanderson Commission Report, paragraphs 27–40.

28. Ibid., Cd.5194, app., p. 124: Memorandum on the Law relating to Indian Immigration.

29. Dwarka Nath, *A History of Indians in Guyana* (London, 1970), chap. 6, pp. 48–55.

30. Quoted in Tinker, *New System of Slavery*, p. 106.

31. Wood, *Trinidad in Transition*, pp. 131–32. Major Fagan's case is discussed further in chapter 6.

32. Nath, *Indians in Guyana*, p. 154.

33. *Port-of-Spain Gazette*, 8 July 1897. Discussed again in chapter 5.

34. See his testimony to the Sanderson Commission, 12 July 1909, #9068–9305, P.P. 1910, XXVII (Cd.5193). See also John H. Harris, *Coolie Labour in the British Crown Colonies and Protectorates* (London: Edward Hughes & Co., 1910), pp. 14–16, for a criticism of Commander Coombs' conservatism.

35. F. H. Hitchins, *The Colonial Land and Emigration Commissioners* (Philadelphia: University of Pennsylvania Press, 1931).

36. See Appendix 2 for a survey of Jamaican immigration legislation.

37. See note 28 above. See also the main body of the Sanderson Commission Report (Cd.5192), paragraph 263.

38. P.P. 1910, XXVII (Cd.5192), Sanderson Commission Report, paragraph 227; also vol. 3 of the same report (Cd.5194), app., British Guiana, p. 7. See also P.P. 1871, XX (C.393), Report of the British Guiana Immigration Commission, 1870–71, paragraphs 107–13.

39. P.P. 1910, XXVII (Cd.5192), Sanderson Commission Report, paragraph 301. See also the section on Jamaican immigration laws in Appendix 2 of this study.

Chapter 4
Life and Labor on the Plantations: The Chinese

1. Tinker, *New System of Slavery*, p. 198.

2. P.P. 1852–53, LXVIII (986), Despatches respecting Chinese immigrants introduced into British Guiana and Trinidad, p. 80: White to Barkly, 19 July 1851.

3. Look Lai, "Chinese Indentured Labor," p. 138.

4. 254 passengers, of whom 251 landed alive. C.O.295/181, Mitchell to Colonial Secretary, 7 May 1853, 13 September 1853.

5. P.P. 1854–55, XXII (1953), Fifteenth General Report of the Colonial Land and Emigration Commissioners (1855), app. no. 51, White to Walcott, 7 April 1854.

6. P.P. 1852–53, LXVIII (1686), Correspondence respecting Emigration from China, pp. 49–95.

7. P.P. 1852–53, LXVIII (986), Despatches respecting Chinese immigrants introduced into British Guiana and Trinidad, p. 44, Abstract of Surgeon's Journal.

8. Ibid., p. 118, letter from Colonial Land and Emigration Office, 14 May 1853.

9. Quoted in P.P. 1854, XXVIII (1833), Fourteenth General Report of the Colonial Land and Emigration Commissioners (1854), p. 68.

10. See P.P. 1852–53, LXVIII (986), Despatches respecting Chinese immigrants introduced into British Guiana and Trinidad, passim.

11. See note 9 above.

12. C.O.295/180, Mitchell to Colonial Secretary, 10 March 1853.

13. P.P. 1854, XXVIII (1833), Fourteenth General Report of the Colonial Land and

Emigration Commissioners (1854), app. no. 76, Report by Agent-General of Immigrants Henry Mitchell, 28 November 1853.

14. Annual Immigration Report (Trinidad) for 1863.

15. P.P. 1859, XIV (2555), Nineteenth General Report of the Colonial Land and Emigration Commissioners (1859), app. no. 42, Mitchell to Johnstone, 1 June 1858.

16. P.P. 1854–55, XXII (1953), Fifteenth General Report of the Colonial Land and Emigration Commissioners (1855), app. no. 51, White to Walcott, 7 April 1854.

17. P.P. 1852–53, LXVIII (986), Despatches respecting Chinese immigrants introduced into British Guiana and Trinidad, p. 129: White to Walcott, 9 April 1853. Ong Soong Seng seems to have stayed on in Trinidad beyond his original five-year appointment. An official letter in 1865 described him as the Immigration Department's senior Chinese interpreter and recommended a salary increase from £150 to £175 per annum. C.O.295/232, Sutton to Cardwell, 23 October 1865. One of the Chinese who arrived on the *Dudbrook* in 1866 also seems to have been privately allotted to him as an indentured servant. Chinese Indenture Contracts, Trinidad National Archives.

18. P.P. 1852–53, LXVIII (986), Despatches respecting Chinese immigrants introduced into British Guiana and Trinidad, p. 147: Report from Agent-General of Immigrants Henry Mitchell, 22 April 1853, enclosed in Harris to Newcastle, 22 April 1853.

19. Annual Immigration Report (Trinidad) for 1856.

20. P.P. 1852–53, XL (1647), Thirteenth General Report of the Colonial Land and Emigration Commissioners (1853), app. no. 50, Report by Governor Barkly, 26 February 1853.

21. P.P. 1852–53, LXVIII (986), Despatches respecting Chinese immigrants introduced into British Guiana and Trinidad, p. 144: Report by Henry Mitchell, 20 April 1853.

22. P.P. 1854–55, XXII (1953), Fifteenth General Report of the Colonial Land and Emigration Commissioners (1855), app. no. 52, Journal of the Chinese interpreter, Wang-Te-Chang, reporting on the state of the Chinese immigrants in Panama.

23. Jacqueline Levy, "Chinese Indentured Immigration to Jamaica during the Latter Part of the Nineteenth Century," paper presented at the Fourth Conference of Caribbean Historians, Mona, Jamaica, 1972.

24. See Tables 23 and 24, Appendix 1.

25. See Table 24, Appendix 1.

26. See Tables 25 to 27, Appendix 1.

27. C.O.111/336, Report from Immigration Agent Crosby, 29 August 1862, enclosed in Hincks to Newcastle, 2 September 1862.

28. P.P. 1871, XX (C.393), Report of the British Guiana Immigration Commission, 1870–71, paragraph 328.

29. Ibid., paragraph 106.

30. Ibid., paragraph 169.

31. *Port-of-Spain Gazette*, 21 June 1865.

32. Ibid. Not strictly true. See the British Guiana Immigration Commission Report, 1871, paragraph 371, "800 Chinese women resident on estates, not under indenture, some of whom work 'very well'": P.P. 1871, XX (C.393).

33. Roughly 88 embarked at Swatow, and 55 at Amoy. The Fukienese were distributed as follows: Aranguez (14), Buen Intento (4), Broomage (16), Concord North (4), Diego Martin (2), Wellington (15). Chinese Indenture Contracts, Trinidad National Archives.

34. Several reputable sources refer to the arrival of 1 Chinese female among the 192 Chinese who came to Trinidad on the *Fortitude* in 1806. These sources include Noel Deerr's *History of Sugar* (London: Chapman & Hall, 1949) and Gertrude Carmichael's *History of the West Indian Islands of Trinidad and Tobago* (hereafter *History of Trinidad and Tobago*) (London: Alvin Redman, 1961). They also include several commentaries in Trinidad Census Reports of the twentieth century. The author has examined the original correspondence in the C.O. 295 Series (Trinidad) and has not been able to substantiate this. See C.O.295/14, Hislop to Windham, 26 October 1806. The error seems to have originated with E. L. Joseph's *History of Trinidad,* first published in 1838, and repeated without confirmation since then in several derivative accounts.

Also, the *Clarendon* which went to Trinidad in 1853 from Canton seems to have had a number of female emigrants available to it, but they were not accepted by the captain of the vessel, on the ground that their presence might have led to quarrels and disturbances on the voyage. P.P. 1852–53, LXVIII (986), James White to S. Walcott, Secretary of the Colonial Land and Emigration Commission, 8 January 1853: Sub-Enclosure No. 1 to Enclosure in Despatch No. 8, Duke of Newcastle to Governor Barkly, 24 March 1853.

35. Annual Immigration Report (Trinidad) for 1863.

36. P.P. 1866, XVII (3679), Twenty-sixth General Report of the Colonial Land and Emigration Commissioners (1866), pp. 19–20.

37. See Table 24, Appendix 1. See also note 34 above.

38. The Annual Report of the Superintendent of Prisons for 1866 revealed that no less than 905 Chinese had been incarcerated for major and minor offenses during that year. Of these, 502 were for "Want of Certificate" (i.e., apprehended outside the plantation without a pass), and 220 for "Breach of Contract." A further 110 were committed for larceny, and 13 for "Damage with Intent to Steal." See Table 28, Appendix 1. The number of Indians apprehended without a pass in 1866 was 623, for breach of contract 245, and for larceny 146.

39. Annual Immigration Report (Trinidad) for 1866, enclosed letter from John Spiers to Henry Mitchell, 26 September 1866.

40. Annual Immigration Report (Trinidad) for 1866, enclosed letter from Louis Leroy to Henry Mitchell, 10 October 1867. For a list of the estates still employing Chinese indentured labor at the end of 1866, see Table 26, Appendix 1.

41. See Table 28, Appendix 1.

42. Henry Kirke, *Twenty-five Years in British Guiana, 1872–1897* (London: Sampson Low, Marston & Co., 1898), p. 154.

43. P.P. 1871, XX (C.393), Report of the British Guiana Immigration Commission, 1870–71, paragraph 888.

44. Kirke, *Twenty-five Years in British Guiana,* p. 160.

45. P.P. 1871, XX (C.393), Report of the British Guiana Immigration Commission, 1870–71, paragraph 328.

46. Brian Moore, "The Settlement of Chinese in Guyana in the Nineteenth Century," *Immigrants and Minorities* 7, no. 1 (1988), p. 44.

47. Annual Immigration Report (Trinidad) for 1863.

48. P.P. 1871, XX (C.393), Report of the British Guiana Immigration Commission, 1870–71, paragraph 272.

49. Moore, *Guyana after Slavery,* p. 171.

50. P.P. 1871, XX (C.393), Report of the British Guiana Immigration Commission, 1870–71, paragraph 290; also app. E, pt. 1, pp. 12–21.

51. Ibid., paragraph 307.

52. Ibid., letter from Des Voeux to Granville, paragraph 15. For further instances of violence against Chinese laborers, see Beaumont, New Slavery, pp. 68–74, sec. 3, paragraphs 2–5.

53. Port-of-Spain Gazette, 15 July 1865.

54. Colonist, 28 June 1866, quoted in Moore, "Chinese in Guyana," p. 43. See also Beaumont, New Slavery, pp. 27–28, sec. 1, paragraph 12.

55. Port-of-Spain Gazette, 31 March 1866, 4 April 1866.

56. Kirke, Twenty-five Years in British Guiana, p. 157.

57. P.P. 1871, XX (C.393), Report of the British Guiana Immigration Commission, 1870–71, app. D3, pt. 1, p. 12.

58. Ibid., paragraph 482.

59. Annual Immigration Report (Trinidad) for 1871.

60. P.P. 1872, XVI (C.562), Thirty-second General Report of the Colonial Land and Emigration Commissioners (1872), p. 7; also, P.P. 1873, XVIII (C.768), Thirty-third General Report of the Colonial Land and Emigration Commissioners (1873), p. 15.

61. Trinidad Legislative Council Papers No. 65 of 1883: Papers relating to the proposed introduction of coolies from China.

62. P.P. 1871, XX (C.393), Report of the British Guiana Immigration Commission, 1870–71, paragraph 184; C.O.114, Minutes of the Court of Policy (British Guiana), vol. 24, 29 January 1867, and vol. 27, 12 November 1877.

63. P.P. 1898, L (C.8655–57), Report of the Royal Commission on the Sugar Industry in the West Indies 1897, app. C, pt. 2, British Guiana, sec. 120. The plantations on which they were employed were:

		M.	F.
Success	Essequibo Islands	7	1
Hampton Court	Essequibo Mainland	12	7
Peter's Hall	Demerara River	5	1
Windsor Forest	West Coast Demerara	23	7
Albion	East Coast Berbice	18	14
Friends	Berbice River	2	0
Mara	Berbice River	9	3
Total:		76	33

64. See Table 30, Appendix 1.

65. Lee Tom Yin, The Chinese in Jamaica (Kingston: Chung San News, 1963).

66. Ibid., p. 8.

67. Levy, "Chinese Indentured Immigration to Jamaica," p. 59.

68. Andrew Lind, "Adjustment Patterns among the Jamaican Chinese," Social and Economic Studies 7, no. 2 (1958), p. 151.

69. P.P. 1867, XIX (3855), Twenty-seventh General Report of the Colonial Land and Emigration Commissioners (1867), p. 29.

70. P.P. 1868–69, XVII (4159), Twenty-ninth General Report of the Colonial Land and Emigration Commissioners (1869), p. 26.

71. P.P. 1870, XVII (C.196), Thirtieth General Report of the Colonial Land and Emigration Commissioners (1870), p. 29.

Chapter 5
Life and Labor on the Plantations: The Indians

1. There is a wide discrepancy in the statistics concerning these 1845–48 arrivals. The figures here are taken from Roberts and Byrne, "Statistics on Indenture and Associated Migration," p. 129, reproduced in Table 6, Appendix 1. Nath, *Indians in Guyana,* and the Comins Reports of 1893 give different figures: 11,841 for British Guiana, 5,305 for Trinidad, 4,551 for Jamaica, making a total of 21,697. The Geoghegan Report of 1873 gave the following figures for departures from India in these years: 22,202 (11,071 from Calcutta, 11,131 from Madras), representing 12,075 for British Guiana, 5,512 for Trinidad, 4,615 for Jamaica. See also Tables 7 and 8, Appendix 1.

2. Cocoa exports went from 6,422,038 lbs. in 1871 to 16,188,493 lbs. in 1891 to 33,880,560 lbs. in 1901, to 83,560,848 lbs. in 1921. Trinidad and Tobago Census Report, 1946.

3. Gerad Tikasingh, "The Establishment of the Indians in Trinidad, 1870–1900," Ph.D. thesis, University of the West Indies, St. Augustine, Trinidad, 1976, p. 96.

4. Annual Immigration Report (Trinidad) for 1876. There was also one coconut estate in St. Patrick County, the Constance, with ten indentureds (six men, four women).

5. Comins Report (Trinidad), p. 12.

6. Annual Immigration Report (Trinidad) for 1905–6. See also Table 13, Appendix 1.

7. For the geographical distribution of the plantations employing indentured labor in Trinidad between 1862 and 1910, see Table 12, Appendix 1. Not included in these estimates were the large number of nonindentured Indians living off the estates.

8. Then twenty-nine years old.

9. Nath, *Indians in Guyana,* pp. 20–21.

10. P.P. 1847–48, XXVI (961), Eighth General Report of the Colonial Land and Emigration Commissioners (1848), app. no. 18, Dr. Bunyun to Governor Light, 6 January 1848.

11. P.P. 1859, Session 1, XVI (2452), Papers relating to Immigration to the West Indian Colonies, pp. 142–43: Walker to Duke of Newcastle, 15 June 1852.

12. C.O.295/160, Harris to Grey, 21 February 1848.

13. Despatch of Governor Harris dated 8 March 1848, quoted in Davy, *British West Indies,* pp. 310–11, footnote.

14. Discussed in chapter 6. See also Wood, *Trinidad in Transition,* pp. 115–16.

15. C.O.295/163, Harris to Grey, 1 July 1848.

16. P.P. 1851, XXII (1383), Eleventh General Report of the Colonial Land and Emigration Commissioners (1851), app. no. 41, Report by Dr. Henry Mitchell, 16 January 1851.

17. Deerr, *History of Sugar,* vol. 1, pp. 201–3. See also Table 1, Appendix 1.

18. Discussed in chapter 6. See also Moore, *Guyana after Slavery,* p. 41. The same applied to Trinidad. Charles William Day reported in 1847 that "the dislike of the negroes in Trinidad to the introduction of the emigrants from either India or Madeira is very great and they take every opportunity to insult and deride the newcomers." *Five Years' Residence in the West Indies* (London: Colburn & Co., 1852), p. 182.

19. P.P. 1852–53, XL (1647), Thirteenth General Report of the Colonial Land and Emigration Commissioners (1853), p. 56.

20. Judith Weller, *The East Indian Indenture in Trinidad* (Rio Piedras, Puerto Rico: Institute of Caribbean Studies, 1968), p. 29.

21. P.P. 1852, XVIII (1499), Twelfth General Report of the Colonial Land and Emigration Commissioners (1852), app. no. 54, Report by Captain Biden, Protector of Emigrants at Madras, 12 December 1851.

22. *San Fernando Gazette*, 16 April 1852, Report by A. Rogers, Assistant Protector at Calcutta, 31 December 1851.

23. John Bigelow, *Jamaica in 1850* (New York, 1851; reprinted 1970), pp. 17–19.

24. Up to 1895, 1 rupee (16 annas) was worth about 1s. 6d. One pound sterling was equivalent to $4.80 (B.W.I.) throughout and after this period. A Spanish dollar was worth roughly $1.04 (B.W.I.).

25. P.P. 1852, XVIII (1499), Twelfth General Report of the Colonial Land and Emigration Commissioners (1852), p. 58.

26. See Table 10, Appendix 1, for repatriation figures.

27. P.P. 1859, Session 2, XIV (2555), Nineteenth General Report of the Colonial Land and Emigration Commissioners (1859), p. 51; see also P.P. 1871, XX (C.369), Thirty-first General Report of the Colonial Land and Emigration Commissioners (1871), p. 13. According to I. M. Cumpston, *Indians Overseas in British Territories, 1834–1854* (London: Oxford University Press, 1953), pp. 143–45, about two thousand Jamaicans had left for Navy Bay and Panama by 1854 to work on the Panama railroad project. An unspecified number of Indians had also gone with them.

28. P.P. 1859, Session 2, XIV (2555), Nineteenth General Report of the Colonial Land and Emigration Commissioners (1859), p. 51.

29. P.P. 1856, XXIV (2089), Sixteenth General Report of the Colonial Land and Emigration Commissioners (1856), app. no. 60, Statistics of Immigrant Population on 31 December 1855.

30. C.O.295/172, Harris to Grey, 7 January 1851.

31. Tikasingh, "Establishment of Indians in Trinidad," p. 100. See also Annual Immigration Report (Trinidad) for 1889.

32. Moore, *Guyana after Slavery*, pp. 120–21.

33. Cited in Comins Report (Trinidad), pp. 12–13.

34. P.P. 1910, XXVII (Cd.5193), Sanderson Commission Report, Testimony of Sir Neville Lubbock, 5 May 1909, #2473.

35. Ibid., Testimony of Sir Sydney Olivier, 1 July 1909, #8029.

36. Table 2, Appendix 1.

37. Table 4, Appendix 1.

38. Table 3, Appendix 1.

39. Table 32, Appendix 1; Annual Immigration Reports (Trinidad) for 1871, 1881, 1891. See also Table 12, Appendix 1.

40. Tables 15 and 33, Appendix 1.

41. Tables 12 and 15, Appendix 1.

42. From £22 4s. a ton in 1883 to £14 11s. in 1884–85 to £10 7s. in 1895–96, and £9 12s. in 1896.

43. Discussed in chapter 6.

44. Tables 32 and 33, Appendix 1.

45. Edward Jenkins, *The Coolie: His Rights and Wrongs* (London: Strahan & Co., 1871), p. 63.

46. W. H. Gamble, *Trinidad, Historical and Descriptive: Being a Narrative of Nine Years' Residence in the Island* (London: Yates & Alexander, 1866), p. 33.

47. Annual Immigration Reports (British Guiana), quoted in Tyran Ramnarine, "The Growth of the East Indian Community in British Guiana, 1880–1920," Ph.D. thesis, University of Sussex, 1977, p. 86.

48. Annual Immigration Report (Trinidad) for 1916.

49. Harinder Sohal, "The East Indian Indentureship in Jamaica, 1845–1917," Ph.D. thesis, University of Waterloo, Ontario, Canada, 1979, p. 84.

50. Gamble, *Trinidad, Historical and Descriptive*, p. 33.

51. Annual Immigration Report (Trinidad) for 1859.

52. P.P. 1847–48, XXVI (961), Eighth General Report of the Colonial Land and Emigration Commissioners (1848), app. no. 18, Dr. Bunyun to Governor Light, 6 January 1848.

53. P.P. 1871, XX (C.393), Report of the British Guiana Immigration Commission, 1870–71, paragraphs 310–11. The Chinese laborers had mainly Chinese drivers. Chief Justice Beaumont suggested in 1871 that many of the drivers, including some of the Chinese ones, enriched themselves illegally by extorting regular payments from the laborers under their control. Beaumont, *New Slavery*, pp. 87–88, sec. 3, paragraphs 17–18.

54. P.P. 1874, XLVII (C.314), Geoghegan Report, p. 72.

55. P.P. 1915, XLVII (Cd.7744), Report to the Government of India on the Condition of Indian Immigrants in Four British Colonies and Surinam (hereafter the McNeill-Lal Report), p. 74.

56. *Demerara Daily Chronicle*, 21–23 November 1888, quoted in Moore, *Guyana after Slavery*, p. 257, note 18.

57. See, for example, Annual Immigration Report (Trinidad) for 1917.

58. Comins Report (Trinidad), p. 37.

59. P.P. 1910, XXVII (Cd.5193), Sanderson Commission Report, Testimony of William Morrison, 7 May 1909, #2828.

60. Ibid., Testimony of Sir Neville Lubbock, 5 May 1909, #2531.

61. Ibid., #2611.

62. Tinker, *New System of Slavery*, pp. 174–75.

63. Ibid., p. 223.

64. Trinidad Legislative Council Paper No. 39 of 1877.

65. Alan Adamson, "The Impact of Indentured Immigration on the Political Economy of British Guiana," in Kay Saunders, ed., *Indentured Labour in the British Empire, 1834–1920* (London: Croom Helm, 1984), p. 43.

66. M. Shahabuddeen, *From Plantocracy to Nationalisation: A Profile of Sugar in Guyana* (Demerara, University of Guyana, 1983), pp. 182–86.

67. Karl Marx, *Capital*, vol. 1, cited in Adamson, "Impact of Indentured Immigration," p. 42.

68. P.P. 1871, XX (C.393), Report of the British Guiana Immigration Commission, 1870–71, p. 4: Des Voeux to Granville, 25 December 1869.

69. Ibid., paragraphs 405–11.

70. P.P. 1910, XXVII (Cd.5192), Sanderson Commission Report, pp. 57, 71.

71. Ibid., p. 57.

72. Discussed in chapter 6.

73. The McNeill-Lal Report of 1914–15 indicated as much, in relation to British Guiana, where the percentage of summonses to indentured immigrants rose between 1896–97 (when it was 18.48 percent) and 1906–7 (when it was 37.8 percent), just around the period of the rise of the rice industry. Indentured immigrants were said to have devoted to the plots assigned to them, or to the land leased by other immigrants, more of their time than their employers thought reasonable. P.P. 1915, XLVII (Cd.7744), McNeill-Lal Report, p. 70.

74. P.P. 1910, XXVII (Cd.5192), Sanderson Commission Report, pp. 77–79.

75. San Fernando Gazette, 3 September 1868, Letter to the Editor from Echo.

76. Beaumont, New Slavery, pp. 39–40, sec. 1.

77. P.P. 1898, L (C.8655–57), Report of the Royal Commission on the West India Sugar Industry, app. C, pt. 4 (Trinidad), sec. 314, Memorandum from East Indian Immigrants to the West India Royal Commission.

78. Trinidad Legislative Council Paper No. 57 of 1895: Report of the Protector of Immigrants on Wages Earned by the Indentured Immigrants.

79. P.P. 1910, XXVII (Cd.5193), Sanderson Commission Report, Testimony of Sir Neville Lubbock, 5 May 1909, #2463.

80. P.P. 1915, XLVII (Cd.7744), McNeill-Lal Report, app. 10, p. 134.

81. P.P. 1898, L (C.8657), Report of the Royal Commission on the West India Sugar Industry, app. C, pt. 2 (British Guiana), sec. 158.

82. George W. Des Voeux, My Colonial Service in British Guiana, St. Lucia, Trinidad, etc., (London: Murray, 1903), p. 133.

83. See Demerara Colonist, 24 August 1868, on Mr. Justice Beete's resignation, quoted in Port-of-Spain Gazette, 19 September 1868.

84. Walter Rodney, A History of the Guyanese Working People, 1881–1905 (Baltimore: Johns Hopkins University Press, 1981), p. 41.

85. San Fernando Gazette, 3 September 1868, Letter to the Editor from Echo.

86. Bridget Brereton, "Sir John Gorrie: A Radical Chief Justice of Trinidad, 1885–1892," Journal of Caribbean History 13 (1980), pp. 44–72.

87. Port-of-Spain Gazette, 8 July 1897.

88. Edward Underhill, The West Indies: Their Social and Religious Condition (London: Jackson, Walford & Hodder, 1862), p. 82.

89. Ibid., p. 89.

90. Gamble, Trinidad, Historical and Descriptive, p. 36.

91. Beaumont, New Slavery, p. 14, intro.

92. P.P. 1871, XX (C.393), Report of the British Guiana Immigration Commission, 1870–71, paragraph 327.

93. Ibid., paragraph 835.

94. See note 92 above.

95. Des Voeux, Colonial Service, pp. 133–39.

96. J. H. Collens, A Guide to Trinidad: A Handbook for the Use of Tourists and Visitors (London: Elliot Stock, 1886), pp. 238–39. A similar comparison with the "ordinary farm laborer in England" was made by the Protector of Immigrants in the Trinidad Immigration Report for 1899.

97. Annual Immigration Report (Trinidad) for 1871.

98. Comins Report (Trinidad), p. 50.

99. P.P. 1910, XXVII (Cd.5193), Sanderson Commission Report, Testimony of Reverend John Morton, 29 July 1909, #10,488–10,601.

100. Ibid., Testimony of W. Alleyne Ireland, 9 August 1909, #10,960. See also W. Alleyne Ireland, *Demerariana: Essays Historical, Technical and Descriptive* (Georgetown: Balwin & Co., 1897).

101. Published works include Basdeo Mangru, *Benevolent Neutrality: Indian Government Policy and Labor Migration to British Guiana, 1854–1884*; John La Guerre, ed., *From Calcutta to Caroni: The East Indians of Trinidad* (St. Augustine, Trinidad: University of the West Indies, 1985); David Dabydeen and Brinsley Samaroo, eds., *India in the Caribbean* (London: Hansib, 1987). Unpublished works include three doctoral dissertations: Tyran Ramnarine, "The Growth of the East Indian Community in British Guiana," 1880–1920 (1977); Dale Arlington Bisnauth, "The East Indian Immigrant Society in British Guiana, 1891–1930," (1977); Gerad Tikasingh, "The Establishment of the Indians in Trinidad, 1870–1900 (1976). These are in addition to the older, more conservative works by Dwarka Nath and Peter Ruhumon.

102. Rhoda Reddock, "Indian Women and Indentureship in Trinidad and Tobago, 1845–1917," *Caribbean Quarterly* 32, nos. 3 & 4 (1986), pp. 40–41. See also P.P. 1915, XLVII (Cd.7744), McNeill-Lal Report, pp. 37–38; Beaumont, *New Slavery*, pp. 74–75, sec. 3, paragraph 6.

103. P.P. 1910, XXVII (Cd.5193), Sanderson Commission Report, Testimony of William Middleton Campbell, 10 May 1909, #3050.

104. Davy, *West Indies*, p. 311.

105. P.P. 1871, XX (C.393), Report of the British Guiana Immigration Commission, 1870–71, paragraph 858; see also P.P. 1910, XXVII (Cd.5193), Sanderson Commission Report, Testimony of Oliver William Warner, 26 March 1909, #690. A recent study pointed out that in India the murder of unfaithful wives was commonplace. In 1872 alone, of 8,840 murders, 2,480, or 28 percent, were of women, and of that number, 1,152, or 46 percent, were murders of wives by husbands. See Sohal, "Indian Indentureship in Jamaica," p. 143.

Spousal violence often assumed bizarre forms. The British Guiana Annual Immigration Report for 1895–96 commented as follows:

> violent assaults on wives in India take a direction unknown in the West Indies or even in Europe . . . quot[ing] . . . from an Indian paper: "Notwithstand[ing the heavy punishment recently inflicted for that particular form of crime, biting off a wife's nose continues to be a favorite amusement in Bombay. Only the other day, writes a contemporary, two men got four years hard labour each for this offence; and at the sessions which are being held at Bombay now, another man has been sentenced to a similar penalty for another such outrage."

106. Annual Immigration Reports (Trinidad) for 1897, 1898.

107. Comins Report (British Guiana), p. 63. See also Basdeo Mangru, "The Sex-Ratio Disparity and Its Consequences under the Indenture in British Guiana," in Dabydeen and Samaroo, *India in the Caribbean*, pp. 211–30.

108. Tyran Ramnarine, "A Hundred Years of East Indian Disturbances on the Sugar Estates of Guyana, 1869–1978: A Historical Overview," in Dabydeen and Samaroo, *India in the Caribbean*, p. 123. See also Nath, *Indians in Guyana*, chap. 13.

109. Annual Immigration Report (British Guiana) for 1903–4.

110. Moore, *Guyana after Slavery*, p. 173.

111. P.P. 1910, XXVII (Cd.5193), Sanderson Commission Report, Testimony of William Morrison, 7 May 1909, #2831.

112. P.P. 1884–85, LIII (C.4366), Report on the Recent Coolie Disturbances in Trinidad. See also Kelvin Singh, *Blood-Stained Tombs: The Muhurrum Massacre of 1884* (London: Macmillan, 1988).

113. Tikasingh, "Establishment of Indians in Trinidad," pp. 133–34. See also Kusha Haraksingh, "Control and Resistance among Overseas Indian Workers: A Study of Labour on the Sugar Plantations of Trinidad, 1875–1917," in Dabydeen and Samaroo, *India in the Caribbean*, pp. 61–80.

114. *Port-of-Spain Gazette*, 16 October 1891.

115. P.P. 1910, XXVII (Cd.5193), Sanderson Commission Report, Testimony of William Coombs, 12 July 1909, #9180–85, 9303–5.

116. P.P. 1915, XLVII (Cd.7744), McNeill-Lal Report, p. 73.

117. Annual Immigration Report (Trinidad) for 1916.

118. P.P. 1910, XXVII (Cd.5194), Sanderson Commission Report, pt. 3, app., pp. 135–36. See also Tinker, *New System of Slavery*, pp. 228–29.

119. Annual Immigration Reports (Trinidad) for 1906–7, 1907–8, 1910–11, 1911–12.

120. Sohal, "Indian Indentureship in Jamaica," p. 121. After 1891, most Indian immigrants to Jamaica were employed in the banana industry, with sugar taking second place.

121. Annual Immigration Report (Trinidad) for 1863.

122. P.P. 1910, XXVII (Cd.5193), Sanderson Commission Report, Testimony of Peter Abel, 4 November 1909, #12,717.

123. Ibid., Testimony of Robert Duff, 18 October 1909, #12,303–10.

124. Annual Immigration Report (Trinidad) for 1862.

125. Annual Immigration Report (Trinidad) for 1863.

126. Annual Immigration Report (Trinidad) for 1864.

127. Annual Immigration Report (Trinidad) for 1897.

128. Annual Immigration Report (Trinidad) for 1898.

129. Annual Immigration Report (Trinidad) for 1902–3.

130. P.P. 1910, XXVII (Cd.5193), Sanderson Commission Report, Testimony of Peter Abel, 4 November 1909, #12,768; see also #12,763–67.

131. Annual Immigration Report (Trinidad) for 1864.

132. P.P. 1851, XXII (1383), Eleventh General Report of the Colonial Land and Emigration Commissioners (1851), app. no. 45, Despatch of Governor Barkly dated 18 April 1850.

133. Comins Report (British Guiana), p. 52.

134. P.P. 1871, XX (C.393), Report of the British Guiana Immigration Commission, 1870–71, paragraph 482.

Chapter 6
Critics of Indenture: Alternative Voices in Creole Society

1. Deerr, *History of Sugar*, vol. 1, pp. 198–99, 201–3. See also Tables 1 and 2, Appendix 1.

2. John Scoble, *Hill Coolies: A Brief Exposure of the Deplorable Conditions of the Hill Coolies in British Guiana and Mauritius* (London: Harvey & Danton, 1840); Isaac Dookhan, "The Gladstone Experiment: The Experience of the First East Indians in British Guiana," Paper presented at the First Conference of East Indians in the Caribbean, University of the West Indies, St. Augustine, Trinidad, 1975.

3. Carmichael, *History of Trinidad and Tobago*, pp. 215–16. See also Carl Campbell, "Thomas Hinde of Trinidad, 1838–1848," *Journal of Caribbean History* 21, no. 2 (1987), pp. 95–116.

4. *Trinidad Spectator*, June–November 1845, passim.

5. *Trinidad Spectator*, 3 May 1848.

6. C.O.295/158, Harris to Grey, 7 December 1847 (with enclosures).

7. C.O.295/153, Harris to Grey, 5 October 1846 (with enclosures).

8. See note 6 above.

9. *San Fernando Gazette*, 16 April 1852, Interview with immigrants returning on the *Eliza Stewart* by A. Rogers, Assistant Protector of Emigrants at Calcutta.

10. *Trinidad Spectator*, 26 April 1848.

11. Article from *Colonial Magazine* reproduced in *Port-of-Spain Gazette*, 9 June 1848.

12. Quoted in *Port-of-Spain Gazette*, 26 May 1848.

13. C.O.295/161, Fagan to Johnston, 6 May 1848.

14. C.O.295/161, Harris to Grey, 3 May 1848; Grey to Harris, 2 July 1848; C.O.295/164, Harris to Grey, 20 August 1848.

15. *Port-of-Spain Gazette*, 15 August 1848.

16. Robert Moore, "East Indians and Negroes in British Guiana, 1838–1880," Ph.D. thesis, University of Sussex, 1970, p. 144.

17. E. A. Wallbridge, *The Demerara Martyr: Memoirs of the Rev. John Smith, Missionary to Demerara* (London, 1848), p. 241.

18. *Creole*, 9 December 1856, quoted in Robert Moore, "East Indians and Negroes," p. 196.

19. Moore, *Guyana after Slavery*, pp. 40–41; Robert Moore, "East Indians and Negroes," pp. 147–49.

20. *San Fernando Gazette*, 19 June 1850.

21. *San Fernando Gazette*, 3 and 10 October 1868, 24 May 1884, 15 May 1886, 15 September 1886; *New Era*, 29 July 1872. See also Singh, *Blood-Stained Tombs*, chaps. 3 and 4; Gerad Tikasingh, "The Trinidad Press and the Issue of Immigration," Paper presented at the Ninth Conference of Caribbean Historians, University of the West Indies, Cave Hill, Barbados, 1977.

22. *Trinidad Free Press*, 9 December 1851.

23. *San Fernando Gazette*, 23 April 1887.

24. *Port-of-Spain Gazette*, 18 February 1871.

25. *New Era*, 27 March, 3 April 1871.

26. *Trinidad Chronicle*, 13 June 1871, 21 March 1885.

27. *San Fernando Gazette*, 14 June 1890.

28. *San Fernando Gazette*, 7 July 1893.

29. Quoted in P.P. 1898, L (C.8657), Report of the Royal Commission on the West India Sugar Industry, app. C, pt. 4 (Trinidad), sec. 295, Memorandum by the Hon. H. A. Alcazar on Indian Immigration, paragraph 12. See also Eric Williams, *History of the People of Trinidad and Tobago* (London: Andre Deutsch, 1962), pp. 112–13.

30. Des Voeux, *Colonial Service*, p. 131.

31. Comins Report (Trinidad), pp. 6–12.

32. *Port-of-Spain Gazette*, 8 August, 15 October 1895.

33. As the next decade progressed, more and more cocoa estates began to import indentured labor themselves, as the industry began to overtake sugar as the primary export commodity in Trinidad. By 1910 these had risen to about eighty. See Tables 12 and 13, Appendix 1.

34. P.P. 1898, L (C.8657), Report of the Royal Commission on the West India Sugar Industry, app. C, pt. 4 (Trinidad), sec. 307.

35. *San Fernando Gazette*, 6 December 1892, 7 July 1893.

36. Trinidad Legislative Council Paper No. 73 of 1896.

37. P.P. 1910, XXVII (Cd.5194), Sanderson Commission Report, pt. 3, app., p. 138: Cane Farming in Trinidad (figures supplied by Sir Neville Lubbock).

38. P.P. 1898, L (C.8657), Report of the Royal Commission on the West India Sugar Industry, app. C, pt. 4 (Trinidad), sec. 295.

39. Ibid., sec. 312.

40. P.P. 1910, XXVII (Cd.5192), Sanderson Commission Report, paragraph 297.

41. P.P. 1898, L (C.8655-57), Report of the Royal Commission on the West India Sugar Industry, 1897, paragraph 302.

42. P.P. 1910, XXVII (Cd.5193), Sanderson Commission Report, Testimony of Sir Neville Lubbock, 5 May 1909, #2475.

43. Ibid., #2484.

44. P.P. 1910, XXVII (Cd.5192), Sanderson Commission Report, paragraph 296.

45. Ibid., paragraphs 289–93.

46. Debates of the Legislative Council of Trinidad and Tobago (Hansard), 19 February 1913, pp. 46–48.

47. For an account of the campaign that culminated in the abolition of indentured immigration from India, see Tinker, *New System of Slavery*, chaps. 7–9.

48. *Creole*, 24 January 1857. See Robert Moore, "East Indians and Negroes," chap. 6, generally, for a discussion on the views of the small newspapers of the Afro middle class.

49. Moore, *Guyana after Slavery*, p. 116.

50. Peter Fraser, "The Immigration Issue in British Guiana, 1903–1913: The Economic and Constitutional Origins of Racist Politics in Guyana," *Journal of Caribbean History* 14 (1981), pp. 22–23, 31–37; Robert Moore, "East Indians and Negroes," pp. 202–6.

51. The 1903 petition and the 1909 memorandum are both in the Sanderson Commission Report, P.P. 1910, XXVII (Cd.5194), pt. 3, app., pp. 18–22, 27–30.

52. P.P. 1910, XXVII (Cd.5192), Sanderson Commission Report, paragraph 240.

53. Ibid. (Cd.5194), pt. 3, app., p. 36, Chamberlain to Swettenham, 10 September 1903, paragraph 6.

54. Quoted in Sohal, "Indian Indentureship in Jamaica," p. 205.

55. See Appendix 2 on Jamaica immigration laws.

56. Correspondence between the Jamaica Baptist Union, the Governor of Jamaica, and the Colonial Secretary of State can be found in the Sanderson Commission Report, P.P. 1910, XXVII (Cd.5194), pt. 3, app., pp. 76–94.

57. P.P. 1910, XXVII (Cd.5193), Sanderson Commission Report, Testimony of Josiah Edwards, 23 July 1909, #10,089–10,193.

58. See note 56 above, especially p. 84. See also Sanderson Commission Report, (Cd.5192), paragraph 302.

59. See note 56 above, especially p. 90, paragraph 63.

60. P.P. 1915, XLVII (Cd.7744), McNeill-Lal Report, p. 214.

Chapter 7
Beyond Indenture: Chinese Mobility and Assimilation Patterns

1. P.P. 1871, XX (C.393), Report of the British Guiana Immigration Commission, 1870–71, paragraph 54.

2. Annual Immigration Report (Trinidad) for 1871.

3. Underhill, West Indies, p. 79.

4. Wood, Trinidad in Transition, p. 166.

5. Underhill, West Indies, p. 79.

6. L. A. A. de Verteuil, Trinidad: Its Geography, Natural Resources, Administration, Present Condition and Prospects (London: Cassell, 1884), p. 160.

7. Hart, Historical and Statistical View, p. 140.

8. C.O.295/195, Memorandum by Charles Warner, 23 July 1857.

9. San Fernando Gazette, 4 May 1878.

10. C.O.295/227, Notes on the Annual Return of Indentured Immigrants in Trinidad for the Year 1863, paragraph 17.

11. Charles Kingsley, At Last: A Christmas in the West Indies, 2d ed. (London: Macmillan, 1889), p. 186.

12. Trinidad Legislative Council Paper No. 39 of 1877.

13. Report of the Inspector of Prisons for 1876: Trinidad Legislative Council Paper No. 27 of 1877.

14. Report of the Inspector of Prisons for 1890: Trinidad Legislative Council Paper No. 65 of 1891.

15. Table 29, Appendix 1.

16. The towns and villages with the largest Chinese presence by 1881 were, in the north, Port-of-Spain (333), Arima (57), Tunapuna (47), Arouca (38), and in the south, San Fernando (138), as well as Princes Town in Savanna Grande (45). Census Report of Trinidad, 1881.

17. Some of the decline in Tacarigua and Arima wards was the result of an eastward shift by the Chinese towards the new urban center of Sangre Grande and environs. The Arima Ward boundary was also redrawn, and the eastern portion became part of the new Manzanilla Ward in St. Andrew County by 1911. The Chinese population in Manzanilla Ward alone in 1911 was 117 (116 men and 1 woman). Census Report of Trinidad and Tobago, 1911.

18. Table 30, Appendix 1.

19. There were 430 large merchants and traders in Trinidad in 1891, only 9.1 percent of whom were natives of a foreign country other than the United Kingdom. There were 1,425 shopkeepers, of whom 42.5 percent were Indians, 23.9 percent Chinese, and 15.3 percent "Trinidadians" (i.e., Blacks and mixed). Of the 2,283 "salesmen, shopmen and clerks," 45.3 percent were natives of Trinidad, 20.1 percent British West Indians, 11.3 percent Chinese, and 9.7 percent Indians. Census Report of Trinidad and Tobago, 1891.

20. The twenty-nine "mechanics and handicraftsmen" included seven barbers, three

tailors, fourteen bakers and cake makers, two carpenters, one goldsmith, one blacksmith, and one woodcutter. Census Report of Trinidad and Tobago, 1891.

21. One interesting fact about the Chinese in 1891 was the total absence of laundrymen, the classic occupation of their North American counterparts in California and the western states. The 1911 census was the first to record the existence of 9 Chinese laundrymen, described by the report as "seriously and successfully competing with the laundresses of the chief towns of the colony for the clothes washing of the people." By the 1921 census there were "no less than 37 Chinese" involved in this occupation, in "most of the populous streets of Port-of-Spain."

22. Tables 31 and 32, Appendix 1.

23. The 1931 census, for example, specifically distinguishes between 2,027 China born, 2,054 born locally of Chinese parents, 1,108 born locally of a Chinese father only, and 50 born locally of a Chinese mother only (p. 27). The same methodology was followed in the 1946 census, which enumerated 2,366 China born, 2,926 born locally of Chinese parents, 3,673 mixed Chinese with one Chinese parent (paragraph 113).

24. C.O.295/236, Mitchell to Bushe, 30 October 1866, enclosed in Despatch No. 123, 5 November 1866.

25. A Chinese-language weekly newspaper in Trinidad in the late 1950s, *Cheng Chi*, claimed to have readers in New York, Canada, Peru, Brazil, Panama, Venezuela, Argentina, and Haiti, in addition to Hong Kong and Singapore. An article on the newspaper's activities and an interview with its editor are recorded in *The Nation* (Party newspaper of the People's National Movement), 12 August 1960.

26. See note 23 above.

27. See *Trinidad Royal Gazette*, 9 March 1887.

28. P.P. 1871, XX (C.393), Report of the British Guiana Immigration Commission, 1870–71, paragraphs 74, 857.

29. Table 33, Appendix 1.

30. Clementi, *Chinese in British Guiana*, p. 331.

31. P.P. 1871, XX (C.393), Report of the British Guiana Immigration Commission, 1870–71, paragraph 837.

32. Reported in *Port-of-Spain Gazette*, 25 February 1865.

33. *Colonist*, 31 January 1865; *Port-of-Spain Gazette*, 25 February 1865.

34. P.P. 1871, XX (C.393), Report of the British Guiana Immigration Commission, 1870–71, paragraphs 850–51.

35. Report by Sub-Immigration Agent Mr. Griffin of Berbice (1887), quoted in Comins Report (British Guiana), p. 74. See also Moore, "Chinese in Guyana," p. 46.

36. Clementi, *Chinese in British Guiana*, p. 312. For a recent account of the Hopetown experiment, see Reuben Kartick, "O Tye Kim and the Establishment of the Chinese Settlement of Hopetown," *Guyana Historical Journal*, vol. 1 (1989), pp. 37–50.

37. Moore, "Chinese in Guyana," p. 46. Lombard Street "Chinatown" was virtually destroyed in December 1913 by a fire caused by an explosion of Chinese fireworks in one of the business places. Casualties amounted to twenty-three (possibly more), and property damage to $750,000. Marlene Kwok Crawford, *Scenes from the History of the Chinese in Guyana* (Georgetown, 1989), pp. 56–57.

38. Clementi, *Chinese in British Guiana*, chap. 14.

39. Tables 31 and 33, Appendix 1.

40. Clementi, *Chinese in British Guiana*, p. 332. The statistics for 1885–1904 do not

include the year 1898, the Immigration Report for 1898–99 being unavailable in the Public Record Office. The difference may be negligible, certainly for those who returned to China in that year.

41. Tables 31, 32, and 33, Appendix 1. See also Jamaica Census Report, 1943. Jamaican "Chinese coloureds" numbered 5,515 in 1943. The China Handbook for 1955–56 published in Taipei put the Jamaican Chinese at 13,000, and the Cuban Chinese at 23,765. See Naosaku Uchida, *The Overseas Chinese: A Bibliographical Essay* (Stanford: Stanford University Press, 1959).

42. Grierson's *Report on Colonial Emigration* comments in paragraph 25: "A Chinaman's idea is to save till he has saved sufficient to start himself as an independent rival to the planter. The Indian coolie's aspirations, on the other hand, seldom rise beyond his being a wellpaid coolie servant, and nothing more. For this reason the Indian coolie is popular, while the Chinese coolie is unpopular, in the colonies."

43. Annual Immigration Reports (Trinidad) for 1861, 1863. In fact, the earliest Chinese returnees were two who embarked on the *Scindian* in June 1855 and three on the *Morayshire* in December 1858, but these were probably not success stories. P.P. 1865, XVIII (3526), Twenty-fifth General Report of the Colonial Land and Emigration Commissioners (1865), app. no. 22.

44. P.P. 1870, XVII (C.196), Thirtieth General Report of the Colonial Land and Emigration Commissioners (1870), p. 22.

45. P.P. 1872, XVI (C.562), Thirty-second General Report of the Colonial Land and Emigration Commissioners (1872), p. 11.

46. P.P. 1873, XVIII (C.768), Thirty-third General Report of the Colonial Land and Emigration Commissioners (1873), p. 22.

47. P.P. 1874, XLVII (314), Geoghegan Report, p. 73. See also Annual Immigration Report (British Guiana) for 1876.

48. P.P. 1852–53, XL (1647), Thirteenth General Report of the Colonial Land and Emigration Commissioners (1852–53), app. no. 50: Despatch from Governor Barkly relative to Chinese laborers dated 26 February 1853.

49. P.P. 1852–53, LXVIII (986), Despatches respecting Chinese immigrants introduced into British Guiana and Trinidad: Report from Immigration Agent-General, 20 April 1853.

50. P.P. 1854, XXVIII (1833), Fourteenth General Report of the Colonial Land and Emigration Commissioners (1854), p. 68.

51. Moore, "Chinese in Guyana," pp. 48–49.

52. Kirke, *Twenty-five Years in British Guiana*, p. 160.

53. *Port-of-Spain Gazette*, 14 June 1865.

54. *Port-of-Spain Gazette*, 31 March and 4 April 1866.

55. *San Fernando Gazette*, 12 October 1889. See also Howard Johnson, "The Chinese in Trinidad in the Late Nineteenth Century," *Ethnic and Racial Studies* 10, no. 1 (1987), pp. 87–88.

56. Howard Johnson, "The Anti-Chinese Riots of 1918 in Jamaica," *Immigrants and Minorities* 2, no. 1 (1983), pp. 50–63. The 1918 riots clearly had spin-off effects in the ensuing years. In 1924, the Jamaica Chinese Benevolent Society in its report to the Chinese ambassador in London complained, *inter alia*, of the subsequent murder of at least nine Chinese by native Jamaicans: Chang Tang, Huang Yuan, Chang Hsin Kwei, Yu Shui Fa, Cheng Kim Lien, Yang Chih, Feng An, Feng Fah, Ma Ping Chuan. In 1928, in

another letter to the same ambassador, the Benevolent Society claimed that, after another spate of murders committed during attempted robberies, the Chinese in Jamaica were "trembling in fear of their lives." Lee Tom Yin, *The Chinese in Jamaica* (Kingston: Chung San News, 1963), p. 10.

57. Johnson, "Chinese in Trinidad," p. 89.

58. P.P. 1852–53, LXVIII (986), Despatches respecting Chinese immigrants introduced into British Guiana and Trinidad, p. 73: White to Barkly, 21 June 1851.

59. P.P. 1854–55, XXXIX (O.7), Despatches respecting Chinese immigrants introduced into British Guiana and Trinidad, p. 7: Winchester to Bowring, 22 July 1854.

60. H. J. Clark, *Iere: The Land of the Humming Bird* (Port-of-Spain: Government Printing Office, 1893), p. 52.

61. P.P. 1854, XXVIII (1833), Fourteenth General Report of the Colonial Land and Emigration Commissioners, p. 69; also app. no. 76, Report of H. Mitchell, 28 November 1853.

62. Annual Immigration Report (Trinidad) for 1857. In fact, Chinese interracial marriages began as long ago as the first experiment of 1806, with the men who landed on the *Fortitude*. A historian who published in 1838 had the following to say about the attitudes of this all-male group towards interracial liaisons: "A few of their descendants by negro and coloured women form a part of the people of Trinidad. They were exemplary parents, and never suffered a child of theirs to be born in slavery—they always bought the mothers, and sent their children to English schools." Joseph, *History of Trinidad*, p. 233.

63. Quoted in Underhill, *West Indies*, p. 79.

64. Hart, *Historical and Statistical View*, p. 100.

65. Kirke, *Twenty-five Years in British Guiana*, p. 160.

66. P.P. 1871, XX (C.393), Report of the British Guiana Immigration Commission, 1870–71, paragraph 328.

67. H. V. P. Bronkhurst, *The Colony of British Guiana and Its Labouring Population* (London: T. Woolmer, 1883), p. 124.

68. P.P. 1871, XX (C.393), Report of the British Guiana Immigration Commission, 1870–71, paragraph 327. The Annual Immigration Report for 1878 even recorded the execution of a Chinese immigrant for the murder of an Indian female, presumably his partner. C.O.114/29, Administration Reports for 1878 (British Guiana).

69. Comins Report (British Guiana), p. 95.

70. That some of the Chinese bachelors in the new environment were not exactly celibate is evident from some of the official reports on the condition of a minority of the 1853 arrivals. The Immigration Report for 1856 stated, somewhat mysteriously, "Very little intercourse has taken place between the Chinese and the women of the country, and that little, as I have been informed by the Colonial Surgeon, generally terminated in an appeal to his mediation." Precisely what that ambiguous reference meant was clarified by a subsequent medical report from the Colonial Hospital in 1862 stating that, in the previous year, no less than 17 percent (217) of them had received treatment at the main public hospital; that half of them had been treated for various forms of opium addiction, and the other half for syphilis; and that one-third of the total syphilitic cases treated for 1861 had been Chinese! The report went on to say:

It is highly probable that the exclusive prevalence of syphilis among these immigrants is traceable to the difficulty experienced by Chinamen in forming matrimonial alliances with the colored creoles of the island, as well as to the nonintroduction to the colony of Chinese female immigrants of their own class simultaneously with the males. This difficulty, however, is gradually undergoing the modification which time usually produces, and though still existing to a large extent, yet, some intermarriages of a recent date shew that the antipathy of the industrial class of colored creole women is not so strong towards the Chinese settlers and immigrants as formerly. Nevertheless, many of them have sunk into an effete state of physical debasement, and illicit association with the most abandoned class of our population is not uncommon amongst them. It is with this class of females they contract the disease referred to.

Excerpt from Medical, Statistical and General Report of the Colonial Hospital for the Year ending 31 December 1861, *Trinidad Royal Gazette* 28 (25), 11 June 1862, p. 9.

71. *Port-of-Spain Gazette*, 20 June 1895 and 16 June 1896. See also Johnson, "Chinese in Trinidad," p. 91.

72. *San Fernando Gazette*, 18 May 1878. The Chinese in British Guiana even formed their own ethnic Freemason Lodge in 1907, known as the Silent Temple Lodge. Kwok Crawford, *History of the Chinese in Guyana*, pp. 67–69.

73. P.P. 1852–53, XL (1647), Thirteenth General Report of the Colonial Land and Emigration Commissioners (1853), app. no. 50, Despatch from Governor Barkly, 26 February 1853.

74. C.O.111/327, Wodehouse to Newcastle, 3 May 1860, enclosing Immigration Report of 25 April.

75. Annual Immigration Report (Trinidad) for 1857. See also Bishop of Barbados, May 1862, quoted in Hart, *Historical and Statistical View*, p. 94.

76. "60 to 70 Hindus, and a sprinkling of Chinese." Sarah Morton, ed., *John Morton of Trinidad: Journals, Letters, and Papers* (Toronto: Westminster, 1916), p. 105.

77. Wood, *Trinidad in Transition*, p. 167.

78. Kingsley, *At Last*, p. 186.

79. Gamble, *Trinidad, Historical and Descriptive*, p. 46.

80. Johnson, "Chinese in Trinidad," p. 95.

81. Moore, "Chinese in Guyana," pp. 50–51.

82. Kirke, *Twenty-five Years in British Guiana*, p. 49.

83. Ibid., p. 158.

84. Arthur Young, "Chinese in the West Indies," *China Weekly Review* 48, no. 11 (11 May 1929), p. 466.

85. Biographical glimpses of his life and career are contained in the autobiography of one of his sons: Percy Chen, *China Called Me* (Boston: Little, Brown & Co., 1979). For a full career history, see Howard L. Boorman, ed., *Biographical Dictionary of Republican China*, vol. 1 (New York: Columbia University Press, 1967), pp. 180–83.

86. P.P. 1910, XXVII (C.5193), Sanderson Commission Report, Testimony of Alfred Richards, 24 June 1909, #7168–7568; 15 July 1909, #9560–9590.

Chapter 8
Sojourners to Settlers: West Indian East Indians, and East Indian West Indians

1. P.P. 1866, XVII (3679), Twenty-sixth General Report of the Colonial Land and Emigration Commissioners (1866), pp. 29–30.

2. P.P. 1872, XVI (C.562), Thirty-second General Report of the Colonial Land and Emigration Commissioners (1872), pp. 11–12.

3. Comins Report (Trinidad), p. 26.

4. P.P. 1866, XVII (3679), Twenty-sixth General Report of the Colonial Land and Emigration Commissioners (1866), p. 28.

5. P.P. 1867–68, XVII (4024), Twenty-eighth General Report of the Colonial Land and Emigration Commissioners (1868), pp. 8–9.

6. See note 2 above.

7. See note 2 above.

8. P.P. 1871, XX (C.393), Report of the British Guiana Immigration Commission, paragraph 52; also app., pt. 1, D3, p. 12.

9. G. Roberts and M. A. Johnson, "Factors Involved in Immigration and Movements in the Working Force of British Guiana in the Nineteenth Century," Paper presented at the Fourth Conference of Caribbean Historians, Mona, Jamaica, 1972.

10. Annual Immigration Reports (Trinidad) for 1861–63.

11. P.P. 1856, XXIV (2089), Sixteenth General Report of the Colonial Land and Emigration Commissioners (1856), app. no. 60, Statistics of Immigrant Population on 31 December 1855. See also P.P. 1859, XVI (2452), Papers relating to Immigration to the West Indian Colonies, Report from Alexander Anderson, Acting Agent-General of Immigration, 24 January 1856, pp. 320–24.

12. See Annual Immigration Report (Trinidad) for 1871 for Statistics on Resident Coolie Estate Labor, 1863–1871.

13. See, for example, K. O. Laurence, "Indians as Permanent Settlers in Trinidad before 1900," in La Guerre, Calcutta to Caroni, pp. 95–114.

14. P.P. 1868–69, XVII (4159), Twenty-ninth General Report of the Colonial Land and Emigration Commissioners (1869), p. 18.

15. P.P. 1854, XXVIII (1833), Fourteenth General Report of the Colonial Land and Emigration Commissioners (1854), app. no. 76, Report by Henry Mitchell, Agent-General of Immigrants, 28 November 1853, p. 262.

16. P.P. 1870, XVII (C.196), Thirtieth General Report of the Colonial Land and Emigration Commissioners (1870), app. no. 20, Return of Immigrants and Liberated Africans who have returned to their own countries from the British West Indies and Mauritius, 1843–1869, p. 87.

17. See note 3 above.

18. Comins Report (British Guiana), sec. 12, p. 19. "Casuals" were paying passengers.

19. Ibid., p. 44.

20. P.P. 1871, XX (C.393), Report of the British Guiana Immigration Commission, app., pt. 1, M3, p. 60.

21. Ibid., paragraph 836.

22. See Table 10, Appendix 1.

23. See Tables 32 and 33, Appendix 1; Comins Report (British Guiana), p. 19.

24. Annual Immigration Report (Trinidad) for 1902–3.

25. Comins Report (Trinidad), p. 25. The emigration agent for British Guiana in India related the following story in his 1899–1900 report:

Immigrants to British Guiana make large sums of money, but when they return to India with their savings, they are generally robbed by their relations. As Mootee said, "My people too much tief." The man has lost caste by crossing the Kalapanee, so the priests sweat him of a large sum of money before they will allow him to recover his caste. Then the whole of his kindred tribes and village community, hearing of his return with, to them, a fabulous sum of money, come down upon him like locusts, and, to use an expressive Eastern phrase, "eat him up."

I remember one family who returned to India on Christmastide with a considerable sum of money, about £800 or 900, enough to keep them in luxury in India for the rest of their lives, came back to the depot in a few months to re-engage and return to British Guiana as indentured immigrants. I asked him how it was and they told me that the priests and their relations had robbed them of all their money, so they wanted to go back to the Colony and earn some more. "Too much bad men in this country," was their description of their native land.

C.O.114/87, Report of the Emigration Agent in India for British Guiana for 1899–1900, 20 February 1900.

26. P.P. 1910, XXVII (Cd.5193), Sanderson Commission Report, Evidence of Oliver William Warner, 26 March 1909, #584–85.

27. Comins Report (Trinidad), p. 25.

28. Annual Immigration Reports (Trinidad) for 1901–2 to 1910–11.

29. Comins Report (British Guiana), p. 22.

30. P.P. 1910, XXVII (Cd.5193), Sanderson Commission Report, Evidence of Sir Frederick M. Hodgson, 14 May 1909, #3528.

31. Laurence, "Indians as Permanent Settlers," p. 96.

32. P.P. 1872, XVI (C.562), Thirty-second General Report of the Colonial Land and Emigration Commissioners (1872), p. 11.

33. Wives of male grantees received a £5 cash grant for themselves from 1869 to 1889, in addition to the grants received by their spouses.

34. Annual Immigration Report (Trinidad) for 1893.

35. Trinidad Legislative Council Paper No. 13 of 1906: Report on the Labour Question in Trinidad 1906, app. H, Reverend John Morton, Memorandum on East Indian Settlements in Trinidad, 25 September 1905.

36. Laurence, "Indians as Permanent Settlers," p. 99.

37. Trinidad Chronicle, 18 June 1875.

38. Up to 1868, very little Crown land was actually sold. The sales for the nineteen years from 1847 to 1865 amounted to 3,423 acres. There was much squatting, though. C.O.295/235, Return of the Number of Sales of Crown Lands in each year since 1847 to 31 December 1865, enclosed in Despatch No. 71 dated 19 June 1866. See also Comins Report (Trinidad), diary entry 1 July 1891.

39. See Table 12, Appendix 1.

40. Comins Report (Trinidad), p. 16.

41. Laurence, "Indians as Permanent Settlers," p. 105.

42. Comins Report (Trinidad), p. 21.

43. See Table 17, Appendix 1.

44. Annual Immigration Report (Trinidad) for 1920.

45. Comins Report (Trinidad), diary entry 8 June 1891.

46. See Table 18, Appendix 1.

47. Comins Report (Trinidad), p. 21.

48. P.P. 1915, XLVII (Cd.7744), McNeill-Lal Report, p. 42.

49. See Trinidad Legislative Council Paper No. 77 of 1882: Immigration Return of Mortality in accordance with Clause 3 of Ordinance No. 9 of 1875.

50. See Table 4, Appendix 1.

51. Comins Report (Trinidad), diary entry 9 June 1891. Montserrat Ward in Central Trinidad produced the most cocoa, and Indians were involved there too.

52. P.P. 1910, XXVII (Cd.5192), Sanderson Commission Report, paragraph 284.

53. Annual Immigration Report (Trinidad) for 1917.

54. Comins Report (Trinidad), p. 16.

55. See Table 18, Appendix 1.

56. Comins Report (Trinidad), pp. 17–18.

57. Census Report of Trinidad, 1891. See also Table 18, Appendix 1.

58. See Table 18, Appendix 1. See also Marianne Ramesar, "The Impact of the Indian Immigrants on Colonial Trinidad—An Assessment at the End of the Indenture System," Paper presented at the First Conference of East Indians in the Caribbean, University of the West Indies, St. Augustine, Trinidad, 1975; and by the same author, "Patterns of Regional Settlement and Economic Activity by Immigrant Groups in Trinidad, 1851–1900," Paper presented at the Seventh Conference of Caribbean Historians, University of the West Indies, Mona, Jamaica, 1975.

59. See Tables 11 and 32, Appendix 1.

60. See Tables 6 and 8, Appendix 1.

61. See Table 10, Appendix 1.

62. P.P. 1910, XXVII (Cd.5193), Sanderson Commission Report, Evidence of D. S. de Freitas, 26 April 1909, #1537–44.

63. See Table 15, Appendix 1.

64. Lesley Key-Potter, "The Post-Indenture Experience of East Indians in Guyana, 1873–1921," in Bridget Brereton and Winston Dookeran, eds., *East Indians in the Caribbean: Colonialism and the Struggle for Identity* (New York: Kraus, 1982), pp. 82–83.

65. Ibid., pp. 73–78; see also Lesley Potter, "Internal Migration and Resettlement of East Indians in Guyana, 1870–1920," Ph.D. thesis, McGill University, Montreal, 1975, chap. 5.

66. Alan Adamson, *Sugar without Slaves: The Political Economy of British Guiana, 1838–1904* (New Haven: Yale University Press, 1972), p. 94.

67. Roberts and Johnson, "Factors Involved in Immigration," table 6.

68. See note 66 above.

69. Key-Potter, "Post-Indenture Experience," p. 86.

70. The Chinese settlement at Hopetown was actually the first, created in 1865.

71. P.P. 1915, XLVII (Cd.7744), McNeill-Lal Report, p. 77.

72. Ramnarine, "Indian Community in British Guiana," p. 128.

73. Key-Potter, "Post-Indenture Experience," p. 89.

74. Comins Report (British Guiana), p. 25.

75. Homestead grants, reduced to 5 acres in 1906, had an alienation restriction period of ten years. They were distinguished from absolute grants, which had no restrictions. Most homestead grants tended to be purchased in the remote North Western and Pomeroon districts of Essequibo and were less popular with the Indians.

76. See Table 19, Appendix 1.

77. Key-Potter, "Post-Indenture Experience," p. 85.

78. Ibid., p. 87.

79. Rodney, *Guyanese Working People*, pp. 84, 251.

80. Nath, *Indians in Guyana*, p. 110. See also Table 4, Appendix 1.

81. Nath, *Indians in Guyana*, pp. 262–63. The main export markets for British Guiana rice were within the larger Caribbean region, in the British, French, and Dutch territories.

82. P.P. 1910, XXVII (Cd.5193), Sanderson Commission Report, Evidence of William Morrison, 7 May 1909, #2867.

83. Ramnarine, "Indian Community in British Guiana," pp. 173–74. See also P.P. 1910, XXVII (Cd.5193), Sanderson Commission Report, Evidence of Charles Sandbach Parker, Managing Director of Demerara Ltd., 28 June 1909, #7787.

84. P.P. 1915, XLVII (Cd.7744), McNeill-Lal Report, p. 78.

85. P.P. 1898, L (C.8657), Report of the Royal Commission on the West India Sugar Industry, 1897, app. C, pt. 2 (British Guiana), Evidence of A. H. Alexander, Immigration Agent-General, #1389.

86. Comins Report (British Guiana), p. 25.

87. Ibid., pp. 27–28. There were also 5,326 sheep and goats.

88. P.P. 1915, XLVII (Cd.7744), McNeill-Lal Report, p. 140. The number of sheep and goats was 3,022.

89. Comins Report (British Guiana), p. 25.

90. P.P. 1915, XLVII (Cd.7744), McNeill-Lal Report, p. 77.

91. See Table 20, Appendix 1. See also J. D. Tyson, Report on the Condition of Indians in Jamaica, British Guiana and Trinidad: Memorandum of Evidence for the Royal Commission to the West Indies, 1938–39 (New Delhi, 1939), paragraph 42.

92. Nath, *Indians in Guyana*, p. 241.

93. Key-Potter, "Post-Indenture Experience," p. 84. See also Tables 14 and 33, Appendix 1.

94. Comins Report (British Guiana), p. 49; Annual Immigration Reports (British Guiana), 1891–1904 (no figures available for 1898).

95. See Table 16, Appendix 1.

96. Comins, *Note on Emigration from India to Jamaica* (hereafter Comins Report [Jamaica]) (Calcutta 1893), p. 23.

97. See Table 22, Appendix 1.

98. See Table 21, Appendix 1.

99. P.P. 1915, XLVII (Cd.7744), McNeill-Lal Report, p. 215.

100. Rodney, *Guyanese Working People*, p. 179.

101. *San Fernando Gazette*, 16 June 1883.

102. Dookhan, "Gladstone Experiment," p. 24. Though the official records do not make mention of it, it appears highly likely that these interracial unions were contracted by the non-Hindu aboriginal elements or "hill coolies" who dominated the earliest migrations numerically.

103. P.P. 1847–48, XXVI (961), Eighth General Report of the Colonial Land and Emigration Commissioners (1848), app. no. 18, Bunyun to Light, 6 January 1848.

104. Quoted in Comins Report (Trinidad), p. 33. The emigration agent for British Guiana in India related the following anecdote in his 1905–6 report:

> In the Annual Report of the work of the United Free Church of Scotland Missions in Madras, for last year, one of the lady workers tells of a convert from Hinduism who adopted a somewhat curious method of coming to a decision. She had been a zealous worshipper of her own gods, but when she heard of the new religion, she determined to put the matter of the choice between it and the old one to the test. So she sat a hen upon a number of eggs and vowed that if when they were hatched they were found to be cocks, she would continue to worship her own gods, but if

they were hens she would adopt the new teaching. In due time the eggs were hatched, and all the chickens were hens. True to her word, the woman placed herself under Christian instruction at once. We are not told whether the Scottish missionaries approve of the method of settling questions of religious belief or not. C.O.114/112, Report of the Emigration Agent in India for British Guiana for 1905–6, 27 February 1906.

105. Collens, *Guide to Trinidad*, p. 233.

106. J. C. Jha, "The Indian Heritage in Trinidad," in La Guerre, *Calcutta to Caroni*, pp. 5–9.

107. Census Report of Trinidad, 1891, table 13.

108. Idris Hamid, *A History of the Presbyterian Church in Trinidad, 1868–1968: The Struggles of a Church in Colonial Captivity* (Port-of-Spain: St. Andrew's Theological College, 1980); J. T. Harricharan, *The Work of the Christian Churches among the East Indians in Trinidad, 1845–1917* (Port-of-Spain, 1976); Brinsley Samaroo, "The Presbyterian Church as an Agent of Integration in Trinidad during the Nineteenth and Twentieth Centuries," *Caribbean Studies* 14, no. 4 (1975), pp. 41–55; Samaroo, "Missionary Methods and Local Responses: The Canadian Presbyterians and the East Indians in the Caribbean," in Brereton and Dookeran, *East Indians in the Caribbean*; Charles Alexander Dunn, "The Canadian Mission in British Guiana: The Pioneer Years, 1885–1927," M.A. thesis, Queen's University, Ontario, 1971; Simon Mangru, "The Role of the Anglican Church in Christianising the East Indians in British Guiana, 1838–1898," M.A. thesis, University of Guyana, 1977.

109. Nath, *Indians in Guyana*, p. 247.

110. Bisnauth, "East Indian Immigrant Society," p. 507.

111. Kusha Haraksingh, "Aspects of the Indian Experience in the Caribbean," in La Guerre, *Calcutta to Caroni*, p. 169.

112. P.P. 1922, XVI (Cmd.1679), Report by the Hon. E. F. L. Wood, Parliamentary Under-Secretary of State for the Colonies, on his visit to the West Indies and British Guiana, 1921–22, sec. E, p. 23.

113. P.P. 1910, XXVII (Cd.5193), Sanderson Commission Report, Evidence of Francis E. M. Hosein, 16 July 1909, #9666–9767; also Evidence of George Fitzpatrick, 1 October 1909, #11,837–12,110.

114. P.P. 1915, XLVII (Cd.7744), McNeill-Lal Report, p. 79; Annual Immigration Report (Trinidad) for 1920.

115. See J. C. Jha, "East Indian Pressure Groups in Trinidad, 1897–1921," and Gerad Tikasingh, "The Emerging Political Consciousness among Trinidad Indians in the Late Nineteenth Century," Papers presented at the Fifth Conference of Caribbean Historians, University of the West Indies, St. Augustine, Trinidad, 1973. See also Tikasingh, "The Representation of Indian Opinion in Trinidad, 1900–1921," in Brereton and Dookeran, *East Indians in the Caribbean*, pp. 11–32.

116. Tinker, *New System of Slavery*, p. 328.

Chapter 9
Conclusion: Asian Indenture in Comparative Perspective

1. See articles by Herbert S. Klein and Stanley L. Engerman, "The Transition from Slave to Free Labor: Notes on a Comparative Economic Model," and Sidney W. Mintz,

"The Divided Aftermaths of Freedom," in Manuel Moreno Fraginals, Frank Moya Pons, and Stanley Engerman, eds., *The Spanish-Speaking Caribbean in the Nineteenth Century* (Baltimore: Johns Hopkins University Press, 1985), pp. 255–69, 270–78, respectively.

2. Stanley L. Engerman, "Servants to Slaves to Servants: Contract Labour and European Expansion," in P. C. Emmer, ed., *Colonialism and Migration: Indentured Labour before and after Slavery* (Dordrecht, The Netherlands: Martinus Nijhoff, 1986), pp. 263–94.

3. Look Lai, "Chinese Indentured Labor," pp. 121–28.

4. See Meagher, "Introduction of Chinese Laborers," and Helly, *Idéologie et Ethnicité*.

5. Morton, *John Morton of Trinidad*, pp. 146–47. See also P.P. 1910, XXVII (Cd. 5193), Sanderson Commission Report, Evidence of Rev. John Morton, 29 July 1909, #10,585–86.

6. Williams, *From Columbus to Castro*, p. 96, quoting the seventeenth-century French historian Père J. B. du Tertre.

7. Cocoa in Trinidad, of course, was not peripheral by the 1880s. The industry utilized indentured and ex-indentured labor, free labor of all races, and contracts with independent peasant cultivators of all races (including Venezuelan immigrants).

8. Rodney, *Guyanese Working People*, chap. 7 generally. Moore, *Guyana after Slavery*, pp. 184–87, 217–19.

9. Bridget Brereton, *Race Relations in Colonial Trinidad, 1870–1900* (Cambridge: Cambridge University Press, 1979), chap. 9 generally. For a more general assessment, see Marianne Ramesar, "Recurrent Issues concerning East Indian Immigrants to Trinidad," in La Guerre, *Calcutta to Caroni*, pp. 135–52.

10. Kelvin Singh, "East Indians and the Larger Society," in La Guerre, *Calcutta to Caroni*, pp. 33–62; also in the same volume, Kusha Haraksingh, "Aspects of the Indian Experience in the Caribbean," pp. 155–72. Bisnauth, "East Indian Immigrant Society," pp. 503–8.

11. Carl Campbell, "Immigration into a Divided Society: A Note on Social Relationships in Trinidad, 1845–1870," Paper presented at the Fourth Conference of Caribbean Historians, Mona, Jamaica, 1972, p. 27.

Bibliography

A Note on Primary Sources

The official records for a study of the indentured immigration can be divided into those of the British government, those of the governments of the West Indian territories involved, and, in the case of the Indians, the records of the government of India. The principal materials utilized from the first category were the Colonial Office records, mainly those containing official correspondence between the Colonial Office and the governors of the respective territories. These are located in the Public Record Office in London, and microfilmed copies of these files can also be found in the respective territorial archives. The main series utilized were the C.O. 295 Series for Trinidad and the C.O. 111 Series for British Guiana.

Vitally important for an in-depth study of the distribution and progress of the immigrants are the annual reports of the Immigration Departments of the colonies involved, each headed by an Immigration Agent-General or Protector of Immigrants, who was charged with overseeing all matters relating to the adjustment and progress of the immigrants on the plantations. These important reports are conveniently compiled, in the case of British Guiana, in the C.O. 114 Series among the annual administration reports. The early Trinidad reports (pre-1870) are interspersed in the correspondence of the C.O. 295 Series; most of the post-1870 reports can be found among the annual collections of the Trinidad Legislative Council Papers, located in the Trinidad National Archives. The India Office of the British Library in London, which houses official records of the government of India in the colonial period, contains copies of all the colonial Immigration Department reports (Caribbean and non-Caribbean) under the Emigration Proceedings Series of the Proceedings of the Government of India and of the Provincial Governments of Bengal and Madras. Also included in the India Office collections, under the same series, are the annual reports of the Protector of Emigrants at the embarkation end of the voyage, Calcutta and Madras. The India Office collections are catalogued in Timothy Thomas, *Indians Overseas: A guide to source materials in the India Office Records for the study of Indian emigration, 1830–1950* (London: The British Library, 1985).

Next to the Annual Immigration Reports, the most vital official records are the Annual Reports of the Colonial Land and Emigration Commission, the branch of the Colonial Office responsible (until its dissolution in 1878) for overseeing and cataloguing the movements of people within and out of the British Empire to various nineteenth-century destinations. Crucial among these were the indentured immigration movements of Chinese and Indians to the West Indies. The reports, which were published as Parliamentary Papers, contain detailed annual summaries of these (and other) migration movements, and the comprehensive appendices include documents ranging from immigration statistics to Governors' and Immigration Agent-Generals' dispatches, to copies of local legislation covering various aspects of immigration regulation and procedure. They are invaluable for the earlier period of the immigration and are conveniently grouped together under the British Parliamentary Papers Publications of the Irish University Press, under the series entitled Emigration. The relevant volumes of the series for this study are Volumes 10 to 18, covering the period 1843 to 1873. In the body of the text, the annual reports are cited under their original Parliamentary Paper designations.

Special investigative reports commissioned from time to time, by the British or the various colonial governments, to study various aspects of the indentured immigration experiment constitute the next major source of information utilized in this study. They were often published as Parliamentary Papers, but several of them were published locally, either as Indian government reports or as West Indian official publications. They are all described in the Bibliography.

Finally, the statistical and demographic data contained in the Decennial Census Reports of the West Indian territories, as well as in the annual Blue Books of Statistics, are invaluable, as are, on a more minor level, the data contained in the various local year books.

Primary Sources

Public Documents

UNITED KINGDOM GOVERNMENT

Annual Reports of the Colonial Land and Emigration Commissioners 1843–73 (Gt. Britain, Parliamentary Papers, Emigration Series, Volumes 10–18, Irish University Press)

Colonial Office Records, Public Record Office:

C.O.295 Series. Original Correspondence (Trinidad), 1800–10, 1838–1920.

C.O.111 Series. Original Correspondence (British Guiana), 1860–69.

C.O.114 Series. Sessional Papers and Administration Reports (British Guiana), 1860–1910.

Parliamentary Papers (annual series):

1810–11, II (225). West Indies—Report from the Select Committee appointed to Consider the Practicality and Expediency of Supplying our West Indian Colonies with Free Labourers from the East.

1839, XXXIX (463). British Guiana—Correspondence re Hill Coolies.

1840, XXXIV (77). British Guiana—Correspondence re Hill Coolies.

1842, XIII (479). Report of the Select Committee of the House of Commons on the Commercial State of the West India Colonies (Lord Stanley Committee).

1842, XXIX (379). Trinidad—Papers re State of Colony (includes 1841 Trinidad Hearings pp. 67–103).

1844, XXXV (530). Papers re Emigration of Chinese Labourers to the West Indies.

1847–48, XXIII, pt. 2 (184). Report of the Select Committee on Sugar and Coffee Planting in Her Majesty's East and West Indian Possessions and the Mauritius (Lord Bentinck Committee).

1852–53, LXVIII (986). Despatches respecting Chinese immigrants introduced into British Guiana and Trinidad.

1852–53, LXVIII (1686). Correspondence respecting Emigration from China.

1854–55, XXXIX (O.7). Despatches respecting Chinese immigrants introduced into British Guiana and Trinidad.

1857–58, XLI (525). Despatches respecting Chinese immigrants introduced into British Guiana and Trinidad.

1857–58, XLIII (481). Correspondence re Chinese emigration to the West Indies, etc.

1859, XVI (2452). Papers relating to immigration to the West Indian colonies.

1860, LXIX (2714). Correspondence respecting emigration from Canton.

1871, XX (C.393). Report of the Commissioners appointed to Enquire into the Treatment of Immigrants in British Guiana.

1874, XLVII (314). Report by J. Geoghegan on Emigration from India.

1884–85, LIII (C.4366). Report on the Recent Coolie Disturbance in Trinidad.

1898, L (C.8655–57). Report and Papers of the Royal Commission on the West Indian Sugar Industry (Norman Commission).

1910, XXVII (Cd.5192–94). Report of the Committee on Emigration from India to the Crown Colonies and Protectorates (Sanderson Commission).

1915, XLVII (Cd.7744). Report on the Condition of Indian Immigrants in the Four British Colonies (Trinidad, British Guiana or Demerara, Jamaica and Fiji), and in the Dutch Colony of Surinam or Dutch Guiana (McNeill-Lal Report).

1922, XVI (Cmd.1679). Report by the Hon. E. F. L. Wood, Parliamentary Under-Secretary of State for the Colonies, on his visit to the West Indies and British Guiana 1921–22.

GOVERNMENT OF INDIA

D. W. D. Comins, Note on Emigration from India to Trinidad (Calcutta, 1893).

D. W. D. Comins, Note on Emigration from India to British Guiana (Calcutta, 1893).

D. W. D. Comins, Note on Emigration from India to Jamaica (Calcutta, 1893).

George Grierson, Report on Colonial Emigration from the Bengal Presidency (Calcutta, 1883).

Duncan Pitcher, Report on the System of Recruiting Labourers for the Colonies (Calcutta, 1882).

J. D. Tyson, Report on the Condition of Indians in Jamaica, British Guiana and Trinidad: Memorandum of Evidence for the Royal Commission to the West Indies presented on behalf of the Government of India (New Delhi, 1939).

Annual Reports of the Protector of Emigrants from the Port of Calcutta to British and Foreign Colonies.

GOVERNMENTS OF THE WEST INDIES

Annual Reports of the Agent-General (Protector) of Immigrants (Trinidad) 1850–1920. (1850–69: in the Colonial Office Correspondence, Public Record Office, C.O.295 Series; 1870–1920: in the Legislative Council Papers of the Government of Trinidad and Tobago. They were also printed in the *Trinidad Royal Gazette* and the *Port-of-Spain Gazette.*)

Annual Reports of the Agent-General (Protector) of Immigrants (British Guiana), 1876–1910 (in the Colonial Office Documents, Public Record Office, C.O.114 Series Volumes dealing with administration reports).
Report of the Special Committee appointed to consider matters relating to the Labour Question in Trinidad, 1906: Legislative Council Paper 13 of 1906.
Legislative Council Papers of Trinidad and Tobago, 1870–1920.
Decennial Census Reports of Trinidad-Tobago and British Guiana, 1881–1946.
Jamaica Census Report, 1943.
West Indian Census Report, 1946.
Immigration Ordinances: No. 18 of 1891 (British Guiana); No. 19 of 1899 (Trinidad).
Debates of the Legislative Council of Trinidad and Tobago (Hansard), 1910–20.
Blue Books of Statistics (Trinidad).
Ship Registers, Trinidad National Archives.
Chinese Indenture Contracts, Trinidad National Archives.

Year Books and Newspapers

The Trinidad Official and Commercial Register and Almanack (1866–96).
The Trinidad and Tobago Year Book (1897–1910).
Trinidad Royal Gazette
Port-of-Spain Gazette
San Fernando Gazette
The New Era
Trinidad Chronicle
Trinidad Spectator
Trinidad Standard

Books and Pamphlets (Contemporary Publications)

Aldus, Don. *Coolie Traffic and Kidnapping*. London: McCorquodale & Co., 1876.
Amos, Sheldon. *The Existing Laws of Demerara for the Regulation of Coolie Emigration*. London: Head, Hole & Co., 1871.
Barrett, Rev. William G. *Immigration to the British West Indies: Is It the Slave Trade Revived or Not?* London: A. W. Bennett, 1859.
Beaumont, Joseph. *The New Slavery: An Account of the Indian and Chinese Immigrants in British Guiana*. London: W. Ridgway, 1871.
Bell, K. N., and Morrell, W. P., eds. *Select Documents on British Colonial Policy, 1830–1860*. Oxford: Clarendon Press, 1928.
Bigelow, John. *Jamaica in 1850*. New York: George Putnam, 1851, reprinted in 1970.
Brierly, J. N. *Trinidad: Then and Now*. Port-of-Spain: Franklin's Electric Printery, 1912.
Bronkhurst, H. V. P. *The Colony of British Guiana and Its Labouring Population*. London: T. Woolmer, 1883.
———. *Among the Hindus and Creoles of British Guiana*. London: T. Woolmer, 1888.
Brummell, J. *Demerara after Fifteen Years of Freedom*. London: T. Bosworth, 1853.
Burnley, William, ed. *Observations on the Present Condition of the Island of Trinidad, and the Actual State of the Experiment of Negro Emancipation*. London: Longman's, 1842.
Butterworth, A. R. *The Immigration of Coloured Races into the British Colonies*. London, 1898.

Clark, H. J. *Iere: The Land of the Humming Bird.* Port-of-Spain: Government Printing Office, 1893.

Clementi, Cecil. *The Chinese in British Guiana.* Georgetown: Argosy, 1915.

Collens, J. H. *A Guide to Trinidad: A Handbook for the Use of Tourists and Visitors.* London: Elliot Stock, 1886.

Cothonay, R. P. M. Bertrand. *Trinidad. Journal d'un Missionaire Dominicain des Antilles Anglaises.* Paris: Victor Retaux et fils, 1893.

Crookall, Lawrence. *British Guiana: Or Work and Wanderings among the Creoles and Coolies, the Africans and Indians of the Wild Country.* London: T. Fisher Unwin, 1898.

Davy, John. *The West Indies before and since Slave Emancipation.* London: W. & F. G. Cash, 1854.

Day, Charles William. *Five Years' Residence in the West Indies.* 2 vols. London: Colburn & Co., 1852.

Des Voeux, George W. *My Colonial Service in British Guiana, St. Lucia, Trinidad, Fiji, Australia, Newfoundland and Hong Kong with interludes.* London: John Murray, 1903.

———. *Experiences of a Demerara Magistrate, 1863–1869.* Georgetown: Daily Chronicle, 1948.

De Verteuil, L. A. A. *Trinidad: Its Geography, Natural Resources, Administration, Present Condition and Prospects.* 2d ed. London: Cassell, 1884.

Edwards, Bryan. *History, Civil and Commercial, of the British Colonies in the West Indies.* 5 vols. London: T. Miller, 1819, reprinted by Ams Press, New York, 1966.

Franklin, C. B. *After Many Days: A Memoir being a sketch of the life and labours of the Rev. Alexander Kennedy 1836–1849.* Port-of-Spain: Franklin's Electric Printery, 1910.

Froude, J. A. *The English in the West Indies or The Bow of Ulysses.* London: Longman's, 1888.

Gamble, W. H. *Trinidad, Historical and Descriptive: Being a Narrative of Nine Years' Residence in the Island.* London: Yates & Alexander, 1866.

Grant, K. J. *My Missionary Memories.* Nova Scotia: Imperial Publishing Co., 1923.

Harris, John H. *Coolie Labour in the British Crown Colonies and Protectorates.* London: Edward Hughes & Co., 1910.

Hart, Daniel. *Historical and Statistical View of the Island of Trinidad.* Port-of-Spain: Chronicle, 1866.

Innis, L. O. *Trinidad and Trinidadians: A Collection of Papers, Historical, Social and Descriptive, about Trinidad and Its People.* Port-of-Spain: Mirror Printing Works, 1910.

Ireland, W. Alleyne. *Demerariana: Essays Historical, Technical and Descriptive.* Georgetown: Balwin & Co., 1897.

Jenkins, Edward. *The Coolie: His Rights and Wrongs.* London: Strahan & Co., 1871.

Joseph, E. L. *History of Trinidad.* London: Frank Cass & Co., 1970, reprint of 1838 edition.

Kingsley, Charles. *At Last: A Christmas in the West Indies.* 2d ed. London: Macmillan, 1889.

Kirke, Henry. *Twenty-five Years in British Guiana, 1872–1897.* London: Sampson Low, Marston & Co., 1898.

Lobscheid, Rev. William. *Chinese Emigration to the West Indies: A trip through British Guiana undertaken for the purpose of ascertaining the condition of the Chinese who have emigrated under Government contract, with supplementary papers relating to contract labour and the slave trade.* Demerara: Royal Gazette, 1866.

Mathieson, William L. *British Slave Emancipation, 1838–1849.* London: Longman's, 1932.

Milliroux, F. *Demerara: Transition from Slavery to Liberty.* London, 1877; translation of 1843 French edition.

Morton, Sarah, ed. *John Morton of Trinidad: Journals, Letters, and Papers.* Toronto: Westminster, 1916.

Peck, Nathaniel, and Price, Thomas. *Report of Messrs Peck and Price who were appointed at a Meeting of the Free Colored People of Baltimore, held on the 25th November 1839, delegates to visit British Guiana and the island of Trinidad for the purpose of ascertaining the advantages to be derived by Colored People migrating to these places.* Baltimore, 1840.

Premium, Barton. *Eight Years in British Guiana, 1840–1848.* London: Longman's, 1850.

Rodney, Walter, ed. *Guyanese Sugar Plantations in the Late Nineteenth Century: A Contemporary Description from the ARGOSY.* Georgetown: Bovell, 1979.

Scoble, John. *Hill Coolies: A Brief Exposure of the Deplorable Conditions of the Hill Coolies in British Guiana and Mauritius.* London: Harvey & Danton, 1840.

Scoles, Ignatius. *Sketches of African and Indian Life in British Guiana.* Demerara: Argosy, 1885.

Sewell, William. *The Ordeal of Free Labor in the British West Indies.* New York: Harper & Bros., 1861.

Swinton, Capt. and Mrs. *Journal of a Voyage with Coolie Emigrants from Calcutta to Trinidad.* London: Alfred Bennett, 1859.

Thorne, John Thomas. *Some Haphazard Notes of a Forty-Two Years' Residence in British Guiana.* Demerara: Argosy, 1899.

Trollope, Anthony. *The West Indies and the Spanish Main.* London: Chapman & Hall, 1860.

Underhill, Edward. *The West Indies: Their Social and Religious Condition.* London: Jackson, Walford & Hodder, 1862.

Wallbridge, E. A. *The Demerara Martyr: Memoirs of the Rev. John Smith, Missionary to Demerara.* Georgetown Daily Chronicle, 1943 reprint of London 1848 edition.

Whitworth, Charles. *State of the Trade of Great Britain in Its Imports and Exports, 1697–1774.* London: C. Robinson, J. Robson et al., 1776.

Secondary Sources

Books

Adamson, Alan. *Sugar without Slaves: The Political Economy of British Guiana, 1838–1904.* New Haven: Yale University Press, 1972.

Beachey, R. *The British West Indian Sugar Industry in the Late Nineteenth Century.* Oxford: Blackwell, 1957.

Brereton, Bridget. *Race Relations in Colonial Trinidad, 1870–1900.* Cambridge: Cambridge University Press, 1979.

———. *A History of Modern Trinidad, 1783–1962.* London: Heinemann, 1981.

Brereton, Bridget, and Dookeran, Winston, eds. *East Indians in the Caribbean: Colonialism and the Struggle for Identity.* New York: Kraus, 1982. (Contains a selection of the papers presented at the First Conference of East Indians in the Caribbean, St. Augustine, Trinidad, 1975.)

Campbell, Persia. *Chinese Coolie Emigration to Countries within the British Empire.* London: Frank Cass, 1971, reprint of 1923 edition.

Carmichael, Gertrude. *The History of the West Indian Islands of Trinidad and Tobago.* London: Alvin Redman, 1961.

Chen, Jack. *The Chinese of America.* San Francisco: Harper & Row, 1980.

Chen, Percy. *China Called Me.* Boston: Little, Brown & Co., 1979.

Cumpston, I. M. *Indians Overseas in British Territories, 1834–1854.* London: Oxford University Press, 1953.

Dabydeen, David, and Samaroo, Brinsley, eds. *India in the Caribbean.* London: Hansib, 1987.

Deerr, Noel. *The History of Sugar.* 2 vols. London: Chapman & Hall, 1949–50.

De Verteuil, Anthony. *The Years of Revolt: Trinidad, 1881–1888.* Port-of-Spain: Paria, 1984.

———. *Eight East Indian Immigrants.* Port-of-Spain: Paria, 1989.

Dutt, Romesh. *The Economic History of India.* 2 vols. New Delhi: Government of India, 1970.

Emmer, P. C., ed. *Colonialism and Migration: Indentured Labour before and after Slavery.* Dordrecht, The Netherlands: Martinus Nijhoff, 1986.

Green, William. *British Slave Emancipation: The Sugar Colonies and the Great Experiment, 1830–1865.* Oxford: Clarendon Press, 1976.

Hamid, Idris. *A History of the Presbyterian Church in Trinidad, 1868–1968: The Struggles of a Church in Colonial Captivity.* Port-of-Spain: St. Andrew's Theological College, 1980.

Harricharan, J. T. *The Work of the Christian Churches among the East Indians in Trinidad, 1845–1917.* Port-of-Spain, 1976.

Helly, Denise. *Ideologie et Ethnicité: Les Chinois Macao à Cuba, 1847–1886.* Montreal: Les Presses de l'Université de Montréal, 1979.

Hibbert, Christopher. *The Great Mutiny: India 1857.* New York: Penguin, 1980.

Hitchins, F. H. *The Colonial Land and Emigration Commissioners.* Philadelphia: University of Pennsylvania Press, 1931.

Horton, V. P. Oswald, ed. *Chinese in the Caribbean.* Souvenir, Thirtieth Anniversary of the Chinese Republic, 1911–41. Kingston, Jamaica: Gleaner Co., 1941.

Irick, Robert Lee. *Ch'ing Policy towards the Coolie Trade, 1847–1878.* Taipei, China: Chinese Materials Center, 1982.

Jayawardena, Chandra. *Conflict and Solidarity in a Guianese Plantation.* London: Athlone Press, 1963.

Jiminez Pastrama, Juan. *Los Chinos en La Historia de Cuba, 1847–1930.* Havana: Editorial de Ciences Sociales, 1983.

Kirpalani, M., et al., eds. *Indian Centenary Review, 1845–1945.* Trinidad: Guardian, 1945.

Klass, Morton. *East Indians in Trinidad: A Study of Cultural Persistence.* New York: Columbia University Press, 1961.

Knowles, Lilian. *The Economic Development of the Overseas British Empire.* 3 vols. London: Routledge, 1928–36.

Kondapi, C. *Indians Overseas, 1838–1949.* New Delhi: India Council of World Affairs, 1951.

Kuczynski, R. R. *Demographic Survey of the British Colonial Empire,* Vol. 3: *West Indian and American Territories.* London: Oxford University Press, 1953.

Kwok Crawford, Marlene. *Scenes from the History of the Chinese in Guyana.* Georgetown, 1989.

La Guerre, John, ed. *From Calcutta to Caroni: The East Indians of Trinidad*. St. Augustine, Trinidad: University of the West Indies, 1985.

Laurence, K. O. *Immigration into the West Indies in the Nineteenth Century*. Barbados: Caribbean University Press, 1971.

Leander, Birgitta, ed. *Europa, Asia y Africa en America Latina y el Caribe: Migraciones "libres" en los siglos XIX y XX y sus efectos culturales*. Mexico City: UNESCO, Siglo Veintiuno Editores, 1989.

Lee Tom Yin. *The Chinese in Jamaica*. Kingston: Chung San News, 1963.

Mandle, Jay. *The Plantation Economy: Population and Economic Change in Guyana, 1838–1960*. Philadelphia: Temple University Press, 1973.

Mangru, Basdeo. *Benevolent Neutrality: Indian Government Policy and Labour Migration to British Guiana, 1854–1884*. London: Hansib, 1987.

Menezes, Mary Noel. *Scenes from the History of the Portuguese in Guyana*. London, 1986.

Mintz, Sidney. *Caribbean Transformation*. Chicago: Aldine, 1974.

———. *Sweetness and Power: The Place of Sugar in Modern History*. New York: Viking, 1985.

Moore, Brian. *Race, Power and Social Segmentation in Colonial Society: Guyana after Slavery, 1838–1891*. New York: Gordon & Breach, 1987.

Moreno Fraginals, Manuel; Moya Pons, Frank; and Engerman, Stanley, eds. *The Spanish-Speaking Caribbean in the Nineteenth Century*. Baltimore: Johns Hopkins University Press, 1985.

Nath, Dwarka. *A History of Indians in Guyana*. London, 1970.

Nehru, Jawaharlal. *The Discovery of India*. Garden City, N.Y.: Anchor, 1960.

Niehoff, Arthur and Juanita. *East Indians in the West Indies*. Milwaukee: Milwaukee Public Museum, 1960.

Rodney, Walter. *A History of the Guyanese Working People, 1881–1905*. Baltimore: Johns Hopkins University Press, 1981.

Rodriguez Pastor, Humberto. *Hijos del Celeste Imperio en el Peru, 1850–1900: Migración, Agricultura, Mentalidad y Explotación*. Lima: Instituto de Apoyo Agrario, 1989.

Ruhomon, Peter. *Centenary History of the East Indians in British Guiana, 1838–1938*. Georgetown: Daily Chronicle, 1947.

Saha, Panchanan. *Emigration of Indian Labour, 1834–1900*. New Delhi: People's Publishing House, 1970.

Saunders, Kay, ed. *Indentured Labour in the British Empire, 1834–1920*. London: Croom Helm, 1984.

Schlote, Werner. *British Overseas Trade from the 1700's to the 1930's*. London: Oxford University Press, 1952.

Schwartz, Barton, ed. *Caste in Overseas Indian Communities*. San Francisco: Chandler, 1967.

Shahabuddeen, M. *From Plantocracy to Nationalisation: A Profile of Sugar in Guyana*. Demerara: University of Guyana, 1983.

Singh, Kelvin. *Blood-Stained Tombs: The Muhurrum Massacre of 1884*. London: Macmillan, 1988.

Thorner, Daniel and Alice. *Land and Labour in India*. Bombay: Asia Publishing House, 1962.

Tinker, Hugh. *A New System of Slavery: The Export of Indian Labour Overseas, 1830–1920*. London: Oxford University Press, 1974.

Trotman, David Vincent. *Crime in Trinidad: Conflict and Control in a Plantation Society, 1838–1900*. Knoxville: University of Tennessee Press, 1986.

Uchida, Naosaku. *The Overseas Chinese: A Bibliographical Essay*. Stanford: Stanford University Press, 1959.

Vertovec, Steven. *Hindu Trinidad*. London: Macmillan, 1992.

Von Albertini, Rudolf. *European Colonial Rule, 1880–1940*. London: Oxford University Press, 1982.

Watts, David. *The West Indies: Patterns of Development, Culture, and Environmental Change since 1492*. Cambridge: Cambridge University Press, 1987.

Webber, A. R. F. *Centenary History and Handbook of British Guiana*. Georgetown: Daily Chronicle, 1931.

———. *Those That Be in Bondage*. Wellesley, Mass.: Calaloux Publications, 1988.

Weller, Judith. *The East Indian Indenture in Trinidad*. Rio Piedras, Puerto Rico: Institute of Caribbean Studies, 1968.

Williams, Eric. *Capitalism and Slavery*. London: Andre Deutsch, 1964.

———. *History of the People of Trinidad and Tobago*. London: Andre Deutsch, 1962.

———. *From Columbus to Castro: The History of the Caribbean, 1492–1969*. London: Andre Deutsch, 1970.

Wood, Donald. *Trinidad in Transition: The Years after Slavery*. London: Oxford University Press, 1968.

Articles

Ankum-Houwink, J. "Chinese Contract Migrants in Surinam between 1853 and 1870." *Boletin de Estudios Latinoamericanos y del Caribe* 17 (December 1974): 42–69.

Bentley, Gerald, and Henry, Frances. "Some Preliminary Observations on the Chinese in Trinidad." In Frances Henry, ed., *McGill University Studies in Caribbean Anthropology*, 19–33. McGill University Centre for Developing Area Studies, Montreal, Occasional Paper Series 5, 1969.

Brereton, Bridget. "The Foundations of Prejudice: Indians and Africans in nineteenth century Trinidad." *Caribbean Issues* 1, no. 1 (1974): 15–28.

———. "Sir John Gorrie: A Radical Chief Justice of Trinidad, 1885–1892." *Journal of Caribbean History* 13 (1980): 44–72.

Campbell, Carl. "Immigration into a Divided Society: A Note on Social Relationships in Trinidad, 1845–1870." Paper presented at the Fourth Conference of Caribbean Historians, Mona, Jamaica, 1972.

———. "Thomas Hinde of Trinidad, 1838–1848." *Journal of Caribbean History* 21 (1987), 95–116.

Chang-Rodriguez, Eugenio. "Chinese Labor Migration into Latin America in the Nineteenth Century." *Revista de Historia de America* 46 (December 1958): 375–97.

Cumpston, I. M. "Survey of Indian Immigration to British Tropical Colonies to 1910." *Population Studies* 10, no. 2 (1956), 158–65.

Dookhan, Isaac. "The Gladstone Experiment: The Experience of the First East Indians in British Guiana." Paper presented at the First Conference of East Indians in the Caribbean, St. Augustine, Trinidad, 1975.

Ehrlich, Allen. "The Interplay of Rice and Cane: East Indians in Rural Jamaica." Paper presented at the First Conference of East Indians in the Caribbean, St. Augustine, Trinidad, 1975.

Ferreira, Jo-Anne S. "The Portuguese of Trinidad." In Gerard Besson and Bridget Brereton, eds., *The Book of Trinidad*, 263–73. Port-of-Spain: Paria, 1991.

Fraser, Peter. "The Immigration Issue in British Guiana, 1903–1913: The Economic and Constitutional Origins of Racist Politics in Guyana." *Journal of Caribbean History* 14 (1981): 18–48.

Fried, Morton. "Some Observations on the Chinese in British Guiana." *Social and Economic Studies* 5, no. 1 (1956): 54–73.

Hall, Douglas. "The Flight from the Estates Reconsidered: The British West Indies, 1838–1842." *Journal of Caribbean History* 10 (1978): 7–24.

Haraksingh, Kusha. "Indian Leadership in the Indenture Period." *Caribbean Issues* 2, no. 3 (1976): 17–38.

———. "Estates, Labour and Population in Trinidad, 1870–1900." Paper presented at the Tenth Conference of Caribbean Historians, St. Thomas, U.S. Virgin Islands, 1978.

———. "Control and Resistance among Overseas Indian Workers: A Study of Labour on the Sugar Plantations of Trinidad, 1875–1917." *Journal of Caribbean History* 14 (1980): 1–17. Also in D. Dabydeen and B. Samaroo, eds., *India in the Caribbean*, 61–77. London: Hansib, 1987.

———. "The Hindu Experience in Trinidad." Paper presented at the Third Conference of East Indians in the Caribbean, St. Augustine, Trinidad, 1984.

———. "Aspects of the Indian Experience in the Caribbean." In John La Guerre, ed., *Calcutta to Caroni: The East Indians of Trinidad*, 155–72. St. Augustine, Trinidad: University of the West Indies, 1985.

Higman, Barry. "The Chinese in Trinidad, 1806–1838." *Caribbean Studies* 12, no. 3 (1972): 21–44.

Hu-De Hart, Evelyn. "Immigrants to a Developing Society: The Chinese in Northern Mexico, 1875–1932." *Journal of Arizona History* 21 (1980): 49–86.

———. "Coolies, Shopkeepers, Pioneers: The Chinese of Mexico and Peru, 1849–1930." *Amerasia Journal* 15, no. 2 (1989): 91–116.

Jha, J. C. "The Indian Mutiny-cum-Revolt of 1857 and Trinidad (West Indies)." *Indian Studies: Past and Present* 13, no. 4 (1972): 419–30.

———. "East Indian Pressure Groups in Trinidad, 1897–1921." Paper presented at the Fifth Conference of Caribbean Historians, St. Augustine, Trinidad, 1973.

———. "The Background to the Legalisation of non-Christian Marriages in Trinidad and Tobago." Paper presented at the First Conference of East Indians in the Caribbean, St. Augustine, Trinidad, 1975.

———. "The Indian Heritage in Trinidad." In John La Guerre, ed., *Calcutta to Caroni: The East Indians of Trinidad*, 1–20. St. Augustine, Trinidad: University of the West Indies, 1985.

Johnson, Howard. "Immigration and the Sugar Industry in Trinidad during the Last Quarter of the Nineteenth Century." *Journal of Caribbean History* 3 (1971): 28–72.

———. "The Origins and Early Development of Cane Farming in Trinidad, 1882–1906." *Journal of Caribbean History* 5 (1972): 46–74.

———. "The Anti-Chinese Riots of 1918 in Jamaica." *Immigrants and Minorities* 2, no. 1 (1983): 50–63.

———. "The Chinese in Trinidad in the Late Nineteenth Century." *Ethnic and Racial Studies* 10, no. 1 (1987): 82–95.

Kartick, Reuben. "O Tye Kim and the Establishment of the Chinese Settlement of Hope-
town." *Guyana Historical Journal,* vol. 1 (1989): 37–50.
Key-Potter, Lesley. "East Indians and the Afro-Guyanese: Village Settlement Patterns and
Inter-Group Relationships, 1871–1921." Paper presented at the Fourth Conference of
Caribbean Historians, Mona, Jamaica, 1972.
———. "The Post-Indenture Experience of East Indians in Guyana, 1873–1921." In
B. Brereton and W. Dookeran, eds., *East Indians in the Caribbean: Colonialism and the
Struggle for Identity,* 71–92. New York: Kraus, 1982.
Laurence, K. O. "The Establishment of the Portuguese Community in British Guiana."
Jamaican Historical Review 5, no. 2 (1965): 50–74.
———. "The Evolution of Long-Term Labour Contracts in Trinidad and British Guiana."
Jamaican Historical Review 5, no. 1 (1965): 9–27.
———. "The East Indian Indenture in Trinidad" (review article). *Caribbean Quarterly*
17, no. 1 (1971): 34–47.
———. "Indians as Permanent Settlers in Trinidad before 1900." In John La Guerre, ed.,
Calcutta to Caroni: The East Indians in Trinidad, 95–116. St. Augustine, Trinidad:
University of the West Indies, 1985.
Levy, Jacqueline. "Chinese Indentured Immigration to Jamaica during the Latter Part of
the Nineteenth Century." Paper presented at the Fourth Conference of Caribbean
Historians, Mona, Jamaica, 1972.
Lind, Andrew. "Adjustment Patterns among the Jamaican Chinese." *Social and Economic
Studies* 7, no. 2 (1958): 144–64.
Look Lai, W. "Chinese Indentured Labor: Migrations to the British West Indies in the
Nineteenth Century." *Amerasia Journal* 15, no. 2 (1989): 117–40.
Mangru, Basdeo. "The Sex-Ratio Disparity and Its Consequences under the Indenture in
British Guiana." In D. Dabydeen and B. Samaroo, eds., *India in the Caribbean,* 211–30.
London: Hansib, 1987.
———. "Stifled at Birth: Private Emigration from Bombay to British Guiana in the
Mid-Nineteenth Century." *Immigrants and Minorities* 6, no. 2 (1987): 190–99.
Mansingh, Lakshmi. "Cultural Heritage among the East Indians in Jamaica." Paper pre-
sented at the Second Conference on East Indians in the Caribbean, St. Augustine,
Trinidad, 1979.
Mansingh, Lakshmi and Ajai. "Indian Heritage in Jamaica." *Jamaica Journal* 10, nos. 2–4
(1976): 10–19.
Moohr, Michael. "The Economic Impact of Slave Emancipation in British Guiana, 1832–
1852." *Economic History Review* 25, no. 4 (1972): 588–607.
Moore, Brian. "The Retention of Caste Notions among the Indian Immigrants in British
Guiana during the Nineteenth Century." *Comparative Studies in Society and History* 19,
no. 1 (1977): 96–107.
———. "The Settlement of Chinese in Guyana in the Nineteenth Century." *Immigrants
and Minorities* 7, no. 1 (1988): 41–56.
Perez de la Riva, Juan. "Demografía de los Culíes Chinos en Cuba, 1853–1874." *Revista
de la Biblioteca Nacional José Martí* 57, no. 4 (1966): 3–31.
Ramesar, Marianne. "The Impact of the Indian Immigrants on Colonial Trinidad—An
Assessment at the End of the Indenture System." Paper presented at the First Confer-
ence of East Indians in the Caribbean, St. Augustine, Trinidad, 1975.
———. "Patterns of Regional Settlement and Economic Activity by Immigrant Groups

in Trinidad, 1851–1900." Paper presented at the Seventh Conference of Caribbean Historians, Mona, Jamaica, 1975.

———. "The Integration of Indian Settlers in Trinidad after the Indenture Period." *Caribbean Issues* 2, no. 3 (1976): 62–65.

———. "Recurrent Issues concerning East Indian Immigrants to Trinidad." In John La Guerre, ed., *Calcutta to Caroni: The East Indians of Trinidad*, 135–54. St. Augustine, Trinidad: University of the West Indies, 1985.

Ramnarine, Tyran. "A Hundred Years of East Indian Disturbances on the Sugar Estates of Guyana, 1869–1978: A Historical Overview." In D. Dabydeen and B. Samaroo, eds., *India in the Caribbean*, 119–41. London: Hansib, 1987.

Reddock, Rhoda. "Indian Women and Indentureship in Trinidad and Tobago, 1845–1917." *Caribbean Quarterly* 32, nos. 3 & 4 (1986): 27–49.

Riviere, William Emanuel. "Labour Shortage in the British West Indies after Emancipation." *Journal of Caribbean History* 4 (1972): 1–30.

Roberts, George, and Byrne, Joycelyn. "Summary Statistics on Indenture and Associated Migration Affecting the West Indies, 1834–1918." *Population Studies* 20, no. 1 (1966): 125–34.

Roberts, G., and Johnson, M. A. "Factors Involved in Immigration and Movements in the Working Force of British Guiana in the Nineteenth Century." Paper presented at the Fourth Conference of Caribbean Historians, Mona, Jamaica, 1972.

Samaroo, Brinsley. "The Presbyterian Church as an Agent of Integration in Trinidad during the Nineteenth and Twentieth Centuries." *Caribbean Studies* 14, no. 4 (1975): 41–55.

———. "Missionary Methods and Local Responses: The Canadian Presbyterians and the East Indians in the Caribbean." In B. Brereton and W. Dookeran, eds., *East Indians in the Caribbean: Colonialism and the Struggle for Identity*, 93–115. New York: Kraus, 1982.

Sebastien, Rafael. "A Typology of the Caribbean Peasantry—The Development of the Peasantry in Trinidad, 1845–1917." *Social and Economic Studies* 29, no. 2 (1980): 107–33.

Shepherd, Verene. "Indians and Blacks in Jamaica in the Nineteenth and Early Twentieth Centuries: A Micro-study of the Foundations of Race Antagonisms." *Immigrants and Minorities* 7, no. 1 (1988): 95–112.

Singh, Kelvin. "East Indians and the Larger Society." In John La Guerre, ed., *Calcutta to Caroni: The East Indians of Trinidad*, 33–62. St. Augustine, Trinidad: University of the West Indies, 1985.

Smith, Raymond. "Some Social Characteristics of Indian Immigrants to British Guiana." *Population Studies* 13, no. 1 (1959): 34–39.

Tikasingh, Gerad. "The Emerging Political Consciousness among Trinidad Indians in the Late Nineteenth Century." Paper presented at the Fifth Conference of Caribbean Historians, St. Augustine, Trinidad, 1973.

———. "The Trinidad Press and the Issue of Immigration." Paper presented at the Ninth Conference of Caribbean Historians, Cave Hill, Barbados, 1977.

———. "The Representation of Indian Opinion in Trinidad, 1900–1921." In B. Brereton and W. Dookeran, eds., *East Indians in the Caribbean: Colonialism and the Struggle for Identity*, 11–32. New York: Kraus, 1982.

Young, Arthur. "Chinese in the West Indies." *China Weekly Review* 48, no. 11 (11 May 1929): 466.

Unpublished Theses and Dissertations

Bisnauth, Dale Arlington. "The East Indian Immigrant Society in British Guiana, 1891–1930." Ph.D., University of the West Indies, Mona, Jamaica, 1977.

Laurence, K. O. "Immigration into Trinidad and British Guiana, 1834–1871." Ph.D., Cambridge University, 1958.

Meagher, Arnold. "The Introduction of Chinese Laborers to Latin America: The Coolie Trade, 1847–1874." Ph.D., University of California, Davis, 1975.

Moore, Robert. "East Indians and Negroes in British Guiana, 1838–1880." Ph.D., University of Sussex, 1970.

Potter, Lesley. "Internal Migration and Resettlement of East Indians in Guyana, 1870–1920." Ph.D., McGill University, Montreal, 1975.

Ramesar, Marianne. "Indian Immigration into Trinidad, 1897–1917." M.A., University of the West Indies, Mona, 1973.

Romnarine, Tyran. "The Growth of the East Indian Community in British Guiana, 1880–1920." Ph.D., University of Sussex, 1977.

Sohal, Harinder. "The East Indian Indentureship in Jamaica, 1845–1917." Ph.D., University of Waterloo, Ontario, Canada, 1979.

Tikasingh, Gerad. "The Establishment of the Indians in Trinidad, 1870–1900." Ph.D., University of the West Indies, St. Augustine, Trinidad, 1976.

Index

Abel, Peter, 81, 135
Abolition: abolitionists, 2, 3, 12, 156; slavery and slave trade, 1–3, 10, 16
Acham, Eugene Bernard. *See* Chen, Eugene
Achong, Tito, 216
African-Americans, 15, 16, 55
Africans, 6, 14–16, 55–57, 117, 247, 302
Agent-General of Immigrants. *See* Protector of Immigrants
Alcazar, Henry, 173, 174
American Revolution, 1, 2
Amoy. *See* Fukien
Anderson, Justice, 160
Andrews, Reverend Charles F., 156
Anguilla, 14
Antigua, 4, 7, 9, 17, 251, 273, 276, 302
Anti-Slavery Society, 54, 62, 95, 156, 157, 167
Apprenticeship, 3, 8, 9
Argos, 216
Argosy, 180, 184
Assam, 26, 27, 31, 34, 227
Austin, J. Gardiner, 59, 71–75, 105, 203
Australia, 89, 91–93, 205, 294–96
Azores, 17

Bahamas, 14
Bananas: industry, 50, 51, 86; workers, 185–87, 252–53
Baptist Union of Wales, 185
Barbados: emigration, 13, 14, 168, 172, 174, 239, 251, 302; free labor, xii, 4, 7, 11; sugar production, 9, 273
Basti, 31, 34

Beaumont, Chief Justice Joseph, 134, 138, 141, 166
Bechu, 133, 142
Beete, Justice Edward, 335n.83
Beet sugar, 10, 171
Bengal: capture of, 20–21; emigration within and from, 24, 26–36, 43, 277, 279; famine in, 26; immigrants in West Indies, 109, 110, 114–15, 122–25, 137, 218
Bengal Hurkaru, 24
Bentinck, Lord George, 13, 160
Bentinck Committee (1848), 18
Bermuda, 14
Bhodu, 160
Bhojpuri, 257
Bihar: emigration, 25–27, 30–35, 279; political unrest, 34; social and economic pressures, 24, 26, 34
Bombay, 20, 30, 32, 35–36
Brahmins, 29, 125–26, 258
Brazil, 2, 10, 16–17, 20, 40, 103, 325n.64
British Emancipator, 156
British Empire, 2, 3; in China, 38–40; in India, 20–25, 321n.2, 322nn.3, 7
British Guiana: anti-indenture lobbies, 154–57, 163–66, 178–84; Chinese laborers, 87–104, 299; immigration into, 13–18, 19, 33–37, 42–45, 47–49, 71–80, 87–96, 276–79, 292–94; indenture system, 50–86, 304–8; Indian laborers, 107–53, 282–83; major export commodities, 273–75; post-emancipation problems, 3–13; post-indenture options, Chinese,

www.ingramcontent.com/pod-product-compliance
Ingram Content Group UK Ltd.
Pitfield, Milton Keynes, MK11 3LW, UK
UKHW042052090325
456014UK00002B/34